Principles of External Business Environment Analyzability in an Organizational Context

Bruno F. Abrantes
Niels Brock Copenhagen Business College, Denmark

A volume in the Advances in Logistics, Operations, and Management Science (ALOMS) Book Series

IGI Global
PUBLISHER of TIMELY KNOWLEDGE

Published in the United States of America by
IGI Global
Business Science Reference (an imprint of IGI Global)
701 E. Chocolate Avenue
Hershey PA, USA 17033
Tel: 717-533-8845
Fax: 717-533-8661
E-mail: cust@igi-global.com
Web site: http://www.igi-global.com

Library of Congress Cataloging-in-Publication Data

Names: Abrantes, Bruno F., 1976- author.
Title: Principles of external business environment analyzability in an organizational context / Bruno F Abrantes.
Description: Hershey, PA : Business Science Reference, [2023] | Includes bibliographical references and index. | Summary: "The purpose of this book on Business Environment Analyzability (BEA) is to provide a learning insight into the theoretical background surrounding the exercise of macro analysis and the challenges of fashioning (and executing) a BEA project"-- Provided by publisher.
Identifiers: LCCN 2022045626 (print) | LCCN 2022045627 (ebook) | ISBN 9781668455432 (hardcover) | ISBN 9781668455449 (paperback) | ISBN 9781668455456 (ebook)
Subjects: LCSH: Strategic planning. | Management audit. | Decision making. | Externalities (Economics)
Classification: LCC HD30.28 .A24747 2023 (print) | LCC HD30.28 (ebook) | DDC 658.4/012--dc23/eng/20221125
LC record available at https://lccn.loc.gov/2022045626
LC ebook record available at https://lccn.loc.gov/2022045627

This book is published in the IGI Global book series Advances in Logistics, Operations, and Management Science (ALOMS) (ISSN: 2327-350X; eISSN: 2327-3518)

British Cataloguing in Publication Data
A Cataloguing in Publication record for this book is available from the British Library.

Advances in Logistics, Operations, and Management Science (ALOMS) Book Series

John Wang
Montclair State University, USA

ISSN:2327-350X
EISSN:2327-3518

Mission

Operations research and management science continue to influence business processes, administration, and management information systems, particularly in covering the application methods for decision-making processes. New case studies and applications on management science, operations management, social sciences, and other behavioral sciences have been incorporated into business and organizations real-world objectives.

The **Advances in Logistics, Operations, and Management Science** (ALOMS) Book Series provides a collection of reference publications on the current trends, applications, theories, and practices in the management science field. Providing relevant and current research, this series and its individual publications would be useful for academics, researchers, scholars, and practitioners interested in improving decision making models and business functions.

Coverage

- Computing and information technologies
- Networks
- Production Management
- Marketing engineering
- Risk Management
- Services management
- Decision analysis and decision support
- Political Science
- Operations Management
- Organizational Behavior

IGI Global is currently accepting manuscripts for publication within this series. To submit a proposal for a volume in this series, please contact our Acquisition Editors at acquisitions@igi-global.com or visit: https://www.igi-global.com/publish/.

The Advances in Logistics, Operations, and Management Science (ALOMS) Book Series (ISSN 2327-350X) is published by IGI Global, 701 E. Chocolate Avenue, Hershey, PA 17033-1240, USA, www.igi-global.com. This series is composed of titles available for purchase individually; each title is edited to be contextually exclusive from any other title within the series. For pricing and ordering information please visit https://www.igi-global.com/book-series/advances-logistics-operations-management-science/37170. Postmaster: Send all address changes to above address.

Titles in this Series

For a list of additional titles in this series, please visit: www.igi-global.com/book-series

Change Management During Unprecedented Times
Kyla Latrice Tennin (College of Doctoral Studies, University of Phoenix, USA & Forbes School of Business, USA & World Business Angels Investment Forum (WBAF)-G20, USA & Lady Mirage Global, Inc. USA)
Business Science Reference • © 2023 • 413pp • H/C (ISBN: 9781668475096) • US $250.00

Multidisciplinary Approaches to Organizational Governance During Health Crises
Carla Sofia Vicente Negrão (CeBER, University of Coimbra, Portugal) Isabel Guerreiro Pimentel Maia (University of Coimbra, Portugal) and João António Furtado Brito (University of Cape Verde, Cape erde)
Business Science Reference • © 2023 • 300pp • H/C (ISBN: 9781799892137) • US $250.00

Considerations and Characteristics of the Millennial Leader in Today's Global Society
Tymon M. Graham (TMGraham Consulting, LLC, USA)
Business Science Reference • © 2023 • 300pp • H/C (ISBN: 9781668447116) • US $240.00

Handbook of Research on Blockchain Technology and the Digitalization of the Supply Chain
Tharwa Najar (Gafsa University, Tunisia) Yousra Najar (Manar University, Tunisia) and Adel Aloui (EM Normandie Business School, France)
Business Science Reference • © 2023 • 315pp • H/C (ISBN: 9781668474556) • US $250.00

Perspectives on Women in Management and the Global Labor Market
Elisabete S. Vieira (GOVCOPP, University of Aveiro, Portugal) Mara Madaleno (GOVCOPP, University of Aveiro, Portugal) and João Teodósio (Polytechnic Institute of Santarém, Portugal)
Business Science Reference • © 2023 • 382pp • H/C (ISBN: 9781668459812) • US $240.00

Perspectives and Strategies of Family Business Resiliency in Unprecedented Times
Hotniar Siringoringo (Gunadarma University, Indonesia) and Ravindra Hewa Kuruppuge (University of Peradeniya, Sri Lanka)
Business Science Reference • © 2023 • 322pp • H/C (ISBN: 9781668473948) • US $240.00

Futuristic Technology Perspectives on Entrepreneurship and Sustainable Innovation
Sanjay Misra (Department of Applied Data Science, Institute of Energy Technology, Halden, Norway) Amit Jain (Amity University, India) Manju Kaushik (Amity University, India) and Chitreshh Banerjee (Amity University, India)
Business Science Reference • © 2023 • 300pp • H/C (ISBN: 9781668458716) • US $250.00

IGI Global
PUBLISHER of TIMELY KNOWLEDGE

701 East Chocolate Avenue, Hershey, PA 17033, USA
Tel: 717-533-8845 x100 • Fax: 717-533-8661
E-Mail: cust@igi-global.com • www.igi-global.com

Table of Contents

Foreword ... vii

Preface ... ix

Acknowledgement ... xiii

Introduction ... xiv

Section 1
Environmental Fearfulness and (Business) Environmental Analyzability

Chapter 1
Human Quest for (Environment) Control and the Microfoundations of Management ... 1

Chapter 2
Organizational Management and Strategic Behaviour ... 26

Chapter 3
Understanding Business Environments (BEs) ... 47

Chapter 4
External Business Environments (EBE) ... 69

Chapter 5
External Business Environment Analysis (EBEA) ... 110

Chapter 6
Systems Analyzability, Analytics, and Business Intelligence ... 191

Section 2
Business Environment Analysis Projects (BEAP)

Chapter 7
Managing a Business Environment Analysis Project (BEAP) 207

Chapter 8
Business Environment Analysis Project´s (BEAP) Capabilities 241

Chapter 9
Project Quality Management (PQM) 252

Chapter 10
Strategic Project Auditing 271

Conclusion 300

List of Acronyms 303

Glossary 307

Compilation of References 313

About the Author 325

Index 326

Foreword

As a business management educator with specialisms in entrepreneurship, organisational strategy, and writing up award-winning case studies on business organisations, I have had the privilege of sharing in the lived experience of businesses of all forms and sizes. In all contexts that I have conducted my research and facilitated learning in, one of the recurrent, yet understated themes of the key to organisational success remains the complexity of the business environment.

Environmental analysis has long been considered the skeleton key of business strategy conundrums. Whether organisations excel or perish, we can often attribute the organisation's excellence or death to the organisation's ability to correctly analyse and appropriately respond to both the internal and external environmental landscapes of the organisation. And yet, how to effectively analyse the business environment continues to be elusive as the limitations of our knowledge in this area are exposed time and time again with any environmental shake up.

In several textbooks on the strategic processes of organisations, this core area of strategic thinking and decision making is often glossed over, in part due to the oversimplification of the implications of the environment on the life of the organisation. Tools like the infamous PESTEL and SWOT analysis frameworks are useful starting points for this strategic exercise of analysing the business environment. Very little thought is given however to how to start thinking about analysing the business environment in the organisational context and what to do with the blueprint of considerations yielded by these frameworks. Strategic management practitioners and organisational leaders have a lived appreciation of the limitations of these tools. Unfortunately, very few textbooks, preceding "Principles of External Business Environment Analyzability in an Organizational Context" attempt to capture this reality sufficiently.

The first part of this textbook, aptly titled "Environmental Fearfulness and Business Environment Analyzability" reveals the inherent challenge of strategizing for success in the first instance; the challenge of attempting to control the unpredictable. The textbook attempts to unpack the philosophical underpinnings of the need for strategic control and the juxtaposition of dynamic environments that at best can only be responded to and not controlled. The textbook explores the strategic management approach to creating the appropriate organisational control levers and provides context for how these levers can be effectively implemented in practice using globally recognisable case studies. Case examples have been integrated in the main chapters and featured as extended contexts for knowledge examination and application.

The second part of this textbook introduces a project methodology approach to effective business environment analysis. This is a relevant perspective compatible with the principles of in-built dynamism and agility. This perspective enables the strategic management practitioner to consider how every strategic operation contributes to effective analysis of and response to the business environment.

This textbook is contemporary in its consideration of the digitalised reality of modern-day organisations.

The style of the chapters is written to bridge traditional generally accepted knowledge and present contexts that serve to at times reinforce the timeless principles that form our knowledge of organisational strategy; and at other times critically challenge the very knowledge we have come to rely on. The text makes appropriate nods to thought leaders in various fields that have informed strategic thought but goes beyond that in introducing fresh perspectives.

The authors are lauded on their ability to present the content in a sufficiently easy to understand manner for a non-specialist audience and yet remain intellectually stimulating and challenging for the audience that is well acquainted with the language and nature of organisational strategy.

Whilst positioned to give guiding principles, the textbook remains non-prescriptive- an essential feature of the reality of strategy and the endless need for adaptability and contextual fit.

Although the chapters are distinctive in their areas of focus, there is a clear flow and logical relationship across the topics covered in the textbook. The chapters are legible with valuable insights as individual stand-alone components and still synergistically come together to give life to the book in its entirety.

The textbook is a go-to for lovers of a trip down a rabbit hole of strategic inquiry with its rich body of suggested further reading.

I have found this text to not be a replacement for existing texts in strategy but a necessary addition to the body of knowledge.

Natasha Katuta Mwila
De Monfort University (DMU), UK

Preface

The purpose of this book on *business environment analyzability (BEA)* is to provide a learning insight into the theoretical background surrounding the exercise of macro analysis and the challenges of fashioning (and executing) a BEA project.

With this ambition, started in the fall of 2020 reflecting upon the likely utility of the book, and with a boost of self-assurance decided to begin. The main point was to unite a body of literature and solve some fundamental issues faced by my undergraduate and postgraduate students for years. Perhaps common to most students in Management Sciences. Moreover, support the planners and management consultants´ activities with an extra layer of BEA theory which extends the earlier scholarly work.

The exponential growth of the domain of business administration and strategic management in recent decades, as in many other domains, both in social and natural sciences, had the virtue of stretching the boundaries of knowledge and likely improve our understanding of your surrounding world, although, the study of a vastness of topics comes side by side with the temptation for generalizations on instruction and on the selection of learning materials. Certainly, all tutors/instructors strive to provide the finest learning experience and equip the apprentices with the most sophisticated tools at their own reach. In this process, the spiraling growth of theoretical foundations leaves the educator with no option but to face this dilemma: *How may I cover all spectrum of ideas in a limited amount of time (for class interaction and coursework)?*

Inevitably, scholars feel many times on a tightrope, having to choose an avenue of learning contents in detriment of other/s, or a model, or to place more emphasis on a certain type of concept or type of critique. Surely this thought crosses the minds of many of my fellow professors: *What is more relevant, the (neo)classicism, the contemporaneity or a broader view of a topic or course?* Being not an exception to this rule, here, I also came across multiple times with challenges alike.

The educator's assumption of the generalizability is a natural one. This means, following the belief of doing a "better job" to a cohort means to provide students with a "man-sized meal" or a full-range of topics against the contrarian viewpoint of the concentration on fewer ones.

Without trying to point out any superlative directions for higher education policy-making, or to opine on "the" optimal performance path, or make any judgements about pedagogical tools and their relation to effective learning or satisfaction, furthermore, I would like merely to underline that the sole reason for giving continuity to this project and writing this book was, in my particular case, to provide a simplified alternative for my students in the future, enrolled at our tertiary education programs at *De Monfort University (DMU)* and *Niels Brock Copenhagen Business College (NBCBC),* and hopefully, assist someone else, with equivalent issues, or whom the topics and contents here addressed could be perceived of relevance to other practitioners across industries, for instance, management consultants, strategists, business intelligence and data analysts, or marketers.

Hence, I embarked on a journey at the end of 2020 to gather from the fairly vast and dispersed amount of literature in the field of Strategic Management and focusing solely on the specifics of theme of this book, customize it through a product blending of a text/reference book not solely due to my permanent quest for theoretical updateness, but also, intending to remedy the holism (panoramic view) of most textbooks though missing some depth. Thus, it may clearly affirmed that this book has no particular aspiration to be a "blind" adopter of none of those book categories.

On the Strategic Management (SM) domain, the sub-theme of *Business Environments,* has been revealed to my understanding a clear deficit one, with some shortage of specific literature dedicated to it, when compared to other sub-fields. Paradoxically, the understanding of the markets, the *locus* where companies compete is seminal for building any rational model of strategy design and achieve organizational success in short and long-term. Hence, the balancing of breadth/depth of content regarding *Business Environments* have been of the most challenging and simultaneously most critical for me as to the SM-teaching. I resolved on my daily scholarly activities by combing the semester or yearly textbook adopted with further literature (reference books) and with the complementarity of journal articles. Yet, this opened the door for further anxiety and frustration on the learners´ side having to deal with the necessity to read, at the same time, multiple sources sometimes accessible on different formats, whether printed or web versions) and placed on different locations, as own physical library, e-libraries/repositories and academic databases). Thus, writing this book, was noticeable, a consequence of the sentiment of student´s population, deriving from a (common-sense) learning environment analysis. Eventually, all citizens or agents in any societal domain need to gauge their surrounding social/professional environment, whether or not, their Business Environment.

Reusing the words of *Dr. Natasha Mwila* in the foreword of this book, "*is a go-to for lovers of a trip down a rabbit hole of strategic inquiry with its rich body of suggested further reading.*" Unquestionably, the book is tailored for an audience of postgrad students enrolled in courses as Organizational Management, Global Strategic Management, International Strategic Management of Markets and Resources, Organizational Behaviour or others alike, as well as, to other scholar conducting research in this domain. Notwithstanding, everyone with a desire to learn more, regardless of its educational background are invited to read it, as again emphasized by the same scholar aforementioned, whom lauded that the content of the book is present "*…in a sufficiently easy to understand manner for a non-specialist audience and yet remain intellectually stimulating and challenging for the audience that is well acquainted with the language and nature of organisational strategy*".

Chapter one dives into individual fears and instincts taken as the antecedents for the perception of natural and social risks are gathered in this chapter to illustrate the microfoundations of Organizational Management and the underlying rationale for the contemporaneity of the management function. Entering the realm of the Philosophy of Management, and following some of the most influential roots in Ancient China and Greece, one may revisit particularly the Xenophon´s contribution to the initial conception of Business Management, and to the consequent evolution of human thought until the neoclassicism of the Scientific Management. Along the way, seminal concepts (e.g. uncertainty or risk) are revisited in the context of Strategic Management, domain which is discussed side-by-side with Governance and Leadership. Furthermore, the case of Haier Group (and Mr. Zhang Ruimin) is used to illustrate the successful intertwine of the three organizational dimensions (i.e. governance; leadership; and, management) for the organizational success.

Chapter two explores the context of business strategy´s formulation and contemporary management, addressing seminal aspects related with: (i) technological disruptions (e.g. artificial intelligence and the internet-of-things; and the 4th industrial revolution); (ii) global business competition (e.g. new business models; mergers and acquisitions; network competition; or, globalization); and (iii) the upsurge of the VUCA business environments. In this context, are depicted the major challenges surrounding the Strategic Adaptation and Strategic Fit to VUCA environments. One addresses moreover the POLC cycle, plus the phases of strategic fit (and the organizational levers of internal/external fit) and the importance of developing multiple organizational capabilities. Lastly, it depicts the association of strategic management practices (Planning vs. Controlling) and their importance for the organizational success.

The previous chapters dwell around the Microfoundations of Management (chapter 1), plus strategy formulation and the challenges contemporary management (chapter 2). key-constructs (fear and thought) are taken as an instinctive-driven and rational-driven configuration of human behavior. In chapter three, one starts to immerse into the realm of business context in our modern world. One starts to focus on business environments (BE) and address seminal concepts, as "environment"; "ecosystem"; or "market" (and underlying ideas, as marketspace, marketplace or e-market). Here, a BE is assumed to fit, at the begging of the 21st century, a dynamic paradigm, and so the chapter discusses the types of business environment´s changes and their inner changing events. Moreover, is presented the strategic paths (to respond to BE´s change), and the tenets of organizational success. With regard to the latter, the analyzability function is introduced as a determinant of success.

Focused on the subset of external business environment (EBE), chapter four explores the EBE´s "layers" and "elements" and the firm´s view of them. Entering the analyzability function it describes the utility of the Business Environment Analyzability (BEA) function and the typology of business environment analyzability projects (BEAP). Furthermore, the Schools of Thought in Strategic Management are interconnected to organizational value, and herein, is emphasized the importance (and competitive implications) of BEA to value-creation. Strategy interfaces, namely the external interface, are associated with prior concepts as "organizational fit" or "strategic drift" and argued on the role BEAPs on the shaping of the firms position in the EBE.

Chapter 5 focuses on entering the realm of analyzability. The chapter begins with a debate surrounding the Philosophy of Analyzability (PoA) around essential issues such as, assumptions and stances. Afterwards, it specifies focuses on the scope of a Business Environment Analyzability Project (BEAP). Here are depicted the phases and the criteria surrounding the factor´s selection (on a BEAP). Moreover, it covers the types of criteria and the notions of balance and dominant criterion. Subsequently, it elaborates on other more specific domains of analyzability. For instance, the phases of the strategic decisions which lead to the choice of criteria (and the dominant one); the selection of sources of data, the use of models for analyzing the External Business Environment (EBE); and the applicability of indexes, ratios and benchmarks.

Chapter six focuses on the influence of information and communication technologies (ICT) in strategic communication and market research. One addresses, among others, the role of computer-based Information Systems (IS) and IS Management in contemporary businesses, the Intelligence Cycle and the types and categories of IS and their utility to operational and strategic activities of a firm. Furthermore, it discusses the increasing digitalization of societies, and herein, the challenges of digital business communication and business digitalization. Seminal aspects are here uncovered with this regard, as the copiousness and overdependence of data analytics, the phenomenon of Big Data, the concentration of economic agents over platforms, the use of web-based value chains, and the shift to "reintermediation".

Approximating itself to project management theory, chapter seven contextualizes the BEAP into the multiple types of project contexts and characteristics. Considerations are made as to the project design, regarding the project brief´s components and the constraints regarding the project´s approval in the context of the portfolio´s pipeline and management requirements. It considers furthermore the 5C´s influencing the project environment and the project structuring, from the simple input-out model, passing through the ICOM, 4-D, the MODest and the 7-S framework. Furthermore, it centers attention in the project´s architecture and on the alignment to the organization, considering seminal aspects as organizational culture; structure and business processes). The phases of project, the structure and roles of each project´s element, and cascades the project´s "architectures" (or systems) into processes and their underlying project/corporate nexus.

Immersing into the Resource-based view (RBV) and Dynamic Capabilities Theory (DCT), chapter eight emphasizes the importance of resource´s endowment function to any project, such as: (i) criterious asset´s deployment; and (ii) capability´s selection. Those are seminal to the approval of the project´s proposal among other portfolio candidates. One explores different views within the RBV and Human Capital Theory around larger conceptions (e.g. abilities; assets; capabilities; core-competences; resources; or skills) and their connection to market value in the form of individual/group´s worth and organizational capabilities and their inherent firm-specific advantages (FSA) transposed to the context of functional or ad hoc project teams. Seminal dynamic capabilities (DC) are brought to the light in the context of a Business Environment Analysis Project (BEAP), as the coordination; knowledge-utilization; or learning capability.

Chapter nine addresses the importance of project quality (PQ) in the mediation of the project governance´s endeavors and its outcomes (of Project Performance). It provides a multilateral vision of what quality is from different stakeholder´s point of view. It intertwines the seminal contribution of Deming´s theories (of profound knowledge and optimization) which influenced decisively the evolution of the project management body of knowledge (PMBOK) with the total quality management (TQM). The chapter addresses moreover the types of quality processes and enters the domain of quality assurance as a system of relevance to ensure the fulfillment of quality standards. Within the PMBOK revisits a few theorizations (as the MODest framework) and enters the realm of the Total Quality Management (TQM).

Historically sparse, the body of literature in Strategy Auditing (SA) has grown in number and array of scholarly endeavors since the 1980s. Dominantly centered upon the instrumentalization of, Robert Grant´s Strategic Management Process (SMP), which linearity and forward-orientation of this framework outlines the number of "processes" and its "workflow", the SA is a disciple of a major school of thought (i.e. the Planning View) postulating that corporate planning and strategic controls are the two most nuclear functions of the strategist. So, where is "the analysis" (and particularly the business environment analysis – BEA) realized in a SA? The Strategy Audit symbolizes the "big picture" outlining a full cycle of the business-level strategy execution, while the BEA is one process within the SA as a system. The embeddedness of the BEA (projects) in the SA is addressed in chapter ten while summarily describing the aspects of contextualization, positioning and association with other SA-processes directly linked to it.

Bruno F. Abrantes
Niels Brock Copenhagen Business College, Denmark

Acknowledgement

First I would like to thank all these people, who along this three-year journey of this project, spared time/energy, shared knowledge and wisdom and somehow instilled me with a restlessness sense towards public service - teaching, research and writing.

I must though praise, at least once in life three people who, affectionately, I cognomen them as a "*triad of supporters*". These knights opened doors that ultimately would shape my professional life to date. Professor *Nelson António (ISCTE-University of Lisbon)* who supervised my Ph.D. research and with whom I have the honor (and pleasure) to keep sharing projects for almost a decade. Professor *Miguel Torres Preto* (*Instituto Superior Técnico – Universidade de Lisboa*) who welcomed me in the first research project I had the opportunity to participate on. Finally, *Lars Askholm* (*Køge Business College)* who kindly received me at *Niels Brock, Copenhagen Business College (NBCBC)* and placed me in the middle of a fantastic faculty team at *NBCBC and De Monfort University*.

An enormous thank-you note goes also to *Charlotte Forsberg (Pro Vice-Chancellor/Executive Vice President Further and Higher Education - NBCBC*), whom always shown a great deal of interest in this project over the last years and her busy professional agenda did not constrained her to write anyway the postface of book. Inevitably, a recognition is also due to *Dr. Natasha Katuta Mwila (Program leader, at the School of Leadership, Management and Marketing - De Monfort University)* whom I have to thank for envisioning the potential contribution of this book and for the brilliant contextualization of the topic in the *Foreword* section, adding gravitas and teasing out the reader for the chapter to come. Moreover, to the interest of the NBCBC´s Library services at Bispetorvet campus (*Gaby Lewin*) and the publisher itself, especially the editorial and book development teams (*Angelina Olivas* and *Rowan Rumbaugh*).

Despite all this, a substantial part of my debt goes to an extraordinary woman (*Julia Abrantes*), someone I managed to be lucky enough to call "my wife" and happens to be a pillar in life.

Introduction

Business environment… "*analyzability*"? The reader might get tempted to an initial judgement: *Here it comes another buzzword*! Fancy jargon on the good old-style adding fuzziness to the existing academic terminology on the spectrum of market "*analysis*".

Indeed, this book covers both, *analysis* and *analyzability*. Apart from being homophonous words with clear grammatical resemblances, they are however two distinctive conceptions with a complementary meaning underlying the analytical framework of any organization. Together, they are the "essence and soul" of the corporate systems architecture and they consubstantiate the role of many experts with different jobs and responsibilities. In a glance, the first (*analyzability*) entails the full scope of options at one´s disposal for the potential examination of an institution and subsequently its business environment (including all the research endeavors of the analyst (commonly referred to, as the consultant) – here is your first definition. The second (*analysis*) identifies the decisional path taken and comprises the actual *options*, and cumulatively, the *action*, as the extent of realized work within the scope of a given task or activity; considering the aim/s set for such analysis, whether simply accommodating new information or crunching raw data, or their subsequent interpretation (and reporting), or even, inferring on their effect on a given project, department, or business unit.

Are you confused…? Surely, the reading of this introduction (and the first part of the book) will dissipate your doubt/s, open further horizons and stimulate you to reflect upon the analysis function.

Furthermore, the initial chapters (in Part One) will immerse into the most fundamental aspects of *Business Environment Analyzability (BEA)* with a particular emphasis placed on the "universe" (past/present/future), as the outer-firm´s reality to be observed as an epilogist object both as a forward and backward process. Hence, the narrative provides an outlook of the natural and social world events (from the primitive to the modern environment), but tunneled towards the realm of *External Business Environment Analysis (EBEA)*. Yet, a dyadic (external-internal) reflection about the external ecosystems (e.g. countries or regions) is constantly observed against the internal ones, taken as a focal entity regardless of its typology (e.g. any private firm; foundation; public authority; agency; bank).

Indeed, the scrutiny of the analysis function is intertwined with the managerial role of an organization (public or private). *Why is that* so? We remind the reader, that the focal point of this book is the "organizational context". The length of coverage of the analysis function unites past with present, ranging from the historical notions of primitive environments (and the underlying human behavioral roots) and the philosophical pillars of management in ancient civilizations until the most operational aspects of a contemporary organization in the beginning of the 21st century. The journey begins with the narrative flying over the evolution of human-thinking/needs/behaviour and the influence of such heritage on modern societies and particularly on the contemporary business sphere. Undoubtedly, the cognitive processes and subsequent behaviour of industry practitioners at managerial-level balances invariably emotions with reason (and memory). In great extent, instincts seems to be (still) a safety net for rational management decision-making, as perceptions (gut feelings) and individual experiences (thus, observation and further learning) are undisputable assets; moreover, with societies and businesses on constant kinesis accentuating their worthiness.

At the end of Part One, you will build a far more clear view of what it takes to conduct industry research, particularly about *External Business Environments (EBE).* Moreover, one should understand better the hazards of ineffective analysis, and worse, the (managerial) implications of overlooking such exercise of observation, i.e. the (lack of) analysis about the exercise of analysis.

Although, this topic (EBEs) is certainly familiar for whom have pursued prior college education on Business Studies, and attended courses on Strategic Management, Macroeconomics or Strategic Marketing. If that is your case, you were already exposed to the ideas of seminal authors as *Albert Humphrey; Francis J. Aguilar; Henry Mintzberg; Heinz Weirich; Robert Grant* and/or many others.

So, as a starting question, one may wonder: *Why a book on external business environments?*

The answer is a straightforward one, because books in this field (BEA) opening further horizons are needed. Despite, the seminal contribution of Francis J. Aguilar in the 1960s opening horizons for further scholarly research in entrepreneurial universities focused on knowledge-development; however, the research in this field became tautological, and worse, research became dull. Scholars have not reached not even in a fictional non-mutating world, the "saturation point" of knowledgeability about the reality. Thus, an aggravating factor of our "epistemic lag" is that the world keeps spinning, and scholarly endeavors have not figured out a 100% ontological explanation "to platonify" (sorry, "to theorize") the universe. On top of this, with all the "epistemic arrogance" of several of my colleagues, many believe we are producing new knowledge as such a pace as a sports car accelerates in a German motorway.

Unsurprisingly, a significant number of more skeptical scholars on Management Sciences sustain the importance of, the organizations on the 21st century, to develop competences on *strategic awareness,* to better grasp the changing patterns of the out there word. Dr. Nassim Nicholas Taleb calls this world an "Extremistan" universe. However, remembering an old proverb, it is a matter of (I shall quote) "*Do as I say, not as I do.*" A vast majority of strategy textbooks fit perfectly such expression. Despite the recognition of the importance of capability-development on *External Business Environment´s (EBE) awareness* for leveraging the organization's strategic decisions and action, the reality is quite contrastingly bizarre. Pardon me the provocation, but short-sight and myopia is the dominant paradigm of EBE theorization on most strategy books. Despite the emergence in the last decades of important bodies of theory (as, the Endogenous Growth; Human Capital; the Resource-Based View or the Dynamic Capabilities View) that supposedly should have pulled this theme forward; nonetheless, it remains fairly unexplored justifying further advancements for the sake of knowledge- development.

Hence, a critique and sophist discussion surrounding newer thoughts on the domain of the Philosophy of Management are here explored. These aim to offset the current scenario of apathy and literary stagnation, with incipient reflections on *analysis* (scope and utility) as one of its philosophical dimensions (and components of the managerial function), as to the present or future, on the light of multiple and accelerated changes realized at the social regimes worldwide. This is not a transversal research gap across Social Sciences, this is a particularly problematic on the areas of corporate governance, organizational behaviour, and strategic management.

In this book is though shown moreover that *strategic awareness,* as an organizational capability to be owned, is not enough, *per se*. "Awareness" means solely to have eyes laid on the universe, plus the comprehension of the inputs of information there from, and at its best, might indicate a more accurate judgment about the surrounding universe. Yet, this does not mean a higher ability to take strategic decisions and act effectively as a manager. Indeed, strategic thinking and rational decision-making are intertwined (cognitive and managerial processes) requiring analytical skills to transform the right data, collected at the right time, into multiple pieces of (operational) knowledge and (strategic) business intelligence, to be able to predict on early-stage environmental challenges and proactively act upon them. This on its own, is a great argument to emphasize, the importance of exercising External Business Environment Analysis (EBEA), since they are so determinant for the prior, even though requiring a collective effort of various knowledge types, skills and abilities.

Forgetting EBEA is like dead sentencing a company for the future, even for the ones whom were designed and born as value-innovation business models (so epithetized, "*blue oceans*") (Kim and Maugbourne, 2011) and followed the canons of assertive business modelling, as the Alexander Osterwalder and Yves. Pigneur´s *Canvas*. In fact, *blue oceans* require an essential component of analysis, as these authors recognize it, prior the launching of the model, i.e. the Key Success Factors (KSF), as majors premises for competitive distinctiveness and innovativeness.

Furthermore, External Business Environment Analysis (EBEA) is even more necessary, as in a contemporary context where business ecosystems are, seemingly, more challenging than ever (as widely recognized by several empirical studies), with increasing *volatility, uncertainty, complexity* and *ambiguity (VUCA*VUCA), at an unprecedented level (of VUCA) as to the nature of business competition, this require an assertive resolution of the players to develop further capabilities as explicit knowledge-bundles to complement their market awareness (as a blending of latent/experiential knowledge with marketing capabilities). Thus, the quest nowadays is, not solely for awareness but for preparation for action, hence for (*strategic) agility*. Here, being s*trategically flexible* is a prerequisite to become agile. Strategic flexibility entails the fashioning of business models, organizational structures, systems and resources´ distribution/allocation, to better accommodate those outer dynamics (that constitute VUCA), yielding above-average returns (a.a.r.) and contribute to the sustainability of the firm. But, this is a linking topic to be explored within internal analysis (of the firm).

Out of curiosity one may raise a seemingly simple question: *what makes a Business Environment to become VUCA*? Firstly, one cannot separate these dimensions and claim, this market is "V", but not "U" or "U" but not "C" and so forth, as dimensions are all intertwined. Secondly, best way to comprehend VUCA is to look at their separate meaning, as certainly, those words look alike, but their meaning is quite distinctive, even though, being interrelated phenomena.

Volatility: Occurs when *environmental change* is a persistently arising (Worthington and Britton, 2009). Thus, a market is volatile when it reveals a tendency for the occurrence of environmental changes on a regular basis, and on a rather continuous manner. One factor to be pinpointed as a cause of volatility is the "technological advancement", as the variable *technology* is a disrupter of the way companies operate and their offerings of goods and services. Consequently, highly volatility markets, commonly adjectivated as being more "dynamic" lead to high uncertainty markets.

Uncertainty: Refers to lack of certainty. *Certainty* being the full availability of information (and at the right time) at the firm´s disposal for taking a rational decision (Boddy, 2017). Uncertainty, is the opposite. Uncertainty is a firm´s unique perception of the extent of sparse certainty about an event in the market for operating therein with a tolerable degree of risk. Under a context of moderate to high uncertainty, the business goals clearly set confront scenarios but little availability of information about the best course of action. As expected, the external influences are in the uncertain context multiple and broad in scope. For instance, the political or technological disruptions brought by recent events as the Brexit or the Covid-19 pandemic are paradigmatic contexts of uncertainty.

The notion of *Complexity*: Entails a large number (almost infinite) and variety of events that constitute the full set of external influences that a firm is exposed to. The reader should consider that no study is likely capable of considering them all. Consequently, the firm´s challenge is to recognize the existence of such influences but then focus on the greater ones. For instance, the most pertinent for a particular business unit, or the ones pressing the most a certain organization. In chapters 4 and 5 this issue of complexity is addressed under the context of *criteria* for factor selection.

Ambiguity, as argued by Van Strallen (2015), is an extension of uncertainty. Boddy (2017) accentuates this primary idea, as a dyad of uncertainties with origin in unclear goals and unclear contexts. This cumulatively uncertainty (or simply, *ambiguity*) can be classified as a *directional uncertainty* (about the business goals´ to set) which intertwines with a *circumstantial uncertainty* (about the course of action – or operational planning ability), as a result of the degree and diversity of the owned human capital. Ambiguity may be then portrayed as the meta-*uncertainty* output of a binary perception about a single event. Here, if the perception is positive, as the firm comprehends fairly well the event, this reveals a state of circumstantial "certainty" which keeps directional certainty aligned. Whenever the perception is negative or the comprehension of an event is low or vague, and the event is taken as opaque, than the event carries a state of "uncertainty" which may escalate it ambiguity.

However, the reality is that firms do not deal with one change at a time on the external environment. Change is often multiple (*x* events per time unit) and multifaceted as to their origin and nature. This means ambiguity, as firms are challenged to find reasonable explanations to multiple events at the same time, and gain some understanding (perception) of them morphology, symbology and evolution.

Despite, *V* triggers *U* and C, in parallel, C influences likewise A. Consequently, lower C which can be rated as *C* minus *(C-)* represents a lower A (*A*-) and lower V (V-) determines lower U´s (U-) and lower C´s (C-).

At this stage, you might have grasped already this idea, that the more a dynamic market is (*V+)*, the more is subsequently the likelihood of appearing uncertain events (*U*+). But, you might have recognized also, that a new event adding to others, not simply tops up on novelty, with more and more changes making it also harder to digest (as more data has to be processed), threatening the ability to understand a full external context on the right time. This makes the job environmental analysis harder and subsequently harder is also the job of strategic re-positioning, as the more complex (*C*+) is the task, more ambiguous (A+) is the overall perception and the level of difficulty to take rational decisions on it. With such a context, one could argue, can we work on "controlling" V to climb sharply and subsequently control the rest, right? The answer is no, there are far too many agents in play, and the sources of volatility-creation have hence a multifaceted origin.

Consequently, the firms do not really (neither fully) "control" business environments. They can simply acknowledge them by analyzing them and have a bounded vision of the game (competition) and the chess board (environment) attempting to influence and turn it into a more favorable one to its side. This is also applied to large enterprises and dominant incumbents with significant market stakes. *Strategical flexibility*, is then a theoretical imperative for better problem-tackling and market fitting, as a state of preparation to further (action), whether before or after a challenging or threatening event hits the "coast" (I mean, the firm). Companies are summoned under VUCA to mobilize real competences towards action as to the analysis of business environments to cope with outer hurdles and opportunities, as challenges are likely to become with time more frequent and larger in scope. The call for organizational flexibility, is a call for *strategic agilization* as a practical need of the 21st century. Invariably, along the book, we will discuss multiple types of EBE phenomena, from *fads* to *wild cards* and *black swans;* and the importance of timely adjustment of the firm to the EBEs.

Organizations need to be able to constantly upskill and reskill themselves as to their ability to deal with challenging events and upcoming change, such as, forming patterns of outer behavior and newer trends. This allows any firm to take more rational decisions and act more effectively, to redefine their competitive position, endure and prosper, especially in markets of higher dynamics. On the contrary, less interest or attention for business environment issues and lower asset investments and capabilization (arguably, a negligent behaviour) sets one firm in a collision course with markets (alias, *strategic drift*). It is a frequent shortcut taken by many players though at a higher cost for all stakeholders.

How come one company is detached from understanding the attractiveness of the industry (even a highly innovative one)? How may one navigate, survive and thrive without knowing in detail the industry structure, the demand-side, the supply-side (especially competition and suppliers) and without understanding the major industry dynamics and evolution traits?. Those are indeed essential issues to be acknowledged; however, is argued here, one cannot drawn them clearly unless the firm possess more "macro-insightful" and updated data and knowledge about other societal aspects shaping the industries, as the public policies, the economic systems, the legal frameworks, the regional and global dynamics, or national/organizational interculturality issues.

In this sense, if your desire is to broaden horizons and know more about the technicalities and virtues of external business environment analysis, then this is a book for you! More than a collection of concepts extracted from prior literature (or a toolbox of practices or models of analyzability, dictated as perfect recipes for a EBE scenario), this book invites you to engage in a critique of both philosophical and management issues, to rationalize the whole management function, and therein the role of strategic management and reflect upon the External Business Environments (EBE) through multiple angles, accounting several options for a critique of the assumptions, views or streams of thought, reasoning and models surrounding the complex task of developing *business environment analysis projects (BEAP).*

Unavoidably rambling back and forth through a theoretical revision, the chapters encompass, case discussions and reflective questions along the book. Two inseparable domains of Organizational and Business Management are key-aspects here addressed. Firstly, the Philosophy of Management depicting (ontological, epistemological, axiological and rhetorical) assumptions and stances, and the continuum of the paradigms. Secondly, the Management function itself and its subsystem of Strategic Management, prior elaborating on the structure and content of a BEAP.

The notion of *BEAP* is conceived from local to a global project dimension, accounting the pre-design stage, the design process, implementation until a post-implementation phase, or after-action review. Fresh conceptions are introduced as to the rationalization of the strategic decisions comprising the BEAP for the maximization of its utility and value, such as the notion of analyzability *criteria.* The latter allowed the objective building of new measurement units and scales for factor´s selection, i.e. something new in the field, and consequently, the patterning of multiple models of analyzability based on goals, analyzability stance and factor selection.

However, the book also reveals some of the "turnkey solutions" for external business environment analysis, (EBEA), presenting a set of most significant frameworks, here explained as to their context and utility for a rather usage through a rational model. Moreover, a plethora of sources of data are provided to guide you through, as in a future role of analyst, as the reader is expected at same point to assume also a market data collection endeavor. A one-to-one revision of made of it takes to analyze a Business Environment and a Business Ecosystem, and are addressed aspects of effective Business Environment analysis, since the elaboration on the conception of organizational success until widget counting aspects of strategic performance related to the measurement of progression or results, in complementarity to the ideas addressed in chapter 2 (namely, 2.4. "*Management Strategic Performance Measurement*").

Bruno F. Abrantes,
Niels Brock Copenhagen Business College, Denmark

Section 1

Environmental Fearfulness and (Business) Environmental Analyzability

Chapter 1
Human Quest for (Environment) Control and the Microfoundations of Management

ABSTRACT

Individual fears and instincts taken as the antecedents for the perception of natural and social risks are gathered in this chapter to illustrate the microfoundations of organizational management and the underlying rationale for the contemporaneity of the management function. Entering the realm of the philosophy of management, and following some of the most influential roots in Ancient China and Greece, one may revisit particularly the Xenophon´s contribution to the initial conception of business management, and to the consequent evolution of human thought until the neoclassicism of the scientific management. Along the way, seminal concepts (e.g. uncertainty or risk) are revisited in the context of strategic management domain which is discussed side-by-side with governance and leadership. Furthermore, the case of Haier Group (and Mr. Zhang Ruimin) is used to illustrate the successful intertwining of the three organizational dimensions (i.e. governance, leadership, and management) for the organizational success.

INTRODUCTION

Since the primitive world, *fear* is assumed to be a survival-responsive function to the external reality one cannot explain, the "unknown". The most unfamiliar the event is, the highest the insecurity and perception of threat, so the need for controlling it. Naturally, fear-control evolved with time, from primal physical fears (of pain, sickness, death, and simple material loss) to others forms, as the (un)recognition of the "self" (loss of identity or meaning), shifting the epicentrum of the concerning phenomena for tangible to intangible fears with spiraling sophistication until modern times.

DOI: 10.4018/978-1-6684-5543-2.ch001

Most of the ancient fears no longer exist in our minds and rituals, whether the offering to the Gods or the worship of the natural divinity. Apart from metaphysics (here excluding the atheists), we are no longer afraid of nature as before. We do not fear, the "mysteries" of the phases of the moon or the solar eclipses. We have no longer a need to control witchcraft, or primeval rituals.

However, the baffling human fear of living on danger is asserted to still exist among us. In the form of modern instinct fear sharpens our sense of survival in modern living. Human nature has not changed! The limbic system in our brain is a vital one. It is involuntarily activated once reaching one positive or negative emotion or feeling; thus, having a direct connection to senses and assuming a *rhinencephalon´*s survival instincts function. This is applicable to any human creature and to any context. Anyone would be petrified of fear if confronted with an eminent attack of a wild animal; or being carjacked in a traffic light. But also in other contexts, not inducing physical fear but social stress (e.g. the panic to fail an oral exam; or the embarrassment of harsh critics when presented your research work in a conference).

Whether you are in life danger, or the danger is the "loss of face" fear is still among us. This applies to all contexts and individuals, from the CEO in Canary Wharf, or a broker in Wall Street, or the teenager in Bronx, or the climber on an expedition to the Annapurna, or even the bravest solder in the battlefield. Fear is always fear, regardless of the size of the threat – relevant is, the perception one makes of it.

FEAR: INSTINCTS AND SURVIVAL

Functioning as a subliminal mechanism of self-protection, fear triggers a cognitive function towards the shielding of a threat (alias, the *instinct*). *Instincts* equip us with gut feelings, as a baseline sense of survival, that tell us which direction to act, whether one needs to respond ("fight"), or to adapt ("run"), or let it go ("relax"), and from there so exercise our instinctive reactions building the individual roadmap of (survival) responses acting in coordination to a set of experienced events. Such inventory of responses constitute our survival function.

Since the world keeps spinning and technology advancing, with the appearance of new gadgets, tools and apparatus molding new habits and ways of living, *fear* will keep mutating in our modern world accentuating the struggle of the "old Joe". This character personifies the fear of the "digital illiterate", the granddad forced to deal with e-mails, software programs, social media, online/contactless payment methods, e- banking systems or creeping digital tax statements. From an initial discomfort, fear escalates to the recognition of some sort of personal intimidation of physical or mental integrity.

In the beginning of the 21st century we experience an intersection of fear with social advancement, and our behaviours turned into a schizophrenic composite response to both. A new world with a strict vision of everything, where the watchword became ....*"control" it*! As the old proverb goes "*A bird in the hand is worth two in the bush*". Over-analytical, and information-centered, the world is in the hands of data brokers, and data analytics´ systems-owners. Some hold private interests, allegedly known as profit-seeking organizations, as *Facebook*, *Microsoft*; or *Google*. Others, go beyond profit agendas (as the *Bilderberg* group; or the *Freemasons*). *Roger Martin*, a famous strategist of our times claims

"The world is on a zealously science-obsessed tangent by which is attempting to apply science to everything whether suitable for scientific analysis or not..."

One may argue that *science became seemingly the mean instead of the end*. The world´s penchant for analytics, is now served on a tray by business schools craving to prepare students with analytical techniques for the business world and form the new generation of technocrats. This s something the philosopher *Friedrich Nietzsche* baptized as the *Bildungsphilister*, as a person devoted to the understanding of the surface without intelectual elevation or erudition to explore the surrounding world. Apparently, the same risk of a philistine culture is (such as in the 19th century) is believed to be more alive than ever! The book of *Shoshana Zuboff* ("*The Age of Surveillance Capitalism: The Fight for a Human Future at the New Frontier of Power*") makes it clear. It is not just a fear but a actual risk and ought to be a wake-up call for individual awareness for the decay of human decency in a battle of values versus power, mediated by the increasing importance of data (datafication) of our societies.

I am not attempting to write an epilogist recreation of (the evolution of the) human history with regard to fear, instincts, risk and survival, nor to distort any retrospective window of the past-present passage. The evidence are though strong enough to express that we are in a particular moment of history experiencing a dominant technocratic view of the world, focusing on the analysis of known events, with an unprecedented valuation of the theoretical framework (over the empirical). The *locus* of interest has though indisputably shifted from nature, art, religion, and mankind´s evolution, as it happened for thousands of years of constant re-civilization of humankind. Hopefully, this a temporary occurrence (aka, a "*fad*" –how strategists like to term it) and reversible, or a passage for a brighter vision of the universe.

Today, *Analyzability* seems to be the answer to everything. Thinking is about the future, the unknown and the unpredictable. Forecasts and orientation to formulate scenarios requires the instrumentalization of science: models, processes and analytical techniques. This is the realm of the philistines! To some authors, this comes at the expense of a "philistine enslavement" (though this is in my own words) of information data and consequently of human rights, as the world is heading towards a path of,

Mediocrity of Values and Excellence of Analysis

With such a dusky micro-reflection shadowing the present of our world, you may wonder, *why a book on Business Environment Analyzability?* You may recall the answer to this question is the first paragraph of the "*Introduction*" section. Scientists believe nowadays the answer for human behaviour is flocking. Research shows that, subconsciously, the crowd (95%) follows a minority of individual humans, so the answer is, *humans flock like sheep and birds*. In Organizational Strategy, as in many other societal domains, the amount of books, e-books and audio-books mostly on organizational behaviour and corporate/ business strategy; corporate responsibility and ethics keeps growing (at a rapid pace), as scholars flock into same themes, models and even examples. Generalist text-books in strategy are the norm these days. An updated book in business environment analyzability is the fish swimming against the stream. The statisticians would call it a Gaussian *outlier*. That´s what this book is (about)!

There is more about the analysis function in this book than in a traditional /generalist "strategy" book. Those you can find plenty on book stores and library shelfs. This is a book for graduate students craving for the alternative view, for the ones who work with strategy analysis (as strategists; planners, researchers), and other business practitioners, the entrepreneur, the business-owner or the manager. The latter ones, are the industry practitioners whom ultimately suffer the pressures and consequences in their organization deriving from the multiple challenges (such as multiple serendipitous opportunities) of the current reality in 21st century: *survival; adaptation; performance; sustainability challenges*.

Regardless of the status quo of societies and the dynamics of the business world, one firm is nowadays constantly defied in goals, systems and structure, by external movements on earth. The latter carries underlying business ethical dilemmas (as, interpersonal conflicts; bargaining disputes; resources acquisition; downscoping; downsizing; integration issues; intercultural; asset´s rotation or alienation, as many others) and further business needs (e.g. information; capabilities; repositioning). For a firm, whatever is not concrete and fully grasped represents an abstraction, and subsequently abstractions carry *complexity* (a concept presented at the *Introduction* section). The business world is full of these complexities one has to deal with on a daily basis, appearing surreptitiously and with blurred contours. They are difficult to grasp, in most of times!

Subsequently, business environment´s complexity is like an unfinished puzzle, regardless of the shape of the pieces (or typology of challenges). The symbology and representativeness of a new event, and impact on the firm, is something to acknowledged, whether likely to constitute a problem or not. Perhaps it comes as an opportunity or a benefit, but those may scumble if not timely grasped. Such assertion is presented by Hans Rosling (2019), not with this same words, in his bestselling book "*Factfulness*" were the author postulates that human instincts seem to bias our perspective toward a darker viewpoint, as humankind seems to be driven by an unconscious attentiveness towards surrounding negativity, which is manning and controlling our fears and subsequently blocking our analytical thinking.

Consistently, the human brain, functions, basically, as a *"scenario generating organ"* (Lindgreen and Bandhold, 2009, p. 39). It has an instinctive need for searching where the grass is greener and spotting any evidence or signals of it, for guaranteeing own security. One needs to constantly scan for any turbulence on the surrounding environment, comprehend the existing phenomena therein and make sense of the existing reality. Furthermore, one has a need to deduce future developments and adapt by creating alternative options, renewing life/business goals and inferring possible actions (including a stepwise planning of them, with all scenarios possible).

One could well compare human instincts to animal instincts, as an antelope on the Africa savannah, or with an Iberian lynx in Europe, as these living creatures share commonalities with humans. Here, we are not taking about the primate menfolk from the Stone Age (2000 B.C), but looking at our contemporary men from the Digital Age on the 2nd decade of the 21st century. Despite the commonalities (instinct-wise), one could though argue that animals are not endowed with thinking and speaking abilities, and their primitive nerve system is rather incomparable. Humans are rational creatures, animal don´t.

Truth is, humankind has seemingly not evolved that much and instincts carved in our genetic code, are deeply crusted in our actions. *Foci* is still the threat and instincts are our safe net, as the most elementary defensiveness mechanism of "*attentive filtering*" against all phenomena and occurrences out of our span of control.

This unconscious level of preparedness is the kickstart for the compulsive attempt to, monitor all insightful material for the understanding of the environment and its dynamics and change, and ultimately, to be able to gain a sense of certainty around it. Jofre (2011, p. 1) contends that is the most basic form of strategy, as a natural human activity, is not exercised as an exact science but as a "*very abstract attribute of the intricate human cognition*".

Indeed, the *"Homo Sapiens is a scenario planning animal"* (Lindgreen and Bandhold, 2009, p. 124), and his/her instinct-level of self-human programming occurs on multiple domains. For instance, as to the *negative instinct*; the *fear instinct*; the *urgency instinct*; or the *generalization instinct*. Rosling´s claims though that six other instincts (*the gap; straight line; size; destiny; single*; and *factfulness*) haze our perception and determine the individual behaviour (Rosling, 2019).

Accordingly, it may be naturally accepted the responsiveness to fear, as a logical behaviour pattern, with outer events fueling our reactions for their delimitation or neutralization of the uncomforted or threat caused by a newer phenomenon one is exposed to. This almost neurotic fear-drive, to establish some sense of influence over the universe is then an ancestral necessity that starts on the knowledgeness of *natural elements* (and the deemed appropriation of their most valuable resources), and is prolonged with the need to grasp moreover the *social elements.*

The first *(natural elements)* imply the comprehension of what was so-called in classic Greek philosophy as the "Four Elements" of nature (i.e. air; earth; fire; and, water), which in modern world has as extended view to other ones (e.g. time; force; darkness; light; thunder; ice, shadow, moon).

The latter (social elements), may be defined as subjective occurrences deriving from real-world interaction across people and events. The "social condition" account though social *goods* (e.g. ideas, thoughts or motivations), a *social state* (e.g. affection, mood, humor) or *social events* (e.g. discussions, reunions or problems). These possess an identical capacity, such as the natural elements, to impact and likely yield some good or harm.

With time, one have learnt to accommodate such elements, adapt to harsh outer circumstances, and control the effects. Furthermore, the competitive nature inherent to humankind, or better said "instinct", accommodated an ancestral mental programming to confront, conquer and/or outperform others, whether competing or not for scarce goods. In management such outlook is labelled as the "rival".

(Re)act upon the surrounding environment, entails then a myriad of chores, to observe, to outline, to monitor and to assess the object/s, as assumed elements with an underlying potential impactful ability and carrying harming effects which require innate or built-in sharpness to safeguard the individual (the "self") or the group ("us/we") (e.g. friends; relatives or team-membership).

This quest for human control over the surrounding space and life was manifested on the evolution of mathematics towards probability theory attempting to model the intuitive notion of "uncertainty" and consequently guiding stochastic models in different scientific domains (e.g. Biology, Economics or Physics) (Geiss and Geiss, 2009).

In the modern world, the fear of underlying to the perception of, "uncertainty" or "risk" led to a complexification of language and the appearance of a business jargon (distinguishing the connoisseur from the crowd) with entrenched meanings, linguistic codes and creating new trends as to the use of acronyms and buzzwords. The contribution of Douglas Hubbard on his book ("*How to measure anything*") clarifies some of those concepts relevant for the context of this book (Hubbard, 2014, p. 84).

Uncertainty is defined as the lack of complete certainty about the future, which is unknown.

And,

Risk is a state of uncertainty where some of the possibilities involve a loss, catastrophe or other undesirable outcome

With such baseline, one may separate the "wheat from the chaff" disentangling key constructs frequently misunderstood.

Uncertainty is not endogenous, is not an individual fear. Uncertainty exists in the *business environment (BE)* regardless of its recognition or not. It is as an exogenous trait to be assimilated and adapted to. Thus, entering the domain of individual perceptions, the idiosyncratic challenge organizations face, with this regard, is to develop a sense of awareness for the recognition of the *uncertainty* and distinguish it from, the likelihood of an event to occur, and likelihood of an event yield a value-negative effect or impact (*risk*) on someone, somewhere, and somehow.

Hence, the perception towards uncertainty refers to a state-of-mind, comprising the alertness and distress about a perceptible hostile matter which may challenge the continuity of a desired status quo. The psychosomatic condition of the individual is dominant aspect shaping the collective view and culture. The perception of risk (not the risk itself) is a consequence of the first. It accounts both, (i) the possibility of an event effectively occur (and its awareness about its likelihood to be realized); and furthermore, (ii) the extent of damage that might cause (and the preparedness to flexibilize the firm´s resources and take an agile response.

These concepts (uncertainty and risk) are again revisited on chapter 5, when addressing the major *criteria* of *External Business Environment Analyzability (EBEA)*. It shall be stated also that, these definitions are part of an overall compilation of concepts gathered at the *Glossary*. The reader is invited to revisit them anytime, as a supporting tool to use back and forth supporting one´s reading, as this book is more than to be read all-at-once, but to consult as a Strategic Thinking or Analysis guide whenever it is of convenience.

Uncertainty is, then, basically this, whenever a gut feeling (or instinct) is confirmed, the company is aware of the challenge and preferably aware of the extent of its effect/s. It is a prediction of occurrence and degree of impact, all together in the same conception. Those ideas are explored during this book and the notion of "impact" is (what is called) a *criterion of analyzability* which we will accompany along the book and will be particularly explored in chapter 4.

Ergo, the instinct to control the surrounding world and mold it to our image and likeness, is nothing more and nothing less than "Management". The management function is something that, mankind practices for over a thousand-years in multiple contexts and with multiple purposes. It is apparently a part of our DNA and our own identity. *Management* is a critical controlling toolkit for surviving the natural and social sphere, and so, much more than an exercise of simply "to manage". This is especially true, as management is mistakenly associated to *Organizational Management*. This explains partly the confusion and myths surrounding it.

Inevitably, "management" taken as merely what is to be managed within the organization´s realm is a far too reductive idea of the spectrum of observation and control of our lives and in consequence reductionist of its breadth. The association of management to the business world is a foreseeable and needed one, since is a critical activity for the subsistence and sustainable enduring of any organization, whether being a social enterprise or profit-oriented. This explains the whole attention given by theorists and methodologists within the fields of Management Sciences and Business Studies to the development of a constant body of literature for the updateness of (new) knowledge for the public good, for furthermore adoption by students, academics, professionals, companies, associations/federations, other industry incumbents and national governments and international authorities.

So, what could one tell about the management in an organization? Surely, one can argue that management is all around, is the invisible hand that glues all objectives and efforts together, and pushes companies into their right direction (according to their fashioned vision and mission statements).

Obviously companies manage nowadays all their subsystems (strategy, finance, accounting, marketing, production, operations or services) and their resources (brands; patents; technology; knowledge; systems; software, facility, equipment; inventory; or people) and stakeholders (clients; communities; investors; open-makers; media; suppliers; partners; upstarters; networks; expert groups; competitors;

employees; subsidiaries; retailers; representatives; or, authorities); however, thinking of management solely in professional terms as an organizational function (or even an asset), it depreciates the real-life prominence, worthiness, complexity and thresholds of what the management function is. Hence, before jumping into the strategic dimension of this function within the organizations (as the context of this book), and depicting its applicability to the theme of business environments, the next section will address first the microfoundations of management and its evolutionary path until modern times.

FROM XENOPHON´S PHILOSOPHY (OF MANAGEMENT) TO THE NEO-CLASSICISM (SCIENTIFIC MANAGEMENT)

In order to better understand contemporary management on the 21st century, one certainly need to go back to the ancestral roots of the dominant philosophic thought, particularly the Chinese and Hellenic civilizations, to comprehend its evolutionary path, and decipher their etymology, influence and role. Undoubtedly, great figures such as *Confucius, Mencius, Sun Tzu, Sun Pin*, or *Lao Tzu* have played an important role in China and other Asian countries, shaping indelibly modern societies, most especially in Far East, as to the way of businesses are done nowadays (Rarick, 2009).

The Confucian moral philosophy represented, with its bioethics principles, the *prima face* pillars of our updated moral values (of *beneficence; justice; non-maleficence*; and, *respect for autonomy*) (Tsai, 2005). Lao Zu (or Laozi) has contributed to, alongside the Confucianism, to a second greater religious/philosophical system, the Daoism (or Taoism), influenced by the follower Zhuangzi (4th Century B.C.) and his meta-ethical reflections and skeptical philosophy as to the limitations in life, and consequently in knowledge, claimed to be foolish the attempt to raise it to an unlimited level. Zhuangzi satirized Confucian disciples and with an anarchist position disregarded the role of governance and management defending that good order results appear spontaneously (Hansen, 2020).

Furthermore, Sun Tzu, considered for many as the first ancient Chinese strategist, argued that strategic management is partially an art and partially a science. His work keeps influencing the Western and Eastern thought of business leaders especially due to his book "*The art of war*" which warfare devotion left an indelible mark on modern strategy, as the topic of battlefield stratagem is considered of great importance as to the understanding of strengths and limitations of those of your foe. Sun Tzu emphasized the importance of *positioning* and its dependence of the conditions of the environment, whether objective/physical or subjective. As to the latter, the subjective conditions of the environment referred to the ideas/decisions of the other competitive actors. For Sun Tzu positioning was more important than planning, as a response which ought to be fast and dimensioned appropriately to address the changing conditions in the environment.

One of the great examples of such heritage that endures on Asian countries, is noticeable on the business networking practices´ domain. The notion of *guanxi* has endured, as a concept and as a business practice, surviving multiple generations until our times. With Confucian roots, *guanxi* refers to "the *drawing on established connections in order to secure favors in personal relationships*" (Dunning and Kim, 2007, p. 329). This management practice has not solely long-lasted, but also spread wings across neighbor countries, and evolved in nature assuming multiple variations. Moreover, it gained a great deal of importance including among large corporations in China and Japan.

In Old Greece, the role of ancient philosophies (and subsequently, the rhetoric, dialectic and sophistry), is likewise recognized on well-known figures, and great thinkers as *Aristoteles*, *Euclid, Plato* or

Socrates. Their blueprint on philosophical and educational spheres, and further work on the development of mathematics, have spread pivotal ideas and methodologies that have influenced markedly the formation of new conceptions and theories worldwide, also as to the domain contemporary business and management (Zanakis et al, 2003).

Nonetheless, within the sphere of Strategic Management, perhaps the most famous example in ancient times revolves around a myth of classic military strategy (the Trojan War), involving the image of *Helen* whom was married the King Menelaus of Sparta but escaped with the son of a Trojan King (Priam). From this event derives a delightful tactical maneuver so-called the "Trojan horse".

The story goes around the city of Troy on the western-coast of Anatolia, on Asia Minor. Here, both Greeks and Trojans entered a deadly conflict because of Helen´s betrayal. On the origin of all this is *Aphrodite*, as this goddess promised Helen to *Paris,* whom ultimately seduced by him abandoned King Menelaus. The king did everything on his power to gain her back entering a war with Troy. During the war, in order to gain access to the Troy and win the war, the Greeks built a giant Trojan horse. A huge hollow wooden horse symbolizing an offering to the Trojan goods, which was left at the entrance of the city; however the horse was a stratagem so their troops could enter the city, besiege the Trojans and ultimately ending the war victorious.

It is a delightful story emphasizing the role of *tactics* and use of tactical maneuvering as a ploy in competition. However, abandoning the context of Military Management and focusing solely on the realm of Business Management, *Xenophon´s* philosophy, is here in an unavoidable reference of the Old Greece´s contribution to modern sapiency, which should not be forgotten.

Considered "*the father of management*", Xenophon was the first philosopher to reflect upon, and conceptualize on *Business Management.* His original ideas were believed to, have been recorded originally on *Oeconomicus,* a book published around 385 B.C. even though at that time, his notion of an organization was still diffused, such as, what it required to be managed. His notion of Management was a restricted idea circumscribed to *Household Management* (Blok, 2009).

Nonetheless, *Xenophon´*s ideas entailed not a simple administration of the private sphere (of the house one lives in). But instead, it accommodated an extended notion of what the administration function is, including all properties owned by an individual in order to make a living, or business management concerned the totality of assets of the owner, acting as a "business manager" with responsibility on own "business operations".

*Xenophon´*s philosophy of management can be depicted then, according to Blok (2009), into *Nine Dimensions of Business Management,* with manifestations ranging from local governance, to management of a complete set of engineering projects (Zanakis et al, 2003, p. 72).

In sum, Xenophon´s primary level of management is the management assumed by the business manager of a *management team,* which entails the assumption that one cannot control all activities (assumption 1). The prior implies the design of a *management system,* in which, the business manager assigns rules for the functioning of businesses and selects/nominates middle managers which shall report to him about their business performance. Business management concerns the extension into "*proper asset management*" (p. 9) which refers to the optimized management of assets out of the direction control on other locations (or building) to be arranged properly in order to make profit and allow the business manager to take advantage in private life of the wealth which has been generated.

Table 1. Xenophon´s philosophy of management (9 dimensions)

Dimension	Description	Goal
1.	establishment and maintenance of a functioning order of the business to make profit	Profit
1.	establishment and maintenance of a functioning order to evoke public admiration	Reputation
2.	establishment and maintenance of a functioning order of the business serves both private and public interests in an integrated way	Cross-benefits
3.	Management consists in the engagement of the business manager in the business operations via direct labor.	Performance
4.	Management consists in the engagement of the business manager in the business operations via the work done by other people (a) Collaboration and partnership with other business managers in a management team (b) Establishment of a management system with internal rules and regulations that employees have to comply with (c) Assigning proper roles to trusted middle managers (d) Direct people management of employees and/or middle managers	Structuring
5.	Management consists in training and teaching of employees and/or middle managers	Development
6.	Management acknowledges the fundamental limitations of the establishment and maintenance of the functioning order of the business, and acknowledges the fundamental role of risk and misfortune	Uncertainty (and risk)
7.	Management consists in *proper asset management* in order to increase profit and pleasure.	Leisure (Wealth for maximization of…)
8.	Management consists in proper asset management in order to serve society	Responsibility and citizenship (to the external environment)

Source: Blok (2019)

Most specially, the principles of Sun Tsu and Xenophon echoed for centuries and influenced decisively their respective fields. For instance, on the 16th century the Ottoman Empire, so spread across a large geography, established an intelligence network to begin a more in-depth and accurate management of information about their enemies (war of information) (Gürkan, 2012). Here, the Ottomans were the first to formally apply the practice of *counter-intelligence* as a set of combined activities to prevent enemy intelligence, developing a set of information management tools to be utilized on further military action and secret diplomacy, such as, *disinformation, information analysis, cryptanalysis, propaganda, bribery, sabotage* or *espionage*. At that time, information became unsurprisingly a key asset and *information gathering* the most elementary activity to be held, with news being conveyed in the form of *nouvelles* or *avisos,* as documented units of data which to be relied on. This opened furthermore a myriad of societal developments as, international exchange; opening of new trade routes; printed press; the founding of public postal system; the intensification of human relations; the development of booking of daily transactions; or the European movement triggered by the 95 thesis of Martin Luther, termed as the Reformation.

On the other hand, the tenets of the Xenophon´s *Philosophy of Management* travelling also for centuries founded disciples in the modern world, including on the 19th and 20th centuries. His followers have developed, for instance, the *Scientific Management*, and an extended version of the scientific approach, based on the logic of economic rationality, giving birth to the so-called *Rational Models* of management applicable particularly to decision-making. The latter is something to be explored on chapter 5, when addressing the models of strategic decisions, as primary determinants of (effective) performance as to the business environment analysis. These disciples have with time been challenged though towards multiple streams of thought, as Business Management evolved in its theoretical framework, with the boost given specially by the Humanists counter-weighting the scientific management, but also seen on the expansion of the reasoning towards *Internal Process Models*, *Human Relations Models*, *Open System Models* and a *Contingency View*, considering the latter, the environment circumstances being a determinant of the manager´s decisions.

The *Scientific Management*, as a School of Management brought major ideas which prevailed along the European ascending industrialization period (industrial revolution), as the *Taylorism*, which envisioned the scientific management as an attempt to create a sense of factory production, in which, emphasized the importance of planning, a best of way of production, a best person for the job, training for specific tasks and the following of procedures and the compensation through financial incentives. In addition, these ideas of Frederick W. Taylor for increasing productivity gained supporters, as Henry Ford whom applied them into an assembly line for increased efficiency (*Fordism*), or Henry Gantt which focused on the planning of work and measurement of tasks (well-known for the "Gantt chart"), or Lilian and Frank B. Gilbreth for their motion and time studies production line´s increased efficiency.

On the corporate governance´s side, an decisive impulse was given by Berle and Means' (1932) study on the separation of ownership and *control* (now known as one essential component of management), as a measure of business operations ("*The Modern Corporation and Private Property*"), arguing that business owners, are the ones with *legal ownership* rights over a firm which shall be distanced from professional individuals (managers) which exercise a controlling function (Tricker, 2000). This allowed in the 1970s, the emergence of the *Agency Theory* to be further incorporated into multiple theoretical domains within the sphere of economics, Corporate Governance and Management, the latter with great application on the sub-field of finance (e.g. Roberts, 2005; Jensen and Meckling, 1976; Bonazzi and Islam, 2007). Such approach (Agency Theory) found though an alternative ground on Williamson's (1979) *Transaction Cost Economics theory (TCE)* foreseeing governance as a business architectural constellation which sets particular mediums for supporting economic transactions (Heide, 1994, p. 73). In this set-up, governance is regarded as a choice between the *traditional market* (*governance- a price mechanism*) and structural configuration and underlying *hierarchy* (*governance - a authority structure*).

MANAGEMENT AND UNCERTAINTY CONTROL

A construct of universal application, *management* seems to exist to provide us with an essential comfort and certainty and adding gravitas to the way we deal with intricate problems in life to be disentangled. Certainly, management alleviate the burden of the unknown and releases individuals from the fears addressed succinctly in the first section.

Management is then definable as the "*activity of intending to add value to resources with the aid of people and other resources.*" (Boddy, 2017, p. 11)

Unquestionably, *management* assumed a fundamental and preponderant role within the business context since the second half of the 20th century (Boddy, 2017). Management spans across a broad range of human and/or automated activities, aiming at ensure a higher alignment, predictability and reduction of uncertainty. Consequently, management it supports micro and macro decision-making, in which the one "in charge" (the *manager*) expects to gain, maintain or renew a sense of physic comfort about potential hazards.

Hence management is all around us, embedded in multiple quadrants of our lives, within a plethora of domestic, social, organizational and political settings, whether wrapped in a personal governance or corporative governance context. Thus, it is worth to clarify at this stage that this definition above, is a general one, extending itself beyond the spectrum of organizational management.

Actually, if we consider management inside and outside the firm´s context, we will certainly come to the conclusion that they are diametrically different, even though, complementary models. The major distinguishable difference separating management in the organizational setting and outside it, as referred in the previous paragraph, linked to the responsibility of corporate governance (organizational context) and personal governance (non-organizational context) is the interpretation of the function (management) itself. Within the organizational realm, management is a conscious exercise, (and likely rationale), deeply rooted on the organization´s specific espoused norms, culture, leadership and structural configuration.

Conversely, as citizens, we vest involuntarily the manager´s hat, as something inherent to an organizing living, an unconscious exercise, equally wide in scope (as in the organizational realm), comprising the administration of a varied range of quotidian life events. For instance, we strive to manage our children´s lives, and influence our friends´ (and relatives) ideas and decisions. Moreover, we manage ourselves, our jobs; career; health; nutrition; household; budget; finance; culture; leisure; or any other aspects in life. We even manage, at the best of our capacity, our free time, and attempt to spare part of it (time) to simply do nothing, administering what we call nowadays the *work-life balance*.

We do literally manage every piece and bit of our life. We are all managers whether we accept it or not. Such an agency is therefore considered an expression of an individual exercise, taken by the individual (the *manager*) regarding his/her aptitude to reflect, act and assume a responsibility upon the shaping of a phenomenon´s progression and outcome.

So, several are the introductory questions we could raise at this stage regarding the organizational management function:

1. Is Organizational management an individual exercise?
2. What is the difference between Management and Leadership?
3. How to distinguish from Management and Corporate Governance?
4. What it takes to be a "good manager" or a "good leader"?
5. And/or, how to identify a successful organization?

All those are questions are legitimate and pertinent ones as they seek to respond to natural curiosity. The reader may have some other to complement these initial 5 ones. In order to answer such questions, is to enter the organization´s realm and funnel the discussion to the subset of *Organizational Management*. In fact, the book is all about this, management on the organizations and so we will start by provided our own defining of it.

[Organizational Management (OM)]: A firm-level function, to be broken-down into multiple processes, utilizing a set of own resources, in other to attain alignment, predictability and uncertainty- reduction, and generate value-addition.

Comparing such definition of *OM* with the one of *management* in general, one may track its consistency and similarity to the conceptual root. It is a set of endeavors (activities), which altogether create one organizational *function* exercised through the combination of various assets to ensure the effective accomplishment of the set goals.

Hence, confined to OM, this book immerses into the depths of collective management following a firm-level perspective with a particular focus upon *Strategic Management (SM)*, as the latter is a critical area with a transversal role, working somehow like the "glue" that ties all other organizational functions (e.g. the sourcing; marketing; production; or distribution) and underlying activities around the organizational goals. Hence, it involves all managerial levels (senior, middle and line managers, external/internal consultants, and other supporting/operating areas.

As referred to in the title, the book bridges Organizations and Markets, while instrumentalizing the Strategic Management function as the mediator between the two proxies (*organization* and *markets*). It intends to focus on concepts, archetypes and practical tools of *business environment analysis (BEA),* since BEA is an iterative activity of strategic management, and a responsibility of all managers, transversal to hierarchic levels. In addition, literature on a specific theme as Business Environment Analysis (BEA), especially strategy textbooks, denotes a necessity for a compilation of theoretical knowledge on the field for the facilitation of the apprenticeship of the theme (i.e. External Business Environment) especially for tertiary education business administration programs. A focus on *Business Environment Analyzability* means then, the reader is zooming-in into the external interface of strategy (i.e. interface strategy - markets).

Indeed, Organizational Management, and particularly Strategic Management, are functions (unlike personal governance) likely not driven by individual fear and human instincts, in which, firms ought to recognize the context of bounded rationality in which they operate within. Thus, assuming such vulnerability coming from the partial comprehension of the markets and consequent inner limitations of it, configures a scenario of embedded uncertainty from which firms cannot escape from.

However, some firms are better than others and utilize uncertainty as a starting point for moving forward, reducing their cognitive "fog" and control their own destiny. This is the case of Hair Group, the case-firm introduced immediately before the "Chapter Highlights" and "Summary of the Chapter" (at the end of the chapter). The humble words of *Mr. Zhang Ruimin*, CEO of *Haier Group* is the proven example of how possible it is to attain a long-lasting successful control of uncertainty over decades, distinguishing in his words clearly the two concepts addressed above in this chapter (*uncertainty* and *risk*) as being two separate ideas, and demonstrating that market uncertainty is not deterministic of risk and financial losses: "*The only thing that we know is that we know nothing…*If you don't *overcome yourself, you will be overcome by others*." (Fischer, Lago and Liu, 2015, p. 6).

Mr. Zhang Ruimin attentiveness of the markets, most particularly the customer needs, is acknowledged by the ability to reinvent *Haier Group* as a consumer-responsive innovation firm, being an appliance´s manufacturer aiming to constantly differentiate itself by the quality of its products and its focus on customer service leadership.

This case is, purposively, an inspiring case of business success, surrounding the ability of this company to sense environmental change, by employing highly-skilled labour capable of, among others, forecasting and foresight activities to fulfill market gaps on customer needs and experience. However, this case is much more than that (success)! In this chapter, it is so far described in general "Management" as an answer to fear and basic instinct´s response, and Organizational Management as the solution for the controlling the business environment uncertainty. However, we will continue with a comparative outlook, distinguishing management from governance and leadership as the latter two functions are like the "armed forces" of successful management. This case, is a brilliant demonstration of the interplay of this triad (governance, management and leadership). Often confused in between as to their scope and boundaries, however their triadic action goes hand in hand with the others.

In Hair Group, the role of Mr. Zhang Ruimin overlaps, being a policy-maker, a real-manager and a change-seeker. Hopefully, this blurb about the case-firm has sharpened your interest for the reading their business story (section "CASE: HAIER GROUP"), besides following the next sections (*1.4. Management and Leadership*; and, *1.5. Management and Governance*). You may note, furthermore, that all chapter are accompanied by a distinctive short-case along with the "Summary of the Chapter" and you are encouraged to make a quick skimmed reading of each case before immersing into the content of the chapters.

MANAGEMENT AND LEADERSHIP

Often applied in the business world lexicon, *leadership* is frequently utilized in a plethora of different contexts. They are confounded many times with management as one single construct. The *ex-ante* understanding both is a compass guiding one through a wider comprehension of this book. Management and leadership are set on two different journeys and have two separate roles.

To understand the boundaries of this concept (*leadership*) in relation to *management* emphasis ought to be placed on two upstream conceptions (*influence* and *power*). The influence of the leader and the power exerted by the leader. Leadership refers to an individual expression of desire to modify the status quo. Such aim of the "leader" is intrinsically dependent on two fundamental ideas, the ability to sway a third person´s ideas, decisions and actions towards a desired direction, and the capacity to make use of tactical tools, as maneuvers for shaping others.

Influence may be then defined by two fundamental skills (or influence-related capabilities):

a) The mobilization of power resources;
b) The modification of the behaviour of other people.

I*nfluence* falls then into the sphere of intentions, as a process of social construction of the outcome (*heuristics of influence*):

Figure 1. Heuristics of managerial influence
Source: Own elaboration

Mobilization (input)	→	Modification (output)

On the other hand, *power*, a concept attributed to Sir Bertrand Russel is consequentialist. It aims to determine the decision-making/behavior on favor of the influencer and produce the intended effects (Boddy, 2017). So, *whom shall the leader influence and why?* Leaders aim to influence any capital/ organizational or product-market stakeholder whom may be deterministic of the result. Combinations of influences are various and changing and according to the endeavor the influencer is projecting for the fulfillment of the vision of change.

Figure 2. Leader´s breadth of influence
Source: Boddy (2017)

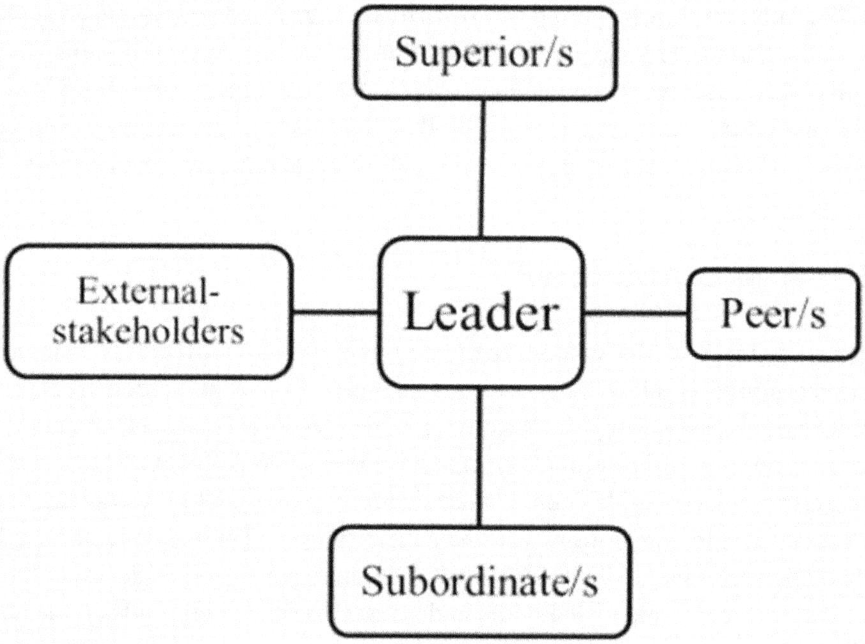

Based on the prior, the definition of *leadership* delivered by Bennis and Nanus (1983) refers to the ability to move an organization from a current to future states, creating a vision for new opportunities, influence other organization-stakeholders to commit to the newer vision of change, and instill new ideas, processes, strategies and cultures. In simple terms, as expressed by *Rosalynn Carter* in 1927, in one of her famous quotes, a manager guides a person, the leader takes one where he/she wants them to go while the "great leader" takes someone to, where don't necessarily wants to go, but ought to be.

Making a comparison between the two functions, it may be advocated that management seeks stability. Aims at reduce the uncertainty and attain a certain output according to the type of input and transformation system in place at the organization. On the other hand, leadership seeks change, to over the organization towards the usage of other type of resources, more efficient systems, processes, activities/routines and technologies, which go beyond the goal´s set, expanding horizons of corporate thinking, creating new opportunities, enhancing the efficiency in the use of resources, creating a new vision and culture for a wealthier, more successful and/or sustainable organizational future.

Hence, Management and Leadership are different functions but not incompatible. They exhibit complementary features. The image of the leader may furthermore be taken by the same person as the manager, as both roles are commensurable, and can be overlapped, taken together, as the manager's personality traits and behaviour are identical to the traits of leader. This is observed on the case of Haier Group, where Mr. Zhang Ruimin (CEO) assumed simultaneously the role of the visionary shaping the future of the company from being simply an appliance manufacturer though a change path for becoming a provider of reliable solutions to its customers' problems. He has increasingly incorporated sophisticated forms of customization, new types of services and new technologies, making Haier group simultaneously a customer-responsive innovator, a niche-innovator and a network-building entrepreneur for enhancing customer intimacy through its *zi zhu jing ying ti* (*ZZJYT*) model of independent operating units, as self-organizing work units (i.e. ZZJYTs) assuming critical functions — marketing, design, and manufacturing (Fischer, Lago and Liu, 2015).

However, the opposite may be also true, as the leader may also exist regardless of whether is formal empowered into a managerial position. Despite it seems incompatible the stability and change are two sides of the coin of organizational success. For instance, imagine the general manager of a successful organization with solid strategic and financial results of the last years. He/she certainly wishes to endure that path and status of stable and continuous returns; however, as a manager recognizes as well that in order to maintain the organized needs simultaneously to change, adapt to market dynamics, take advantage of new knowledge and technologies, conduct further research, develop new processes, products and innovate for extending the longevity of prior success. They could be seen (management and leadership) as to parallel dimensions, in which, the company manages the present (the ability to currently transform resources into value) and explores the future (changes towards different resource bundles, systems and objectives).

Table 2. Management vs. leadership

Dimensions	Manager	Leader
Status	Stability	Change
Vision	Continuity	Rupture
Function	Commands, instructs, empowers, monitors and motivates	Acts, engages, motivates, inspires
Role	Formal	Informal
Position	Job	Self-made Intrapreneur
Direction	Strategic and Financial goal´s accomplishment	Challenge the strategic direction, create new opportunities, business models/processes and/or culture
Business Model	Institutionalized	Fashioned
Activity	Secures the direction	Opens new routes
Coaltion	Subordinates	Followers.
Influence	Legitimate power and authority.	Expertise power and role-model
Power	Authority	Influential
Change	Reactive	Proactive
Goal	Maintain the status Succeed (be the hero)	Modify the status New vision of success (seed heroes)

Source: Own elaboration

Leaders instill a rupture, using informal power (if not a/the manager) to convince others to build a coalition, and to become the champions of change, spreading the word across the entire organization, and eliminating obstacles along the journey. For instance, the *8-Step Model* developed by the Harvard

Business School´s professor, Dr John Kotter is a reference as a method implementing the heuristics of leading change through the adoption of the following sequence of procedures (Kotter Inc., online):

1. Create a sense of urgency
2. Build a guiding coalition
3. Form a strategic vision
4. Enlist a voluntary army
5. Enable action by removing barriers
6. Generate short-term wins
7. Sustain acceleration
8. Institute change

Short note, just to recommend, in connection to the above, a delightful reading of a book ("*Our iceberg is melting*") in which the author above makes a great analogy with the life of penguins assisting a changing event, walking the reader through a smooth transition across the steps of model, as penguins are forced to change (while attempting to discover a new home and way of living).

In this sense, the leader is a self-made intrapreneur, which inside the organizational realm, possess specific traits of personality, which will determine decisions and behaviour. McCrae and John (1992) have group those leader´s traits them into five main domains, which labelled of *clusters* (and designated them of *The Big Five*). Accordingly, the behaviour of the leader ranges along each of those clusters of *agreeableness (A); conscientiousness (C); extraversion €; neuroticism (N);* and, *openness (O)*, from which personality traits vary between extreme positive and negative (+/-) poles. Here five negative *(X -)* positions are assumed per cluster and five positive positions *(X +), representing* different separate behavioral traits. See below the example for the A clusters:

Figure 3.
(Note: A1 - unfeeling; A2 - oppositional; A3 – quarrelsome; A4 – straightforward; A5 – compliant; A6 –sympathetic; O1 - narrow-minded; O2 – disinterested; O3 – unimaginative; O4 – creative; O5 - open-minded; O6 – intellectual) Source: McCrae and John (1992)

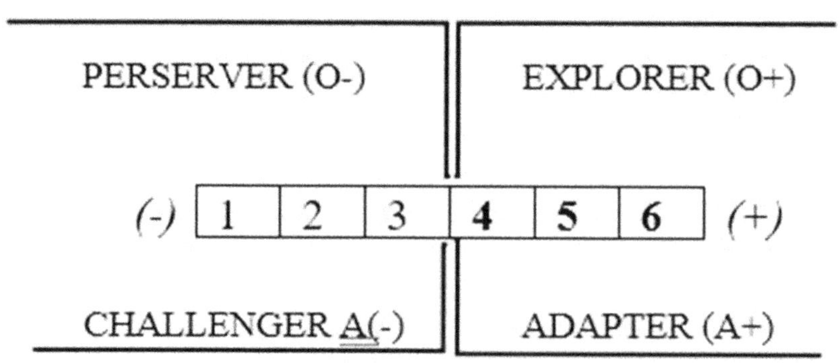

The leader is then assumed, regardless of other variations in traits, as a proactive individual aiming at modifying a status, ambition to set (and reach) newer goals, pursuing heroic projects/achievements.

Often, mistakenly taken by the other, management and leadership are clearly distinct but complementary (*commensurable*). Both functions, and capabilities-owned and built by both are required within the organization, to get the work done in day-to-day basis, and to idealize, create and inspire others to change. Using here the analogy of the sea, both tranquil and wavy waters, are equally important for further learning, development and evolution.

Lindgreen and Bandholm (2019) assert though that regardless of the principles and styles, leadership ought not to be confused to a formula in unison. Two-brain halves, a *creative leadership* and an *effective leadership*, share a common denominator. Although, the first (creative) is oriented towards reconfiguration and renewal for development purposes. The latter (efficient) oriented towards production and results. Their guiding principles are naturally disparate, with the first being the process and vision control while the latter being the management of objectives.

Naturally, the case of Haier Group combines accentuated creative leadership traits perceived on the launching of unconventional products/services or products with unconventional design, as the *Tianzun,* a cooling device with an obelisk-like shape with a small wind tunnel. Yet, this is accompanied by remarkable effective leadership traits observable, for instance, on the marketing campaign with a slogan highlighting the design as a unique selling proposition (USP) for the Chinese market: "cool, not cold"; but also, on the manufacturing activities accommodating customer-interaction´s data with the *Tianzun* devices for developing further product features; or even on the procurement and after-sales services integrated the latter with sourcing feasibilities and follow-through plans (Fischer, Lago and Liu, 2015, p. 3).

MANAGEMENT AND GOVERNANCE

Another common source of misperception, is to label *management* with the epithet of *governance* and vice-versa. Both concepts, exactly as in the previous section, in which we distinguish management and leadership, cover two separate concepts with two separate roles in business.

One might consider though the boundaries of governance and management more subtle than the previous comparison, as public/private governance of any organization is not devoid of the managerial hand, and such confusion arises especially when we focus on single functions in which governance are intertwined, and one determines the other (Abrantes and Fernández, 2023; Abrantes, 2020). Perhaps, the broader scope of governance is a confounding one, touching a plethora of different theoretical domains (e.g. economics; political sciences public administration or sociology). Hence, the term *governance* in the context of the organizations refers actually to what is dubbed as *corporate governance,* which shall not be confused with other typologies, or even, with a government itself, as a federal institution with responsibilities within *executive, judicial* and *political* governance.

In turn, governance is a broader agency than a government, configuring the design, maintenance and monitoring of the "rules of game" (Rhodes, 1996). Hence, the government´s body is a discrete nomination assisted by rotation of individuals in power while governance continues "*ad eternum*" and follows the longevity of the governing institution. Noteworthy is, non-governmental entities in civil society, are also entitled to "governance" just as any public/private enterprise, as a municipality or a private-equity firm. Thus, we may find it on any other enterprise and organization such as, an accreditor body; a board of a charted profession; a chamber of commerce/trade/industry; a central bank; a foundation; a professional association; standard development organization; union, and so forth.

Governance is associated, not with societal *growth* but instead is focused on *development*. Let's say that within the business context while management administers resources to achieve goals and accumulate wealth, on the other hand governance focus on the drawing the path to a better organization. The common ground of them (management and governance) and inclusively leadership lays on centering attention on the *strategic direction* for a better future, despite aiming at set different destinies and milestones.

Governance is tied to two main sets of activities:

(i) Policy-making;
(ii) Processes (for polices´ implementation);

On the etymology of the word governance, is the first utilization attributed on the old Greece´s time to Plato, in which the term "*kubernan*", meaning to "pilot", referred to, the design of a system of rules. Here, the term was circumscribed solely to the sphere of political governance.

Governance issues came to the spotlight in our contemporary societies mostly in 1980s, brought by the public reforms taken by the United States of America (USA) in which principles of corporate management got replicated under the auspice of public-private development and government bureaucracy (Ruhanen et al., 2010). On the academia, the field evolved fast, driven by strives on political sciences, notoriously influenced by the classical foundations of Greek philosophers and further developments in modern society. Corporate governance, as in other theoretical fields, maintained an accentuated proximity to a political approach. Unsurprisingly, the definition of *governance* absorbed such background: *"the self-organizing inter-organizational networks characterized by interdependence, resource exchange, rules of the game and autonomy from the state"* (Rhodes, 1997, p. 15, cited in Ruhanen et al., 2010).

A straightforward definition of *corporate governance* (CG) transposing the tenets of the above definition to the organizational context is given by the Cadbury Report (1992, p. 15), as "*the system by which companies are directed and controlled*".[1] Hence, after a description of what CG is, it may be established a comparison of Management-Governance, similar to the one in the previous section (Management-Leadership) (see Exhibit 6 below).

Table 3. Management vs. governance

Dimension	Management	Governance
Goal	Administer resources; Goal´s accomplishment, and Corporate vision´s alignment Maintain the status	Design the rules (policies, processes and rights) Fashion the status
Vision	Continuity (corporate vision´s alignment)	Set a universal system and its standards
Power	Authority	Law
Hierarchy	Dependent on an upper system	Decrees the management tenets
Influence	Legitimate power and authority.	Universal
Coalition	Senior/middle/line manager; supervisor; Program/project or team leader	Stockholders / Board of directors

Source: Own elaboration

Crossing the two functions per dimension, governance seems to be tied to the *design* of policies whether management to the administration of resources towards the goal´s accomplishment deriving from the corporate vision of the direction of those policies, and the adopted model of their implementation in a given moment in time.

Hence, governance is broader in scope and it comes at the upstream of organizational management though mediated by the action of strategic leaders.

Figure 4. Interrelation governance-management - leadership
Source: Own elaboration

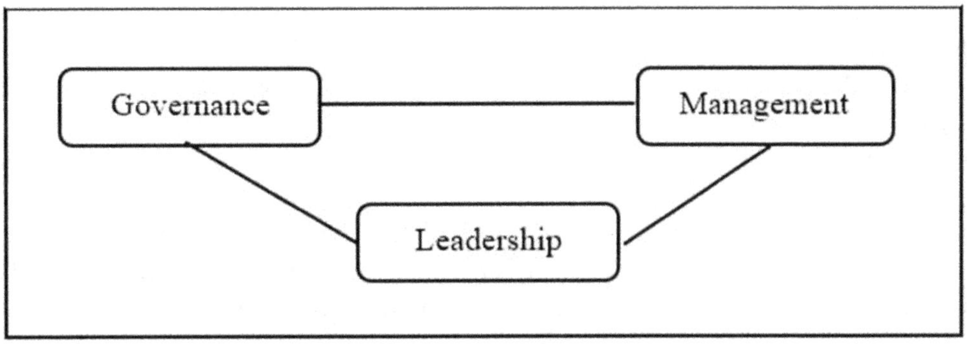

Hence, management provides continuity to governance. It brings *feasibility* to the universal system and standards created by the governing laws. Management ensures that the corporate vision is realistic and endurable, though being challenged or mediated by the internal "hunters" of discontinuity (i.e. leaders), both by their thoughts *(how´s the organization idealized?)* and emotions (*how´s the organizational felt/experienced?*), referring to the "hearts and heads" of the idiosyncratic system of decision-making of each leader.

In this sense, governance refers to a holistic view of the firm, as whole system of rights, processes and controls, which is established over the internal and external sphere of the organizational management for protecting the interests of all stakeholders (Centre of European Policy Studies, 1995).

Tricker (1984, pp. 6-7) argues that corporate governance ''*emphasizes giving overall direction to the enterprise (private actor), and overseeing and controlling the executive actions of management*''. In the case of Haier Group, the direction of the company, pointed towards a customer-centric view, in which products/services, capabilities, activities and even the organizational structural is managed according to the direction followed by the CEO. Even the shift of the organizational structure and the creation of ZZJYTs implied an adaptation of the business model towards the go-to-market governance guidelines. Thus, as referred by Nickols (2016) corporate governance is all about determining the *ends* of the enterprise, in which, those who govern are responsible for the setting those ends, communicating them to the stakeholders in a clear manner, and ensure these ends are legitimate and contribute to the wealth of the organization and its members.

Hence, corporate governance is embedded, according to the author, on multiple spheres of action. Some authors label them as *dimensions of governance*. However Nickols (2016) consider 4 major spheres (*communication*; *economic*; *ethical; and strategic direction).* Those seem to derive from the Graham et al. (2003) ten (10) governance dimensions:

1. *Accountability* (to organizational and external stakeholders)[2];
2. *Consensus*-orientation;
3. *Effectiveness*[3];
4. Efficiency[4];
5. Equity;
6. Public participation;
7. Responsiveness to stakeholders;
8. Rule of law;
9. Strategic vision;
10. Transparency.

However to gain a deeper understanding of the theoretical scope covered by governance the reader is suggested to have a look at a deeper mapping of the characteristics of governance, or the so-called *dimensions*, presented in the study of Ruhanen et al. (2010) ("*Governance: a review and synthesis of the literature*"). The study of these (four) authors may be particularly appealing for the reader, aiming at dissipate, any existing doubts until this stage, as to the thresholds of governance and management. Their in-depth coverage of the dimensions of governance through a systematic literature review over 53 journal articles in the field is a clear contribution for the broad understanding of the governance role.

In the figure above, it may be observed that the dimensions are dually categorized, as the bar chart contains two colors, corresponding to the two most influential theoretical bodies (Political Science and Corporate Management) which affected the evolution of governance-related theory. Here, a revision of 40 main factors (dimension) are roughly summarized into a ranked list of the most influential dimensions, filtered by its theoretical root.

It is clear that most scholars are concerned with rather holistic aspects of what we have classified as the "greater governance" more than the heuristic aspects of "minor governance". Here, this classification, separates, by governance scope, the sphere of action of the govern body into two separate tiers, the greater governance referring to the overall (vision and action), while the minor governance as the locus of the attention is specific. For instance, the direction set upon the dimension training, in most organizations, pertains an immediate impact to the department (and its projects and teams), having a specific nature, per each division or business unit, mostly felt by the line manager, the training candidate and the human resources area responsible for the training. On the other hand, the accountability dimension, related to the overall targets set for a business, as the quantitative standard of achievement of goals (often called strategic goals), are shared across the organization by all internal stakeholders, being so a component of greater governance. Indeed, the benefits and drawbacks of the minor governance decisions hits indirectly across units, yet their influence is rather heuristic than overall strategic. However it shall be also acknowledged that, despite of the degree of influence (firm-specific - or minor governance, or firm-wide impact, greater governance) of an individual policy or rule, governance has though a broad-scope and implies the preparation of a organizational "recipe" with a strategic nature, hence, the array of coverage of multiple arrangements deriving from dimensions may naturally vary

Figure 5. Dimensions of governance
Source: Ruhanen et al. (2010)

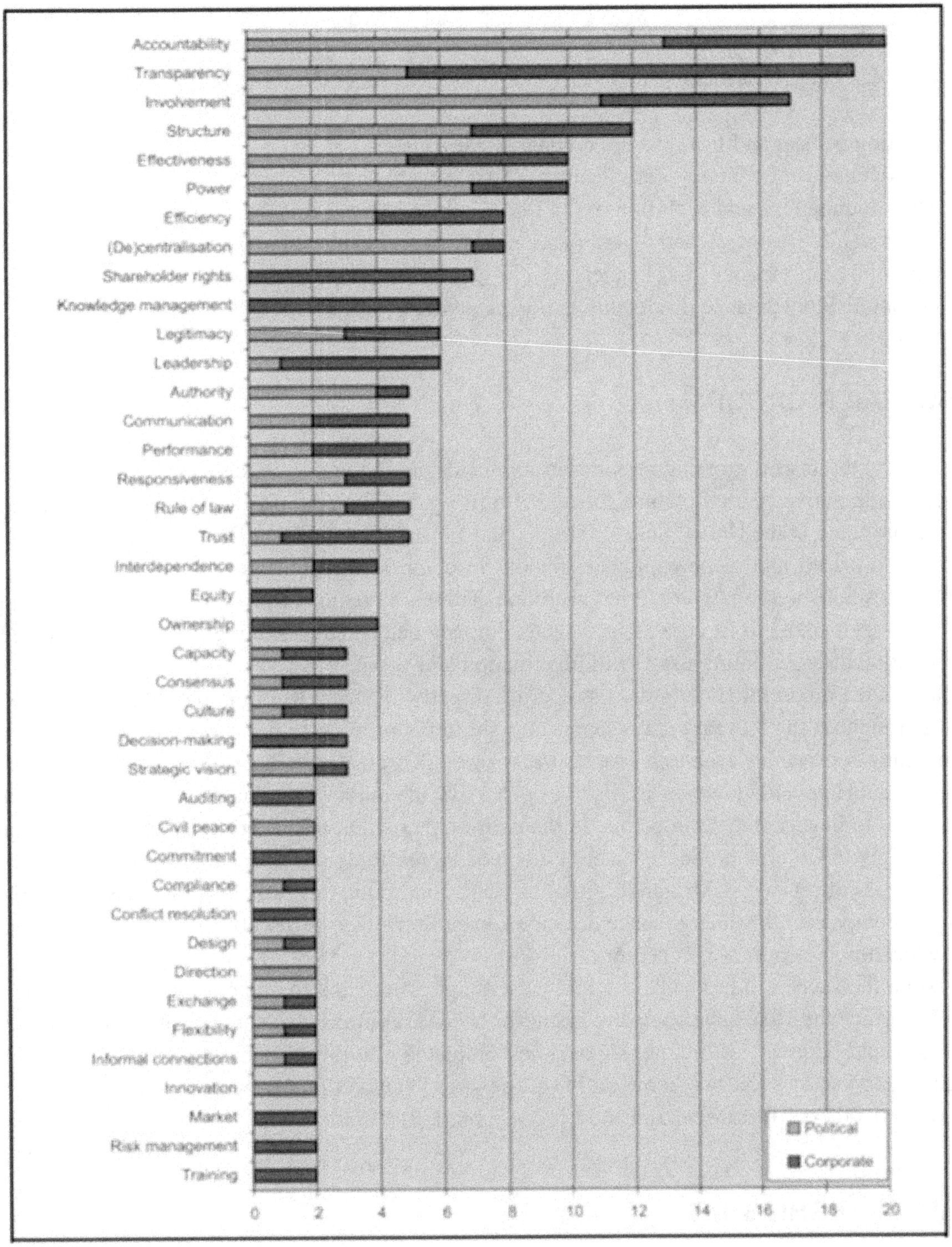

in their coverage, with some actions being whole-corporate resolutions and others targeting particular functional/geographical areas and activities.

LEARNING OUTCOMES

- Relation of Fear and Instincts in Personal Governance
- The dynamics of contemporary business (VUCA)
- Microfoundations and evolution of the Philosophy of Management
- Understand Business and Organizational Management; Strategy; Strategic Management; Corporate Governance; and Leadership
- Distinguish governance, leadership and management

CASE: HAIER GROUP

Haier is now the fastest-growing provider of appliances in the world. Since 2011, it has held the largest worldwide market share in white goods. With its upscale brands in China, such as Casarte, and its growing presence in the United States, Europe, and Japan, this US$38 billion company has moved out of the value-priced and niche appliance domain to compete directly with top-of-the-line appliances from more established companies. It has accomplished this by being a consistently coherent and capable company: staying true to its core identity as a company dedicated to solving problems for consumers, while continually reinventing itself with imagination and verve.

Much of the credit for Haier's success accrues directly to Zhang Ruimin, the company's CEO since 1984. Throughout the 30 years of his tenure, his sharp focus on customer service leadership has given the company consistency even as it propels Haier through dramatic changes. Zhang was the leader who proposed that Haier should never see itself as just a manufacturer of products, but instead as a provider of solutions to its customers' problems. In the earliest years, that meant bringing new levels of quality and reliability to Chinese products. Later, it involved increasingly sophisticated forms of customization and new types of services. Through its simplicity and continuity, this principle has given all employees a reliable compass with which to make decisions, even in the face of disruptive market challenges such as new technologies or new competitors.

Despite the success it has achieved, and its willingness to stick to one core value proposition (and one CEO) since the 1980s, the company has never become complacent. Zhang established early on that changes would be a way of life, not soon-to-be-completed episodes that must be traversed. "The only thing that we know is that we know nothing," he says. "If you don't overcome yourself, you will be overcome by others." (Fischer, Lago and Li, 2015, pp. 1-8)

CHAPTER HIGHLIGHTS

- The ten (10) human *instincts*
- The Environment: *natural* and *social* elements
- The notion of environmental *uncertainty* and *risk*

- Xenophon´s philosophical foundations of Business Management
- The concepts of *Management*, *Organizational Management*, *Strategy* and *Strategic Management*
- From Scientific Management approach to Contemporary Management
- Links between Governance, Management and Leadership
- Environmental dynamics, and managing change

CONCLUSION

Fortunately, the evolution of science and the empirical knowledge increased our understanding of human fears, deepened our comprehension of natural and social interactions and consequently increased its predictability, and moreover, gradually reducing the uncertainty both on tangible and intangible transactions. This is also applicable to the organizational management realm, whether public or private ones and their business and operations.

On this chapter, we have made a smooth entrance into Corporate Management and Business Environments, as we have addressed general ideas and concepts, within the spectrum of Management Sciences and Business Administration. The reader had the occasion to get acquainted with (or revisit) the microfoundations of business management and so accompany the evolutionary path of the scientific thinking, from the roots of the Philosophy of Management until our modern times, plus the neoclassicism of the Scientific Management approach and their influential role on the unravelling of other contemporary models of management. Moreover, we looked at other concepts (as uncertainty, risk, governance and leadership) in the context of the organizations, and took some time to dissect leadership and governance, prior an immersion into the topic of this book (i.e. Business Environment).

Hence, considering the content addressed in this chapter, one may naturally deduce from the evolution of the management function, that the organizations have also evolved and so as the business environment. It is true that the philosophy of management has gone through a long journey since the original idea of *household management* in Ancient Greece, so as the practice of the scientific management dominated by the Taylorism in the 19th century. Surely, (Contemporary) Management is now a discipline much more sophisticated than a century ago, and the same happened with the contemporary business environments. Surely, the role of science has been decisive, and it may be claimed a true inverse relation (of *scientific knowledge* and *uncertainty reduction*) valid expressly when considering the environment as a static one.

Nonetheless, contemporary business environments are assumed to be, especially on the rather innovation-driven or efficient economies of the first world, as dynamic business spaces, where the nature and pace of agents' maneuvers may be truly unpredictable.

Prior knowledge, market experience, or even the sharpness of the medical gaze of some agile organizations, do not always guarantee the governing body/senior managers the full resolution of future upcoming challenges. In fact, several are the theorists on the domain of international business (IB) who claim that markets are increasingly *volatile, uncertain, complex and ambiguous (VUCA)* and firms ought to acquire and/or build cognitive and managerial (dynamic) capabilities to accommodate potential risks of strategic drift, and to gain a sense of awareness of the dynamics of environment change an attain strategic flexibility to (pre)act and (re)act upon it.

In the next chapter, the reader is introduced to business environments and the problematic of business *environment analyzability* (BEA) and effective *business environment analysis*. In fact, the latter two concepts are quite distinctive and we will start our immersion into this topic by making a distinction of them. Nevertheless, after a smooth introduction to organizational management-related concepts and theory in this chapter, the next one will begin by bridging *management* and *strategy, as the two functions* are intrinsically related.

The management function is broken down into its four (4) major components. Afterwards, organizational strategy is introduced through the Mintzberg notion of *5Ps*, and followed by a discussion about *Strategic Management*. Herein, the reader has a short incursion into *Strategic Planning* and Strategic *Controls* as some insights are provided about goal´s setting and planning, plus Strategic Performance Management (SPM), as these two activities (plan and control) are essential in organizational management. Moreover, both are connected to business performance and corporate wealth. Herein, one may already find a connection between the activities of planning/performance measurement and performance evaluation/diagnosis with the Xenophon´s 8th dimension of his Philosophy of Management as a tenet of profit and pleasure-seeking and their maximization.

REFERENCES

Abrantes, B. F. (2020). Governance of academic laboratories and the capabilisation of higher education students. *International Journal of Management Education*, *14*(2), 135–158.

Abrantes, B. F., & Fernández, R. L. (2023). Digital competition and capabilities' augmentation on international cohorts: Evidence from the 'case competition 2019'. *International Journal of Education Economics and Development*, *14*(1), 100–122. doi:10.1504/IJEED.2023.127628

Bennis, W., & Nanus, B. (1985). *Leaders: The strategies for taking charge*. Harp & Row.

Boddy, D. (2017). *Management: Using practice and theory to develop skill* (8th ed.). Pearson Education Limited.

Cadbury, A. (1992). *The Financial Aspects of Corporate Governance (Cadbury Report)*. The Committee on the Financial Aspect of Corporate Governance (The Cadbury Committee). http://www.ecgi.org/codes/documents/cadbury.pdf

Fischer, B., Lago, U., & Li, F. (2015) *The Haier Road to Growth*. Strategy + Business. https://www.strategy-business.com/article/00323.

Geiss, C., Geiss, S. (2009) *An introduction to probability theory*. Jyväskylän yliopisto.

Jofre, S. (2011). *Strategic Management: The theory and practice of strategy in (business) organizations*. DTU. https://backend.orbit.dtu.dk/ws/portalfiles/portal/5705108/rapport1.11.pdf

Lindgren, M., & Bandhold, H. (2009). *Scenario Planning*. Palgrave MacMillan.

Martin, R. (2022). Why Planning Over Strategy? *Medium*. https://rogermartin.medium.com/why-planning-over-strategy-88555015af3c

McCrae, R. R., & John, O. P. (1992). An introduction to the five-factor model and its applications. *Journal of Personality*, *60*(2), 175–215. doi:10.1111/j.1467-6494.1992.tb00970.x PMID:1635039

Nickols, F. (2016). *Four Strategies for Managing Change*. Nickols. https://nickols.us/four_strategies.pdf

Rarick, C. A. (2009). The historical roots of Chinese cultural values and managerial practices. *Journal of International Business Research, 8*(2), 59–66.

Rosling, H. (2019). *Factfulness*. Flammarion.

Ruhanen, L., Scott, N., Ritchie, B., & Tkaczynski, A. (2010). Governance: A review and synthesis of the literature. *Tourism Review, 65*(4), 4–16. doi:10.1108/16605371011093836

Tricker, R. I. (1984). *Corporate governance: Practices, procedures, and powers in British companies and their boards of directors*. Gower Publishing Company, Limited.

Tsai, D. F. (2005). The bioethical principles and Confucius' moral philosophy. *Journal of Medical Ethics, 31*(3), 159–163. doi:10.1136/jme.2002.002113 PMID:15738437

Zanakis, S. H., Theofanides, S., Kontaratos, A. N., & Tassios, T. P. (2003). Ancient Greeks' practices and contributions in public and entrepreneurship decision making. *Interfaces, 33*(6), 72–88. doi:10.1287/inte.33.6.72.25177

Zuboff, S. (2019). *The age of surveillance capitalism: The fight for a human future at the new frontier of power: Barack Obama's books of 2019*. Profile books.

ENDNOTES

1. (Corporate) Governance as a system is explored in the Part II – chapter 7. In such chapter the focus on Project Governance, in relation to "Business Environment Analysis Projects (BEAP) incorporates a seminal body of theory of system´s architecture denominated "stage-gates" here briefly referred to.
2. Refers to the due responsibility to organizational and external stakeholders
3. Effectiveness as to the achievement of goals
4. Efficiency as to the decision-making and problem-solving (regardless of resource allocation/administration)

Chapter 2
Organizational Management and Strategic Behaviour

ABSTRACT

This chapter explores the context of business strategy´s formulation and contemporary management, addressing seminal aspects related with: (i) technological disruptions (e.g., artificial intelligence and the internet-of-things; and the 4th industrial revolution); (ii) global business competition (e.g., new business models; mergers and acquisitions; network competition; or globalization); and (iii) the upsurge of the VUCA business environments. In this context, the major challenges surrounding the Strategic Adaptation and Strategic Fit to VUCA environments are depicted . One addresses moreover the POLC cycle, plus the phases of strategic fit (and the organizational levers of internal/external fit) and the importance of developing multiple organizational capabilities. Lastly, it depicts the association of strategic management practices (planning vs. controlling) and their importance for organizational success.

INTRODUCTION

On the previous chapter, we have introduced the management function, crucial for controlling the outer uncertainty. In addition, management is distinguished from governance and leadership, two interrelated functions within the organizational sphere commonly misinterpreted as to their boundaries and threshold of their theoretical frameworks. Moreover, it included some relevant ideas, such as: (i) to the evolutionary path of the body of theory on Management Sciences; and (ii) non-static nature of business environments. Perhaps, this may lead to a question, whether theory modified the industries and businesses, or vice-versa, practitioners pushed research towards a newer reasoning. Such, assertion may be naturally contested, but in our study of internationalization model´s endurance, it is concluded a mutual and reciprocal influence (Abrantes, 2020).

It is relevant though to acknowledge that most of these ancestral fundaments of management practices are still valid as knowledge-gained references in the field, nonetheless, the context has been altered with time, and consequently the assertions of academics and practitioners on the way to administer a firm. For instance, the disruption of information and communication technologies (ICT) and the dissemination

DOI: 10.4018/978-1-6684-5543-2.ch002

of digital technologies worldwide and their generalized utilization have brought the world together in a global interdependence with commerce becoming more web-based, trade shifting to platforms. In fact, these two factors (technology and globalization) are seminal attributes of businesses in the 21st century.

CONTEXT: RELEVANCE AND DETERMINISM

In current times, the orientation to service industries has reached an exponential growth and development, with an unprecedented optimization triggered by big data analytics software applications and artificial intelligence powerful algorithms. Thus, the uprise of the tertiary sector has inevitably transformed the primary and secondary sectors towards a second economy comprised of a *4th industrial revolution (4IR)* also known as the Industry 4.0, interconnecting the real and digital world. The prior has shaped the factory production and the transactional industries for the future.

Hence, a growing number of companies in the secondary sector have adhered to "cobotization" (as a human-robot interaction´s phenomenon at the workplace of co-working and sharing of activities) or even transformed production into full robotized units. Production became also gradually a commonly dispersed global activity. Grant (2021) provides a good example of the such *globally-dispersed production* by described in his book the *Boeing 787 Dreamliner* aircraft model, in which, several of its parts being nowadays produced all over the world; for instance, the central fuselage (in Italy); the forward fuselage (in Japan and USA); the escape slides (in USA); the raked wing tips (in South Korea); the electric brakes and landing gear (in France); the cargo doors (Sweden) or the flight deck seats (in UK). So, one may wonder (specially the buyer) were thus my purchased product comes from? Yes, the business realm is more sophisticated and intertwined than ever before, and the current paradigm of supply-demand balance across industries only increases the pressure on industry (or better said) intra-industry competition, in which, typically production life-cycles assist a downward trend in time, such as the (lead) time on post-launching phase of the product with early-imitators/followers being able to copy and replicate ideas and products at a faster pace.

Companies eager to subsist, grow and to become a dominant incumbent or a sustainable firm have developed furthermore methodologies towards process innovation tools, in addition to product-innovations, focused on the operation's continuous improvement and on their supply chains, but also, on transactional and reporting systems, with added apparatus on business intelligence, and even, idealized new strategic innovations as to their business models adopting a multiplicity of options, for example, the *freemium*, *meter-based*; *razor-and-blade*, *blue ocean* and so forth).

Other organizations, especially large-firms shifted to an alternative reasoning, a *non-organic growth logic*, in which, business growth or development (as innovation processes, competition maneuvers and goals) are achieved by instilling alternative approaches for boosting the division´ s competitiveness and sustainability of the corporation, enhancing market opportunities, opening new foreign market-entry doors, modifying strategic (re)positioning or even regulating competition.

These approaches seem to have gained traction in last decades in the western world. One of those approaches are the utilization of merging and/or acquisition (M&A) of their firms. This popularized non-organic growth instrument has assisted a steep upward tendency in the last decades, as the number of operations, both in transactions and value involved in the operations, including on cross-border acquisitions, overcoming, since 2015, the 47K mark on annual transactions and the 4,92 trillion USD since 2007(IMAA, 2021).

Figure 1. Number of mergers and acquisitions (M&As) worldwide
Source: IMAA (2021)

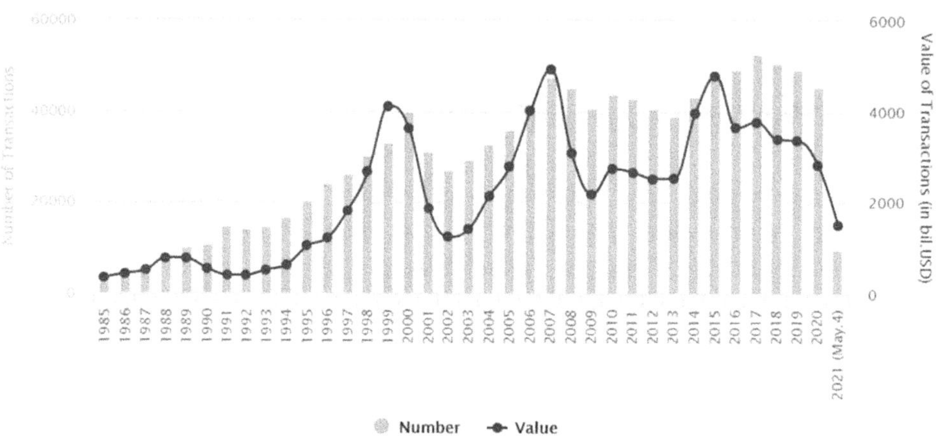

These numbers above are though challenged by a recent fall in number of deals in 2018, even though increased by 4% in the market value of these transactions. Surely, the COVID-19 pandemic as though accentuated a most recent trend as to the variable "number of transactions". This was triggered by a sudden decline in market values, with buyers reconsidering sales opportunities, especially in private company targets, with more depth *due diligence* endeavors over earn out structures, equating future performance risks and adopting a rather risk-aversion positions to avoid rebounds. This data is gathered for three decades at the *Institute for Mergers, Acquisitions and Alliances (IMAA)* which provides clear insights and confirms such upward trend (Fenwick, 2020).

Definitely, firm´s growth difficulties have been attenuated by market opportunities which have created a context of alternative growth. In addition, large corporations have become familiar with the strategic use of M&As as an instrument at their disposal as a logic of portfolio enlargement, diversification strategies (in order to enter into other niches, segments or industries) and/or maintain the competition at distance, namely the innovators from the startup ecosystem. A good example of the strategic use of M&A is given by *Cisco System Inc.* is a great example of leveraged long-term corporate-level strategy´s growth objectives through systematic acquisitions, the extension of portfolio of products/services, segments of coverage and even industries where they compete on (Volberda et al., 2011). For instance, since the year 2005 until 2021, their number of acquisitions have exceeded more than one hundred transactions (Cisco, online; Volberda et al., 2011; Fenwick, 2021).

In addition to M&As, as a non-organic growth business strategy, is also the accentuating trend observed on *cooperation* strategies being increasingly used with time, as several companies, especially multinationals, seems to have shifted in the last five decades the western paradigm of *solo-playing* to a *networking playing* or competition, and celebrating multiple forms of cooperation from strategic partnership (non-equity ones) or alliances (equity alliances), join-ventures or consortia. Those have mostly a dual purpose, *uncertainty-reduction* or *competition-reduction/collusion strategy*. Going back to *Cisco System Inc.* above referred as an example of strategic M&A, their non-organic growth model is pillared though on both instruments, M&As and cooperation. Here on the latter, the emphasis is placed on strategic partnerships. Cisco have celebrated in the last decades multiple strategic partnerships with other knowledge/tech-based corporations (e.g. *Accenture; BearingPoint; Capgemini; EDS; Fujitsu; HP; IBM; Intel; Microsoft Itatel; Motorola; Nokia; SAP; Wipro*, and so forth). as a key source of innovation development and focused on activities such as R&D and patenting, ensuring strategic allies with cutting edge technology-development expertise and strategic resellers of their goods.

Regarding the contribution of business networks to growth or development, ought to be made a note to the authors Jan Johanson and Jan-Erik Vahlne, whom have emphasized an the alteration of traditional business practices, as they acknowledged a paradigmatic shift of the internationalization of the firms, from (solo-player´s) *process internationalization* to a *business network view (BNV)* (Abrantes, 2020). In their model ("*Business Network Internationalization Process*" - BNIP) these authors, whom have developed the Uppsala process model of internationalization in the 1970s, which gave origin to the "Uppsalian School of Thought", consider business *relationship* as a key element of success, and defined it as a cumulative process, continually established, maintained, and developed to provide short-term returns, create network positioning and ensure the long-term survival of the firm (Abrantes, 2020; Johanson et al, 1988; Johanson and Vahlne, 1977). Here, the *BNIP* model considers that strategic positioning is firstly defined in opposition to the counterparts in foreign markets. Secondly, companies competing abroad face a double setback dubbed as the *liability of foreignness* and *liability of outsidership*, two phenomena related with correlation of foreignness with economic rent´s losses. Here, the authors claim and mitigation of these risk of financial losses through a BNV, in which, *networking position* opens new avenues for business opportunities and the extent of *network power* therein may, not solely, reduce the risk of losses created by both phenomena but also contribute to the stabilization of the firm on a foreign market and the growth of its business, explained by an increase of *market commitment.* More centralized positioning means then more power and more benefits of direct and indirect social exchange flows between network affiliates in the form of higher social capital or intelectual capital gains. These ideas considers international business as being country-specific was updated with a country-wide reasoning as business relations are borderless.

However, this Western Perspective of the BNV seems to have though great discrepancies to an Eastern Perspective. Firstly, the Eastern Perspective seem to be rather anchored on the national culture heritage and the espoused norms it entails, with business networking assuming dissimilar contours and exercise. For instance, one may recall on section "Roots of Management" on the first chapter, the Confucian rooted Chinese concept of *guanxi* (Dunning and Kim, 2007). In Far Asia the benefits of business networks are exploited for hundreds of years (Abrantes, 2020). The same happens with other forms of business networks (e.g. the *keiretsu*, or *zaibatsu*).which their virtues incorporating two major principles: the *principle of cooperation* and the *principle of solidarity* below described (Brouthers, Gao and Napshin, 2014).

Table 1. Business networks: principles of cooperation of solidarity – Easter perspective

Characteristics of the Principle of Cooperation	Characteristics of the Principle of Solidarity
Information exchange and Co-development	Reciprocal monitoring
Management exchange mechanism	Supporting financial stabilization
Participation in senior management committees	Credit lending
Interlocking of board memberships	---
Cross-shareholding	---

Source: Abrantes (2020)

According to such perspective, the principle of cooperation aims at contribute to the co-development of its members, as an inclusive logic encompassing the exchange of information and knowledge-sharing supporting common managerial best practices and innovation (ranging from systems and processes, to procurement and purchasing or selling opportunities).

The central positions within the network are generally taken by top-managers, non-executive officers or chairmen of larger corporations (or their representatives – commonly family members) which assume a patriarchal of network self-protection armored by ample local power relations, in which, the weakest links of its series of relations are assumed by upstarters, early-stage or small business units which adherence to the network is likely to attenuate their perceived *liability of newness* and/or *liability of smallness*. Hence, this self-protection aims at solve unexpected or unpredicted risks, undercut the lack of external legitimacy due to the limited reputation due to short existence or smallness, however, playing a contributive part for the extension of the thresholds of influence of the network (Abrantes, 2020; Xin and Pearce, 2016) .

In this sense, the Eastern´s business networking logic seems less *formalized* but more *hierarchical* than Western business networking practices, deeply rooted on, what Schneider and Barsoux (2002) classified as, the "family/tribal culture" inspired on the two cultural dimensions, *uncertainty avoidance (UA)* and *power distance (PD),* of Geert Hofstede´s 6-D Model (Hofstede Insights, online). Those differences are perceived on multiple quadrants of the more occidental(ized) practice, which higher formalization entails, not the protection of a wider circle of private/social relations on a business sphere, but instead, a more institutionalized collaboration, accounts practices as sharing of intelligence (also seen on Orientalized networks) and other apparatus, as development of communities of expertise, open innovations systems as joint industry-research, co-product development, consortia, or joint internationalization.

In sum, it is unavoidable for practitioners in any industry the context of business on the 21st century, which is dynamic and harsh for any organization, regardless of its structure, dimension or location. The context imposes multiple, and somehow indistinct, challenges to the governance and management boards, and require from the organizations an awareness as to the subtleness of change and the requisites to comply with them. I will not enter into the idiosyncrasies of different economic systems and industry structures, however, it shall be acknowledged by the reader that different nations with dissimilar market conditions configure a scenario of a specific *absolute* and *comparative advantages*.

Yet, taking solely into account the generalization above made, in which, markets are business environments holding a *volatility; uncertainty; complexity*; and *ambiguity (VUCA)* reality, then they hold four (4) separate types of traits shaping the perceived context by a firm. The *Trait 1 (Volatility)* is a firm-specific challenge related to the upholding of a desirable/solid position on the market. *Trait 2 (Uncertainty,)* is a context in which firms are specifically challenged by the difficulty of prediction, since is hard to keep one´s eyes open about the whole surrounding dynamics and be aware of possible (future) events - as to the time an event is expected to occur and the source that originates or causes such incidence. The *Trait 3 (Complexity)* refers to a context, in which, firms might be affected by a multiplicity of different events whose intertwining challenges the firm to a multiple reaction upon various fronts for generating competitive parity or competitive distinctiveness, typically accomplished through one´s innovation in product or services and so creating organizational-specific value. The *Trait 4 (Ambiguity),* implies the perception of a context of high uncertainty though associated with a high degree of abstraction of its problematic; thus, being of difficult circumscribe the reality and comprehend its problematic to take any decisions and act upon it.

Challenges are often blurred and hard to circumscribe, as to the impact and time-horizon, which makes it is difficult to follow in terms of technology and capabilities to be acquired, build or reinforce.

Hence, managers have to deal on a daily basis with the certainty of "uncertainty" and the hypothesis of having it changed on a frequent basis. This requires a preparation for constant change (flexibility) and to control the scope and degree of change in order to deal with potential strategic drift from the markets. Thus, VUCA business environments require on this century an upstream full attentiveness towards a myriad of co-existing threats as, the rapid technological acceleration (as we are fully embracing the digital era), the reduction of product-innovation life cycles, the upsurge of big-bang disruptions, the intra-industrial convergence of product attributes, the proliferation of e-businesses.

ORGANIZATION´S STRATEGIC FIT

The contemporary management function encompasses the combination of a set of activities, or major components, to ensure the avoidance of derailing from desired vision and direction (governance) and from the established goals (management). These major managerial activities are summarized into four categories of management: *planning, organization, leading and controlling (POLC):*

Figure 2. Components of management
Source: Boddy (2017)

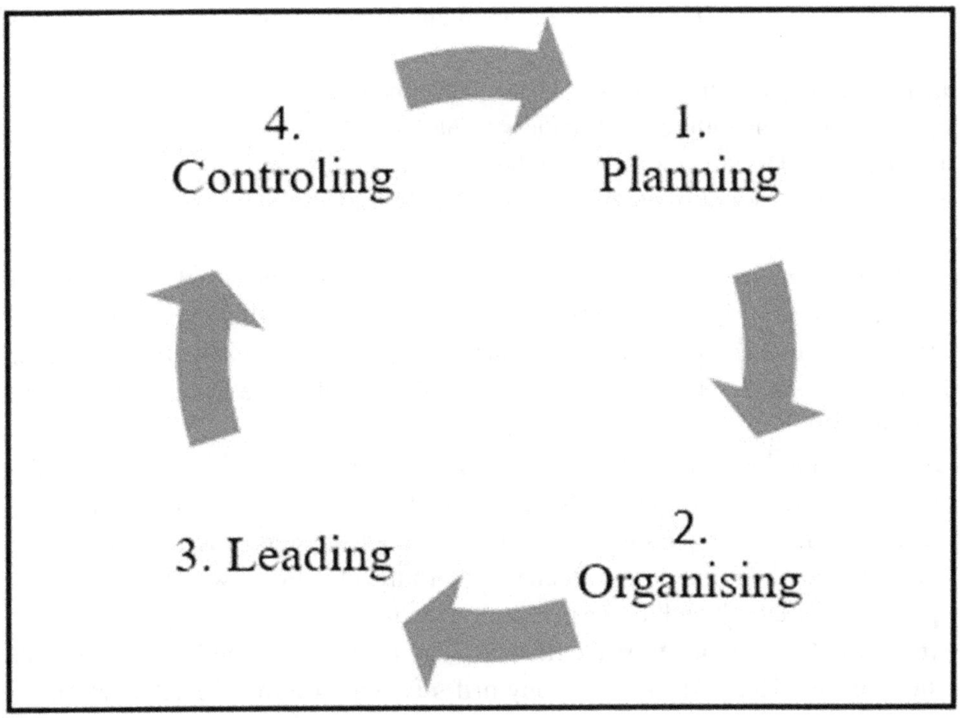

The four components *(POLC)* are considered "the" major managerial activities, resembling their alignment a cyclic workflow, as they are a cumulative set of activities to be taken by the manager, but not randomly as they obey to a certain order. These are naturally interrelated, as serial/chain of responsibility with an uninterrupted timeframe. The heavy burden of the general management of the whole myriad of managerial components, has accordingly, an identical chain of command, as the multiple objects of management, the structure, culture, goals, resources, processes and outputs in an organization are likely to be shared. Firstly, within the top-management team (TMT), then divided by respective areas, within divisions, by departments with middle-managers and subsequently distributed to other sub-parts, as the program managers and project/nucleus/team managers or supervisors, as the ones assuming a line management responsibility towards a certain part of the whole operative line.

Accordingly, the management as a whole (or the full POLC cycle) to be able to function as a well-oiled machine, ought then the parts to be aligned (S*trategic Alignment)*. Moreover, this internal alignment requires an equivalent external alignment toward the dispositions of the business environment. Thus, the strategic alignment of the firm, requires a degree of strategic fitness between multiple parts (Abrantes and Venkataraman, 2022). For instance, the resources have to be allocated in such dimension and typology, which the type of allocation it allow the fulfillment of the business goals. Beer at al (2005) have mapped the *organizational* levers (L_n) of such alignment *(A)*. The function is represented as follows (Abrantes and Venkataraman, 2022):

$$A(f) = \sum(L1; L4)$$

These organizational levers (L_n) of internal alignment are the following:

- L1: Business Strategy → Internal Business Environment
- L2: Organizational Capabilities → Business Strategy
- L3: Organizational Design → Leadership behaviour
- L4: Organizational Culture → Organizational Capabilities

Consequently, management entails at be able to align a constellation of multiple variables. Here making an analogy to the a ship sailing in the ocean, one could argue that to be able to "sail" on a right direction our boat (the organization) requires preparing all resources, as navigation equipment to interact (levers) with different components assertively (alignment), regardless the climate and weather conditions (business environment).

The L1 organizational lever (strategy – internal environment) refers to the overall internal fit of the remaining levers to the accomplishment of the business strategy´s goals. This is identical to an external fit (strategy-environment) encompassing the ability to strategically reposition a company´s business according to the perceived mutations on the business environment, namely with a response in consonance to the emergence of new events and the formation of new trends.

The external fit is the contrary to strategic drift. The latter corresponds to a bad external fit with a business environment. Thus, when a company drifts is getting into a deviated spiral, in which, the environmental change adopts a divergent direction and/or degree of mutation which the company is not capable of sensing and/or accommodating it internally. This is the case of *Kodak,* not being able to sense the upcoming changes in the industry, but also, not being able to implement the new technology in portfolio of products. Firstly, Kodak was the inventor of this new technology (digital camera) but despite that potential advantage, was not willing to commercialize it to not harm the film camera industry. Thus, Kodak ignored both the customer´s willingness to receive the product and the competition´s digital technologies skills and reverse engineering to copy or develop it.

Secondly, ignored the conclusions of the business environment analysis´ (BEA) report produced by Mr. Vince Barabba (Head of Market Intelligence) which foreseeing a maximum 10-year window of opportunity to adapt their portfolio of products. Unlike, Haier Group (the success case presented in chapter 1), Eastman Kodak Co.´s senior management was reluctant to change, this resulted in an accentuation of the drift, loss of performance (period of flux) and final death, illustrating the typical phases of strategic drift.

External or organizational fit, requires the acquisition of resources and development of skills for market research and intelligence-building as an upstream requirement for avoiding this phenomenon of *strategic drift* which occurs in four steps (Johnson, Scholes, & Whittington, 2008) as to the degree of change and time:

- Phase 1: Incremental Change (contrary direction of strategy to environmental change)
- Phase 2: Strategic Drift (continuous change in strategy – path dependent – accentuating the non-alignment with the business environment
- Phase 3: Period of Flux (drift in strategy triggered a downturn in performance)
- Phase 4: Transformation or death (dramatic scenario where the company dies, or is acquired or transformational change in markets, market focus, products, and capabilities)

In this sense, the way a *strategy* is formulated and implemented is paramount for the organizations and their businesses, and ought to be sensitive to what is happening on the external business environment. Noticeably, the latter can affect the goal´s setting (as its deliberate strategy). Hence strategy (or better said, strategic management) is a critical system within organizational management. Whether in scenarios of high or low market dynamics and facing higher or lower predictability (or VUCA), two most elementary elements are undoubtedly present at every organization´s general managements, i.e. the design of a *strategy* and the controlling of that same strategy *(Strategic Controls).* One may naturally deduce that these are components of the POLC and so also components of Strategic Management, and the latter is a by-product or a subset of management, and such idea is totally correct.

Let us contextualize then strategy with the management function, and so, we better start by the beginning, which defining *strategy*. The MIT Press´ definition of *strategy* provided by Alfred Chandler (1962) puts emphasizes on three attributes:

(i) Determination of goals (x);
(ii) Adoption of courses of action (y); and,
(iii) (iii) Allocation of required resources (z) (of achieving such goals)

Thus, strategy (S) as a function may be represented through a simple axiom as,

$$S_{(f)} \equiv \{x, y, z \in S: x +(y+z) >0\}$$

Chandler´s definition, seem to place goals as the attribute *x* as the center and the other components deriving from the prior.

Figure 3. Component´s Chandler´s definition of strategy
Source: Chandler (1962)

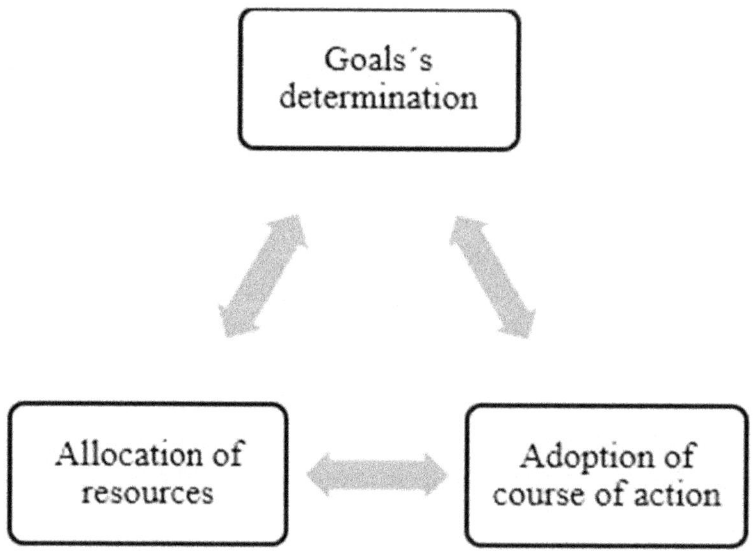

The keynote of this definition of strategy is prescretionism, as it emphasizes resources ownership as a remedy essential for creating new opportunities for change and/or growth. Chandler suggests that more favorable combination of resources may be accomplished by the refashioning of the organizational structure either by redeploying or expanding its resources.

In more contemporary literature, strategy is defined as "an integrated and coordinated set of commitments and actions designed to explore core competences and gain competitive advantage" (Volberda et al. 2011). This definition seems rather holistic and aiming at cover both strategy within and without an organizational context. A third definition is here added from other author, also with the benefit of being applicable to the organization´s realm. Thus, instead of a rather abstract definition of strategy, Boddy´s (2020) definition can be claimed to portray the notion of organizational strategy.

"about maintaining a balance between ends, ways, and means of surviving and thriving – providing a framework for making choices and trade-offs; and identifying resources, methods, actions, and value-creating objectives that sustain the organization over time within an ever-changing context."

The two constructs (strategy + management) cross-checked into a specific spectrum (strategic management), are as a matter of fact, a sub-function of the first (management) maintaining a whole-firm circumscription while focusing on competitive-gains and (above-average) returns.

Despite the most common myth, to look at strategist as the ones whom work on the "planning the future", something that I normally tend to deconstruct on my classes, as strategists are not innate visionary people, but trained stakeholders to have a keen or sharpen eye, since their job consists onto the analyze of the strategy proxies (i.e. the firm and market components), and lead managers to implement rationale models of decisions toward better future competitiveness and profitability. The complexity of the job (strategy-making) is addressed by Mintzberg´s (1987) on a seminal article ("*The strategy concept I: Five Ps for strategy*") with over a thousand citation-mark.

The 5Ps of strategy refer here to the multiple dimensions of strategy (plan, ploy, pattern, position and perspective) of what strategy accounts for, encompassing the components of the management function planning (i.e. POLC) and entailing the arrangement of future target goals and emergent tactics against direct/indirect competition, screening own resources and capabilities (R&C) bundles, structural configurations, systems and processes, culture and leadership, and the way those are closely tied to the external interface (the business environments), as to the industry structures and their economic systems, attractiveness, evolution, to the competition and demand´s knowledgeability and to the critical factors that determine the firm´s success and wealth. With Mackay et al. (2020) the 5Ps have grown into 12Ps (*plan, purpose, perspective, priority, problem-solving, possession, process, position, plasticity, practice, pattern and preparation*).

Accordingly, strategic management (SM) follows the all-round management cycle (POLC): planning, organization, leading, and controlling. This means that the companies have the ability to, on their own, determine their goals as to the when/how they are supposed to be reached (plan) considering the targets which are set for a certain moment, communicate and involves the whole parts of the company to contribute to the achievement of its vision and making the necessary arrangement to succeed, including setting, in many cases, motivational instruments in place (e.g. most common, showcasing best practices; role model playing or implementing meritocracy tools) so that each one is expected to deliver a positive contribution for the organizational success. It shall be noticed though that the different models of management may eliminate, for instance, external motivational factors of motivation related to the meritocracy of the individual or team, if rather centered on shareholders gains and maximizing the return on shareholders. So, the *POLC* is intrinsically rooted on the SM, as an underlying "tenet" of SM practice, and the same with any other sub-organizational system (e.g. financial management; human resources management; production management, etc.).

STRATEGIC PLANNING AND STRATEGIC CONTROLLING

Hence, two seminal dimensions of SM are quite clearly inferred, i.e. *Strategic Planning* and *Strategic Controls,* as opening and closing the POLC cycle. This means also that if they follow the POLC, they are iterative activities, repeatedly taken across business cycles. Here the concept of *planning* refers to design of three of the following:

(i) The setting organizational and business goals
(ii) Implement operative courses of action (on how to achieve them)
(iii) Evaluating the progression and/or outcomes/results

Furthermore, the notion of planning, based on Boddy (2016), is here defined as, an iterative activity comprising, the setting of organizational, and implementation of a course of action for their achievement and evaluating of the outcomes. Thus, SM´s starting point (*planning*) and closure are intrinsically connected, as one dictates the other and vice-versa. For instance, the degree and type of goals influence the instruments to be put in place as to the measurement of their accomplishment. However, the results deriving from the strategic control function, are also taken as a "diagnostic" of performance, as the firm puts in practice an overall mechanism of observation of internal and external factors, also called a *strategy audit* process (as designated by Wheelen and Hunger, 1987, p. 6), with the purpose of reducing risks and approximating vision and goals to results, and also, building strategic decision making intelligence for future decision-making processes. This means, using strategic controls for further strategic planning, hence uncovering a strategic loop (the "*Strategic Decision Making Process*"). In this context, the purpose of planning is:

(i) Clarify the direction *(P)*
(ii) Create an efficient use of resources and capabilities (R&Cs) *(O)*
(iii) Motivate the employees *(L)*
(iv) Measuring progress/outcomes *(C)*

As it may be observed, the SM accounts as well, in its sub-functions the POLC cycle, with *ex ante* and *ex post* dimensions as to an-going business strategy. Then, *goal´s establishment,* as the first element of planning is a pillar for all planning activity and a task of enormous responsibility, often disregarded as to their importance. A *goal* may be defined as, a desired future state for an activity or organizational unit. Setting goals ought to consider that, they should be clear, challenging and motivating and oriented toward action for facilitating their implementation across the organization (Locke and Latham, 2002). Using a simple mnemonic, desirably goals are fashioned to be "*SMART*":

- *Specific*
- *Measurable*
- *Attainable*
- *Rewarded*
- *Timed*

SMART goals require firstly a specific nature, which implies a threefold attention to the: (i) clear identification of its purpose; (ii) circumscription of the stakeholder´s responsible for their accomplishment; and, (iii) drawing of initial guidelines for further action.

However, these 5 interplaying properties (*specification; measurability; attainability; rewarding; and time-bounded*) are *cumulative* ones, otherwise, a goal neglecting one of these properties compromises the fashioning of a SMART goal. It might seem well-fashioned, yet is "non-smart". Thus, it has furthermore to be measurable. As the this property of a goal (measurability), one need to bring in the notion of *target,* which corresponds to a degree of accomplishment which can be observed whether it was achieved or not based on qualitative or qualitative instruments. Let´s take one example. A *Company X* at the steel industry in Germany defined as a strategic goal for the year 2020 "*to reduce by 50% their greenhouse gas (GHG) emissions*" in all their business operations, including direct production activities, energy production and transportation of goods. Such new goal, deriving from the strategic planning exercise, is evidently a *strategic goal* or (also called) a *business goal* (not an operational goal) since its scope affects transversally the whole organization or at least most of its activities. In this example, the aggregate figures of the carbon dioxide (CO_2) footprint of the firm accounted for the year 2019 constitute the baseline of calculation for 2020, for measurement of the desired target. From that baseline, the *standard* or full target attainability corresponds to a reduction factor *(r)* representing a cut to half. In this sense, whether being a tangible or intangible goal/objective, easily quantifiable or not, important is, that the prior specification of the goal is well fashioned to make it observable, as to its full achievement or partial achievement.

$$Target\left(x\right)=\left(\frac{GHG2020}{GHG2019}\right);\leftrightarrow \Delta_{(GHG2020)=} (GHG_{2019} \,.\, r);\; r \geq 0{,}5$$

In case of partial deviation *(d > 0)* to the target, the partial achievement function may be represented as,

Partial achievement $(\Delta_{(GHG2020)} = (GHG_{2019} \,.\, r)$ or $r < 0{,}5$

And, in case of failure to reach a goal or total deviation ($d = 1$)

$(\Delta_{(GHG2020)} = (GHG_{2019} \,.\, r)$ or $r = 0$;

Or, $r < 0$, as r variation range goes from $(-\infty, \ldots]$

As postulated by Douglas W. Hubbard, everything came measured. So imagine alternatively that in the previous example case, the company has designed, not a *specific goal*, as a strategic goal, but instead, what is called a *directional goal*. For instance, if the company had simply decided towards the *"reduction of greenhouse gas (GHG) emissions in 2020"*. So, if the goal is not specified it requires initially a simple interpretation of the meaning. In this case "reduction" corresponds to:

$GHG_{2020} \leq GHG_{2019}$; or $r > 0$, as r variation range goes from $[\ldots, \infty)$

The "attainability" refers to the likely realistic nature of the specific + targeted goal. If a new goal is not feasible (e.g. a local coffee shop to become the largest retail company in the world) then is not attainable, as the strategic design of the goal is detached from the reality. However, one may be made aware that a realistic goal (feasible) may also be unrealistic, in this case of, the target was set too high, being too ambitious and is unreachable for the organization in a certain moment in time. Setting high targets for a goal can make it challenging, but if too high, may be an illusion, so being demotivating for the employees and subsequently abandoned. When a milestone or a "point in destiny" for the future is set on a "pedestal", the organizational reality is ignored and started to mix it with own dreams.

Hence, it is essential to consider the context of attainability, the resources at disposal or to be acquired, and the industry and firm´s internal context. Moreover, goals ought to be relevant to the firm´s growth, development and sustainability, otherwise, are merely meaningless goals which may not lead to any benefit. Moreover goals, such be motivating to encourage employees to good the "extra-mile" of effort to accomplish them, and companies shall consider the use intrinsic/extrinsic motivational factors to stimulate their accomplishment, from the mere the facilitation of conditions to the rewarding of the merit of the direct contributing units and individuals. Their fashioning requires from the planner to account the "large picture" of the division/corporate´s vision. Finally, goal´s setting, requires, target setting, but also time-setting, or a *deadline* for their attainment. Strategic goals are time-bounded, as a standard, a goal to be achieved in a certain degree (or target) in until a certain moment in time (t_o). Setting SMART goals facilitates the understanding, implementation, and execution.

In sum, planning the future of a firm, and its businesses is a tough job of enormous responsibility and at its start setting goals, demands ambidextrous capabilities, to be able to look holistically at the whole organization, within a temporal context of past/present and future and visualize (or envision) the evolving path, changes and predicts scenarios, considering the accountabilities of each functional area and the influential hand of the external context, for instance, the industry´s dynamics, competition, supply and demand and so forth. Thus, goal´s setting is indelibly connected with goals´ administration. The second follows always the first, as goal´s setting is an *ex ante* analysis dimension (planning) while the latter an *ex post* analysis dimension.

Goal´s administration are focused on the output, measuring the progression and results and on the modelling of new opportunities, scenarios and real options. In this sense, the activities of *measurement* and *analysis* are two major ones in the strategic management domain, as a process. Consequently, a distinction shall be made between them, and furthermore, between *analysis* and *analyzability*. Starting with the latter ideas, *analyzability* refers to the whole spectrum of what the analysis activities comprise. For instance, a *business environment analyzability (BEA)* exercise encompasses the observation of a dual layer of external environment aspects, general and industry environment, with several components therein likely to be accounted. Yet, each firm decides arbitrarily the way they perform their business environment analysis in time, by whom, when, what, how, where and why. This is called a *Quintilian hexametric* decision. Hence, this book focus rather on BEA ("analyzability") (see definition in Glossary).

MANAGING STRATEGIC PERFORMANCE: MEASUREMENT, EVALUATION AND DIAGNOSIS

As noticed by Andersen (2013) managing performance means also managing people. Such as, the allocation of physical and human resources per project (plan), establishing standards and procedures (organizing), motivating and rewarding (leading) and verifying outcomes (control). Thus, strategy-making implies a significant and time-consuming activity of measurement, both, general *or strategic performance measurement (SPM)* and *individual performance measurement (IPM)*. The latter is, the one providing more operational insights, for instance, customer-wise, with regard to goods and service delivery being then assumed as a critical type of performance to be diagnosed. Consequently, firms learnt over time to developed and ameliorate own specific methodologies. Here, Human Resource Management (HRM) departments played a vital role on such improvement. Nowadays, it is acknowledged a myriad of methods, which firm´s combine casuistically, for the purpose of individual performance management (IPM), as follows: the *Critical Incidents Method*; the *Management by Objectives (MBO)* Method; the *Narrative Method or Form*; *Graphic Rating Scale Form*; the *Behaviorally Anchored Rating Scale (BARS) Form*; or the *360 degrees evaluation*. As a rule of thumb, the measurement occurs at IPM-level (individual) for the past (t_{n-1}), as companies' run such evaluation every half-year or yearly, focusing on past events during that time span, using a scouting mechanism for monitoring the performance outputs, circumscribed of pre-determined indicators dubbed as *lagging indicators*. On the other hand at SPM-level (strategic) the measurement is mostly an on-going process, targeting present activities (and their relation to organizational goals) through the using of key-performance indicators (KPIs) that measure the direction (leading indicators) as to the degree of assertiveness or full compliance or deviation. Thus, the progression of performance outputs, are not necessarily results, as events are still on its march and the target (or standard performance) occurs on the future (t_{n+1}).

Figure 4. Performance measurement: standard, acceptable deviation, and range
Source: Boddy, 2017

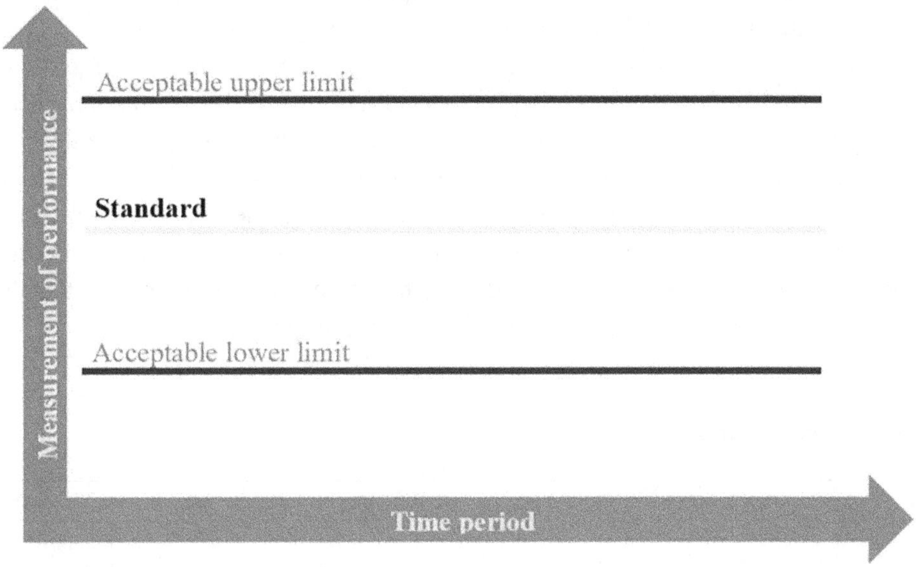

Figure 4 represents the acceptable variation up to acceptance limits, within the acceptable upper limit (AUL) and the acceptable lower limit (ALL). Only beyond such figures, firms establish a course of action for its corrective alignment, from which, derive then implementation plans and the underlying suitability, feasibility and acceptability (SFA) evaluation of those procedures, as an after-action review analyses phase.

Measurement is then a primary analytical exercise, as to the controls of somewhat, requiring the use information from our past/present to attain enhanced present and future outcomes. Hence, measurement within organizational realm, is a seminal process holding the role of uncertainty control, yet not necessary succeeding on its full elimination.

The notion of measurement has naturally evolved with time. Albert Einstein referred to the purpose of measurement, since the reality is dynamic or not certain. Complementarily, George A. Miller from *Massachusetts Institute of Technology (MIT)* separated three components, the object (the *input*), the mechanisms – or medium and tasks (the *channel*), and the data of progression or result (the *output*): *Nature provides the input, the process of measurement is the channel, and the measurements themselves are the output*." (Miller, 1953, p. 7)

Noticeably, measurement as a (whole) process, is intrinsically anchored on a set of fundamental upstream/downstream activities, which encompass, observation; evaluation; and, diagnosis. These are, as a matter of fact, the tenets of strategic performance management (SPM), which fit on the general principles of management (*planning*; *organizing*; *leading*; and, *controlling*) (Boddy, 2017).

As you have discerned from the 5Ps, and from the explanation above (focused on "measurement", one of the tasks comprised of the controlling sub-function), strategy ought to be recognized beforehand as a function with a broad scope, categorizable in multiple ways as different *types of strategies*. The fundamental idea regarding what strategy is, is then comprised on its multiple *interpretations*. For instance, the "analysis", within the control sub-function, is a colossal processes which unravels in multiple forms, according to its objectives containing multiple activities on subsequently different tasks.

Hence, on the context of business environment it comprises also multiple *parts*. So, a natural question to be posed is, what´s the (workable) definition of strategy here suggested in the book? Let´s compromise into workable definition, in short, complementary to the one above. "*an integrated and coordinated set of commitments and actions designed to explore core competences and gain competitive advantage*".

Naturally, such definition deeply rooted on *management* and the underlying rationale of administering the inputs and transforming them into outputs (with competitive gains for the firm) requires planning, organization, leadership and controlling. Consequently, the management has its own value, intrinsic to the transformation processes of the firm´s businesses (*Resources* → *Value-addition* outputs). So, within this context, the role of the *control* as a sub-function, exemplified above, is to analyze the ability to fulfill goals, improve profit pools and extract from them higher (in)tangible value.

Table 2. Cascading the management function

Function	Sub-function	Activities	Tasks
Management	Strategic Management	Controlling	Measurement Evaluation Diagnosis

Source: Own elaboration

In the previous paragraph is mentioned that management is mostly "analytical". To comprehend it, we bring here the example of the cascading of the SM sub-function. Crossing the role of the strategist with the POLC cycle, depict for instance, the control, it I observable that an organization´s strategy implies measuring results, evaluate deviations and determine the impact on designing goals. The same happens if we start the POLC cycle on the SM. Strategic planning implies after-action reviews of previous strategic designs; new goal´s setting, and tactical and implementation planning. Again, is an analytical job, requires cognition, but most of all is determined by a context (external and internal) as previously observed and grasped about the markets and the firm, and the ability to act upon their alignments and intended strategic direction.

One the question the readers may naturally pose then is, w*hat is the perspective of "analysis" here adopted?* The answer is a straightforward one. The analysis of the what/when/how/by whom and why is casuistic, varying on the nature and complexity of the locus of attention being so a multivariate one. It depends on the multiple *interpretations* of the manager and its team and in the vast majority of the occasions it encompasses several possibilities as to the methodological procedure and *parts* of the analyzability. This an issue to introduced on the next chapter we are there entering the realm of business environments.

Miles at al. (1978) showcased four different types of organizational strategies, *defensive, analysis, prospector* and *reactor* one. Those influenced the *5Ps* of firm´s strategic design (*plan, ploy, pattern, position and perspective*) as multiple interpretations of what strategy is. Furthermore, Hill, Ireland and Hoskisson (2017) asserts that the analysis may vary into nature, as for instance, companies may conduct different types of environment analysis (further discussed in chapter three), *scanning, monitoring, forecasting,* and *assessing*.

Another complementary idea is, environment analyzability might be interpreted in a diverse way. For instance, as an activity belonging to multiple dimensions of strategy. For instance, the "analysis" function, whether is considered a type of Miles et al.´s (1978) strategies or not, may be simply considered a component of strategy. For instance, the analysis as a "process" (an analytical procedure) where the manipulation of data is a critical part of the strategist work. Or a practice, preparation or plan (e.g., data collection, intelligence-building, methodological or application).

Similarly, the conduction of an analysis, considered as a *part,* for gaining further insights and (re)build market knowledgeability, may observe different "targets" (*what to analyze?*) (E.g. scanning the market segments) or even different "tiers" (*where to observe?*) (E.g. a country; or product) as incumbents fashion strategies at different level (corporate, business and functional level) and the "scope" as to the endeavor of investigation might be possibly general or specific (*what to know?*). Another aspect of analysis as a part of strategy, is the fact that in various cases the projects are in-depth observations with a static nature, build scenarios for a highlighted reality reported as a picture of the reality, but neglecting the reporting of environment kinesis, which is crucial for the future of the organization´s decision-making or revealing no connection to the strategic objectives defined. Consequently, it is here is peremptorily refuted the idea of an "analysis strategy" per se, since in modern management, analysis is a part of all types of strategies, whether the model of competition is more disruptive than others (e.g. blue ocean strategies or big- bang disruptions) in which the analyzability side still exists prior the company undertaking any maneuvers. On the other hand, it seems adequate the logic of process, as analysis is a systematic processual attribution of thinking, reflection, selection of sources, collection of data, manipulation of information, interpretation, generating of options, outputs, findings and conclusions.

Considering the definition above of what an organizational strategy is, and crossing it with a parsimonious idea at this stage of what the analysis of business environment might be (as addressed in chapter 3), it may be already clarified that the perspective of analysis here adopted is an instrumental one.

CONCLUSION

Analysis is considered as a tools at the organization´s disposal, with significant utility for the strategy function for the setting of goals and further courses of action. It applicability is valued at different time periods both before the decision-making, and after the decision-making. The first (before decision-making) as a preparatory analysis and the latter (after-decision-making) as a dyad of on-going analysis, and after-review analysis, comprising processes of data collection, controlling and interpretation. Hence, an instrumentalization of environment´s analyzability perceives the environmental context as being dynamic, which means that the analysis ought to be also dynamic as well, crossing different realities, and therefore requiring a cross-sectional data gathering, but also, considers the possibility of observing different timeframes, which means that data gathering shall incorporate, as a theoretical principle, longitudinal data. Such combination of cross-sectional and longitudinal is postulated to bring richness to the analytical endeavors, allowing:

a) Pinpoint current and upcoming changes, and its outputs (i.e. societal trends);
b) Extrapolation of the impact of changes to a focal firm

c) Uncover a plethora of potential opportunities and threats, accounting new options, and forecasting newer (future) scenarios.

REFERENCES

Abrantes, B. F. (2020). Are Neoclassic Internationalization Models Enduring? A Case-Review of the Uppsala Paradigm. *SAGE Open*, *10*(2). doi:10.1177/2158244020932535

Abrantes, B. F., & Venkataraman, A. (2022). Environment kinesis and organizational adaptability: Effects of EU's General Data Protection Regulation on the Danish software industry. *International Journal of Learning and Change*, *14*(1), 22–45. doi:10.1504/IJLC.2022.119516

Andersen, P. (2013). *Performance management: A handbook for small business banks and microfinance institutions*. Practical Action Publishing. doi:10.3362/9781780447926

Boddy, D. (2020). *Management: Using practice and theory to develop skill* (8th ed.). Pearson Education Limited.

Chandler, A. D. (2020). *Structure and strategy*. Harvard University Press.

Cisco (online) *Acquisitions by year*. CISCO. https://www.cisco.com/c/en/us/about/corporate-strategy-office/acquisitions/acquisitions-list-years.html

Fenwick (2020) *Coronavirus Impact on M&A and Other Strategic Corporate Transactions*. Fenwick. https://www.fenwick.com/insights/publications/coronavirus-impact-on-m-a-and-other-strategic-corporate-transactions

Grant, R. M. (2021). *Contemporary strategy analysis*. John Wiley & Sons.

Hitt, M. A., Ireland, R. D., & Hoskisson, R. E. (2016). *Strategic management: Concepts and cases: Competitiveness and globalization*. Cengage Learning. Hofstede Insights (online) National Culture. https://hi.hofstede-insights.com/national-culture

Johanson, J., Mattsson, L. G., Hood, N., and Vahlne, J. E. (1988). Strategies in global competition. *Strategies in global competition*, *14*, 75-81.

Johanson, J., & Vahlne, J. E. (1977). The internationalization process of the firm—A model of knowledge development and increasing foreign market commitments. *Journal of International Business Studies*, *8*(1), 23–32. doi:10.1057/palgrave.jibs.8490676

Johnson, G., Scholes, K., & Whittington, R. (2008). *Exploring corporate strategy: Text and cases*. Pearson education.

Miller, G. A. (1953). What is information measurement? *The American Psychologist*, *8*(1), 3–11. doi:10.1037/h0057808

Mintzberg, H. (1987). The strategy concept I: Five Ps for strategy. *California Management Review*, *30*(1), 11–24. doi:10.2307/41165263

Mui, C. (2012) How Kodak Failed. *Forbes*. https://www.forbes.com/sites/chunkamui/2012/01/18/how-kodak-failed/?sh=778c51d76f27

Schneider, R. S., & Barsoux, J. (2002). *Managing Across Cultures, 2nd*. Upper Saddle Rivier.

Startup Talky. (2021) Why Did Kodak Fail?: Kodak Bankruptcy Case Study. *Startup Talkey*. https://startuptalky.com/kodak-bankruptcy-case-study/

Volberda, H. W., Morgan, R. E., Reinmoeller, P., Hitt, M. A., Ireland, R. D., & Hoskisson, R. E. (2011). *Strategic Management: Competitiveness and Globalization (Concepts & Cases)*. Cengage Learning.

Xin, K. K., & Pearce, J. L. (1996). Guanxi: Connections as substitutes for formal institutional support. *Academy of Management Journal*, *39*(6), 1641–1658. doi:10.2307/257072

APPENDIX

Learning Outcomes

- Comprehend the main phenomena (tech and globalization related) challenging businesses in the 21st century
- Firm´s fight back: strategic innovation (for inciting change) and strategic fit
- The POLC cycle of contemporary management
- The planning function and SMART goal´s setting
- The control function and performance management: types of measurement; performance indicators; standard and limits

CASE: EASTMAN KODAK CO.

With a dominant position in photographic film industry Kodak failed though to adapt with the onset of digital photography in the 1990s. Kodak is often hailed as a great example of a firm which failed to take advantage of the business environment´s dynamics. "*Few are the corporate blunders as the staggering Kodak's missed opportunities in digital photography, a technology that it invented*". (Mui, 2012, online)

In 1975, a Kodak engineer, Mr. Steve Sasson, invented the first digital camera, but his invention faced an odd corporate response, with lower enthusiasm than expected.

The Head of Market Intelligence at that time (Vince Barabba) conducted an extensive research looking at the core technologies and likely adoption curves around silver halide film versus digital photography, and concluded in 1981 that digital cameras would inevitably replace film camera, but the good news was, it would take roughly ten years for that to occur. During this 10-year window of opportunity until the early competitor´s arise, Kodak did little to prepare for the later disruption. Only in 1991, Nokia has launched the DCS-100, the first-ever digital SLR, however, facing in the short-term the competition of others players which quickly launched other products, as in 1994 *Apple* launched the *QuickTake* (considered the first mainstream digital camera), and in 1995 *Ricoh* did the same with the RDC-1. On the year 2000, *Fujifilm* came with the FinePix S1 Pro. However, as digital technology was evolving fast, and furthermore, in other societal domains, the industry of digital cameras was shaken by Apple´s launch of the iPhone in 2007. It was not the first mobile phone with an incorporated camera, but its quality and convenience factor made it a game changer.

Kodak standing on denial over such technology and trying to convince their customer-base to use film cameras instead of digital ones had a devastating effect on the ability to compete in the future.

The company´s management had not fully grasped at that time the importance of the technological transition and how to explore the new technologies to stay ahead of competition. The firm´s inability to keep with the pace of technological changes led to its failure, with a accentuated loss of market share with the company finally declared bankrupt in 2012 (Mui, 2012, online; Startup Talky, 2021).

CHAPTER HIGHLIGHTS

- The context of the Business Environment: VUCA traits and the quest for uncertainty-reduction
- Firm-environment relations: *strategic alignment*, *organizational fit*; and *strategic drift*
- The POLC cycle of Contemporary Management
- Organic and non-organic growth strategies of competition
- Business networks (Western vs Eastern networks) and the ancient Asian *guanxi*, *keiretsu* and *zaibatsu* networks
- Strategic *planning* and "SMART" goal´s setting
- Strategic control: *performance*, *target* standards, and *widget counting*

SUMMARY OF THE CHAPTER

On this chapter, one revisited the idea of dynamism of the markets and described the VUCA traits environments (introduced on the initial chapter) of a turbulent environment. From the VUCA, a discussion was began on the context of businesses on the 21st century and its relation to the organizational strategy.

As to the business context, the chapter describes some of the most relevant aspects of business dynamics within four categories: competition, culture, globalization *and* technology. *Moreover, some insights were provided regarding organic and non-growth approaches to cope with the pace of change and type of dynamics of experienced nowadays in such context of contemporary businesses. On the latter (*non-organic growth*) we have elaborated on the most common approaches,* M&As *and* cooperation *supported on the example of* Cisco Systems Inc.´s *non-organic approach to leverage their corporate growth. Here, a seminal cooperation-related phenomenon is introduced (*networking), as *being key for the success of any cooperative model, as alliances, joint-venturing or consortia.*

Within business networks, relevant conceptions were introduced, as affiliation/membership, position, power *or* social capital. *Moreover, a discussion is brought to light, as to the paradigms of* Western *and* Eastern business networks, *and addressed the* principles of cooperation *and* solidarity, *and Far East concepts of* liability of smallness *and* liability of newness *and three models of Eastern business networking, the* guanxi; zaibatsu*; and,* keiretsu.

On the second half of the chapter, it is explored the connection of the context with organizational strategy, with the purpose of bringing the reader close to seminal ideas regarding the impact of social regimes on the firm´s path and success, before immersing into "business environments", something to be initiated on chapter three. We have started by cascading the ancestral Xenophon´s dimensions of management into the modern tenets, or the main responsibilities of the manager (i.e. the POLC cycle*).*

Afterwards, it is presented two most pertinent conceptions related to *Strategic Alignment (A)*, designated as *internal alignment* and *external alignment*. In the next chapters, you will see the function being explored in terms of their *proxies* and *interfaces*. Moreover, in connection to this function *(A)* is introduced the Johnson, Scholes & Whittington´s (2008) notion of *strategic fit* and the Beer at al ´s (2005) idea of *organizational lever*. Both will be well explored along the chapters, with the first (*strategic fit*) unravelling one of the most important reasons why organizations ought to analyze its surrounding environment, i.e. to keep them "fitting in" and so, avoiding deviating avenues, becoming crystalized in time with obsolete portfolios, which may seriously affect their goals and treasury. As to the second (*organizational levers*), this chapter provides some insights onto their internal alignment (L1 to L4) indicating the boundaries where firms need to strategize within (*culture; resources and capabilities; structure; strategic positioning*).

The chapter proceeded within the management function, exploring the subset of *Strategic Management*, and exploring fundamental areas of SM *(strategic planning* and *controls*) as opening and closing parts of the POLC cycle. Herein, the notion of *goal*, *target*, and *performance* are introduced. Furthermore, special attention is given to the strategic goal´s setting (and different types of goals) and strategy auditing of the business performance (i.e. *performance measurement*; *performance evaluation* and *performance diagnosis*) and their acceptable ranges of variation, and the looping cycle of planning – controls.

The next chapter focuses on *business environment´s* key-concepts, followed by the context of analysis of BEs and *ecosystems*. Then, it proceeds with the enlightening of the morphology of the business environments, the major human *assumptions* about business environments (BEs), *perspectives*, *interfaces, layers, ontology* and *elements of analyzability*. Afterwards, you will enter into more specific analyzability aspects with a particular emphasis on data sources, current frameworks, methodological application and future modeling.

Chapter 3
Understanding Business Environments (BEs)

ABSTRACT

The previous chapters dwell around the microfoundations of management (chapter one), plus strategy formulation and the challenges contemporary management (chapter two). Key-constructs (fear and thought) are taken as an instinctive-driven and rational-driven configuration of human behavior. In this chapter, one starts to immerse into the realm of business context in our modern world. One starts to focus on business environments (BE) and address seminal concepts, such as "environment;" "ecosystem;" or "market" (and underlying ideas, as marketspace, marketplace or e-market). Here, a BE is assumed to fit, at the begging of the 21st century, a dynamic paradigm, and so the chapter discusses the types of business environment´s changes and their inner changing events. Moreover, is presented the strategic paths (to respond to BE´s change), and the tenets of organizational success. With regard to the latter, the analyzability function is introduced as a determinant of success.

INTRODUCTION TO BUSINESS ENVIRONMENTS (BE): KEY-CONCEPTUALIZATIONS

Before narrowing down to the specifics of a *business environment* (BE) is, it is here covered first some related ideas, which their meaning seemingly a matter of common-sense, yet give origin to some misperceptions which we wish to avoid as they touch the domain of strategic management (SM). Thus, we do start by defining them and discussion their boundaries.

Hereupon, the first idea connected to the BE here introduced is the notion of *market*. The term is frequently used and interchangeable applied with other close ones, as *marketplace, marketspace.*

Moreover it is frequent the blending of these concepts above with other related ones, as *business ecosystems, sector, industries,* or even with *organizational ecology,* often with a senseless meaning.

Especially for someone with no background on business studies (or perhaps to a most unwary reader about such terminology) this section is especially relevant. However it is also works as a recapitulating exercise for others, since these foundational terms (and ideas) here expressed, are often used by media

DOI: 10.4018/978-1-6684-5543-2.ch003

on news about the state-of-the-art of businesses and the economy, sometimes with blurred connotation. So, let us raise this simple open-end question:

Question 1: What is a market?

One shall acknowledge at first that this is concept perceived differently across scientific areas within the realm of Social Sciences. A multiplicity of definitions co-exist and could be seen then as an obstacle hindering its comprehension. However, here we will explore the richness of conceptual diversity by bringing two (2) major perspectives. Naturally the *Marketing* perspective and the *Industrial Economics* perspective.

Starting by the latter, for scholars on industrial economics a market entails a set of companies producing an identical product or service or a bundle of interrelated products and/or services (Varum et al., 2018). Here the market structure and relations of power among agents is dictated by the rule of elasticity of the demanded quantity versus its price, which has dominated the vision of market competition. This corresponds to the dominant paradigm of *Structuralism*. In this perspective the variable *concentration* (of the market), is a seminal component for comprehend the structure, plus the degree of competition and efficiency therein.

Frequently, due to the ease of access to data per industry, a firm is classified into a market being associated to a specific code that classifies its economic activity by the sector it competes on. Just as a matter of curiosity, firms can hold more than a code as their activities may span across various businesses, or better said, companies might hold businesses in several industries at the same time, something that in corporate-level strategies is dominated as a *diversification strategy*. Here, two (2) major international classification measures co-exist. The European one, termed with a francophone expression, as the *Nomenclature Statistique des Activités Économiques* (NACE), referring to the Statistical Classification of Economic Activities. Also the classification offered by the Organisation for Economic Cooperation and Development (OECD), denominated as the *International Standard Industrial Classification* (ISIC). At national-level, several countries developed also their own metric systems, such as, the *Nomenclature d' Activités Française* (NAF), or the *Classificação de Actividades Económicas* (CAE) in Portugal, both with a similar structure as the General Industrial Classification of Economic Activities within the European Communities, i.e. the 2nd revision of NACE (or *NACE rev. 2*). Nevertheless, the current versions of NACE and ISIC are the most commonly adopted instruments worldwide in scholarly practice and international reporting.

Yet, returning to the definition of *market,* the second perspective is the one delivered by Marketing theorists. Marketers have delimited the "market", and distinguished it from other similar conceptions, as the *marketplace* and *marketspace*. Indeed, joining these three (3) concepts, some doubts may naturally arise. Especially when trying to draw a line and pinpoint what are the attributes participating in one concept but not in the others, or establishing what are their points of contact, or their thresholds. On the perspective, marketing theorists abandoned though the generalizations of a "business market" or "investment market" as the underlying *foci* here observed, and to make a broader reflection about what a "market" might be.

Before moving forward, it ought to be emphasized that these two streams of industrial organization and marketing theories share some commonalities. Their ideas converge as to the context, as both recognize, as a point of contact that, a market is indelibly shaped by the attributes of the economic system, namely the significance of the regulatory and legal framework, which interplay with industry-specific dynamics of competition.

As a mere exercise of reflection, consider a virtual organization, without any purpose or means of existence, holding no staff and having zero interactions with third parties. Finally, this company has no physical or digital assets, and has no resources whatsoever (beyond the initial equity). Also it has no buyers, no sellers, no products, and so forth. I am sure you would say, this is impossible.

There is no such thing, as completely empty firms. It is definitely a utopia (and perhaps, a dull exercise). Hence, the point is, organizations do not exist isolated from the outside world. As firms are not remote islands located in the deep ocean forgotten or segregated from the rest of us.

An *organization* is a collective arrangement with a specific purpose, which guides its ventures and social exchange with third parties (*aka*, stakeholders). To know who one is, comes as the initial point to start understanding the second perspective.

Despite intuitive, the definition of *market,* gets often blended and mistakenly used in the context of a *marketplace* or *marketspace,* as mentioned before. Over the years, I observed several of my students in Strategic Management (SM) courses struggling with these terms and using them unreasonably. Indeed, the hazard of their misuse can be comprehensibly assigned to the phonetic similitude of these words obscuring their conceptual distinction.

Nonetheless, the relative proximity of the three (3) concepts, imply simultaneously their distinctiveness as to their separation of ideas and meanings, but also the sharing of some commonalities between them. In *latu sensum*, a "market" corresponds to the physical or geographical radius of territory where the agents, organisations and individuals, interact therein.

This may comprise an ample range of physical and network boundary delimitations, according to what the perception of strategist/analyst is:

- Market as, a nation (e.g. China, England, Germany, Japan, USA, and so forth)
- Market as, a region (e.g. The Canary Islands-Spain; or Jutland-Denmark; or Hampshire-UK)
- Market as, a meta-region (e.g. Central Asia; Iberian Peninsula; Balkans; Maghreb; Scandinavia)
- Market as, a trade agreement (e.g. European Free Trade Association; Mercosur; North American Free Trade Agreement)
- Market as, a political association (e.g. African Union; Association of Southeast Asian Nations; Community of Portuguese Speaking Countries; Commonwealth; European Union)

In *stricto sensum*, the market is understood to be the background scenario from which agents gathering into, interact, exchange information, negotiate, and realize business agreements between parts, for both buyers and sellers. This is much closer to the first perspective (economic), despite more detailed, than the first perspective asserting to be the context in which firms produce and sell goods. Moreover, we may refer to, for instance, auction houses; professional fairs; outlets; showrooms; supermarkets; or retail stores. Yet, we are entering into the realm of the *marketplace.* Here, the market place (as a location for those activities taken inside markets), is however, bluntly and frequently used as synonym as markets, in *latu sensum* associated with a (set of) nations (e.g. a foreign marketplace or global marketplace). Yet, the marketplace is a primary belonging of the first (markets).

Marketplaces are though concurrent with *marketspa*ces as the latter can be defined as a virtual environment enhanced by information and communication technology (ICT) were the parts interact in an electronic (synchronic or asynchronic) mode, commonly referred to as "online markets", in which, account firms are represented through institutional websites, e-businesses, online stores, web-based software and related web applications.

Within the spectrum of marketplaces and marketspaces, *platforms* have been gaining traction as the fastest grown marketplace type, with an exponential grow rate (worldwide) in the last years. Thus, platforms fit into a category not covered here yet, labeled as *Internet-Mediated Trading* (IMT) markets, as online hubs where buyers and sellers mutually find information, partners and products. Hence, these IMT´s do not fit into none of the types of physical or offline markets presented above. Instead, they belong to the category of an electronic environment (or *e-marketplace)*. Here, within the pure business platforms, we can distinguish them, between, *business-to-business (B2B)* e-marketplaces. Some of the most well-known B2B platforms are*Alibaba; EC21; Taobao;* or, *ThomasNet* on the *business-to-consumer (B2C)* side while on the B2C´ side (e.g. Amazon; E-Bay; the most well-known as B2C are, for instance, *Best Buy; eBay; JD.com*; *Home Depot*; or, *Wallmart).*

Other e-marketplaces could be here pinpointed, as *blogs*, *social media*, or even the *virtual realities*. The latter, are in fact starting to attract several companies due to the advertisement opportunities. *Social media* platforms are definitely the second dominant category of e-marketplaces, sharing the attention of the consumer with business platforms. *Instagram; Pinterest; TikTok; Tumblr; Twitter,* are among others, some of the largest social media providers. These two types of dominant platforms (business and social media platforms), as large virtual places housing gigantic numbers in terms of units of global communication and trade, are managed by a platform provider administrator, often the platform administrator (Bakos, 1991). Some of the most known examples of those platforms, manage to apply an *Aggregator Model,* in which, the service provider acts as a huge vacuum-cleaner that pulls up data from other competing sources/platforms, working as a meta-platform of trade. That is the case of *Alibaba, Amazaon*, or *Taobao*. Others platforms, rather concentric, by option or need, do not further aggregate data from third parties. For example, the case of *Airbnb*; *Barnes & Noble*; *Spotify*; *Wish*; or *Zalando* (Webretailer, online).

Until this point, "markets" have gained full attention, at the beginning of this chapter, and, naturally, the external business environment has been relegated to a secondary position. The word "environment" was above employed a pair of times, referring to the marketplace/space yet without disclosing what, as a matter of fact, what an environment is, or better said, without distinguishing the notion of a "Market" from the "Business Environment"; or even, "External Business Environment" as identified in the heading of the chapter.

To make such distinction less complicated, I may share here a quick story. A few year ago, one of my co-author´s in one of my journal articles about organizational capabilities received the initial feedback of a reviewer from a reputed academic journal´s editor to whom we have submitted a manuscript at that time. The reviewer invited us to provide a clarification of the difference between a *Business environment* and *Business ecosystem*. The reviewer´s comment made total sense, since what was a clear to us, hence invested less time on such distinction, was not so clear to the reader/reviewers. Frequently, my students get also confused with both terms and have difficulties in separating them.

Actually, both concepts are sometimes misused in strategy literature, and discerning their meaning and boundaries in a precise way, was essential for the publishing of that study. As to a strategy book focused on business environment analyzability, as is here the case, the elucidation of these two concepts is paramount. Although, before jumping straight into their conceptual distinction, the reader is here invited to observe carefully the Exhibit 16 below illustrative of some differences and commonalities, and furthermore descriptive on how a company perceives a *business environment* versus a *business ecosystem*.

Figure 1. Diagrammatic Representation of a B. Environment & B. Ecosystem
Source: Own elaboration

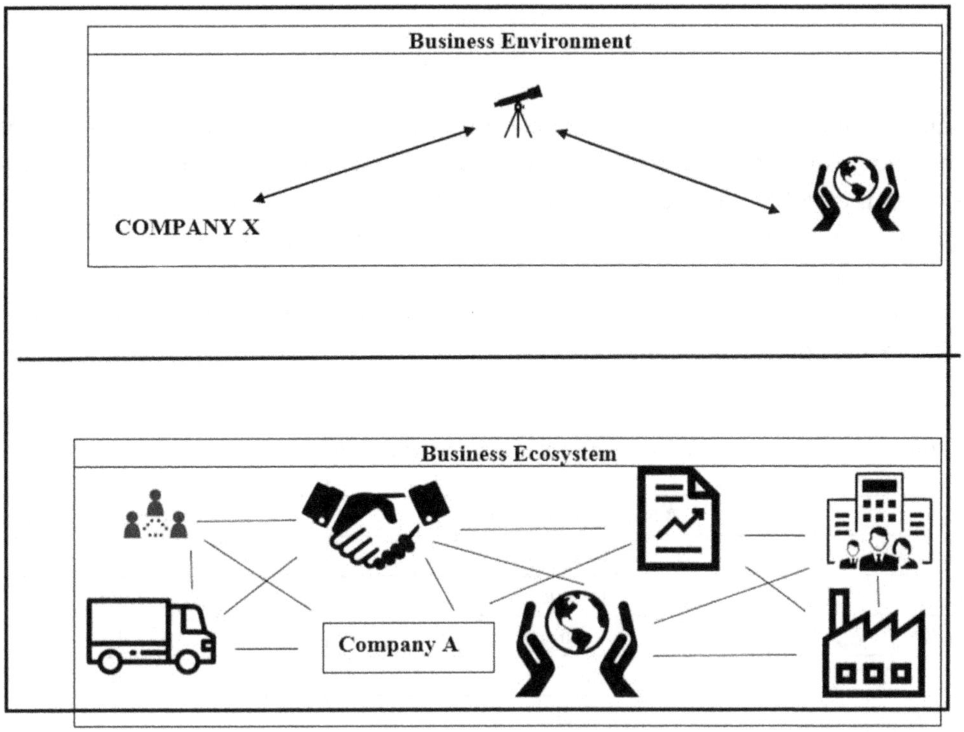

Looking over the figure above, at first glance, you might believe that the distinction of "Market" and "Business Environment" was simply abandoned; or, transformed into an explanation of the differences Business Environment and Business Ecosystem. In fact, the market (considered in *latu sensum*) is underlying to first part, as to the business environment, whether it is a nation, region/meta-region; a free trade agreement (FTA) or a political association.

Taking as an example of a market as a country of establishment and/or competition, then the business environment is the country itself and both constructs are overlapping.

Country X ⇔ Market X ⇔ Business Environment X

It is commonly called *Business Environment,* to describe a distinct (external) reality that ought to be acknowledged (co-existing distinctively from a focal organization), with its own nature, attributes and comprising likely impactful factors which may result into a dyad of (positive/negative) externalities. This definition corresponds, in fact, to an *External Business Environment (EBE)* that corresponds to the external context to a focal firm, in which companies are born-in, and being embedded into them they cannot abstract from it (e.g. the national culture; the technological conditions; or the geo-political positioning). However, the symmetric environment also co-exists with the EBE, which is an *Internal Business Environment (IBE),* as the inner reality of the organization, which defines its existence (e.g. assets; culture; goals; processes; strategy; systems; values; and, vision).

Hence, the *Business Environment (BE)* is a social construction of a business paradigm designed for a focal company, as follows:

BE = (EBE + IBE)

Each company and business unit has a unique BE. On the external business environment reside the various competitors, suppliers, buyers, and other agents. Hence, this most simplistic representation of BE´s is not the real paradigm of attesting the breadth of what the EBE is.

The B*usiness Ecosystem* is termed as, an "economic community", encompassing a set of agents (organizations and individuals) and culture, organized in a network of symbiotic relations of competition and/or cooperation, to produce valuable goods and services to and from the ecosystem. Their many distinctive features are depicted below.

Table 1. Business environments and ecosystems´ analysis: Main proprieties and locus of attention

	Business Environments	**Business Ecosystems**
Mode	Outside-in	Inside-out
Focus	Holistic	Embedded
Procedure	Static	Relational
Dimension	Multi	Mono
Properties	Breadth	Depth

Source: Own elaboration

It is noticeable in Table 6, that business environments and ecosystems possess dissimilar attributes, withal complementary, summarized in the functions below:

$\text{Business Environment}_{(x)} \neq \text{Business Ecosystem}_{(x)}$

$\text{Business Environment}_{(x)} \geq \text{Business Ecosystem}_{(x)}$

$\text{Business Environment}_{(x)} = \sum (\text{Business Ecosystem}_{(x1)\,+}\ \text{Business Ecosystem}_{(x2)\,+}\ \text{Business Ecosystem}_{(x3)\,+\,\ldots}\ \text{Business Ecosystem}_{(xn)})$

The representation of the business environment in Table 6 is one of a manifold interpretation for it; however, the presented here is the dominant one in the Strategic Management (SM) field. The BE is realized through an *outside-in* lens of a focal firm allegedly standing at an outside position and looking into the universe under analysis. On section 1.2. *External environment´s morphology* these BE perspectives are furthermore explored.

On the light of this dominant paradigm, a BE indicates one single market examined separately from others, in terms of, for instance, its country-specificities, in which the observer/s aim at gather insights on the major BE-properties descriptive of its nature, in order to, be able to picture the main properties and profile it. The BE is acknowledged as general and a static construct possible to be acknowledged, regardless of the dynamics of the agents and its specificities, as the structure of the dynamics (the network) and the outcome (the change and evolution). Hence, a constant need of intelligence from the same BE_x requires multiple scanning of it, in multiple time horizons, since the data collected as same point represent solely a snapshot of the reality at a certain moment and with a certain configuration of factors.

Being holistic, a business environment covers though not merely the economic landscape of most relevant pieces of information supposedly more relevant to the firm, but also, other societal quadrants. These may be natural and human forces, occurring at a local, regional or global scale, as the demographics, technology, socio-cultural (and ethical) traits, and the political, regulatory and legal forces (Janes and Sutton, 2020).

Consequently, BE Analysis is a typology of studies comprising relative complexity, encompassing these forces (e.g. demographics, culture, or regulation) as driving mechanisms of change determining how companies position themselves and compete in business. Therefore, BE analysis requires the cross-use of multiple sources of information, and being frequently confused with the broad idea of a market in *latu sensum* as a state or nation.

As to these components of the macro business environments, the Exhibit 18 (below) shows some example of their attributes.

According to Janes and Sutton (2020) the likelihood of external events, such as the ones exemplified above, being more uncertain and pressure more than less an organization, has to do with the degree of the effect, as a driver of change. Consequently, this effect is dependent on the extent of *dynamism* and the *(dis)order* of the business environment.

These scholars associated the first (dynamism) with the market volatility (or "V") and the latter (disorder) with market complexity (or "C"). The intertwining of these two elements of VUCA (*V* and C) as to a cross-observation exercise (of *dynamism X disorder)*, unraveled four patterns of possible changing events, requiring accordingly responsive business strategies.

Forces with higher dynamism lead to, either, creative or radical change. The creative (or also called fluid) change is pushed by the firm (or internally-generated) and this occurs in context of low turbulence of the markets in which positioned on.

Naturally, on such rather semi-stable markets comprised of low turbulence, the organizational capabilities are key- First, they determine the inner ability of the firm to learn faster than competition and the ability to absorb new knowledge and upskill itself. These two determinant factors (pace and upskilling) works as an internal force towards creative change, with problem-oriented or simply new ideas, concepts or inventions. Together these combinative sets of knowledge to generate novelty are bigger or smaller waves of change.

The radical change is geared by high levels of turbulence, mitigated internally by the effectiveness of resources´ administration, particularly their acquisition and allocation, plus through the development of competences have the power to reduce the effects of such disruptions hence destroying their impacting potential.

The intermediated or punctuated change refers to high levels of external competences introduced in the markets by competitors, suppliers, customers, authorities, or any other agents, participating even in different markets, but which effects have a transversal repercussion market-wide. These destructive competences, lead to competitive shifts, especially observed on the most affected firms, often on the verge of losses, focusing then on core-competences with perceived value for safeguarding their positions and subsistence.

Table 2. Examples of BE traits per component

Component	Examples
Demographics	• Aging and life expectancy • Associative patterns and habits (as hobbies) • Distribution of income • Geographical distribution of population and firms (and insularity) • Education
Economic conditions	• Conditions for bonds and stocks • Household income and savings • Inflation rates • Interest rates • Private companies´ debt • Trade deficits/surpluses • Rate of growth
General global forces	• Degree of international trade and investment (inward/outward) • Embargos • Import restrictions • Policies on international trade • Tariffs • Trade barriers
Natural environment	• Borders, frontiers, and air/maritime circumscription • Calamities and disasters • Conditions for farming • Climate and weather • Connectivity, remoteness and/or insularity • Diseases and exposure to pathogenic bodies/microorganisms • Quality of air, water and soils • Orography of land (e.g. coast, mountains, rivers and water resources) • Resources abundance/scarcity
Socio-cultural forces	• Access to leisure and knowledge resources (e.g. libraries or health-club) • Attitudes (e.g. towards immigration; health; technology) • Cultural diversity, landmarks and traditions (e.g. equality in workforce) • Gender roles • Lifestyle features • Values
Technology	• Accessibility to public infrastructures (as computers, phones and other gadgets) • Cyber-security, data accessibility and intelligence protection networks • Computing and telecommunication literacy and utilization • Degree of digitalization of services in society • Extent of knowledge/tech-based entrepreneurship (and surrounding conditions of its ecosystem) • Free access to international platforms and services • Intelectual propriety rights • Wi-Fi coverage and typology

Source: own elaboration

Events generating progressive change, yielded in typical contexts of low dynamism and low disorder, occur then in stable markets where changes are in general incremental, or evolutionary ones, mostly circumscribed to resources, capabilities and business models, with lower depth of change and lower pace of incidence, allowing some complaisance as to the time taken to their perception and accommodation on the firm.

Figure 2. Four broad change paths
Source: Janes and Sutton (2020)

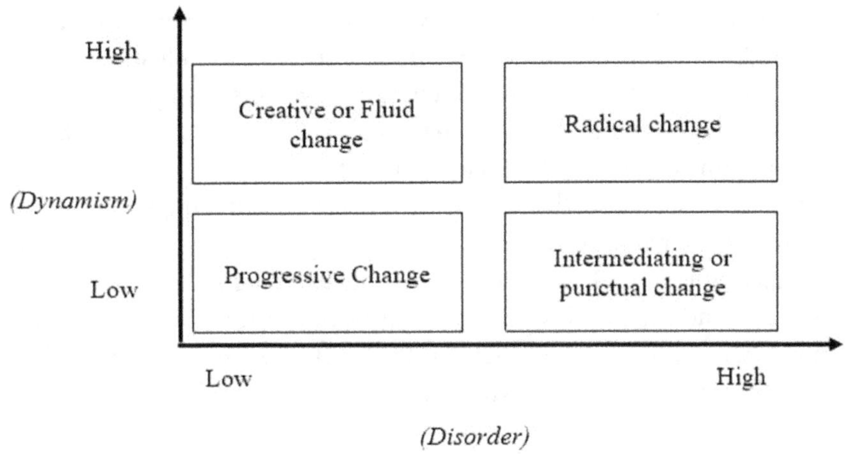

Needless is to say, that the anticipation of the occurrence of those events, especially in context of high turbulence is essential, if not, at least, their identification at an early stage of appearance in the market. However, equally important is, the detection of the impact of each event. Thus, comprehend what type of forces it may exercise on the firm is vital to build awareness about the direct and indirect pressures to be suffered and the degree of their effects.

Nonetheless the morphology of the event is assumed to constrain also the firm´s ability to grasp its nature and recognize its risks. On chapter one we have introduced three types of events with different effects: the *black swans;* the *fads*; and the *wildcards*. What distinguishes one from the other is its nature but also the firm´s perception of it.

According to Taleb and Blyth (2011), a *black swan*, an unpredictable event which is unlikely to occur. *Fads*, are short-term observable shifts with a short-living before fading away, and usually, have a reduced power, and mostly indirect one, to become a real threat. *Wild cards*, are event generating which are perceived as impactful ones, generating discontinuities in the development curve of the firm (Lindgren and Bandhold, 2009).

Understandably, what distinguishes the black swans from the fads and wild cards is the unpredictability. Business environment analysis is then a key function for spotting those events and identifying the disruptive potential of the others, specially the Wild Cards (WS).

Business Ecosystems[1]

As a subset of the BE, a *business ecosystem* is dissimilar but also complementary to the former (environment). The BE entails a macro sphere (e.g. the politics or the socio-culture sphere) which serves as background determining the conditions of the markets. The business ecosystem represents the micro sphere where the agents play therein. The business ecosystem entail an intricate dynamic framework of cross-sector interaction of multiple types of agents (or production factors), as manufacturers, suppliers, competitors, distributors, customers, opinion-makers; outsources, wholesalers, banks, investors, associations, unions, government authorities or regulatory agencies.

Here, the job of the analyst, whenever focused on the ecosystem implies a zooming-in of the observing lens into a micro environment, at industry-level, in which, the market research may be mono-dimensional (e.g. focus on one single industry) or multi-dimensional (i.e. several industries). Relevant is that business ecosystems are generally complex cosmos were the analysis is in-depth and all components of the ecosystem are intertwined and require an attention to other variables, often, not intended to be analyzed, yet participating in the same dynamic influence other parts.

For instance, an analysis of competitiveness of an industry does not imply a simple comparison of the competitor´s base. Actually, it requires the incorporation of many other aspects of the business ecosystem determining the competition game. This means, observing each individual competitor (i.e. the strategic position, business goals, and capabilities); and moreover, the surrounding reality of potential entrants, conditions of competition, as follows: products on the market; existing technologies and innovations; knowing the multiple segments; patterning strategic groups; and so forth.

PERFORMANCE AND SUCCESS: EFFECTIVE BUSINESS ENVIRONMENT ANALYSIS (BEA)

At the previous section, we have drawn the general properties of a *business environment* and compared then roughly against an ecosystem. So, at this stage, one would expect an initial (intuitive and straightforward) enquiring, surrounding the analyzability of a business environment:

Question 2: How can a firm (successfully) grasp a business environment (BE)?

It is indisputable that "*success…*" is an adjective associated with the judgement of quality of a venture.

The case of Haier Group (presented at the end of the chapter one), as you may recall, is indisputably a case of business success. Their success is anchored on the coherence of a triad of functions (governance-leadership and management). Moreover, consistency is ensured by a sharp focus on capabilities (up and reskilling of high-qualified employees) and the agility of the sophisticated structural configuration of this organization, abdicating from the traditional hierarchy to implement the ZZJYTs independent units hybridizing the business model.

In this chapter, it is presented the case of Nokia Corporation. This centenary Finish Company which held multiple tech and non-tech centered business units focus on the production of among others, pulp, paper, rubber, telephony, television sets, radios, and other electronic products. The firm took a seminal decision in the 1980s to concentrate efforts on electronics businesses, especially with a primary focus on the telecommunications sector as a dominant business and assisted a steep rise on this business unit but also an abrupt fall a few years after.

Considering the tenets of success addressed below, here resides the first aspect to be pointed out to Nokia (see case at the end of the chapter) is the *unrelated diversification strategy* followed by the company at corporate-level; thus, maintaining presence, at some point, in a broad range of other industries. Secondly, over-emphasizing market attractiveness in business competition choices. It revealed a likely excessive "sympathy" towards an I/O[2] model to attain high economic rents). This is *per se* not a mistake! To diversify is good (do not get me wrong)! I won´t enter here into further considerations of pros and cons of multiple types of diversification; yet, is noteworthy to mention that several are the Strategy theorists advocating a curvilinear relationship between the degree of portfolio´s diversification´ and the effectiveness of business to attain higher performance ratios measured in profitability. Surely, the diversification into further product markets can reduce the uncertainty-level about future cash flows. As a principle, better is the value created by different business units when synergies are based on a *related constrained* diversification types. The issue on the stake here is, to maintain other businesses as peripheral while its direction remains unfocused and/or unmanageable may create a storm for the future. As a result, one of the decisions of Nokia´s CEO´ at the time (*Kari Kairamo*) to keep the paper industry, ended up to be reversed, as this business unit was in 1989 finally sold off.

Furthermore, Nokia has disregarded the analysis of the external business environment (EBE), going against another tenet of success, i.e. to constantly have a profound understanding of the business environment conditions and dynamics of change. This was determinant for their subsequent fall. Firstly, the firm ignored the early 2000s pressure from low-end competitors triggering early signs of problems. The company was initially dismissive of these new offerings in the market and in 2007 suffers the direct competition of Apple (with the first iPhone).

Hence, *success* requires the fulfillment of four (4) tenets*: long-term goals´ definition; profound understanding of the competitive environment; resources appraisal* and efficient allocation; and, *implementation* of business strategy with its auditing on a regular basis. Nokia missed two of those tenets: long-term goals; and, profound understanding of the business environment. With regard to long-term goals, their corporate strategy became unclear at some stage and subsequently the business strategies for non-tech units subsequently unfocused. The ignoring of emerging events in the market, as the appearance of new players, products and technologies, has then comprised the future success of the company.

In this context, it shall be clarified that one thing the organizational success of an entire business unit, and another is the success of a BE analysis procedure. Such confusion of both is an erroneous and misleading association. Furthermore, the success of the environment analysis is placed on the outputs the individual obtained from the market. Thus, it is built on the proficiency of the analyst to deliver an impeccable piece of research, communication of data and reporting at a standard of organizational excellence, which entails:

(i) Providing a broad picture of the hermeneutic unit/s of analysis; and,
(ii) Accomplishing the pre-established goals of the project.

This is the professional responsibility of management consultants, especially the strategy consultancy firms, such as, the "big-10 league" of strategy consultants (the *Boston Consulting Group*; the *McKinsey & Company*; *Bain & Company*; *A.T. Kearney*; *Oliver Wyman*; *Roland Berger*; *L.E.K. Consulting*; *Monitor Deloitte*; *Strategy&* - former *Booz & Company*; and *EY*). However, in case of the reader is an apprentice enrolled at a higher education institution´s (HEI) undergraduate or post-graduate business program, his/her ascending knowledge-building trajectory, implies a lower responsibility as an analyst, due to the degree of sophistication of business methodological toolbox which is acquainted with on this theme. Early business researchers are thus, at smaller extent, liable to the above referred.

As a matter of fact, the label "success", it indicates a compliance measure of its completion, as a fully executed project, in line with its initial problematization, aims of the investigation, and conducted within the boundaries of ethical principles (deontology/teleology) and qualitative principles (of validity and reliability). In this context, and transposing directly strategy theory into its methodological application (for analyzing BEs) to comprehend what entails such endeavor, let us consider that a successful organizational strategy ought to safeguard the 4 elementary pillars of success (Grant, 2016). Thus, the Table 8 below, crosses these tenets of a success to the domain of business research.

Table 3. Tenets of success: The organizational strategy and the BEA

Success of a Business-Level Strategy (BLS)	Success of Business Environment Analysis (BEA)
1. long-term goals´ definition	→ *corresponds to:* Set the general or strategic goals (SG) and objectives (SO)
2. profound understanding of the competitive environment	→ *corresponds to:* context surrounding the realization of the project (firm and client, competition, and available methods)
3. resources appraisal	→ *corresponds to:* resources allocated to the projects and constraints
4. Implementation	→ *corresponds to:* planning and break-down structuring of the tools, methods utilization, phases, processes, initiatives, operative goals, resources and time horizon

Source: own elaboration

As observed in the table, the (strategy) management consultant project is associated with the accomplishment of its goals (principle 1) and inherent preparation of its realization (principles 2, 3 and 4). The general aims of a *business environment analyzability project (BEAP)* are associated with the profiling of the BE, regardless of the nature and relatedness of any other specific goals or objectives. Here, the distinction of a *goal* and objective is crystal clear. A *goal* is the qualitative definition of intentionality and will (or drive), while the strategic *objective (SO)* expresses the degree of fulfillment (or target). Thus, the goal it may be represented with the drive (d) and the target (t) as follows:

$$SO_{(x)} = (d\,.t)$$

Thus, the success (S) function it is has this specific model:

$$S_{(BEAi)} = \alpha_0 + \beta_1 + \beta_2 + \beta_3 + \varepsilon_i \ldots$$

Here the constant of overall success of the BEAP is determined by the constant alpha *(α),* combined with the beta *(β)* coefficients of objectives. The objective it may be accomplished within a performance measurement evaluation of partial or total accomplishment according to the figures of result (R) or progression (P) of their widget counting.

$$SO = x\,(1 - r) \textit{ or } SO = (d\,.\,t).\,(1 - r)$$

I shall say, each project is a project, and therefore it requires a casuistic immersion of the observer/s into its specificities and constraints. Generally, the understanding of how a BE, implies carrying out of a descriptive study (or a descriptive-evaluative one), as a 360 degrees inspection, since all spheres of the BE have to be accounted as to their mapping of major general factors, as a prerequisite for portraying it or updating its profile. This contrasts substantially to the studies of an ecosystem containing a plethora of different options, and normally are consubstantiated in a deeper or full immersion into one or few characteristics. Thus, *ecosystem analysis* has a rather short radius of circumscription. Yet, a rule of thumb it may be here considered for further studies.

The more dynamic are the agents, the higher its evolution, and the perception of uncertainty surrounding any commitment. Consequently, the higher is also the need for further research, namely as to the evaluation of the motion´s impact on the firm and its underlying opportunities and threat. In this sense, higher environmental kinesis demands for the agents involved, the *organizational ecology*, a reinforcement of (adaptive) dynamic endeavors and strategic repositioning. Here the human capital is key, as extensive competences and capabilities are crucial for such adaptability. Unsurprisingly, "evolution" is frequently associated with an action-reaction spiral chain, categorized by some scholars as a set of four major constraints of the markets: volatility, uncertainty, complexity, and ambiguity (VUCA), which is somewhat a theme to be revisited on another part of the book.

Hence, the "success" of the BEAP, as a quality performance label of its accomplishment, is though influenced *ex ante* by the capacity of the firm to learn further, by its ground knowledge, by its own evolution or historical track and path dependency on the prior, plus an apprenticeship upon real-time faced circumstances as an effective learning curve (on an ascending slope), and its cultural openness for setting the roots and ground for further learning. Here, the organization´s strategy, their capabilities and assumptions hold about the universe under study it may also thoroughly shape the final output. Later on, you will have the chance to explore the factors influencing the BEAP outputs. Still, it may be argued that any BEAP´s output is determined in general by the whole set of tangible and intangible resources and its constraints by the firm (e.g. organizational capabilities; bounded rationality of market researchers; accessibility to existing sources of data; fuzzy and concealed information; corporate directives; time constraints and so forth).

Although, it is worth mentioning that a BEAP is a representation of the reality, a projection of the ontological attributes of the universe under study, aiming at illuminating in general its essence. Thus, are not "the universe" itself. Roy Bhaskar on his book "*Dialectic a pulse of freedom*" expresses a view of a (critical realist) stratified ontology, in which the object of the research is foreseen as the "real", which to be acknowledged requires a study of its structural causes and mechanisms shaping everyday´ s lives. Yet, Bhaskar (2008) asserts also that not social facts (the "events") are reachable and acknowledgeable, being furthermore, its understanding dependent on direct interaction with social actors, and partially not able to be observed (the "empirical"), even when the researcher strives to make a optimal study minimizing bias and objectivizing the content.

In sum, using here a cliché, you may suppose there is no perfect studies. The idea of perfection it embodies the observation of the full range of information, as the reaching of a saturation point of data units, where the one hundred percent of events are fully observed at a full range of properties. This seems an impossible mission under a constrained scenario, and specially supporting the author´s advocacy that not all events are observable, being of a transcendental comprehension. Thus, optimal studies may also be seen as utopic projections of real successful studies, accounting a triad of properties, *suitability, feasibility, acceptability (SFA)*. With this in mind, you are recommended whenever undertaking a strategic evaluation to conduct a SFA potential analysis, and pour such exercise to the formal reporting and documentation-delivery of the BEAP. You may note that such tool is further explored in chapter 3, in which, it will be depicted the components of this tool.

Hence, recalling the question no. 2 above *("How can a firm (successfully) grasp a business environment (BE)?)*" the context of the outside-researcher is noticeably complex, and just following in thesis, the four tenets of a strategic success may not get in a snap a company in the path to success. The reasons for this is, these tenets establish a minimum ground, as principles of corporate liability, to align the firm with the environment. However, they do not provide a compass as to a better of strategic direction, or corporate/business strategy. As generic principles, these are forward-feeding milestones of alignment of governance policies and strategy-making exercise with performance and success; and moreover strategy controls backward-feeding measures of the same alignment.

In this context, another aspect accountable in the business environment, apart from the tenets of success, is the market´s *dynamics*. Within the word dynamics it is included the following four aspects: *motion*; *evolution; reconfiguration*; and, *renewal*. The motion stands for the kinesis or flow of daily changes occurring with a gradualist pace introduced day-by-day or incremental change; but also exists whenever disruptive events alter the social regimes modifying its norms, being therefore transformational of culture and habits, systems and processes and consequently revolutionary as to the nature and functioning of the organizational strategies. The first type of motion (incremental change) is observed both in an indelible operational alteration of time and/or methods (e.g. as a workplace reconfigurations), or a systemic operational change (e.g. a concurrent reengineering of production processes; the launching or diffusion of a new technological advancement), or even on a strategic maneuver of an incumbent with legitimate organic growth intentions, as portrayed at the four quadrants of Igor Ansoff´s strategic planning tool known as the "*Ansoff matrix*", which has the purpose of devising strategies for business development and growth.

Figure 3. Ansoff Matrix (or "product/market expansion grid"
Source: Ansoff (1965)

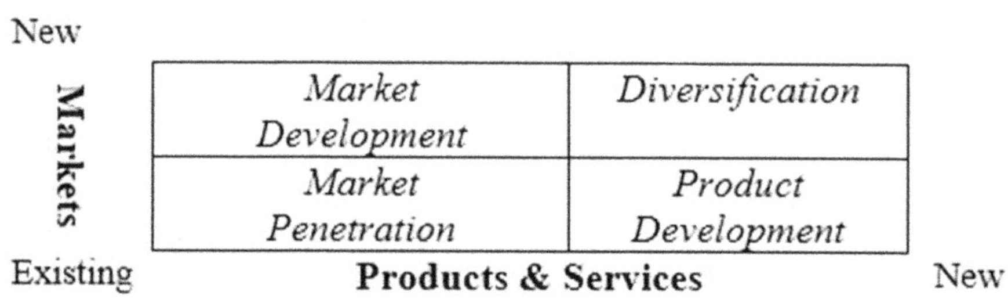

This tool, also denominated "*product market expansion grid*", is a change trigger with origin at the firm-level instead of an externally instilled one. Here, the firm is perceived as a trigger of BE changes by reinforcing a market position, opening new market horizons, new product developments (NPD) or introducing a business-level diversification components with a triadic reasoning, *horizontal diversification*, as the extension to new target groups of clients/consumers, or *concentric diversification*, related to new product lines or services or *conglomeral diversification*, as the launching of goods of technological novelty and embracing other consumption target groups).

Yet, in most cases the change is instigated from the outside to the focal firm. An unavoidable aspect with regard to the accomodation of environmental change seems to be, what it is here labelled of, the "*dynamics´ paradox*". Strategists and management consultants, eager to build relevant intelligence based on sophisticated data and market knowledge illustrative of the reality tend to, often get trapped into a solemn error of *staticity*. This does not mean that senior consultants and strategists believe that market are static (not at all), but it is argued that involuntarily they take in many cases a “snapshot” of the reality, by gathering multiple bundles of cross-sectional data with analytical depth, but lacking on vision, normally neglecting the range or breadth of the projects´ influence in time (past-present-future). Normally, business environment analysis projects look at their core concern (the present) ignoring past contexts explicative of the extant, or overlooking their determinism of the past and present in future possibilities, actions, opportunities and threats. Likewise, the aspect of “evolution” is in some cases another issue, as the connection of past-present, being perceived as a vulnerable side of strategy-related reporting, being partially liable for the phenomenon of strategic drift addressed in chapter two. Instead of, focusing on the collection and analysis of continuous longitudinal data to comprehend the consequences of change or evolving aspects; some projects are subdued by multiple cross-sectional datasets, as “multiple snapshots” of the reality with discrete content, as separate observation with limited connectivity despite any contextual/temporal linkage however not allowing an extrapolation of an evolutionary path, and discontinuity or emergence of trends, and/or even the serendipitous seizing of opportunities or threats.

The bundles of changes constitute the collective phenomenon of partial mutation (reconfiguration) or total mutation (renewal). As in the case of *adaptive reconfiguration* and enduring reconfiguration changes, for instance, the one leveraged by the promulgation of the new *general data protection regulation (GDPR)* which came to force in May 2018 in the European Union (EU) compelling all firms within the Eurozone and with exchange with the European-Union State Members to undertake several alterations in terms of digital processes and products/services, with impact in multiple organizational functions, to be able to comply with the personal data protection of users and securitization measures regarding their information and communication technologies (Abrantes and Venkataraman, 2022; Abrantes and Ostergaard, 2021). Similarly, the Covid-19 pandemic appearing at the end of 2019 in China forced a *reactive reconfiguration* of societal rules in the short-term (e.g. exponential growth of online training, teaching and video-conferencing; forced work-from-home; lay-offs; or even, alteration of produced and sold goods, such as restaurants becoming “take-away” services). Thus, the adaptive and reactive reconfiguration changes refer to an enduring or short-time length of changes but with a partial nature. This contrasts with the renewal which is a type of change that represents a total mutation or a full reconfiguration, as in the case of Nokia Corporation which until the middle of the 80s in last century held a handful of different strategic business units (SBUs) spread across economic sectors or industries, such as, cables, chemicals, electronics, machinery, pulp, paper, power, and rubber, deciding under the CEO´s *Simo Vuorilehto* reign to divest on multiple industrial activities shifting the corporate scope of such unrelated diversification strategies towards an SBU, phasing out the prior businesses and focusing on mobile phone technologies.

In this sense, it may be easily understood that market dynamics are a source of firm´s uncomforted and unwilling form of living the social experience within the markets of commitment. This phenomenon forces the organizations to deal with the underlying spillovers of this dynamism, as the uncertainty, in special of gaining or maintaining solid positions, or the potential risks and externalities, as the reputational or financial losses, the complexity of relations, products, standards, competences and systems of value addition and appropriability, and their underlying ambiguities, and the obscurity of the combinations of resource and capability-bases introduced in products and business models.

The cognoscibility of the business environment, is furthermore influenced by two dominant and interchangeable traits: globalization and technological development. First, the convergence of societies towards a global interdependence, of cross-nation multiple synergies and the ascension of meta-regional dimensions of interculturality, brought by a more ample and faster physical and digital communication and national culture´s exchange, shortened distances, even between countries of lower geographical and psychic proximity, and gradually building a sense of global acculturalization. The first is empowered by the second, since great technological advancements in the ITC domain where technologies of virtualization of physical environments, associated with intra-objects communication, cobotization/ robotization, big-data overwhelming storage magnitudes (e.g. as the zettabyte = 1000^7 bytes; or the yottabyte = 1000^8 bytes), the uprise of the fintech anchored on block chain technologies, and furthermore, the proliferation of societal innovations brought by the advent of artificial intelligence and machine learning are rapidly changing the life of citizens and companies. In such a horizon of society of information and knowledge the intangibilities gained prominence, such as the importance of datasets, business analytics or business intelligence, the information economics, behavioral economics and applied information economics (AIE). Yet, humans being on the epicenter of the large majority of business decisions experience though a lack of full rationality or an optimal position of context acknowledgement with decisions being taken within a bounded rationality context, even though, the crescent availability of information not accompanied by augmentation of human capacity to process it. This, is consubstantiated into what is termed as an *availability of information paradox*, since globalization and technological advancements, as both privileged contexts of accessibility to new target groups of clients/consumers and decisional information than ever before in previous decades, does not configure per se an immediate capacity of the firms to extract those benefits, requiring also further adaptation to such changes, in terms of capabilisation (upskilling/reskilling) of labour, not merely technical competences but cognitive and managerial capabilities, ordinary and dynamic capabilities (e.g. ambidexterity; creativity; international coordination; or patching).

BUSINESS ENVIRONMENTS AND BUSINESS ECOSYSTEMS

Certainly, the reading of the previous sections may sharpen your curiosity for the connection of both (environment-ecosystem), which is an issue revisited and addressed more in detail at the section "*External environment´s morphology*".

For the sake of straightforwardness of the book´s structure, we could at this stage consider a much simpler question:

Question 3: Are (the analyzability projects of) business environments (BE) and business ecosystems intertwined?

Answering this question objectively, imposes the establishment of three prior epistemological assumptions:

a) Whether the environment encompasses:
    i. one ecosystem (business environment ≈ business ecosystem)
    ii. or multiple (> 1) (business environment ≠ business ecosystems)
b) The ecosystems are embedded on the BE
c) And so, the ecosystems are related to it

Considering these assumptions above, it may be inferred a predictable positive relation between both, justifying their crossed analysis. So, the answer (accounting these assumptions) is clearly yes, they are associated.

Yet, before jumping into any in-depth studies (*ecosystem´s analysis*) it is critical for the analyst to comprehend the ontology of the object (environment). Likewise, the business environment it may explained by the sum of events, casual structures and mechanisms that reside at the "actual" ecosystem (e.g. the incumbents´ functions; agency roles; network configurations; entrepreneurial orientation and so forth). Hence, as to a kick start of a Business Environment Analysis Project (BEAP) or an Ecosystem Analysis Project (EAP), and using here the simple analogy of the chicken and egg dilemma to indicate what it came first, is suggested a methodological option (the funnel approach) whenever you are on the eminence of initiating a BEAP. This implies you start by a general observation before initiating any particular observation, as the observation of the general events set a foundational ground for further learning, under the thesis of the virtues of building a *potential absorptive capacity (PACAP)* for the future realization and success of further research. projects.

Naturally, the success of market research (regardless of its typology), lays partially on the understanding of the ontological aspects constituting the social regime of the BE. Thus, any BE regime is populated with multiple spheres (i.e. segments and factors[3]) such as:

- Laws, taxation or political systems (environment/market as a country)
- Agreements, state-membership and quotas (market as a political association)

As to the business ecosystem, these agents configure the notion of *organizational ecology*. This concept refers to the demographics of the ecosystems, and it may be assumed that number of incumbents may vary from one to another, as a result of the VUCA phenomena identified at the end of the previous section.

The organizational ecology, indicates then the typology and quantity of affiliated firms that are their (re)presented at a given moment in time (e.g. investors, suppliers, consultants, competitors, distributors, wholesalers, retailers, or buyers). Their variation is mediated by regulatory and competitive barriers at their entry or exit, which in turn, make their variation to be significant when compared in between. Here, their level of concentration is primarily dictated as to the vertical concentration (suppliers and buyers), and horizontal concentration (e.g. competitors) by regulatory barriers. Here, closed markets are the ones assisting a marked interference from the authorities, imposing obstructions, barriers, trust opportunities and collusion, instigating or sponsoring "p" emperies – monopolies, duopolies and oligopolies. The market is protectionist, concentrated in few, polarized and/or entails no competition whatsoever. By opposition, open markets do not assist prohibitive of significant constrains (regulatory barriers) but solely competitive barriers.

Furthermore, the open markets´ organizational ecology is furthermore influenced by the dynamics, evolution and VUCA perception of the current established firms and potential new entrants. Here, competitive barriers, such as technological or capital-requirements, or accessibility and/or preemption to resources constitute decisive factors for forecasting the attractiveness and liability of outsidership guiding establishment, and further investment/divestment. Here, the knowledgeness of the ecosystem is determinant for the controlling risks and a mediator of commitment decisions.

Although, commencing a research project about a business environment and/or ecosystem analyzability (BEAP or EAP) based on singular attributes is reductive of what the business world is all about in the 21st century, and consequently, is restrictive of the requirements of business intel. Of course, I have started by addressing these concepts separately, but at this stage, after "rolling the dice" of what markets and business environments and ecosystems are, is worth acknowledging that BEs, such as firms, are not "desert islands" with fully armored access to (at most they are "peninsulas"), instead, they are reciprocal connectors of information, goods and funds with other agents.

Technological advancements and the globalization transformed the business world towards a digitalized competition each time more a platform-based (destroying the brick-and-mortars), and subsequently, extending the horizons of target consumers across continents. Nowadays, businesses are more interdependent and connected then ever since, and have transformed the social regimes across the globe on fundamental aspects on what people think and act and believe, spreading the seeds of the established espoused habits and norms of a global culture. To what the SM is concerned, these two factors (technology and globalization) extended the boundaries of BE´s knowledge-requirements, since the markets grew in complexity, requiring an extension of *simple analysis* to a *composite analysis*, the latter touching the outskirts of information of the initial one. *What does this mean in practical terms?* For instance, the extension an ecosystem´s boundary to a regional, meta-regional or global dimensions, implies added tiers of analyzability which makes the studies more challenging and time and cost-consuming.

Let us just pinpoint a few bulleted ideas of added complexity of ecosystems:

- Increasing frequency of "black swans"
- Intra-industrial convergence
- Globally dispersion of the supply chains
- New economic sectors, strategic innovations and business models
- Shift from solo-competition to network competition

A *black swan* is definable as a highly implausible event which holds three (3) major characteristics: high unpredictability; high impact; and its occurrence triggers the architecture of an explanation which makes it less random (Taleb and Blyth, 2011).

Several are the occurrence of unpredictable or uncontrolled events to be identified termed as "black swans", unrelated between each other, and with significant chronological distance in between registered in the last and current century. However, an increasing pace or aggravated frequency of occurrence is observed in recent decades of humankind history, as an enormous list of events (natural and manmade ones) could be here be enumerated in different fields, as in ecology, economy, medicine, politics, technology and in many other domains. For instance, the disasters occurred in the nuclear power plants in Chernobyl (Russia) and Fukushima (Japan); the Asian flu (in the 1950s); the HIV/Aids (in the 1980s), more recently, the Severe Acute Respiratory Syndrome (SARS) in 2003, and the Ebola virus disease (EVD) outbreak of 2014/16 or the 9-11 in USA.

Perhaps, other examples of events with swiping socio-economic effects could be brought to light, as the Great Depression of 1929; the Dotcom bubble; the 2008´s world crisis (triggered by the collapsing of the US real estate market), the commercial battle US-China in 2016, and the recent global economic slowdown with devastating recession effects brought by the coronavirus pandemic. In the business world one could highlight the incredible success of Youtube, the meteoric ascension of Zoom in 2020 or the unbelievable success story of Coupang, the latter being in fact one the cases presented in this book.

Another source of further complexity on business ecosystems besides black swans is the phenomenon of acceleration of the industry evolution. Geared by research, development and launch of innovations, in products, processes and business models, it has been accelerating the pace of products life cycles (PLCs), shrank lead times and pushed economic rents down, including the ones of the pioneer firms. Moreover, trembling the boundaries of value networks, since several are the firms developing in the last couple of decades hybrid portfolios of products crossing multiple industries and appropriating value of firms in which were not allegedly in competition with, yet hard-to-account threats and risks for practitioners; and even more, questioning the utility of *International Standard Industrial Classification (ISIC)* when modern competition have derailed the pre-conception of one industry-specific competition, as products are set across economic sectors.

Likewise, a shift from solo-playing towards network-playing mode, altered the traditional market competition to a hypercompetition, in which, corporate decisions are interdependently taken, dispersed across shared centers of decision and power (then more diffuse), dragging with them the operative activities mutating their location a to b towards an optimal location, with primary activities fragmented into parts and globally dispersed exploring the benefits of offshoring/outsourcing such as:

- exploring local centers of competence and expertise
- exploiting the benefits for (glo)calization
- arbitrary choices mostly with financial gains
- synergies across organic units

At last, value networks hitherto linear in its genesis (*upstream →downstream* logic) are challenged by the convergence of industries and dissipation of products boundaries. Moreover those challenges have spillovers on the appearance of new strategic innovations with new business models leapfrogging phases of value chain (e.g. the *drop shipping)*, or transforming the supply chain into non-linear value propositions. Here, the notion of business model entails an architecture describing how a firm creates and delivers value to its stakeholders and captures a share of it (Teece, 2018).

Non-linear value propositions entail the adoption of C2B (customer-to-business) and C2C (customer-to-customer) models brought by the advent of the sharing economy and circular economy related activities; or even upstarters testing new innovative goods which may appeal to a customer base and with a rapid dissemination, overturning big corporations as dominant incumbents of a marketplace/space with *big bang disruptive* ((BBD) product-offers which might alter very quickly and drastically the consumption habits, and comprising intrinsic risks of destroying commercial empires and dragging them into a big crunch and entropy.

LEARNING OUTCOMES

- Conceptualize, in *latu* and *strictu sensum*, market, marketplace and marketspace
- Distinguish business environment and ecosystem: Properties and *locus* of attention
- Comprehend the main commonalities and differences of Business Environment Analysis (BEA)
- Recognize the dynamics and evolutionary path of the markets, its drivers and effects upon competition
- The notion of *success* in Business Strategy and Business Environment Analysis (BEA)

CASE: NOKIA GROUP

The conglomerate established in 1967 (Nokia Group) deriving from three independent business units: a wood-pulp mill (1865), the Finish Rubber Works (1898) and the Finish Cable Works (1912), rapidly expanded into expanded into digitalization and wireless, and telecommunications.

The Nokia's transition to a primary focus on telecommunications as a dominant business unit began in the 1980s. During the successful period of growth on the telecommunication sector, between the 1990 a 2006, Nokia's focus on design and functionality gained it a worldwide reputation. It in this period that the company launched the first mobile equipment making a GSM call, incorporated ringtones and incorporated the first camera on a phone device.

The spectacular rise of the company took it in 1998 to become the first smartphone manufacturer assuming the status of a best-selling mobile phone brand in the world. In 2001 was an undisputed market leader with over 35% of market share, position held in the sector through the early-mid 2000s.

However, their spectacular rise in the global mobile phone business gave place to a steep fall when the game changed in 2007 with Apple's iPhone, and subsequently, with other mobile phone brands powered by Google's Android operating system, as HTC or Samsung. A combination of external factors and internal decisions culminated on the company's handset business being sold to Microsoft. The firm ignored first in the early 2000s the pressure from low-end competitors triggering early signs of problems. The company was initially dismissive of these new offerings. In 2007 appears the first iPhone. In 2008 Google launches the first Android operating system (the T-Mobile G1). But, on the other side, Nokia had no equivalent product to fight back against the first shipped iPhone, and its operating system, Symbian was ageing. Moreover, its app store (Ovi) was far from Apple´s.

By mid-2011 Nokia was making one tenth as much money on its phones as Apple. Its market capitalization stood at US$43 billion, compared to a high of nearly US$250 billion in 2000. The CEO (Stephen Elon) circulated then a memo admitting that the company was in deep trouble due to changes in the competitive environment. In September 2013, Microsoft Mobile acquired Nokia´s phone unit, the devices and services division in a deal valued at €5.4 billion (Duke and Birkinshaw, 2011; Nokia, 2021).

CHAPTER HIGHLIGHTS

- The notion of market: Industrial Economics vs Marketing perspectives
- The clarification of *market, marketspace, marketplace* and *e-marketplace* (Marketing perspective); and markets in *Latu sensum* and *Stricto sensum*
- External Business Environments (EBE) vs. Business Ecosystems
- The major attributes of an EBE´s VUCA traits: the notion of *dynamism* and *disorder*
- Janes and Sutton´s four (4) organizational *change paths*
- Tenets of *Organizational Strategy* and *Business Success*
- Ansoff´s Strategic Planning matrix
- EBE´s unpredictability and likelihood of events: the *black swans, wild cards* and *fads*

SUMMARY OF THE CHAPTER

The chapter addressed the core concepts of *market, marketplace, marketspace, business environment, business ecosystem* and *organizational ecology*, as these concepts are often miscomprehend and misused. Then, it addressed the market in *lato* and *stricto sensum* and addressed the main properties and *locus* of attention of *business environments* and *business ecosystems* in a comparative manner.

Moreover, we have looked into *market dynamics* and crossed it with the *strategic planning toolkit* of the firm, revisiting the foundation framework of Igor Ansoff´s matrix and the case of *adaptive/ reactive reconfiguration* of Nokia Corporation.

Furthermore, we have proceeded into the definition of what a *business environment analysis project* (BEAP) is, and an effective BEAP, comparing the characteristics of a successful business strategy with a successful BEAP and modelled the (BEAP) success function.

In the last section of this chapter we have looked at the context of BEs and intertwined them with ecosystems and looked at the morphology of both and their dissimilar rationale (outside-in versus in-side out logic of analyzability) On the next chapter, we will into the realm of external business environments (EBE) and therein, we will explore the BE´s attributes, namely the *assumptions* and *interpretations*; *interfaces*; *layers* of analyzability; *ontology* and *elements of BEA*.

REFERENCES

Abrantes, B. F. & Ostergaard, K. (2021) Digital footprint wrangling: are analytics used for better or worse? A concurrent mixed methods research on the commercial (ab)use of dataveillance. *Journal of Marketing Analytics, 10*(2022), 187-202. https://doi.org/ doi:10.1057/s41270-021-00144-5

Abrantes, B. F., & Venkataraman, A. (2022). Environment kinesis and organizational adaptability: Effects of EU's General Data Protection Regulation on the Danish software industry. *International Journal of Learning and Change, 14*(1), 22–45. doi:10.1504/IJLC.2022.119516

Ansoff, H. I. (1965). *Corporate strategy: An analytic approach to business policy for growth and expansion*. McGraw-Hill Companies.

Bakos, J. Y. (1991). A strategic analysis of electronic marketplaces. *Management Information Systems Quarterly, 15*(3), 295–310. doi:10.2307/249641

Bhaskar, R. (2008). *Dialectic: The pulse of freedom*. Routledge. doi:10.4324/9780203892633

Duke, L., & Birkinshaw, L. (2011) *The rise and fall of Nokia*. Think at London Business School Magazine. https://publishing.london.edu/cases/the-rise-and-fall-of-nokia/

Karampatsis, R. M., Babii, H., Robbes, R., Sutton, C., & Janes, A. (2020, October). Big code!= big vocabulary: Open-vocabulary models for source code. In *2020 IEEE/ACM 42nd International Conference on Software Engineering (ICSE)* (pp. 1073-1085). IEEE.

Lindgren, M., & Bandhold, H. (2009). *Scenario Planning*. Palgrave MacMillan.

Nokia. (2021) *Our history*. Nokia. https://www.nokia.com/about-us/company/our-history/. Accessed on the 22/10/2020.

Varum, C., Valente, H., Resende, J., Pinho, M., Sarmento, P., & Jorge, S. (2018). *Economia industrial* (2nd ed.). Edicoes Silabo.

ENDNOTES

1 The introduction to Business Ecosystems is complemented in section 3.3. by an association of the former to EBEs

2 The I/O model of above-average returns (a.a.r) is further discussed in chapter 4 (section 4.1) and compared with the Resource-Based model of a.a.r. and the Positioning School

3 The concepts "segment" (or "landscape") and "factor", surrounding the description of an External Business Environment (EBE) are defined and critically distinguished in chapter 4.

Chapter 4
External Business Environments (EBE)

ABSTRACT

Focused on the subset of external business environment (EBE), this chapter explores the EBE´s "layers" and "elements" and the firm´s view of them. Entering the analyzability function, it describes the utility of the business environment analyzability (BEA) function and the typology of business environment analyzability projects (BEAP). Furthermore, the schools of thought in strategic management are interconnected to organizational value, and herein, is emphasized the importance (and competitive implications) of BEA to value-creation. Strategy interfaces, namely the external interface, are associated with prior concepts such as "organizational fit" or "strategic drift" and argued on the role BEAPs on the shaping of the firms position in the EBE.

INTRODUCTION

Any strategic management (SM) book addresses, unavoidably, business environment analyzability (BEA) issues at some point, even though, the author/s may blandly address it (and involuntarily) as the elected theme might hold other agenda on related topics. For instance, a book on *Design Thinking; Dynamic Capabilities*; *Enterprises Business Architectures*; *Digital Businesses*; *Organizational Culture; Utilitarian Ethics*; and in many other domains is linked to BEAs.

Against what one might think, Business Environment is not a sub-field to discard (at all). Actually, is part of what some scholars have denominated as the *external audit* function, as the evaluation of events and emerging trends, beyond the span of control of a single firm (David et al., 2017). Arguably, these exemplified topics are in fact pieces and bits of the sub-field of BEA in strategy theory, and the latter, is the center nerve of the external audit. Whatever the scholarly focus is, zooming in requires inevitably to go through external business environments (EBE), as they are always present in any study, directly or indirectly, in the areas of business management, economics or marketing strategy.

DOI: 10.4018/978-1-6684-5543-2.ch004

MORPHOLOGY, ASSUMPTIONS AND INTERPRETATIONS

Without realizing, most of the common observed features of strategy theories and even observed practices in the industry, hold a natural tendency to take parts and to adopt (what is believed to be) the best strategic *course of action* (CoA). Hence, two major streams of thought are dominating the hearts and minds of strategists regarding the best CoA for the rational creation of value. One is a *market-based view (MBV)* centered on the comprehension of the industry structure, competition and dynamics. The other, with an opposing rationale, is the *resource-based view (RBV)*, in which, is claimed that high returns are stimulated better of through the development of the firm´s own resources and capabilities. The notion of "value" regards the surpluses that the two primary economic agents, buyers and sellers (representing the demand and the supply-sides) are capable of appropriating.

So, *What the difference in such approaches (MNB vs. RBV)?* The distinction resides not on the objectives, as both hold the aspiration of yielding the highest value, or generating *above-average returns (a.a.r),* but on their way to get there, as to the process of generating value. So the ends are equal while the means are divergent, and here I advocate are a different way of getting the job done, with interdependencies as to the acquisition of further knowledge and building of intelligence bundles, and consequently, complementary ones. However, they adhere to what is called a *pure approach* (of analyzability), in which the strategist focus rather on the *External Business Environment (EBE)*, as advocated by MBV, or instead focus on the *Internal Business Environment (IBE)* as antagonized by the RBV. Comprehensibly companies deal with limited resources, and often decisions require the choice of one of these course of action.

Yet, regardless of the preconceptions of the reader as to virtues and benefits of both, or to a mediating stream here identified, as a *hybrid approach* of (analyzability), i.e. the *Positioning School*, here the author refrains himself from further judgements of importance, and the same with their underlying philosophical stances ("view") and epistemological preconceptions. Then, a question may be self-imposed

Question: Is market-focus "the" (best) way of strategizing?

The answer is a straightforward one. It is a round no (nope)! There is no single or best way to do so! Strategizing is nor solely about *marketing-knowledge* gains or *resource-ownership* or accumulation of large resource-bundles. Otherwise, the reality would have proven to be far simpler, with incumbents assuming a ranked position according to their possession of deeper market knowledge, or inversely, a larger position secured by larger number of resources in-house.

None of those streams of thought (MBV or RBV) have absolutely dominated the competition´s game. So, the reality is, a firm´s behavior towards the *modus operandis* in a market and the way to position itself and compete therein is not a "black and white" paradigm. Contexts diverge, and markets are not static and/or isolated from others.

In this sense, strategizing is does not follow a dichotomic route, of organizational development or marketing knowledge. On the first chapter, we saw the broad scope of the management function as an organizational system. The same happens with strategic management as a sub-system gluing all other parts of the organization. It relies cumulatively on other interdisciplinary fields (e.g. Finance; or Human Resources) and other sub-system as People Management; Supply Chain Management; or Project Management, which are likely its most visible edges. But, also on a thick body of Strategic Management theory, comprising areas such:

- Business ethics
- Corporate governance

- Entrepreneurship
- Functional structures and organizational configurations
- Leadership and managerial succession
- Organizational culture
- Strategic planning
- Ploy, defensiveness and short-term maneuverability
- Resources & Capabilities (R&C)
- Sustainability
- Strategic performance management (SPM)
- Strategic controls and auditing
- Strategic direction
- Strategic innovation
- Strategic controls and performance analysis
- Strategic thinking
- Strategic evaluation
- Structural flexibility, agility and adaptability
- Systems and processes

The "focus" of business environment may range from a continuum of a totally centered projects (or pure analysis) on one of the poles (environment or firm) or comprise a blending of them (Figure 14).

Figure 1. SM: Spectrum of BE research
Source: Own elaboration

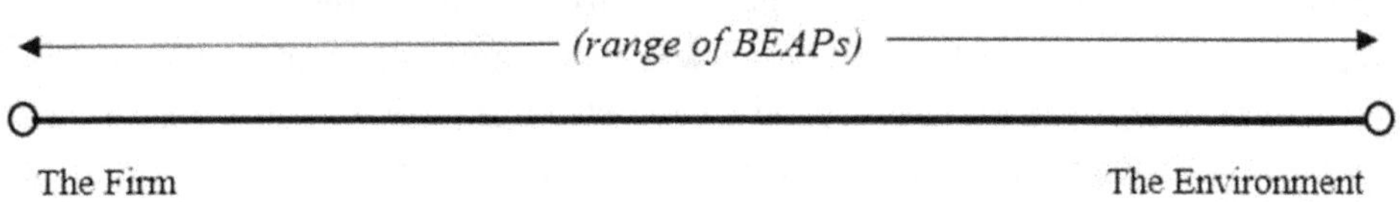

Consequently, it is worth to consider that "the real" is hazy, as the events to be studied are not solely placed within the firm or outside of its borders, as indicated in chapter one when presented the critical realist perception of a stratified ontology. Thus, the complexity of the phenomena implies a duality of *interfaces* furthermore presented in the next section.

In this sense, it may be added to the ontological assertion above the reality, the complementarity of the BEAP, denying the expression of *incommensurability* of business research sociological perspectives of Burrell and Morgan (1981). These authors advocated in their sociological perspectives of regulation and radical change that the research purpose fluctuating between objective phenomena and subjective would fit into a specific research purpose rejecting outright their commensurability or a proportional distribution of parts of the research to respond to events with dissimilar ontological attributes. Here, a contrary epistemological assumption is followed, in which, "the empirical" adjusts to the observation of the "real" to better comprehend "the factual" and adopts a system thinking logic aligned to the post-positivist philosophical position in which critical realism adjusts to.

Hence, the view here followed is not a pure market perspective, despite the content of the book has a focus on a part of market-related research (i.e. the business environment). Thus, it should be stressed that, the book accept the pluralism of multiple perspectives with *pure* or *hybrid* focus, as follows:

- Dynamic Capabilities View (DCV)
- Market-based-view (MBV)
- Technological-based view (TBV)
- Knowledge-based view (KBV)
- Resource-based view (RBV)
- Attention-based view (ABV)
- Ecosystem view (EsV)

MBV and RBV are opposing perspectives, postulating the mutually exclusive focus, respectively, on the environment and the firm. Their reasoning is commonly associated in strategy books with an *industrial organizational (I/O) model* and a *resource-based model (RB)* model of strategy-making.

The MBV, also accepted by the *Positioning School (PS)* of taught, is an adopter of the microeconomic studies of industrial organization (IO) centered on the functioning of the markets. Here, this I/O model has clear neoclassical influences upon the latest wave of industrial organization, the *theoretical wave* leaded by the Chicago tradition emphasizing the need for rigorous theoretical analysis and empirical development of investigation focused on competing theories, paving the way for a plethora of studies related to the analysis of market behavior.

However, the theory of industrial organization is pillared on two streams of thought. Consequently, this theoretical tradition stems from the push given by the *empirical tradition*, criticized by a lack of theoretical ground, though focused on investigating the *market structure* in general as to multiple aspects such, the number of sellers, or degree of product differentiation, the cost structure or the degree of vertical integration. The angle of their research was dominantly upon the understanding of *market performance* (e.g. efficiency; price-to-cost; product variety; innovation ratios; profits; distribution) in which, a typical regression would cross a concentration ratio (CR) (as a measure of non-competitiveness) and the barriers-to-entry (BTE).

$$II_i = f(Cr_i, BTE_i, \ldots)$$

This empirical tradition so epitomized in Edward Mason´s (1939) *structure-conduct-performance paradigm*, demanded though the balancing with theory substrate to be explanatory of empirical evidence. Thus, a second wave of the industrial organization studies led by the Chicago School brought a theoretical tradition emphasizing competitive theories and market behavior. For instance, preconized in Arrow and Debreu (1954) and Debreu´s (1959) *competitive equilibrium paradigm:*

$$\frac{dV}{da} = \frac{\partial f}{\partial a}(x^*(a), a)$$

In this theorem, the derivative of the value as to the optimization problem equals the partial derivative (∂) of the objective function, in which x*(a) is the control variable.

$V(a) = \max f(x, a)$

The *V* represents a function of the maximization of *x* in *a*. In, the next section, it is revisited then the notion of competitive equilibrium to the understanding of *organizational fit* in highly changing environments with VUCA attributes. This concept already introduced in chapter 2 has briefly referred to the function of alignment and organizational levers.

It may be then inferred that the Positioning School retained the heavy heritage from the industrial organization studies by maintaining a marked focus on market competition. In this context, the MBV and the RBV assumed themselves as dominant neoclassic approaches, confronting each other as to the corporate rationale for addressing a potential market, despite fulfilling a distinct role as stated by Martin (2014) of *how-to-win* (the RBV) and where to-play (the MBV) as cumulative reasoning of the modern strategic definition of an organization.

Table 1. Comparison Market-based view (MBV) and Resource-based view (RBV)

Dimensions of comparison	RBV	MBV
Emphasis	Resources (internal)	Market (structure, competition and dynamics)
Rationale	Outside-in	Inside-out
Orientation	Strength driven	Opportunities and risk-driven
Focus	Advantage positioning	Distinctive positioning
Reasoning	How to succeed?	Where to compete?
Role	"Strategic stretch"	Strategic fit

Source: Own elaboration

Here the *strategic stretch* refers to the leveraging of resources, tangible but also intangible assets as branding, knowledge, or reputation, in which, the different types of knowledge, as described by Blacker (1995) as the *embrained, embodied, encoded, embedded and encultured knowledge,* articulated to build on both individual and collective competences and organizational capabilities (OCs) considered as the anchor of organizational success, and take advantage of identified scenarios of distinctiveness of these R&Cs constituting an advantages for their owners. On the other hand, as further described below, the strategic fit aims at identify environmental contexts and their dynamics, including the underlying forces, leading to change, and therein, beforehand, or on an on-going basis, to develop preparatory or reactive actions to ensure the adaptability of the firm to the business environment, and an efficient management of risk and opportunities.

However, the MBV asserting a pure appraisal of the structure and behaviour of the markets to comprehend their efficiency, is nowadays connoted in the 21st century with the label of myopia, since it neglects the self-determination of the firm to pursue rationale strategic designs, undervaluing the importance of the markets (structure, competition and efficiency) to uplift the capacity of the firm to influence those markets. This opposing reasoning (the RBV), with roots on the Penrosian theory of the growth of the firm, is pillared on the resources endowments which ought to be explored without market-positioning restrictions, whether these tangible/intangible and human endowments can be exploited more efficiently, i.e. where these assets represent opportunities against peers, to be exploited as they constitute firm-specific advantages generating higher economic rents.

The RBV evolved towards other forms, as the dynamic capabilities view (DCV) advocating these first-order capabilities deliver above other (ordinary or operational capabilities, and other physical and financial resources) long-term advantages to a firm, then being a source of sustainable competition. The DCV it has a hybrid reasoning, such as for instance the KBV, which elevates the knowledge in its different forms of singular or collective, explicit and tacit (as embrained, embodied; encoded and embedded) playing different roles convertible into different forms and leveraging further learning. Similarly, the TBV as a subset of KBV advocates the merits of specific technical competences, harder-to-imitate, as they might easily obscured (especially combined in complex sets of combinative capabilities) being sources of positive-sum logics of competition more effectively oriented (than the KBV) onto the generation of innovations in new product developments (NPD), operational processes of production and distribution, and of highly innovativeness on business models (Abrantes and Ostergaard, 2022; Abrantes, 2020).

BUSINESS ENVIRONMENT (BE): INTERFACES

As to what the Strategic Management field is concerned, an *interface* identifies a direct interaction of, the strategy function with a part of the business environment, whether that part is on the internal domain (the firm) of on the external domain (the market). Naturally, strategy is a function assuming a pivotal role (among several other organizational functions) through the administration of the social and physical exchange between *proxies*: the firm and market/s. These interfaces are, as follows (Exhibit 24):

(i) An *external interface (EI)*
(Strategy → External Business Environment (EBE): The market/s) ⇔ Strategy concerning the <u>external</u> context of the firm)

(ii) An *internal interface (II)*
(Strategy → Internal Business Environment (IBE): firm) ⇔ Strategy concerning the <u>internal</u> context of the firm)

The external interface associates the multiple dimensions of strategy-making with an external context, comprises the interaction of a focal firm with its outside world (including the business ecosystems), as the selected countries or industries of competition, according to the firm geographical spanning and the positioning of its economic activities.

Here, the firm, as an arrangement with a commercial purpose or profit-orientation, it is comprised of following characteristics:

- An organizational **structure** with a specific configuration or organizational design
- A particular corporate **thinking/**mindset
- A strategic **direction** (vision, mission and goals)
- A general organizational **culture** and multiple sub-cultures
- A corporate **scope** (a choice of industries were to compete in)

Figure 2. Strategy and interfaces
Source: Grant (2016)

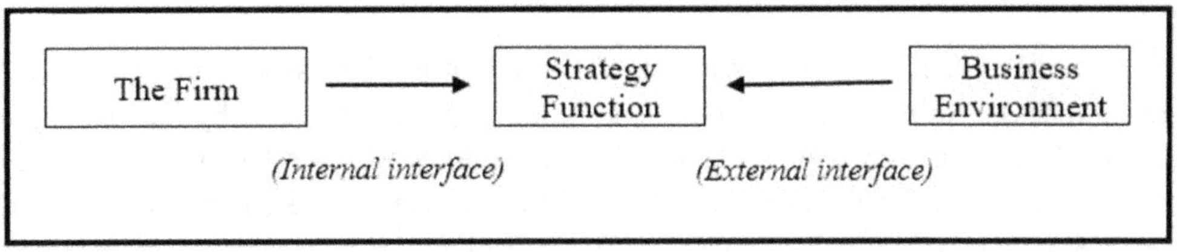

- *n* number of business **strategy/ies** with a given competing rationale, varying in number according to the competitive scope, or number of competing sectors
- Short/medium-term **goals** per business units
- Various organizational **functions** (as sourcing; operations; marketing; and distribution)
- Numerous **systems** (e.g. CRM; ERP; GPS; MRP; POS, etc.)
- Several business **processes** (e.g. customer service; order fulfillment; which, within the SM domain, *strategic controls* shall be emphasized as a critical one)
- And, tangible, intangible and human **resources**
- And, activities, routines, competences and (ordinary and dynamic) **capabilities.**

This internal interface (II) presupposes then a thorough understanding of the organizational characteristics aforementioned, for future strategy design, since an inattentive exposure to a BE can dictate the failure of a business venture. Recalling the "*tenets of success*" (in Exhibit 20), the success of a business is dependent on the self-understanding of resources and capabilities (R&C) of each organic unit of the firm, or *strategic business unit (SBU)*, which is key for comprehending their relative importance, materialized in the set of strengths and weaknesses (SW).

Moreover, the R&Cs, in the remaining context of the organization´s realm determine subsequently the definition of new goals. Nevertheless, the comprehension of the relative importance of the firm is intrinsically dependent on the peers' endeavors performance (aka competitors), which is the same of saying that, the internal interface is vital but not unseparated from the external interface (EI). Thus, it may be claimed to be a summative function of joint analyzability projects of EI/II properties.

$$\text{Strategy}_{(f)} = \sum (\text{EI} \,.\, \text{II})$$

Such mutual and cumulative influence of these proxies (proxy1: The firm; and, proxy 2: The business environment) and their interfaces (II and EI) with the strategy function may raise then several questions (Q) to the reader, for example:

Q1: Can organizations maintain a favorable strategic position in a market?

Q2: How can a firm be more prepared to compete, especially in dynamic business environments and ecosystems?

Q3: Is there a way an organization may become more robust against environmental hurdles, scathes and/or other unpredictable events?

The answer to these questions resides inevitably on a bottom line issue, the need for analyzing the surrounding business environment. Nonetheless, a frequent gaffe committed by top-management teams (TMT) in terms of strategic thinking is to consider BEA merely as a temporary technical instrument to be applied (internally or hiring a consultancy team) in a discrete manner, which means whenever it is believed to be needed as to a methodological response to reduce *uncertainty* and *risk* related to a certain venture. Here, it shall be borrowed from Hubbard´s (2014, p. 84) definitions for distinguishing these two concepts for avoiding any blurriness, since both ideas are complementary.

Uncertainty: *"The lack of complete certainty, that is, the existence of more than one possibility. The true outcome/state/result/value is unknown."*

Risk: *"A state of uncertainty where some of the possibilities involve loss, catastrophe or other undesirable outcome."*

Discrete, or episodically conducted BEA, is then a scenario orientated towards the control of potential risks, based on the ontological assumption that the "out there" reality may be adverse and harmful and may encompass subsequently significant financial losses. As a defensive behavior in line with the prior, mediated by the risk profile of the firm and their decision-makers, organizational responses in this context are organized for the prevention of losses rather than maximizing profits. This instrumentalization of BEA is common for instance, in the following context: (i) whenever is intended to initiate a business venture overseas; (ii) in case of an expected business opportunity; (iii) for the (re)assessment of an investment project; (iv) when a due diligence is required for realizing a merger or acquisition of a firm; (v) occasioned by real risks.

On the contrary, is here recommended the replacement of the short-term (or project) logic of thinking as to the conduction of BEAPs with a temporary nature, by the adoption of a posture of active learning through the continuous or permanent assessment of the environment, which has a triad of virtues: anticipates risks; seizes opportunities, and enables the on-going correction of strategic deviating trajectories (*drifting*). This is achieved by the integration of any activities of business environment analysis in the organization´s systems, fashioning the set of processes (as the several BEAPs), with multiple activities, tasks and responsibilities to be held in a repeated manner to update previous information bundles.

In the next sections, you will have the occasion to look into critical aspects that have a nexus of causality on the strategic position of a firm, or its performance, as possible classifications for the "success" of the strategy interfaces. By opposition to the latter (the notion of success), the conceptions introduced in the latest paragraph, (strategic drift and business failure) it will be additionally depicted in the light of the current frameworks. Here, it shall be accounted, for the comprehension of the success of the strategy´s interfaces, the importance of the company´s past, history and evolution, as a reference framework explanatory of organizational success. This is as relevant as, firms are involuntarily dependent upon their historical track determining, as follows:

- Knowledgeability and competence-base;
- Learning potential (for up and reskilling itself);
- Firm-markets adjustment, fitness´s dilemma and gaps
- Strategic alignment, flexibility, agility, positioning
- Current and future financial returns.

The figure above (Figure 15), places the SM in a mediating role of exchange (interfacing) as a determining factor of planning, as the way companies decide to market themselves and their products, based on conjoint understanding of themselves and the surrounding universe. Beer et al. (2005) and Abrantes (2020) labelled this as an *organizational lever,* which is explanatory of the *strategic fit* towards the BE. To comprehend how can organization be more or less fit, it is required to introduce the notion of *organizational levers,* as they are the explanatory variables of organizational fit(ness), which exist, not solely between the firm and the outside world (firm-environment), but also within the organization (firm-firm). These authors argue that *organizational fit* corresponds to a full stage of agility of the firm, comprised of a preparation to further adaptation against fast-moving environments, change and competing threats (*strategic agility*) and a type of agility within intra-functions, agents and actors inside of the organization (*internal organizational agility*). In this sense, it may be claimed:

Strategic agility → External/Strategic fit

Organizational Fit = +

Internal organizational agility → internal fit

Here, a confusion might be made as to the terminology fit/fitness. The organizational/strategic *"fitness"* expresses a theoretical condition of being agile in a certain moment in time, while the *fit* express the degree of fitness. Thus, the spin-off idea of "being fit" it is considered an outcome, as a realization of the fitness potential of the organization.

In this context, a firm ought to develop a dual-tier of *organizational fitness* (internal and external). This refers for instance, to the ability to:

Example 1 (internal fit): adjust their systems, processes and/or assets distribution in response to alterations of corporate leadership (as in the case of transference or succession of a top executive position to other personae)

Example 2 (external fit): Organize itself for accommodating higher sourcing inputs, for instance, in case of, a steep increase of clients order or sales causing an unbalance of strategy-structure, as the company may not be flexible in response to change.

Example 2.1.(external fit): Quickly adapt, as a new disruptive technology enters the market, with a rapid dissemination, pressuring the firm to react or otherwise parish with a real (or eminent) shift of its own´ s client demand.

Here, we recall, the organizational levers (L_n) advocated by these authors:

L_1: external interface of business strategy/ies and environment traits and trends
L_2: internal interface of business strategy/ies and resources and capabilities-allocation
L_3: internal interface of leadership behaviour and organizational design
L_4: internal interface of organizational design and culture with the organizational capabilities

One might want now to "dot the i´s and cross the t´s" to understand what the organizational lever (L_1) means, as a proxy of an external interface (firm-environment). The $L_{1(\text{business strategy- environment})}$ refers to the symbiotic relation between the overall business environment traits and company´s response to them. Thus, in order to succeed in a certain environmental context the organizations are required to attain (and maintain) a profound understanding of the environment and act accordingly to it, by (re)designing its structure and business strategy to better fit into a certain environment reality, whether more or less adverse, more or less dynamic and innovative, but in which the firm is able to tackle the existing threats and anticipate the upcoming ones, and seize opportunities "to shine" as being perceived as possessing valuable *(v)* products by its target customer-base.

To better comprehend the importance of the business strategy´s adaptability (L_1) as an organizational lever, it is used here the example 2.1 above (about a competitor´s product-innovation launch). Moreover, to depict this example I shall borrow some ideas from the theory of industrial organization to introduce the notion of competitive-equilibrium, value (*v*) and price (*p*) (Tirole, 1988).

In this example, you may start by considering that the market is in competitive equilibrium, each good is sold at a marginal cost or price (represented by p→0; or p0), with a certain perceived value (*v0*), in which the $v(x0) = p(x0)$. Here, the notion of value of the product is equalized to its price, thus, projecting the following competitive equilibrium paradigm (*p0q0*) in a demand curve.

In addition, considering the notion of economic surplus of the seller, as the *producer surplus* (as the amount that producers benefit by selling at a market price) it may help us to better understand the impact of this L_1 in the example 2.1., in which, an environmental change (the product-innovation) is a trigger of the need for business strategic adaptation. If a consumer increases the perception of value delivered by the supplier in a function v1 or v2, then following the arithmetic principle of transitivity, as $v1 < v2$, $v1 > v0$ and for a constant price structure the consumer attains a net Marshallian surplus, regardless of the quantity (q_n) sold. On the other hand the firm (defied by this competitor move) gets capped in value since the shift in consumption represents a modification of q_0 to q_{-n} and potentially accompanied to a revision of v0 to v_{-n} and a loss of appropriated surplus (S) represented by:

$$\Delta S^n = \sum(v_{-n} \cdot q_{-n}); \text{ or } \Delta S^n = (v_{-1} - p_o) + (v_{-2} - p_o) + (v_{(1-n)} - p_o)$$

On the other hand, whenever the demand-side is able to purchase a good for a price that is lower (p_{-1}) than the highest price ($p_{\geq 0}$) this leads to a customer surplus as well. Yet the demand (*d*) of a single good *h* (and its generalization to a groups of products), is given by the q_n function, influenced by the price vector and consumer´s income (*I*):

$$D_{h=}(p, I); \Delta S^n = \sum \Delta S_h = -\int_{p0} \sum q_h \, dp_h$$

In this sense, the dynamics of business ecosystems lead to symmetric benefits of suppliers and buyer, in which the competitor appropriates value for its direct competing incumbents. Unsurprisingly, technological innovation represents, as claimed by the economist Joseph Schumpeter in his book "*Capitalism, Socialism and Democracy*" (1942), a perennial gale of creative destruction. At that stage Schumpeter has foreseen a shift in firm´s positioning from price competition to quality competition pointing out a clear route, which stands as a solution for this example. Companies shall conceive quality-based (counter)actions for obtaining new sources of advantages through, as follows: (i) new technologies; (ii) new sources of supply; and, (iii) new types of organization.

In sum, the notion of *strategic fit (sf)* refers to the external interface of the company, and the internal a *structural fit (strf)* (see example 1) which may be represented as follows:

Organizational fit $(i_t e) = [(sf + strf) / k]$; $sf = [(of - strf) / (1-e)]$

Here, the *i* represents the firm, the *t is* a snapshot in time (*t=0*) and *k* the kinesis or change is given by the expression *k(1-e),* observed in the context of the business environment. Here, the *strategic fit* (with the business environment) is defined by Johnson, Scholes & Whittington (2008, p. 3) as "*the need to appropriate a positioning in their environment*".

Conversely the strategically "non-fit" to the environment, also termed as the *strategic drift*, is defined as the firm´s inability to attain a favorable position and conceal itself from offensive and threatening ploy. *Strategic drift* furthermore understood as a tendency of the firm to develop business strategies in which solely incremental changes are incorporated, based on cultural influences, creating then a gap between the reality of the business environment critical factors of competition and its own strategic design, and so failing to keep pace with the changing environment.

In this sense, it may asserted a variation of *sd* and *sf* between 0 and 1 (*sd=(0; 1); sf=(0; 1),* and sd and sf are opposite propositions $sf = -(-sd)$, and *sd* is represented as follows:

$$sd_{i\,(t=o)} = \Delta BLS^{n}\,(1\text{-}e)/e;\ k \Leftrightarrow 1\text{-}e > 0;$$

In this notion of strategic drift (*sd*), it is considered the variation of the (business) *strategy (BLS)* of the firm against the changing environment, in which, *strategy* is considered to be the direction and scope chosen by a firm at a given moment in time, as to the achievement of short and long term goals and yield *above average returns (a.a.r.)* or higher profitability above others. The problem of strategic drifting, associated with the following of incremental strategies, has allegedly origin on the business historical influences and on the corporate culture´s influences, creating a cultural web of national, institutional and organizational cultural features guiding future strategies and imposing significant challenges to the managers (Figure 4).

INTERFACE EQUILIBRIUM AND STRATEGIC DRIFT

On this section, rather attention is given to opposite the phenomena of organizational adaptation and strategic fit to a business environment (i.e. *strategic drift),* as we will discuss the external interface of a firm´s strategy with its external environment and explore the negative side of the strategic drift and the inherent consequences to the firm´s competitiveness.

A firm's ability to conduct market research over business environments and ecosystems is a determinant kickstart factor on building competitive intelligence, on which the strategic decisions are anchored on, and consequently shield strategic drift. Actually, industrial research has other virtues as the reduction of the perceived uncertainty over the markets and avoid building a competitive blind firm over the markets.

Recalling the definition strategic drift introduced already in the previous section, it refers to a firm´s inability to comprehend market change, manifested on a tendency to implement business strategies disregarding the mutations occurred on the business environment. Needless is to underline how harmful strategic drift is for the future accomplishment of the company´s vision, mission and objectives and for the future wealth of whole stakeholders.

Preventing strategic drifts requires an effort from the internal interface (firm–strategy) to endow employees with a set of competences to be able to sense the change, comprehend its direction and mutational properties and respond accordingly to them.

However, regardless of whether the company is market-centered or company-centered, strategic drift is a phenomenon which may arise from multiple sources:

(i) misinterpretation of the inputs received from the occurring outer events,
(ii) poor analysis of the markets,
(iii) managerial and/or operational inaction.

The latter is also denominated in Strategy theory as *institutional isomorphism,* arguably defended by some scholars to be directly linked with the non-updateness of organizational capabilities (or internal interface deficiencies), configuring a scenario of *competence rigidity*.

For exploring such ideas and the thresholds surrounding the concept of strategic drift (whether or not, as a consequence of core-rigidities and/or isomorphism), we will start by immersing into the context of the book retailing industry, and herein utilize the real case-study of *Toys R Us*. Hopefully a case-firm will facilitate the comprehension of the problematic of the deficiencies on interface systems and the negative impact on the future of the organizational performance, success and wealth.

The case of *Toys R Us* presented almost at the end of the chapter, is also the case of many other well-known large companies (e.g. *Atari*; *Barnes and Noble, Inc.*; *Blackberry*; *Blockbuster; DeLorean Motor; Enron; HMV; Kodak; Motorola; MySpace; Netscape; Nokia*; *Nortel*; *Pan Am*; *Polaroid*; *Sears*; *Tie Rack; Xerox;* or *Yahoo*). The problem of the strategic fit it seemed to reside on, an *historical lock-in*. The company has an insider comfortable position in the markets, and in many cases, is a dominant player and a large multinational enterprise.

Indeed, *Toys R Us* revealed notorious difficulties to cope with business environment raw data and timely recognize early signals of change (i.e. the appearance of big-box retailers; or the emerge of online retailing). Moreover, the company revealed some myopia, as to the diagnose of emergent new events and their forming trends, as a real threat and opportunity. One of those events, above pinpointed is the emergence of online retailing as a new, but nowadays mainstream, way of purchasing goods.

Brick-and-mortar price wars between large companies together with the emergence of online retailing, this shuck the waters of the baby products and toy industry and especially of Toys R Us, which was manifestly unprepared to deal with them. Toys R Us did not grasp (on time) the changes of market behaviour towards the new digital platforms, for example, as Amazon did. Likewise, did not foresee (on time), the importance of digital competition, not as a simple online channel of product selling, but as a new electronic business model, were e-commerce and e-businesses, brought new agents into the game (platforms) and a new ways of positioning (platform competition) since 2000.

Conceivably, the debilities in Toys R Us may be due to a lack of organizational capabilities (OCs) to work with external changes and their accomodation internally within the foundations of their organizational cultural, in order to integrate change in a positive way and "routinize" the dealing with change as an ordinary (but key) trait of market competition.

Such drift of the case-firm observed in this chapter may be especially blamed to the most subtle (or incremental) changes, not always easy to grasp when analyzing an External Business Environment (EBE). Furthermore, strategic drift is a symptomatic indicator of an organizational state of unawareness to "digest" newer events and its unpreparedness to take timely decisions upon them, preventively or reactively, which drags the firms toward a process of drifting culminating either on a full (successful) transformation or death. Hence, avoiding strategic drifts and ensuring constant organizational success requires equilibrium. The balanced attention given to both interface systems, are then two part parts of an effective strategy for ensuring organizational success. You may recall on the chapter 2, is depicted the tenets of organizational success, and there we made reference to the importance of such attentiveness towards the strategic balancing of the interfaces.

Toys R Us. are at a critical stage (last phase – see Figure 16 below), trapped between the "sword and the wall" attempting at regaining a lost competitive hegemony (as described in the case, attempting a "resurrection"). The battle is though for subsistence of the firm in the short-term. This requires a profound transformative solution for gaining back a place in a quite different industry from what they were used to compete in. The current industry market is dominated by large and digital sellers (i.e. Amazon, Target and Walmart) and getting back in the game requires a re-adaptation of skills to an altered reality, the company was blind to in the past. Thus, earlier core competences have to be both up and reskilled, as their dominance in the past, no longer represent the same value in the present.

The phases of strategic drift of what *Toys R Us* went through are depicted below. The first corresponds to an initial phase of distancing to the direction and pace of environmental change (phase 1). This corresponds to the paradigmatic shift of the appearance of digital retailers triggered by technological advancement on ICT, as to e-commerce and security web shopping protocols.

Figure 3. Phases of strategic drift
Source: Johnson, Scholes, and Whittington (2008)

Such incremental change, described in the figure below (*"The origin of strategic drift"*) is materialized into an organizational entropy to break with the continuity of past strategic options and respond to present market stimuli. Hence, this entropy, emphasizing a corporate´s *historical lock-in,* is argued to be motivated by a deviation of the organization´s behavior, revealing traits of a lagged reaction to the business environment circumstantialism, portrayed into an isomorphism, inertia and/or a myopia to identify environmental trends and kinesis, and timely act upon to anticipate or solve divergence of positioning towards the state-of-the-art of business environment requirements. This results into the accentuation of the divergent path (*strategic drift* – phase 2).

This pure strategic drift is manifested not exclusively on the continuity with past real options of competition, but on the extent and adequacy of the response, as the change may not be in line with the environment. If so, a period of *flux* is observed (phase 3), where failure to meet market environment´s requirements is consubstantiated into different outcomes, as a failure in the accomplishment of strategic goals and/or financial goals, as observed in down tendency of the sales figures of Toys R Us in the case above. At this stage, the abandonment of phase 3, is only possible by taking a step forward towards *transformational change* or otherwise perish (phase 4).

Here, the organization is require to cut their ties with past and abandon the innovation model of logical incrementalism and focus on the alignment with the environment. The re-appraisal the utility of R&Cs is essential, namely to comprehend the sources of advantage-formation and past-successful products and competences have not become crystalized in time as core-rigidities instead of its strengths.

Figure 4. The origin of Strategic drift
Source: Johnson, Scholes and Whittington (2008)

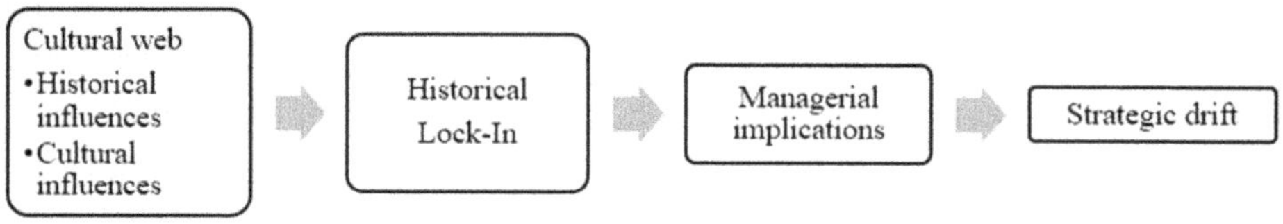

At the stage four (4) of strategic drift (transformational change or death), three possible outcomes may occur:

1. The organization may die
2. Gets taken-over by another one
3. It will go through a period of radical/revolutionary change:
   a. In products
   b. In markets
   c. In focus, as to the segmentation, target and (competitive) positioning (STP)
   d. In capabilities
   e. In top management
   f. In structure and its configuration

If the three (3) initial phases emphasize the deviation against environmental change, the phase 4 unravels a simultaneous degree of adjustment and an outcome of the prior.

Here, the outcome at *Toys R Us* is already acknowledged, it got taken over by a third company (*Tru Kids Brands*), whom purchased the rights to the company. Their acquisition triggered then a transformational process, which is essential to solve the drifting issues. Yet, their transformation followed a hybrid approach combining a turnaround corporate strategy posterior to the selling of the company.

Such processes gravitate in general around the solving of the following five issues: (i) the overvaluing of the familiar inputs from the past; (ii) the problem of the hindsight, as managers tend to find clarifications in the past, instead of defining a clear strategic future direction; (iii) lagging performance effects from real drift; (iv) replacement of core-rigidities; (v) solving relationship´s shackles with product-market stakeholders (e.g. clients; suppliers; outsources).

Table 2. Environmental change: phases of strategic drift

Phase	Description	Properties and Adjustment
1	Incremental change	Historical lock-in and logical incrementalism Unawareness to environmental change Lack of marketing-related capabilities
2	Strategic drift	Myopia to recognize environment kinesis Inertia or lagged reaction to change Rigidity implementing changes in strategic direction and/or design No sense of importance or urgency towards adaption
3	Flux	Strategic and operational performance downturns Failure to accomplish strategic goals (including financial goals) Inaptitude to fulfill environment´s requirements
4	Transformational change or death	Distancing from cultural influences Blocking of historical determinism Equation of options (e.g. competition models, innovation system or partnerships) Revolutionary changes and innovation Reengineering of operative processes New leadership and rupture with dominant paradigm of governance

Source: Own elaboration

EBE: LAYERS

Innate to human behavior it seems to be, as brought at the beginning of the book, the need to conceptualize every phenomenon in nature. Yet, the complexity of the real does not fit into a "single box" of a simple definition. This seems to be the case of the Mintzberg notion of strategy-making when in chapter 2 we have seen the multiple facets of strategy, and defending the accomodation of five dimensions/definition (the 5 Ps) (Mintzberg, 1987). Within the field of strategic management, we saw earlier on that the same happens in the context of business environments. The approach of a company, as the way it opts to face a population of potential buyers, partners, competitors, suppliers or any others agents is intrinsically dependent upon the fourth "P" (of *Positon),* referring to the Hofer and Schendel´s notion of *match* (of firm → environment), describing the attitude of the firm, furthermore explored in the previous section, as to the conceptions of organizational fit, external organizational lever (L_1) and strategic drift.

Concordant with the Mintzberg assertion of the fallacy of SM as being exclusively a synonym of a plan, this delusion of the single-definition, is addressed in chapter one, rejecting such idea while exposing the dual perspective of BEs, in *latu sensum* and *stricto sensum*, in which the latter (representing the place of) mostly defended by marketers opposes to the SM theorists (representing the reality of, with a circumscription larger than the location), even though, marketing exists as an organizational function of value-added activities complementary (not antagonistic) to the strategy function with the SM aiming at create value to all stakeholders (including the product/market stakeholders) through competitive advantage formation/maintenance and delivering above average returns.

However, the dominant paradigm in most strategy books, considering "the" basic framework of strategy-making the existence of strategy interfaces (internal and external) and proxies (the firm and the environment), convey an underlying impression that firms are placed in a difference sphere or reality in comparison with their business environment. Therefore, as argued in chapter one, companies do not exist as islands, as their position, both in terms of location and/or space. This is the same of saying that companies are not isolated and subsequently inaccessible physically (location) or in communication (space) since they interact constantly with third parties. Such interaction occurs within the realm of business ecosystems, regardless of the interaction´s configuration: country-wise (country-specific or cross-country); competition-wise (solo-playing or network-playing mode); product-wise (tangible or intangible) and structure-wise (physical or platform/digital market).

Such scenario of detaching the firm from the universe, as to the existing theoretical background dominating the SM literature must at least be questioned, for the sake of the clarification of this theme wrapped in substantial complexity, demanding some sense of *critique of tradition* and *critique of authority* (Mingers, 2000). Hence, it is with this purpose introduced a section on the *layers* of business environments, intending to clarify as to the fourth p (position) of the firm, the real context of their strategic positioning.

In this sense, two major opposing models of observation co-exist: the *detached* above discussed and by opposition the *circumvented* or *outflanked*. Before bringing their visuals, as a fuzzy cognitive mapping with a visual representation of the competing reality of them, it shall be referred that this book does not refute the logic of the strategy interfaces, since it does not postulate a contrarian reasoning of it. Instead of any contrarianism, it is intended to challenge the apathy in the field and open the horizons to alternative prisms of observation. Such as Henry Mintzberg (1987) did three decades ago when arguing within the context of the 5Ps, the existence of the *"Egg McMuffin" syndrome* (Exhibit 28), of great utility for understanding the morphology of the BEs.

Figure 5. Egg McMuffin Syndrome (perspective constraining position)
Source: Mintzberg (1987, p. 18)

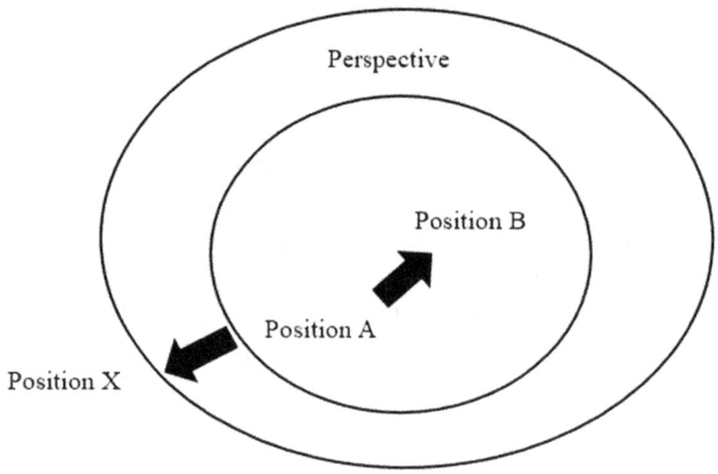

Here the *Egg McMuffin syndrome* is associated with the *perspective* (the fifth p) of the firm, as the ingrained way of seeing the world and contradict the espoused norms of culture, business ethical principles and the collective strategizing mindset, which is surrounding of an immutable property, as organizations do not alter so often their assumptions about the real or universe. This occurs when perspectives are fairly installed in a company, especially observed in most mature incumbents, something acting subconsciously and colliding with the willingness to change a position or a plan. In sum, shifting the culture and corporate thinking is an enormous task, substantially tougher than to alter a competitive position. The way to overcome such dilemma is compatibility. Only, through a scenario of alignment as to the internal fitness of the company, offers a compatible position-perspective outcome, so that the organization may undertake true transformational changes in terms of business change options grounded in structure´s configuration, culture systems of activities and capabilities. As mentioned in the previous section, this is intrinsically related to the organizational levers (L_2-L_4), most especially, the internal interface of organization design and culture with the organizational capabilities (L_4).

However, its shall be emphasized also that the quest for a perspective and position´s compatibility, is a transversal challenge to all organizations, regardless of their stage of development (from upstarters to mature incumbents) and corporate thinking archetype. In this sense, the inclination of a leader towards the adoption of a specific strategic thinking logic for the endogenous growth of an organic business unit, pure or hybrid one, focusing whether on an industrial organization (I/O) model or on a resource-based (RB) so called resource-based view (RBV) or even balancing both perspectives, it ought to be considered that none of them is undoubtedly proven in SM previous scholar contributions to reduce the extent of the challenge of such internal fitness (external-internal; perspective-position). Despite the prior, contemporary literature in the field, has been praising an hybrid reasoning, the balancing of I/O and the RBV, since places the external fitness to the business environment in the center of organizational success, and by opposition the RBV, attributes the assets of the firm as the real centrality, as an internal fitness challenge to be able to better compete in the markets, uncovering two opposing streams of thought; which is the supremacy of market knowledge and business intelligence from one side (the I/O´s outside-in approach) against the capabilisation as a differentiating path for success (the RBV´s inside-out approach).

Figure 6. Dilemma position/perspective of the firm
Source: Own elaboration

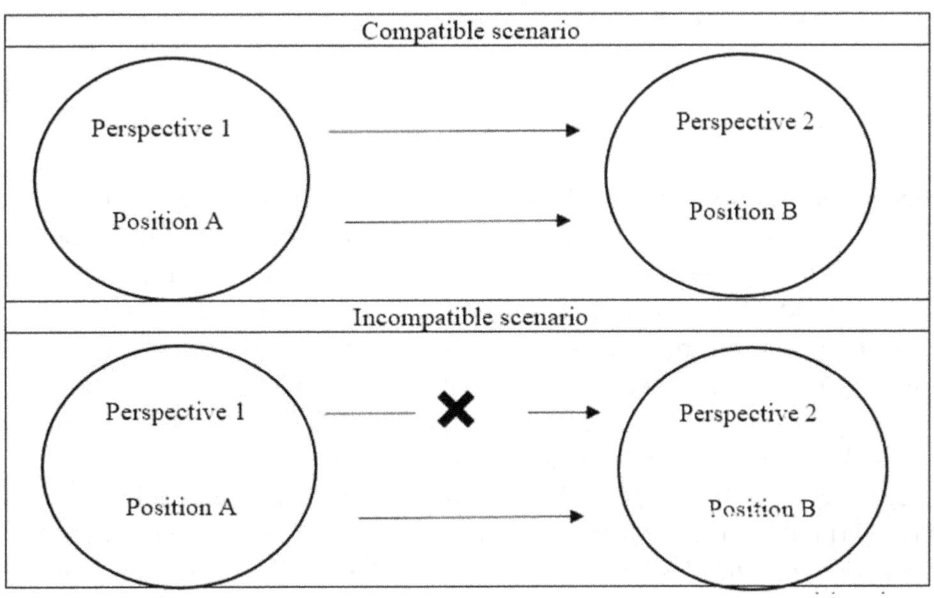

Potential incompatibilities uncover a profound dilemma, of organizational values confronting future organizational success, questioning whether the company is willing to demit the first in favor of the last (organizational success). This refers to the *Lapierre´s* pinpointed clash of the "dream" against the "reality" of competition. Thus, changing a position is relatively of ease to pursue; however, changing the perspective, as in the case above of Toys R Us (see *2.2. Business Environment – Interfaces*) and overcome Amazon´s disruptive model seemed to be a most complex task.

Taking into account the prior dilemma, the visual representation of the business environment layers adopt a static vision, freezing market´s dynamism, which purposively facilitates the exposing of these two models (the detached and the circumvented/outflanked).

Figure 7. Detached and circumvented vision of BEs
Source: Own elaboration

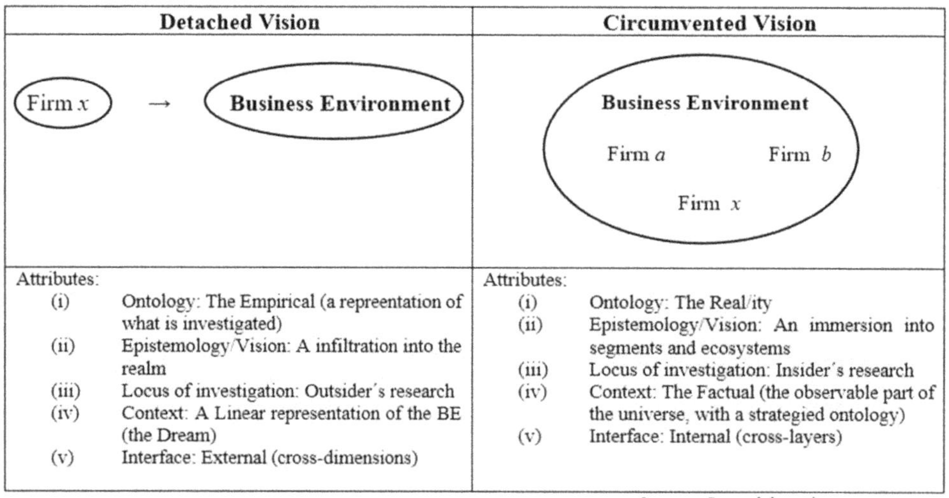

The detached vision of a BE represents the focal firm´s observation of the BE, or alternatively, their representatives outlook through the lens of, for instance, of management consultants; capital stakeholders; investors; or, stock/shareholders. It is a fabrication of the reality as to the firm´s discernment of how something existing outside their frontiers, i.e. the BE may look like. In the figure above is pictured as a linear representation of the environment, so just a representation of the reality not the reality in itself. However the real business environment is not heterarchical, as represented in the detached vision, or deprived of hierarchy. Instead, the reality contrasts with its representation, since it encompasses a hierarchical design as observed in the circumvented vision of it (Figure 20).

Hence, the epistemological assumption about the business environment is, a linear one requiring an infiltration into it (on the detached perspective), against the immersion into different layers of the business environment, referring to a stratified ontological nature of the real (on the circumvented perspective). Thus, only the circumvented perspective is explicit as to the acceptance of "layers" and recognizing a multiple-tiered BE with stratification or hierarchy. The detached perspective has a silent or latent expression as to their recognition of different layers of analyzability. In this sense, the discussing the "layers" denote an underlying acceptance of the circumvented or outflanked perspective of a business environment which is an expression of acceptance of strata in nature or universe under analysis, the BEs.

Figure 8. General representation of business environment layers
Source: Own elaboration

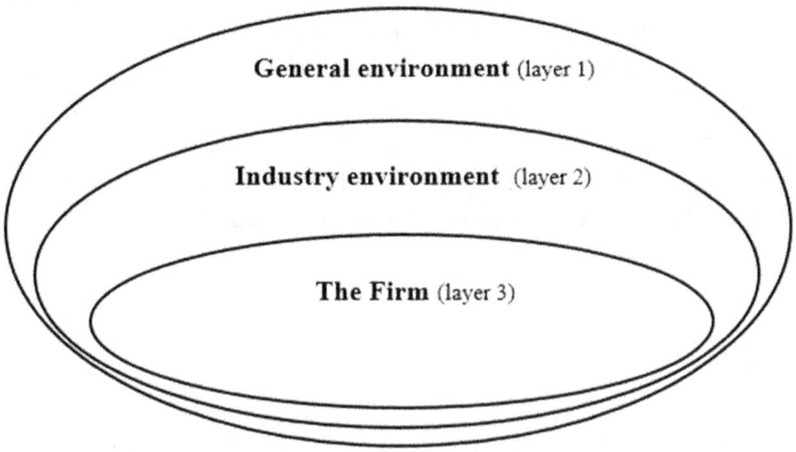

The outer layer represents the business environment (e.g. the meta-region; region; or, country) while the mezzo layer represents the business ecosystem´s context (e.g. the cluster, economic sector or industry) with all its attributions and agents (e.g. banks; customers; national authorities; outsourcers; suppliers and so forth) and micro layer represents the focal firm layer.

Figure 9. Business environment: layers
Source: Own elaboration

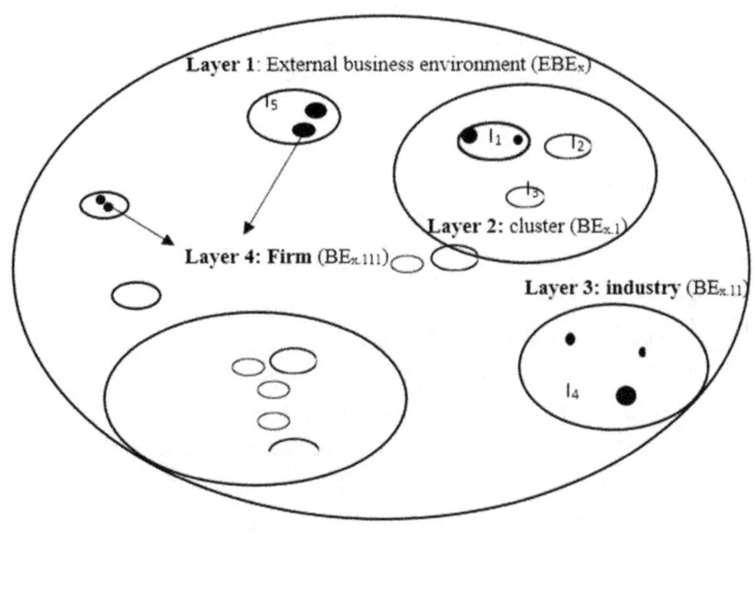

Here the BEA focus mostly on Layer 1, the general environment, which, is in turn an external context to the firm. Layer 4 corresponds to an internal interface of strategy with the firm as one of the proxies of the strategy function. Layer 3 corresponds to the ecosystem of business, namely the economic system (public policies, economic environment and legal framework) and industry structure and agents, and Layer 3 to the industry clusters of businesses, regarding the logic of network-playing addressed on chapter 2.

Hence, Layer 1 and Layer 3 are interrelated (such as Layer 1 and 2), with the structure of the industries varying from *perfect competition* to *imperfect* competition (i.e *monopoly*; *oligopoly*; and *monopolistic competition*) according to the business environment´s determinants of industry´s accessibility to the new entrants on the organizational ecology´s side (i.e. the number of competitors); and its influence on attractiveness, competition, competitiveness and profitability (Keat, Young and Erfle, 2014). Thus, whether BE analysts are adopters of a detached or circumvented view, relevant furthermore, is practitioners comprehend their points of connection which be summarized to the market structures s above and their essentials aspects of entry, exit and competition barriers and opportunities for long-run (non-price centered) competition.

EBE: ELEMENTS

In the previous section we have rambled over the EBE´s layers and positioning of the firm on each layer according to the perspective ("vision") of the observer, but without focusing on its morphology and underlying characteristics. This requires beforehand from a candidate to the development of a BE analysis or from a market researcher/analyst, the initial understanding that any BE has a stratified ontology as depicted on section 4.3. *"Business environment – Layers"*.

Such attribution of the EBE (i.e. *stratified ontology*), posing it with a hierarchical configuration with strata, is a universal and latent attribute of the environment accepted transversally by scholars and practitioners across industries. If one recalls the notion of *Critical Realism*, a philosophical stance addressed in the previous section (*2.1. Business Environment - Assumptions and interpretations),* postulating that a (business) research project assumes a *post-positivist* perspective of the universe under observation, being therefore built on an epistemological assumption that the universe possesses multiple strata (the *real;* the *factual*; and, the *empirical*). Then, the comprehension of the ontology of the EBE, not the research project itself, but nature of a certain environment under analysis, is identically also stratified.

Firstly, the strata of the BE refer to the following three (3) types of elements of analyzability accountable in a BEAP:

(i) Elements of *profiling* (descriptive):
   a. *Segments*
   b. *Sub-segments*
   c. General *factors*
   d. Specific factors (including critical factors)
   e. Parameters (of attributes of a factor)

(ii) Elements of *interdisciplinarity* (evaluative and exploratory):
   a. Factor *relations* (within and across sub-segments, segments and interfaces)
   b. Agents and factors relations
   c. The design of the framework of environment analyzability

Secondly, assuming that the External Business Environment is connoted with the external interface of the strategy function of an organization, and moreover, that the industries, or their clustering constitute an ecosystem, which is a part of the whole, so the business environment analyzability projects may configure two (2) strata:

- Strata 1: An *General Environment*
    - Type of projects: of *Macro External Environment Analysis* (MEEA)
- Strata 2: An ecosystem or industry environment
    - Type of projects: of *Micro External Environment Analysis (MiEEA)*

The *General Environment,* also labelled as *Contextual Environment* by some authors, is the equivalent to the outer layer of the EBE. It comprises all the macro environmental factors, such as, the ones related to the socio-cultural traits, economy, politics, ethics, ecology, or technology, which emanate not only from regional or national sources but also from international, supra-national and/or global developments (Worthington and Bitton, 2009).

The Industry Environment, also termed as *the Immediate Environment,* is also, denominated as the *Operational Environment.* This is the ecosystem where the actual business interaction across agents occur. It holds a large diversity of entity archetypes, which converge towards this environment to create most immediate forms of value, by developing goods, services, patents, or knowledge. It is at this operational environment where other agents converge to (e.g. freelancers; employees; managers; opinion-makers; governments; social/artistic or enterprise foundations; and, other regulating/certificating/accrediting authorities). Moreover, it also here in this environment where the resources converge into, for its combination and joint-transformation, as inherent assets to the activities leading to the value-added to the markets.

Operational Environments might be conceived as, simultaneously, off-marketplaces and e-marketplaces, as the supply and the demand-sides jointly instrumentalize them both ways. Despite, not orchestrating such effort, those two parts, altogether, gain benefits from these dyadic morphology of this environment. Firms offer, cumulatively, their portfolios of products/services within physical and digital channels of distribution on the street and off the street and customers benefit from this convenience of access, facilitating their scrutiny and purchase. Marketers, would label this options, certainly, as, *below-the-line* or *above-the-line* marketing strategies. Typically, firms choose combined options, as retail stores or a direct salesforce, combined with website visibility.

However, the firm-specific scenarios shapes their choices at each moment in time. For instance, their sector specificities, the industry norms, and the typology of management practices may one point towards dissimilar solutions of market positioning. A myriad of existing instruments are out their easily accessible for making goods/service available, both on brick-and-mortar, and alternatively, on the Internet in multiple selling points. For example, as to the first category, firms can consider, for instance, public tenders; sales´ meetings; events – including professional fairs, groups of influence and expertise; or printed media. While acting digitally, may account other options, such as, newsletters; online ads; landing pages; blogs; institutional websites; web stores; social media; or business platforms). These represent at this business environment-specific level, a broad range of alternatives for the attraction of several targets groups, whom benefit and convenience of purchasing whether customized care and personalization attention and a "click-and-go" experience.

Here we shall emphasize that studies focused on this micro environmental layer ought to, unavoidably account, the demand-side (customers) and the supply-side (competitors). The figure of the "customer" either seen on a business-to-business (B2B) logic or business-to-consumer (B2C), is central for the analytical work on this tier external environment tiers to:

a. Identify customer needs (to be able to meet them in the future)
b. Comprehend the many reasons explaining individual and market demand (and possible shifts).

Two central tenets that evolved in recent years is *customer knowledgeability* and *consumer sovereignty* and recognizing them is crucial for any BEAP, as they are fundamental for the functioning of the market economy. The competitor´s analysis also vital to comprehend the profile of installed incumbents in an economic sector, being dominant or non (inclusively small or niche competitors), being whether direct or indirect competitors, or potential competition. The latter are commonly referred to a as "potential entrants". The analysis function allows the consultant/analyst to comprehend whom may alter significantly the structure of an industrial economy, or understand the distribution of strengths and skills, the strategic direction of their businesses, and responsiveness to competitive practices and public policies and regulation.

All the projects (BEAPs) surroundings a description of the General Environment are holistic, aiming at, with a helicopter perspective, to present a general description of the focal reality, whether being a single country or numerous. These projects, are considered "macro", and so labeled as *Macro External Environment Analysis* (MEEA) projects. Some scholars term them also as a *Environmental Factor Analysis* (EFA) projects. Their purpose is descriptive. Yet, descriptive projects allow the conduction of projects with different typologies, from *environmental scanning* to *environmental monitoring,* as they intend at profile EBE and extract a compound set of market data which together work like a puzzle tell the story how the market/s is/are like. This is when projects have a single focus on the general environment (strata 1). One may note that the typologies of BEAPs are a theme covered on the next chapter as we will focus on the analyzability of EBEs.

The Strata 2 is focused on business ecosystems and industry environments, which a composing part of the EBE, positioned on the middle layers (Layer 2 and 3), in which the analysis is equally time-consuming (equivalent to a BEAP on Strata 1), but on this case, the components and attributions are more specific (then with a narrower scope), detailed in content and requiring a higher degree of information per theme and issue. Such an demanding exercise to a market researcher, analyst or strategist, is dependent on prior knowledge about (know-how) technical and research knowledge, but also dependent on the medical gaze and training of those professionals, to be able to deal with the depth of content, navigate through complexity and build a business intelligence (BI) frameworks which are exploratory, and subsequently, in most cases evaluate projects.

Hence, a BEAP focused on strata 2, assumes a cascaded forms of analysis looking into the particularities of the EBE, for instance, into a problematic such as, *networks*; *industry clusters*; *industry structures*; *segmentation*; *competition*; *strategic groups*; *product*; *consumer*, and so forth. In this book, we focus rather on pure EBEs (strata 1) then the latter which is occasionally revisited but not the core object of our attention here. Our focus is pure EBE analysis, which has an antagonistic nature (i.e. holistic) and fits solely into the Strata 1.

However, it shall be stressed that BEAPs possess in many times a hybrid nature, as the goals/objects of the project demand the portraying of strata 1 with embedded data from strata 2.

In this section we have introduced above, as to the type of elements of an EBE. Here, we start with the notion of s*egment.* According to Hitt, Ireland and Hoskinsson (2019) its definition presents it as, a part of all the dimensions of a broader society, which in turn, will influence, the industry and subsequently the firms. I shall emphasize that this definition is specific for the Strategic Management domain. The Marketing discipline depicts also "the parts", not of the general environment, but of the industry environment, breaking it into multiple *categories, types* and *variables* of segmentation, in which, each strata constitutes one segment. In this sense, Marketers are rather focused on the micro environment above denominated as the Strata 2. Thus, both definition share commonalities but are incommensurable, as the segments portrayed in Strata 1 are distinctive from Strata 2.

Indeed, all units of analysis of data are then suggested to be virtually isolated for observation purposes, and classified within a part or a category, called a *segment.* The underlying logic of such thought is, separate the wheat from the chaff, the data needed from the unnecessary one, plunging to the societal specifics one-by-one, as an approach to move away from the chaos of the unknown and move forward towards the order of built knowledge, gained piece by piece, expecting on the way to be molded and adapted. Conceiving in this way a BEAP as a process until getting the "big picture" of, and having an EBE profiled.

In this sense, one may look at multiple dimensions of one EBE and take an equivalent analytical procedure on other market. Hence, BEAPs despite holding a descriptive purpose however allow one to conduct phronetic projects with a high degree of depth, and incorporate in the process, comparative designs, resembling in fact, as to the EBE architecture, exploratory industry projects. We will return to this when we address "analyzability" on chapter 5.

Breaking down societies into dimensions (segments) entails then an exercise of mapping its major categories, as follows:

- Culture
- Demography
- Ethics
- Economy
- Environment
- Health
- International exposure (openness)
- Law
- Policy
- Safety/Risk (national)
- Social norms
- Technology (development)

Hence, talking about these twelve (12) segments, we are referring actually to the multiple roles of each in modern societies. Naturally, all those dimensions are significant to be able to fully profile an EBE in its unity. Moreover, they are associated or *interdependent.* For instance, public policies determine national laws, such as culture, demographics, environment, health and safety shape the economy, and determine the attraction of new talent or new firms, which turn, determines capacity to innovations and generate new patents, knowledge and societal development. They are all interconnected. Hence, organizational resources are scarce, as BEAPs are time-constrained by deadlines and budgets, and moreover, by the ability to grab and process all information. Consequently, it is critical to elect before initiating any project, what are the segments to focus on, and what type of information to extract. Thus, each BEAP is a unique project with specific attributions. Even its iterations vary and the market´s dynamics forces the observer to incorporate external changes occurred with time.

Segments apart from *interdependent* are also *complex*, possessing different types of sub-segments with no equivalent pairs in other segments and accounting a myriad of factors (f) co-exist, with a dissimilar shape and dynamics. Here, the sub-segment refers to a by-product or a sub-categorization of the whole segment.

A *factor* may then be seen as, a unit of a segment which per se, regardless of the whole segment, may have the power to influence the competitive action/response of a firm. So, a segment is composed of multiple factors, such, as societies are composed of *n* segments.

For example, the economic (ECO) landscape is a segment. Herein, all economic information of the countries may assume multiple quadrants, such as:

- Corporate investment´s stimuli
- Income and Purchasing Power
- Macro-economic overall indicators (Performance)
- Taxation to corporations
- Trade balance and deficits
- Unemployment
- Etc.

Within one of those sub-segments, for example, "taxation…", one BEAP may opt to include or exclude multiple factors, such as:

- Corporate income taxes
- Environmental taxes
- Excise taxes
- Labor work taxes (individual income taxes)
- Property and Estate taxes
- Sales taxes
- Taxes over imports/exports
- Value-added-tax

In turn, a sub-segment, may account for multiple factors, which in turn, are multiple pieces of information to be collected to be able to better comprehend the sub-segment and the segment in total. Often, some of those, stated here as factors are sub-segments (Ss), in the case of the existence of multiple factors *(F)*.

So,

$$Ss = n\,(f) \Leftrightarrow n(f) = F$$

And, naturally each f is contained in Ss being a real (natural) number

$$Ss = \{x \in Ss: x > 2\}$$

One may be then on the eminent moment of collecting data to a topic, which you believe to be a single factor, but then it appears to emerge more than one source of data, this means it is instead a *sub sub-segment (Ss)*. For instance "environmental tax" as indicated in one of the bullet-points themes above, in this case, it is a sub sub-segment as one discovered the existence of several taxes in the country within this category (environmental taxation), for example:

- consumption delimitation
- energy consumption
- pollution
- transports
- resource extraction
- waste incineration

To be on the safe side, whenever a BEAP requires data, which by its own means, firms are not able to yield, by their own staff and/or with their internal resources, better to outsource the task. I would dissuade managers to attempt unnecessary collections of partial information as well; or even, full information bundles when one is struggling to assembly it with a minimum standard, avoiding bias or error-free. The insufficiency of data units, or qualitative doubts, does not safeguard the company from future financial rebounds. The same with untrusted, non-validated, and unguaranteed data sources. Also, the same happens with incomplete sets of data. I would advocate, that is always better in those cases to hire the services of an external consultancy firm to assist with the such to whom responsibility and risks may lastly be endorsed to, whenever the circumstances of the project allows that to. Here, an advice for the setting of contractual terms supporting service level, as *service-level agreement (SLA)* terms, and over financial risks, bonus and penalty terms.

Moreover, BEAPs may entail ambidexterian focus or even a multiple-*locus* centrality (several EBEs), a common angle of interest to multinationals or global firms. In fact, as the global interdependence of the markets, associated with network competition models, including industry clusters, make the analyzability a task likely to assume more country-wide contours (*EBE1 vs EBE2; or n EBEs)* than the simplistic country-specific one (1 EBE).

This implies that the extent of intelligence built from, on country-wide projects, not solely accounts the usage of comparative designs on a one to one logic (1:1 - *EBE1 vs EBE2*), but also, may increase the degree (global or regional) market knowledgeability, increasing in this way the extent of sense-given to the information gathered, adding a regional or global level sense-making. Thus, you may have BEAPs, as macro project focused on Strata 1, or a macro external environment analysis (MEEAs) project, with a *regional, national, multinational, meta-regional* and *global* dimensions, as a result of a single effort, concurrent BEAPs taken by separate teams or momenta of wok, being "assembled" afterwards, or a stepwise building of a larger overview of multiple EBEs.

Considered the above options of analyzability, pure or hybrid, country-wide or specific, the typologies may vary, as observed, according to the typology of data required. However, whether as a pure BEAP, solely focused on macro-factors (and segments) or a hybrid project, blending them, their aims/objective and scope of the analysis, as to the choice of segments + factors and models of analysis it is dependent on a dyad of aspects. Firstly, the rationality of the decision-maker as to the strategic planning task, as to the preparation of any activity related to the management information system (MIS) of the company, such as fashioning a BEAP. This entails, all the underlying decisions as to the setting of goals/

Table 3. BEAPs´ general classification

Category	Typology	Dimensions	Focus
Pure	Country-specific	Regional National	1 EBE (and multiple regions) 1 EBE (overall)
Pure	Country-wide	Multinational Meta-regional Global	More than (> 1) EBE More than (> 1) EBE – regional detail More than (> 1) EBE – dispersed by ≥ continents
Hybrid	Country-specific	Regional – Industry focus National – Industry focus	1 EBE (and multiple regions) 1 EBE (overall)
Hybrid	Country-wide	Multinational – industry focus Meta regional – industry focus Global – industry focus	More than (> 1) EBE More than (> 1) EBE – regional detail More than (> 1) EBE – dispersed by ≥ continents (+ industry info – critical factors)

Source: Own elaboration

objectives; course of action and instruments to adopt). Secondly, decisions are taken in organizations, in most large majority by human-beings, especially at middle and senior-level ones, in which, individuals are incapable of detaching their decisions from their hearts and minds, and decide only by pure reason. Hence, decisions, *strategic decisions* or *operational decisions* are also taken into a scenario accounting the one´s *intuition.*

Humans are intuitive by nature and struggle to undress that coat inside the organization. Needless to explain, I believe is, that organizational management decisions are in many cases emotional exercises of experience, as more dogmatic statements, based on perceptions or gut feelings. Hence, decision reflect in many cases, both on success and failure cases (as some shown along the chapters, the reflection of the use of such intuition and emotional decision-making.

Here *intuition* refers to the usage of cognition (as past-experiences, judgments or feelings), as an assumption built upon experiential knowledge from the past. This means without a valid rationale thought, thus a supposition, used as a gut feeling to a specific context to the analysis of a context or a simple piece of evidence to support that a decision is taken on a particular direction. In consequence, the decision-making model, strategic or operational, as to the configuring of the BEAP may vary, according to the external business environment, as to the extent of VUCA conditions, according to the firm´s structure and culture, according to the managerial hubris and personality of the manager or decision-maker. Hence the preparation of a BEAP, may account an array of decisions ranging in structure (*structure/programmed decisions*), association (*dependent* or *independent decisions*). As a consequence, the intertwining of these conditions of decision (below indicated) will influence the design and the success of the project:

a) Elements required and availability of information
b) VUCA external conditions
c) Predictability of outcomes and quantifiable risks
d) Managerial hubris
e) Organization´s culture and assumptions towards risk

A rigorous assessment of decision conditions take into account those parameters prior the establishing the terms (namely the sum of, *objectives* + *course of actions* + *instruments*) of the BEAP. Some companies adopt different techniques as a strategic decision toolbox, incorporating exercises to promote effective decisions, to rationalize their process, or even unravel out-of-the-square solutions, such as the *Devil´s advocacy*; the *Casual Mapping*; the D*ialectic enquiry*; or the *Delphi method (*McKay et al., 2017). These are examples of those instruments to tackle multiple issues and take decision. The most relevant to acknowledge is, that the design of the BEAP varies, according to the elements in interplay and there interpretation by the stakeholders. Consequently, the project may adopt a different format, fitting different models as summarized in the picture below (Boddy, 2017).

Figure 10. BEAP: design conditions (uncertainty x agreement) and modelling
Source: Boddy (2017)

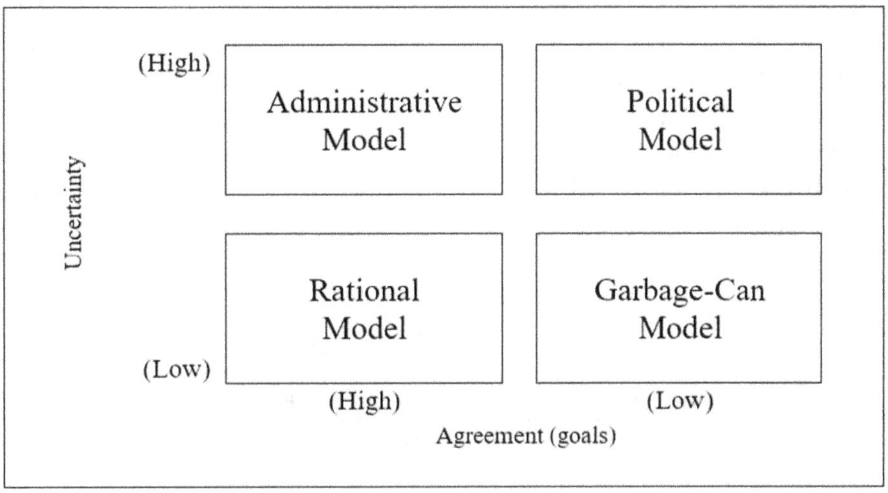

From the Exhibit 34 (above) a set of 4 main decisional models may be observed. These models assess the output of individual managerial behaviour, as to want extent is rationale, creative, mechanic or a palliative one. Thus, projects fitting into The *Rational model* or the *Economic Model of Rationality* encompass consistent decisions taken based the maximization of economic value within a specific set of constrains. Decisions result from a process of structured revision of information (as pro/cons of a goal and cost benefits against other options). However, the goals are set in a directional way, as the uncertainty of the context or the access to information demands from the manager a model of bounded rationality, based on intuition, were decisions may not be structured (Simon, 1956). The purpose of this model is *satisficing*, getting a first solutions which is good enough for a specific uncontrollable context.

The third model (Political) reflects the views of the organization based different interests, thoughts, goals and values, which had to be negotiated between parts so that the project was able to move forward in a satisfactory way to both parts (a *win-win* outcome). The decisions are generally a balancing of interest which negotiation resulted from a discussion of alternatives. Imagine, for instance, a multinational company (MNC) which is willing to conduct a study to determine whether to explore an opportunity revealed to itself on an emergent market. The study of a market may involve different stakeholders, as the organization has a multidivisional form (*m-form*) characterized by a structure comprised of *strategic business units (SBUs)*. A case of a MNC organized by divisions and sub-divisions. The head of division has this project on the table and requires inputs from the SBUs, as to what they considered to be a relevant requirement of analyzability. Certainly, conflict will arise, as SBUs compete for the conquering of superior benefits from the project and their alternatives have to be set at some point. The role of the strategist, as an external consultant may be of great utility to advise the head of division of this company. The same with use of a method such as the *Delphi*, of great interest for the establishment of a framework for the forecasting of what is essential, accessory, common and contradictory arguments and bring some economic rationality to the fashioning of the project, based on likely unbiased professional expertise.

The *Garbage-can model*, tailored to a scenario of high uncertainty and low internal agreement as to the route to be designed, is focused on Cohen, March and Olsen´s (1972) simplistic principle of *choice opportunity* bringing together the ideas of *participants, problems* into a single *solution (PPS)*. Without a better (desirable) model and under an unlike and rather short-termed necessity of decision-making with a short window of opportunity surrounding the solution, the decision is one possible ending contrasting to the absence of decision (no solution). However, decision require the PPS to come all together to a commitment within a highly uncertain environment.

The table below brings though a comparison of the elements of analyzability of these two types of projects, macro (MEEA) and micro (MiEEA) to settle any existing doubts as to the scope of those two types of BEAPs, regardless of the context and model of decision as to the design of the project.

Table 4. BE layers and the projects (of environment-related research)

Layers	Project types	Elements of analyzability
General environment	Macro (MEEA)	General attributes Attractiveness Interdependences (with peers and the focal firm) Comparative positioning Relations Dynamics and evolution
Industry environment	micro (MiEEA)	Structure and general attributes Attractiveness Competitiveness Innovativeness Other interdependences (with peers, general environment and the firm) The agents The parts Other specific phenomenon Dynamics and evolution

Source: Own elaboration

Regardless of the elements of analyzability having a profiling or other interdisciplinary purposes, an initial idea to retain prior the conduction of any BE research is to understand the notion of segments. The *segment* (also referred to, in SM literature, as *landscapes or macrolevel factors)* are the parts of the business environment. Here, the BE is composed of a broad-scope, as there are multiple parts.

These segments, cover multiple societal quadrants, from which one may collect a variety of different sets of data (i.e. *factors*). Typical segments that firms analyze are, for example, the *Legal Environment,* as to the framework of law on a specific context, including policy-developments and legislative changes.

The *Ethical Environment* to understand the firm´s responses to governance and legal affairs, regarding the social contribution to local communities, their relation to nature and the impact of their operations on people and the natural environment. Another relevant segment is the *Technological Environment.* Here, the analysis is focused on the comprehension of the differences of relative competitiveness across markets. Furthermore, as technology is used both as an input and output of business organizations, it should be taken into account, namely, with regard to investments, in innovation and intelectual property, as to matters such as, rights, skills and infrastructures.

In the context of a *Business Environment Analysis Project (BEAP),* the segments correspond to the typical categories or "dimensions" of analysis, as follows:

- the demographic segment
- the economic segment
- the political segment
- the legal segment
- the socio-cultural segment
- the ethical segment
- the technological segment
- or, the global segment.

Despite, research in Strategic Management makes no significant assertions as to the distinction of these segments, as to their contribution to the whole societal system, differences are though acknowledged and not merely circumscribed to the content across segments (or factors, as addressed below), but also, in their morphology and their perceived importance (or relative weight). It ought to be asserted the existence of direct causal relations across segments, in which, the *ex ante* features of the segments´ configurations play a decisive role shaping the others segments dynamics, as an *ex post* effect, in result of one-to-one interrelations.

Here, would surely be relevant to make a few considerations about these segments aforementioned. I will focus then on a couple of seminal ones (the Political and the Economic landscape). Often, the first is disregarded in detriment of the second (the Economic segment). As elaborate below, politics works like the nerve center for the whole society´s functioning. Therefore, I would like to highlight the real importance of this segment for the rest of the macro-environmental context. Furthermore, underline, especially for postgraduate students in Strategic Management or Junior Strategy Consultants, how critical is to get your data right and accomplishing to get this segment thoroughly observed for the success of any future business ventures, most especially in markets with reduced exposure to or null professional/ business experience inside and about them.

Yet, without wanting to underestimate the latter segment (economy), as to its influence on business management; however, it is important to stress that the properties of the economic systems are, as in other segments, fashioned by the underlying political context.

Hence, the existence of causal relations across segments is a *factum*, so is also the dominance of politics over the remaining ones. For instance, the political direction set by the vision of the Trump´s administration, during the presidency from Jan-2017 until Jan-2021, had an accentuated impact on the global agenda´s fight against climate change, representing a setback for avoiding the unbearable rise of global temperatures in the planet (or global warming) that affected the global environmental segment.

Likewise, the political has a clear manifested influence in the economy; subsequently, molding the business dynamics and firm´s performance. These close links between the political and the economic systems, derive from the governments´ action (and local authorities in decentralized political systems), emanated by the set of rules, determining the economic sphere at macro environment level, and consequently, determining the micro business ecosystems´ dynamics. Altogether, they guide the commercial activity across sectors (Boddy, 2017).

Economic systems, (whether capitalist, central planning or mixed) are consequently a mirror of the political contexts and their underlying legal frameworks. Scholars in economics have this association (of politics-economics) quite close on their theoretical background since the early classic thesis. There is indeed a strong influence of political decisions on market regulation, particularly in the microeconomics´ realm. National policies interfere in economic activity, ultimately being the architects of market inefficiencies, a phenomen in microeconomics termed as the *dead weight loss* (DWL), or *efficiency loss*.

Hence, the equilibrium of demand (*d*) and supply (*s*) behaviour curves are, not simply affected by the political direction, but entirely determined by political risks. This market equilibrium (*e*) can be represented by these two (2) functions (*d* and *s*) and is expressed by the vectorial positions of price (*P*) and price equilibrium *(Pe)*, plus quantity (*Q*) and quantity equilibrium *(Qe)* in a given relation represented below, as follows:

Figure 11. Supply and demand behavior
Source: Own elaboration

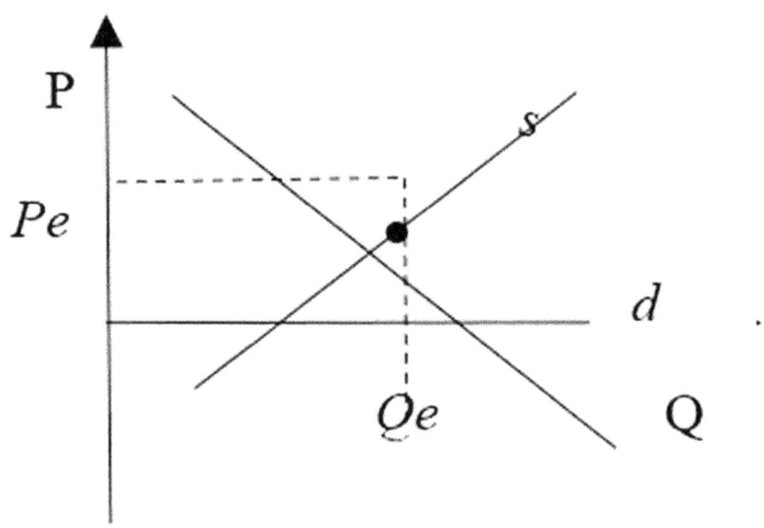

This equilibrium asserts the existence, in such a context, of a consumer surplus, refers to the difference between the price effectively paid for an item and the price he would be willing to pay for it.

Figure 12. Consumer surplus
Source: Own elaboration

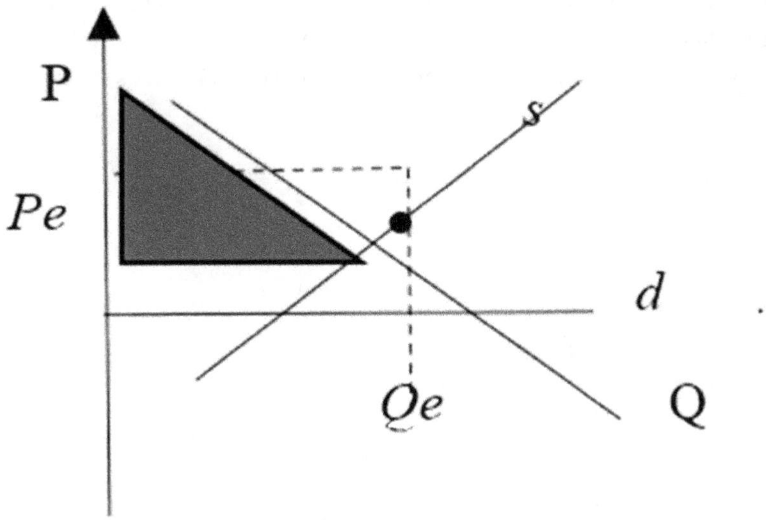

Symmetrically, the producer surplus, as presented in section 4.2, demonstrating to the amount that the producers benefit by selling at a certain market price for a given quantity.

Figure 13. Producer surplus
Source: Own elaboration

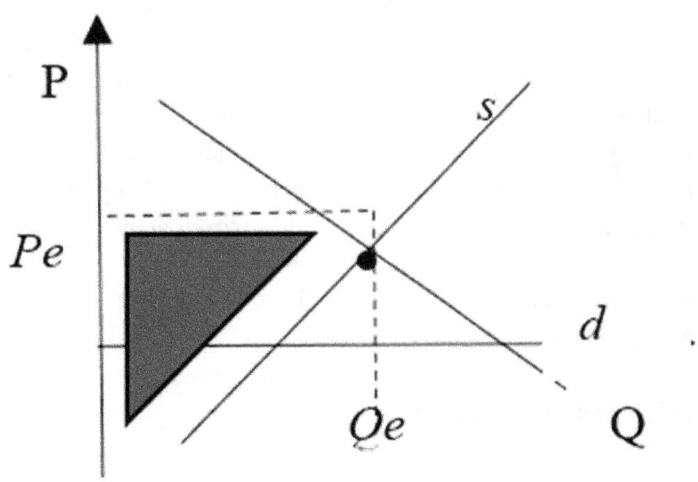

The efficiency results from this perfect match of the economic agents. The consumers being the ones who want to purchase a good above the price, while the seller is equally willing to market it (Tirole, 1988). However, whenever the agents are "forced" externally, to shift to an alternative behaviour, as the *d´* and *s´* functions, this is when inefficiency arise. Here, quantity may be the result, for example, of changes/ increase of corporate taxes, or even additional regulation over goods for selling, such as, limitation of the acquired quantity (q´) of a good; price range limitation (p´); or prices being locked to a fixed sum.

Figure 14. Dead weight loss (DWL)
Source: Own elaboration

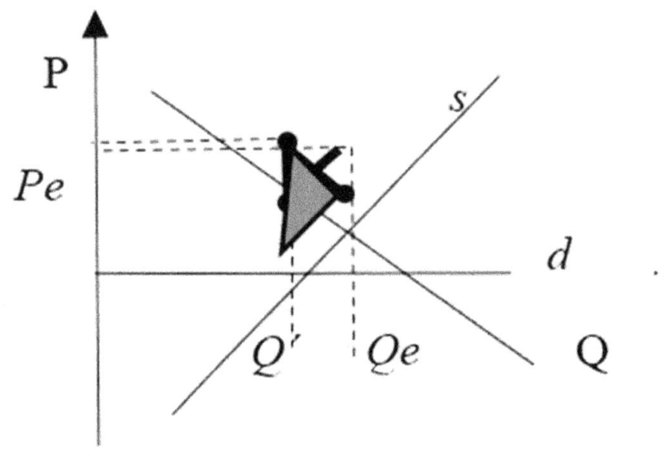

The DWL represents thus the loss of the value appropriated by each side, designated as the *producer surplus* and the *consumer surplus*, resulting from the inherent loss of earning´s power verified because of the political context and political actor´s intervention, surrounding a certain event. On the contrary, such inefficiency would not be observed in an efficient market.

In sum, these political risks matter to local and international businesses, and shape the characteristics of the (macro and micro) External Business Environment (EBE). They represent the political events or actions taken by a government with direct impact on the firm, materialized into the loss of:

- managerial control over current business operations,
- assets (including earnings)

Moreover, with an indirect impact upon:

- business strategies´ realization
- earning power
- potential competition and the dynamics of market segments and strategic groups present competition

Hence, the political content affects thoroughly the market structures and determines the number (or concentration) of the firms constituting its organizational ecology; namely shaping the balance of state-owned and private-held enterprises (Boddy, 2017).

Undoubtedly, political direction and actions of a government are molded by the dominant political thoughts of the (political) apex and its influencers. Moreover, the prior and their inherent operational actions deriving from this political setting, executed by other legal representatives of the governance and top-management spheres, as state official, public servants or company´s managers, have the power of influencing transversally the social regimes. Such political intervention, more than a feature of the national culture, or leadership traits, encompass a grounding assumption, which is an individual and voluntarily adherence to *ideologies*. The notion of ideology entails then a "*set of beliefs about the proper order of society and how it can be achieved*". (Erikson and Tedin, 2003, p. 64).

Furthermore, the political segment may comprise a specific corporate taxation framework or define stimuli programmes to the exploration of the business, concerning its operations (e.g. research and development activities) or investment activities (e.g. internationalization). Moreover, it sets the context and rules for inward investment of foreign companies as to the establishment of a wholly owned subsidiary or the acquisition of stakes in local firms; and subsequently, as to business practices regarding health and security at work (e.g. employees conditions or job protection). Indeed, politics matters, as it influences the whole competition practices, plus the firm/industry-level barriers to enter and engage into competition and abandon the "game".

Besides the ideology, another determining condition of the direction that sets the political context, is *corruption* (Jost, Federico and Napier, 2009; Kurer, 2005). One of the biggest concerns as to the political landscape is brought by the perception of the degree of *individual* and state *corruption*, accepted by citizens either lightly or not. Corruption is all about the use of entrusted power for private gain (Transparency International, online).

With origin in multiple quadrants of society (e.g. as governments, courts, media, politicians, public servants or representatives of business organizations), this definition unravels a roll of negative externalities that come at the cost of erosion of societal trust (social segment), weakening democracies (political segment) and hampering economic development (economic segment). The bill is heavy to all citizens (e.g. social division and inequality; poverty; and even, environmental crisis) particularly in a scenario where corruption practices may flourish, as the consequences are directly proportional to the degree of the phenomenon/problem. The question here is, *How do corruption practices flourish in modern societies*?

They grow especially in political environments which give ample room for individuals least unscrupulous to develop opaque schemes (e.g. unclear public tenure requirements and ad-hoc selection of suppliers); supported by sophisticated financial and digital technological systems; and because someone is willing to incur into illicit practices (e.g. documents forgery; or money laundering). Rodriguez, Uhlenbruck and Eden (2005) introduced a framework for understanding the implications of corruption practices in business organizations, which cross observes two (2) critical concepts: *pervasiveness* and *arbitrariness*.

Corruption´s pervasiveness represents the extent of which a firm is likely to encounter corruption practices in the course of normal transactions with state officials. The arbitrariness corresponds to the extent of opacity or ambiguity associated with corrupt transactions.

Certainly, a relevant association for MNCs may be established within the context of international business´ development, i.e. the degree of financial rebounds due to the extent of arbitrariness. Here, this global civil society organization (Transparency International) developed already some metrics not exactly about the prior (financial rebounds and arbitrariness´s interrelation) but a couple of more general instruments to measure the sub-category of *corruption risks* within political risks. Those are the *Corruption Perception Index (CPI)* (as addressed in next chapter) and the *Global Corruption Barometer (GCB)*. However, corruption controlling is not enough to fight this endemic issue. The antidote is really on a triad of pillars: *integrity*; *accountability*; and *transparency*. Definitely, a larger discussion than the scope of this book intertwining several scientific domains, with a clear epicenter on Business Ethics and Governance.

Embedded in this universe of macro segments, one may so immerse into a myriad of *factors,* multivariate in their nature, inside each segment, which similarities allow for a further sub-categorization into *sub-factors* (Yüksel (2012). A factor corresponds to the element of information within each segment, which all together build a virtual "tile" portraying the reality, as a descriptive profile of the segment. Hence, one (1) segment contains then multiple types of information first selected from, then collected and analyzed. These factors constitute the units of traceable observation as signifiers of the factors, or benchmarks (as discussed in section *5.6. Indexes, ratios, and benchmarks*). An exemplified list of factors per segment provided below:

Table 5. Segments and factors´ correspondence

Segments	Factors (examples)
Political (Pol)	Political system and/or parties Regulatory bodies and (de)regulation Business-related policies Stability of political landscape Impact of (own) corporate policy (e.g. corporate social responsibility, environmental issues, and customer protection) Proposals on legislative changes
Economic (Eco)	Currency exchange fluctuation Gross domestic product (GDP) Inflation rate Mortgage interest rate Taxation Trade deficits or surplus
Social (Soc)	Disposable income Education Life expectancy at birth Lifestyle trends, habits and espoused norms Women in workforce
Political (Pol)[1]	Anti-trust laws Deregulation Political system(s) and stability State ownership of business and attitude towards competition Trading policies Taxation laws
Technological (Tec)	Average Expenditure on R&D Current communication technologies Extent of product innovation and usage of knowledge Patenting and or intellectual property rights

Source: Own elaboration

As suggested by Yüksel (2012), the grouping of factors into sub-segments corresponds to the exercise of clustering information according to the similarity of each piece of data, to be casuistically done according to each BEAPs requisites as to the ability to profile a sub-segment or even data requirements (see figure below).

Figure 15. General environment representation (segments and sub-segments)
Source: Own elaboration

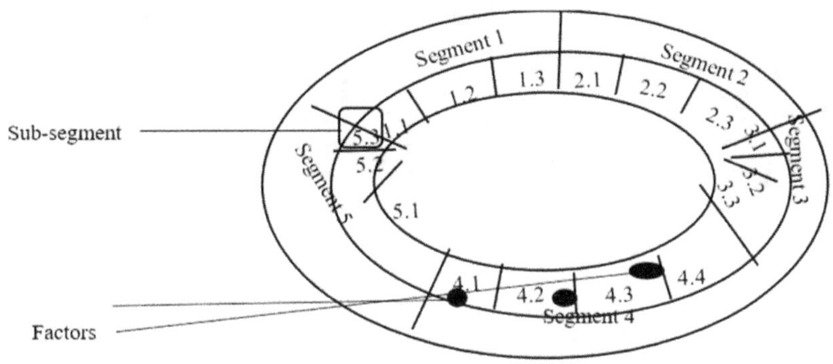

As observed, each segmented may contain multiple segments, segments (and sub) are a hosting place for factors. Yet,

How do we comprehend a diagrammatic representation of a single tier of the EBE, i.e. the general environment does ones closer and more distant to a company?

This would lead us to the concept of *criteria* in factor selection, which it is introduced in chapter 5. Relevant to retain at this stage is, the exercise of sub-segmentation allows the extrapolation of further conclusions, enlarging the quality and depth of the observation for strategic decision-making, hence reducing uncertainty and risks and enhancing business opportunities, since the disaggregated information allow the refinement of the manipulation of the data and the emerge of patterns of information beyond the undistinctive factor analysis on the segment. For instance, all information collected about the segment *Econ*, if you wish to have an insight on let us say "taxation", if for sure, more detailed information is collected on multiple factors of taxation as a sub-segment (e.g. as an *Econ1 – taxation*). Thus, just collecting information on one factor of taxation, as rather specific piece of nuclear information (e.g. corporate tax ratios) does not tell about the overall national taxation framework of a country. In this case, when a BEAP defines "taxation" beforehand as a valuable source of information, and so targeting it as a sub-segment, then this requires the collection of deeper data from a broader range of taxation elements to better illustrate the sub-segment, as a vital component or block to describe the economic landscape/segment.

Hence, drilling down taxation into several elements may comprise the collection of, information about sales taxes, foreign trading and customs taxes, labor taxes, property taxes; and/or capital gains taxes. For such exercise of sub-segmentation Yüksel (2012) the following format:

Figure 16. Sub-segments (PESTEL)

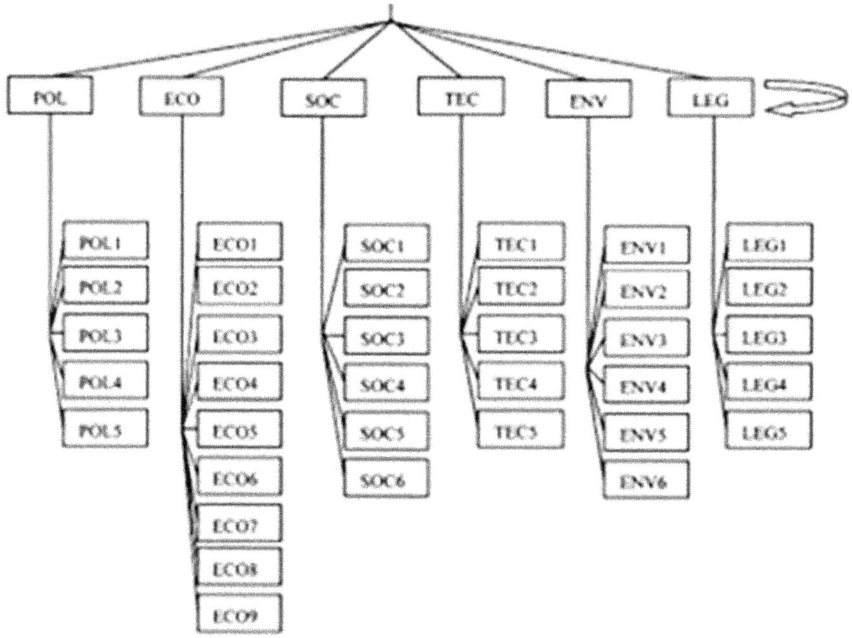

These segments express the following structure:

1- Politic Sub-factors (POL) - focus on the Political system, political parties, and regulatory bodies:
- Relations with European Union (POL1)
- Regional relations (POL2)
- Democratization process (POL3)
- Regional Developments (e.g. Africa and Middle East) (POL4)
- Political stability (POL5)

2- Economic sub-factors (ECO):
- National income (ECO1)
- Investment incentives (ECO2)
- Monetary policy (ECO3)
- Fiscal policy (ECO4)
- Foreign investment (ECO5)
- Current deficit (ECO6)
- Energy cost (ECO7)
- Foreign debt (ECO8)
- Unemployment (ECO9)

3- Social-cultural sub-factors (SOC):
- Life style (SOC1)
- Level of education (SOC2)
- Awareness of citizenship (SOC3)

- Obey the rules (SOC4)
- Will to work of the people (SOC5)
- Democracy culture (SOC6)

4- Technological sub-factors (TEC)

- Technologic investment policies of government (TEC1)
- New patents (TEC2)
  ◦ Number (and/or its tendency) of patents
- Support the research and development activities by government (TEC3)
- Adaptation to new technologies (TEC4)
- Rate of change in technology (TEC5)

5- Environmental sub-factors (ENV)

- Transportation infrastructure (ENV1)
- Traffic safety (ENV2)
- Public health (ENV3)
- Urbanization level (ENV4)
- Disaster management (ENV5)
  ◦ Green issues (ENV6)

6- Legal sub-factors (LEG)

- Competition laws (LEG1)
- Judicial system (LEG2)
- Consumer rights (LEG3)
- Implementation of laws (LEG4)
- International treaties (LEG5)

One of the issues faced as to the gathering of this type of broad information is the multiplicity of sources available to their collection, recalling the phenomena mentioned previously as an *information´s availability paradox*, as excessive amount of sources does not necessarily mean more intelligence. Here, I have two recommendations. Firstly, to start your market research using online market research tools which offer a "full service" in a single report with data already extracted from a multiplicity of different sources. This is the case of, for example, *Marketline* or *Passport* (by *Euromonitor*) which offer a general and updated reporting scheme. However, on the next chapter, we come back to this issue, as there is a section built on sources of data to supporting your research, and helping you create contrived datasets without using any predefined market research tool.

Secondly, commonly, is the need for further data. Apparently, is an easy task in theory to predict your data requirements; however, the collection momenta often observe a gap between requirements (or expectations) and utility. This happens frequently briefly after an initial crunch of figures. The problem may arise from a need for more (information) and build a bigger sample (with more units of data – or data records) or to build parallel sampling with other datasets. Hence, a BEAP requires many times, either the use of *concurrent data*, or *embedded data* collection moments complementary to your initial plans. Let´s say that your BEAP, requires a specific information, on the ECON segment, such as, the currency pairs between X on a specific period $t_{(0,1)}$ against major currencies (e.g. EUR; GBP; or USD) as to their fluctuations, of course, of non-locked pairs. Here, the Yüksel (2012) categorization (ECO1 to ECO9) mentioned above, does not help you to profile fluctuation ratios of country X, as you project requires. You will then need to tap into other, rather specific, reliable sources of official data, as central/ national banks or a statistics bureau (e.g. *European Central Bank*; *Federal Reserve; National Bank*) or other international organizations or regulating agencies (e.g. International Monetary Fund or the World Bank) or even other non-official data sources on exchange markets (e.g. *Bloomberg*; *DailyFx*; *Oanda*) .

LEARNING OUTCOMES

- Relation of Fear and Instincts in Personal Governance
- The dynamics of contemporary business (VUCA)
- Microfoundations and evolution of the Philosophy of Management
- Understand Business and Organizational Management; Strategy; Strategic Management; Corporate Governance; and Leadership
- Distinguish governance, leadership and management

CASE: TOYS R US

Founded in 1948 by Charles Lazarus, a world war veteran, Toys R Us was once one of the largest toy store chains in the world. It grew from a single store in Washington, D.C. into 1,484 stores around the world—nearly half of them in the United States, and another 245 licensed stores in 37 other countries at the time of its liquidation in 2017.

Lazarus inspired by his war friend´s desire, to return home, get married and have children, he anticipated a baby boom and envisioned it as a business opportunity. Having saved some money during his service, Lazarus rented his father's former bike shop to sell cribs, strollers and all the other essential baby equipment, managing to open his first baby goods and furniture store. The rest of the story answers to these three (3) questions, as to the rise, fall and resurrection of the company:

(i) Rise: *How did Toys "R" Us become America's most loved toy store?*
(ii) Fall*: What caused it to be dethroned of its dominant presence in society?*
(iii) Resurrection: H*as the store Charles Lazarus founded risen from the dead?*

In the subsequent years, Lazarus began expanding and soon rented a supermarket to expand into toys and the company officially adopted the name Toys R Us (with a backward R) in 1957. This was almost too-good-to-be-true toy paradise, a new "supermarket of toys", became the go-to place for toy buying. Toys "R" Us became the first big-box store of its kind.

In 1966, Lazarus sold the company to Interstate Sales to help finance a larger national expansion, and transitioned from chief executive to head of the Toys R Us division. Unfortunately, the parent company (Interstate Sales) filed for bankruptcy in 1974, and Lazarus assumed a decisive role handling the firm´s restructuring process. Lazarus sold off struggling pieces of the business and got the company back on track. In 1978, Toys R Us was able to file its initial public offering (IPO). Under Lazarus command, the company opened in 1983 a clothing store spinoff (Kid R Us) and the empire continued steadily to expand, capturing 25 percent of the toy market and was worth $12 billion. Building upon the success of Kids R Us, the company diversified also into baby clothing with Babies R Us in 1996.

Yet, Lazarus have stepped down as a chief executive in 1994. Moreover, since late 90s Toys R Us began to experience mounting competition from fellow big-box stores and their fortune started to change. Three colossal retail competitors—Amazon, Target and Walmart—started steeply discounting baby products and toy prices. In 1998, Walmart became the top US toy seller. Moreover, Walmart and Target also had better online experience in the early days of the Internet.

In 2000, Toys R Us signed its own "death sentence". Instead of investing on developing an online presence, established a 10-year partnership to be an exclusive vendor of toys on Amazon. Amazon received $50 million a year and a percentage of sales in return for exclusivity. Despite the deal, Amazon allowed other toy vendors to sell on their platform too. This created the "perfect storm". In 2003, the spinoff Kid R Us faced the closure of its 146 stores, and by 2005, Toys "R" Us had a 1.86 billion dollar debt, falling profits, and lackluster sales figures. The board of directors took the company from public to private by selling it to a conglomerate of private equity firms — including Bain Capital, Kohlberg Kravis Roberts, and Vornado Realty Trust — purchasing it for $6.6 billion USD. This apparent smart move of restrategizing revealed to be a disaster as the two million dollars debt turned quickly into $5 billion soon after the contract was signed. This crippling debt limited its innovation options, stifled its investment opportunities, and made it impossible for Toys "R" Us to produce a profit sustainably. The company continued to struggle both commercially and financially in the next years. The company officially filed for Chapter 11 bankruptcy protection in September 2017, but the physical stores continued to be open until March 2018 when announced that it would liquidate and permanently close all of its 700-plus stores across the US.

In February 2019, Toys R Us appeared to rise from the dead when Tru Kids Brands purchased the rights to the company (Biron and McDowell, 2021); Roberte, 2020). Later that year, Tru Kids Brands announced it would open a series of holiday pop-up stores under the Toys R Us name. In October 2019, the company announced it was back online. Toys R Us technically still exists online and on social media, however, the brand is a shadow of what it once was.

CHAPTER HIGHLIGHTS

- Opposing models of above-average returns (a.a.r) - resource-based (RB) and industrial organization (IO) and the Positioning School (PS)
- Spectrum of analysis of the External Business Environment (EBE)
- *Strategy interfaces*: equilibrium, and *organizational levers*
- Organizational isomorphism or myopia: *Strategic drift´s* phases)
- Elements of External Business Environment Analysis (EBEA): *Segments* and *Factors*
- Philosophy of Analyzability and differences in Business Environment Analysis Projects (BEAP)

CONCLUSION

This chapter clarifies the scope of the macro and micro external environment analysis, by distinguishing first the two layers and the main focus and utility of each.

Within the "General Environment" (or "Contextual Environment"), is introduced, as to the Macro external environmental analysis (MEEA) function, the notion of *segments* and *factors* of analysis, crucial for running any Business Environment Analysis Project (BEAP). Accordingly, a correspondence was made between segments and sub-segments, with factors (and sub-factors) selection decisions in these projects.

Moreover, is addressed the available modes of data collection and typology of sources. Herein, a discussion enters the realm of Philosophy of Analyzability, as a subset of the Philosophy of Management, and explores the possible design that a BEAP can adopt, considering the interaction of *uncertainty* (of the external business environment) and *agreement* (across organizational-stakeholders) involved in the decision-making around the fashioning of the project.

Since a business environment holds multiple types of information, with origin on multiple factors, hence recognized as complex, due to the number of events to be analyzed, we have also tapped into a seminal concept (i.e. *factor selection*). This concept is a determinant one for comprehending in the next chapter the "criteria" of analyzability.

REFERENCES

Abrantes, B. F. (2020). Tech-innovation and spillovers on corporate-defensiveness: Evidence from the Lisbon startup ecosystem. *International Journal of Business Competition and Growth*, *7*(1), 68–100. doi:10.1504/IJBCG.2020.108439

Abrantes, B. F. & Ostergaard, K. (2021) Digital footprint wrangling: are analytics used for better or worse? A concurrent mixed methods research on the commercial (ab)use of dataveillance. *Journal of Marketing Analytics*, *10*(2022), 187-202. doi:10.1057/s41270-021-00144-5

Arrow, K. J., & Debreu, G. (1954). Existence of an Equilibrium for a competitive economy. *Econometrica*, *22*(3), 265–290. doi:10.2307/1907353

Biron, B., & McDowell, E. (2021) Inside the wild and tumultuous history of Toys R Us, a once beloved children's brand that just closed its last 2 stores in the US. *Business Insider*. https://www.businessinsider.com/the-tumultuous-history-of-toys-r-us-photos-2020-8?r=US&IR=T

Blacker, F. (1995). Knowledge, knowledge work and organization: An overview and interpretations. *Organization Studies*, *15*(6), 1021–1046. doi:10.1177/017084069501600605

Boddy, D. (2020). *Management: Using practice and theory to develop skill* (8th ed.). Pearson Education Limited.

Burrell, G., & Morgan, G. (1979). *Sociological Paradigms and Organisational Analysis*. Heinemann Educational Books.

David, F. R., David, F. R., & David, M. E. (2017). *Strategic management: concepts and cases: A competitive advantage approach*. Pearson.

Debreu, G. (1959). *Theory of value*. Wiley.

Hitt, M. A., Ireland, R. D., & Hoskisson, R. E. (2016). *Strategic management: Concepts and cases: Competitiveness and globalization*. Cengage Learning.

Hofer, C. W., & Schendel, D. (1978). *Strategy formulation: Analytical concepts.* West Publishing.

Hubbard, D. (2014). *How to measure anything: Finding the value of intangibles in business.* John Wiley & Sons, Inc.

Johnson, G., Scholes, K., & Whittington, R. (2008). *Exploring corporate strategy: Text and cases.* Pearson education.

Jost, J. T., Federico, C. M., & Napier, J. L. (2009). Political ideology: Its structure, functions, and elective affinities. *Annual Review of Psychology, 60*(1), 307–337. doi:10.1146/annurev.psych.60.110707.163600 PMID:19035826

Keat, P. G., Young, P. K., & Erfle, S. (2014). *Managerial Economics* (7th ed.). Pearson Education.

Kurer, O. (2005). Corruption: An alternative approach to its definition and measurement. *Political Studies, 53*(1), 222–239. doi:10.1111/j.1467-9248.2005.00525.x

Lapierre, R. (1980). *Le changement strategique: un reve en quete de reel* [Doctoral dissertation, Ph. D. Management Policy course paper, McGill University].

Mason, E. (1939). Price and Production Policies of Large-Scale Enterprise. *The American Economic Review, 29*(1), 61–74.

Mintzberg, H. (1987). The strategy concept I: Five Ps for strategy. *California Management Review, 30*(1), 11–24. doi:10.2307/41165263

Roberte, L. (2020) The Story of Toys "R" Us' Growth, Decline, and Resurrection. *Alabrava.* https://alabrava.net/the-story-of-toys-r-us-growth-decline-and-resurrection/

Rodriguez, P., Uhlenbruck, K., & Eden, L. (2005). Government corruption and the entry strategies of multinationals. *Academy of Management Review, 30*(2), 383–396. doi:10.5465/amr.2005.16387894

Simon, H. A. (1956). Rational Choice and the Structure of the Environment. *Psychological Review, 63*(2), 129–138. doi:10.1037/h0042769 PMID:13310708

Tirole, J. (1988). *The theory of industrial organization.* MIT press.

Worthington, I., & Britton, C. (2009). *The business environment.* Pearson education.

Yüksel, I. (2012). Developing a multi-criteria decision making model for PESTEL analysis. *International Journal of Business and Management, 7*(24), 52–66. doi:10.5539/ijbm.v7n24p52

ENDNOTE

1 Includes also legal and administrative factors due to their intertwining of the three categories.

Chapter 5
External Business Environment Analysis (EBEA)

ABSTRACT

Entering the realm of analyzability, the chapter begins with a debate surrounding the philosophy of analyzability (PoA) around essential issues such as, assumptions and stances. Afterwards, it specifies focuses on the scope of a business environment analyzability project (BEAP). Here the phases and the criteria surrounding the factor´s selection (on a BEAP) are depicted. Moreover, it covers the types of criteria and the notions of balance and dominant criterion. Subsequently, it elaborates on other more specific domains of analyzability. For instance, the phases of the strategic decisions which lead to the choice of criteria (and the dominant one); the selection of sources of data, the use of models for analyzing the external business environment (EBE); and the applicability of indexes, ratios, and benchmarks.

INTRODUCTION

According to Kenichi Ohmae, "*analysis is the critical starting point of strategic thinking*" (Ohmae, 1982, p. 12). The outside world is perceived to hold a myriad of events, trends and problems which ought to be recognized by any firm. For this scholar the role of the strategic thinker or analyst is to dissect them into their constituent parts. This entails the following:

- Knowledge: know more, about yourself (the company) and your strengths and weaknesses; the market; the industry; the customers; competitors – plus strategies and products; the key success factors (KSFs); and what separates winners and losers
- Depth: make a real analysis, penetrate appearances and do not focus on symptoms but on the real essence of the problems
- Infer: build on strengths for your capabilities; and, think as entrepreneur;

DOI: 10.4018/978-1-6684-5543-2.ch005

Moreover, Ohmae (1982) stems that a successful strategy stems for creative minds, capable of strategizing in a creative ad intuitive way rather than simply a rote stepwise process, in order to differentiate itself from the competitors making use of own relative strengths to the satisfaction of its customer-base. This scholar may be also argued to have set principles of what a strategic audit is, covering strategic formulation and controlling, while advocating the seminal importance of, knowledge; depth of analysis; and develop an inferential thinking.

An initial question one may ask is, How/why should one use this for…: *Why to conduct environment analysis?*

Ohmae´s rationale on to the mindset of the strategy analyst provides a decisive insight as to the importance of the analysis function, assertive and adopting a flexible and sophisticated thinking process able to process data and conceive new ideas outside-of-the-box.

Lynch (2009), furthermore, offers a clear answer for the "whys", for the most skeptical candidates and for the most fundamentalist followers of the resource-based model, which by principle devalue totally the importance of external information outside of the thresholds of the firm. This scholar suggests that, environment analysis, as a as mechanism of market examination, for the purpose of organizational learning, as the virtue(s) of:

(i) developing a sustainable competitive advantage (SCA);
(ii) identifying opportunities and threats; and,
(iii) approximating the firm to others, providing opportunities for (productive) co-operation

In sum, risk-controlling and competitiveness purposes suggest the suggest an attentiveness to market dynamics to measure these phenomena (risk; competition) in favor of the future economic rents, financial health, survival and a long-last existence.

As to the "hows", this section will explore several models with a complementary typology to provide the reader with a toolbox of ready-to-use solutions for replication in own firm´s projects and/or on for your clients.

CRITERIA SETTING AND FACTOR SELECTION

Defining the profiling of the business environment may require a different array of conditions according to the goals of the BEAP. On the previous section, we introduced, among others, the notion of segments and factors, and discussed the general factors against critical factors plus the type of BEAPs (pure or hybrid). The BEAPs being focused on the general environment, entail the application of a model of analyzability identified as, a *Macro External Environment Analysis (MEEA)*. Pure or hybrid BEAPs, are then project of macro analysis of BEs, in which, the hybrid ones, are a sub-set of MEEAs incorporating also, market research endeavors and information inputs, deriving from industry-specific data requirements (critical factors), i.e. partial bundles of information eligible from the *Micro External Environmental Analysis (MiEEA)*.

Generally, any BEAP serves a descriptive purpose of demonstrating the way a market is like. Making an analogy, the initial perception from the BEAP is like a "mask", an image created of it. However, the conduction of macro research allows the visualizing of how the BE is like, as uncover the "face". Better to picture the face behind the mask, or be more knowledgeable about its rules, dynamics, risks and opportunities. The idea is to observe the "face", digest its features and profile it at the end.

Consequently, we introduce here the concept of *criteria*, originally drawn by David Cotton on his book "*The Business Strategy Toolkit*" (Cotton, 2012). Cotton advocated a higher logic of rational observation. With this in mind, every BEAP, in order to be assertive as to its goal/s´ achievement, ought to consider prior the collection of any data, the criteria which are considered in greater accounted according to the purpose of the project.

Data for a BEAP varies though casuistically from one to another, even inside of the same company, division, or even with an identical BE target. For instance, a consultant that runs an iteration of a BEAP with the same contours of a previous MEEAs (e.g. a pure project; identical goals; and, on market) may suffer substantial changes in content, as the time (t_{+1}) modifies already the context of observation and the data collected. Recalling an idea set before, EBEs are not static.

Hence, are here presented three (3) types of most significant *criteria* to consider as to the selection of factors when attempting to profile a segment. These criteria, are drawn on the assumption that the companies fashion their BEAPs under an *Economic Model of Rationality* as defined on the previous section.

Business Environment: Criteria

- Criterion 1: *Importance*
- Criterion 2: *Impact*
- Criterion 3: *Time horizon*

Importance refers to the self-assessment of the contribution of a factor, as an isolated piece of information to allow a fairly accurate profile of a segment.

Impact considers the degree of influence of a factor in relation to a focal company.

The *time horizon* considers the length of observation or effect of a factor.

The usage of those criteria for factor selection may be spatially represented on a diagram of the external business environment, on a circumvented vision, as follows:

Figure 1. Criteria setting and factor selection
Source: Own elaboration

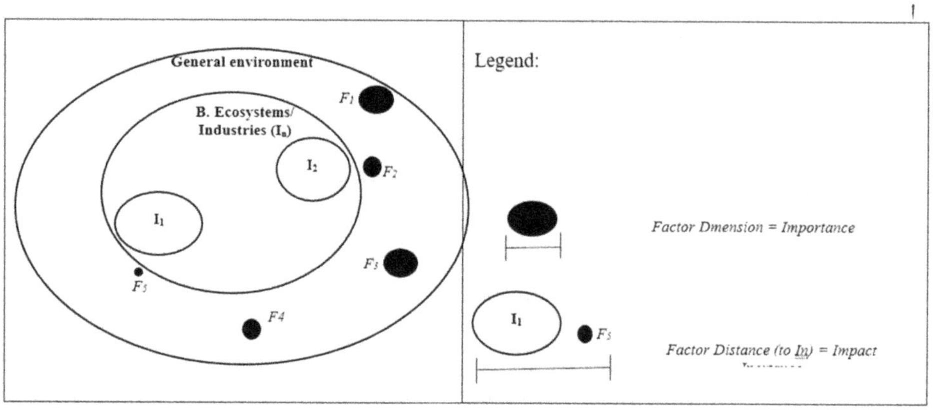

The two tiers (general and industry) are represented by the outer and inner rings. The factors (F_n) populating the outer ring, regardless of the segments (or sub) they belong to, possess an intrinsic value which is partially explicative of the segments. Here, it is introduced the concept of *factor dimension*. The amount of space occupied by a single factor representing the *relative importance* (RI) for the segment. Such relative importance may be described on the following axiom as:

F(RI) = Fx / ∑ *F * 100; or, F(RI; sub-segment) = Fx / ∑ FN * 100;*

The factor dimension provides a ratio ranging from 0 (if inexistent) to 1 (maximum utility) explaining per se alone the segment. The latter is theoretically possible on relativistic projects, yet this implies a perception which devalues the other factors. The relative importance (RI) of the factor within a segment implies then accounting of the number *(N)* of segments, equivalent to a statistical measure of an absolute frequency *(F) (N⇔ F)*. Factors with a larger contribution for comprehending a segment (i.e. *nuclear factors*) are here drawn with bigger dots, while factor with less contribution or with less representativeness for enlightening a segment are then *peripheral factors* and drawn with smaller dots.

In consequence, BEAP tending for a Universalist philosophical stance may naturally privilege the nuclear factors, as the ones with higher importance (as "critical" or "important" factors). On the contrary a relativistic reasoning may give preference to nuclear or peripheral factors. The most significant aspect for their selection/incorporation in the BEAP is the proximity/distancing to the focal firm. This proximity is diagrammatically represented (not as a virtual but) as a real geo location (as the distance between a factor and an industry X). Of course, this is an algebraic abstraction, since for real one cannot determine physical proximity of a factor to an industry. In this context, a company-centered BEAP privileges the factors which may be more impactful for the company and constitute a higher risk or opportunity. As you may already naturally deduce:

i) Important factors to describe a BE may not result into any business opportunities or threats, as to their impact on a specific firm
ii) Specific data, impactful for a firm, may not be of relevance to profile a BE
iii) Effects may long-last or not.

The reader might at this stage ask him/herself,

Question: How one can gauge importance, impact and time?

The answer is simple and optimistic. One can certainly do it even when factors seem hard to grasp and goals far to be reached.

It is a matter of design, whether the BEAP is intended to be universal, aiming at descriptive the most important factors portraying the segments, or be relativistic or specific and cover in a larger extent some specifics of data which may benefit, as to the one´s perception, the focal firm. So, BEAPs have traditionally one (1) dominant criterion (either, *importance* or *impact*) and two (2) secondary criteria (*importance & time horizon*; or, *impact & time horizon*).

Figure 2. BEAP fashioning: Criteria utilization
Source: Own elaboration

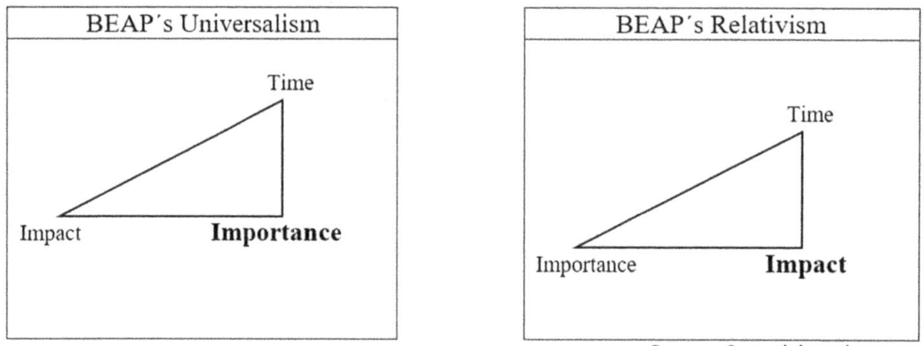

Source: Own elaboration

As to the figure above, the focus on importance of the factors, (universalism) illustrates the desire of the company to portray the reality, isolated from the firm, accounting the set of factors and data which best describes the reality (ontology) as the firm is merely represented therein in the BEAP as the observed the topic of the study. Such dominance of the "importance" macro factors delimitation contrasts with the preference given rather to "impact" as a dominant criterion. Here the projects are relativistic (or specific), as the data is adapted to, and the adaptability is focused on the grasping of "hopes and hazards", as the factors are set particularly to cover all that company believes to be more important to the control of risk. This, factor´s choice accounts all potential beneficial, harmful characteristics of the EBEs, and the oriented towards the determining of what does constitute an opportunity and/or a threat to the company. Ultimately grasp all opportunities (O) and threats (T).

Figure 3. BEAPs: General criteria and the dominant criterion

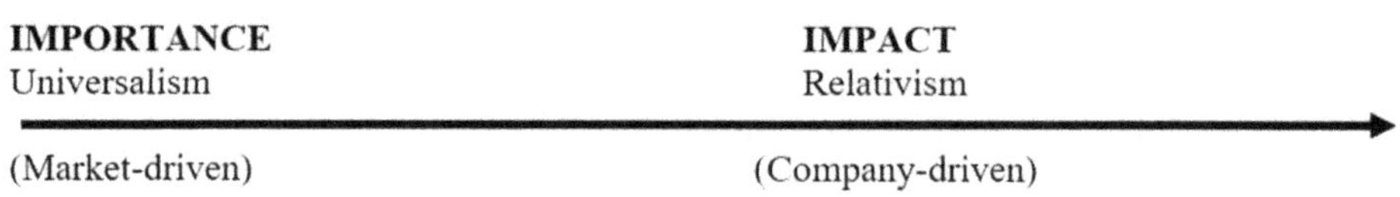

Hence, the dominant criterion can naturally swing from one pole (importance or impact) to another, as companies may decide to adopt a model of analyzability fully focused on one criteria or the other. Nevertheless, the dominant paradigm of industry practitioners across industries and regardless of their structures, is to follow a logic of *acquiescence*, in which, projects are fashioned to be in-the-middle of continuum of the universalist/relativist philosophies, and attain a fairly balanced (and wise) position, accounting both criteria, as their willing to portray the EBE/s but at the same time, comprehend its influence on a focal firm, customizing so the analyzability to own goals. Consequently, BEAPs, accounts as a rule one (1) dominant criterion and two (2) secondary criteria, as follows:

i. One Dominant criterion (importance, or impact)
ii. Two Secondary criteria (time and impact; or time and importance)

Time-led projects are scarce. As the analyzability is not driven at comprehend simply time variations, regardless of what (factors), but instead, to grasp how the reality, including the timing of their effects, being or not impactful for a certain firm.

Such a fluctuation of a BEAP from market-driven to company-driven, exhibits, with regard to the universalism or relativism of corporate thinking, the adoption of a management philosophy where the seniors mangers value rather (dominantly) a *best-fit* or a *best-practice* approach (Boxall and Purcell, 2000). Here, the Best-Practice School intends at gather the overall segments and factors which best portray the universe of analysis. This is anchored on an epistemological assumption that markets exist regardless of the focal firm, which in turn, (the firm) has a likely low or null impact on the environment. Hence, Universalists consider a best-fit model a biased exercised of customization to the firm aiming at meet desirable financial objectives. The relativists start with a dissimilar self-questioning (not what are the factors that better portray it/them, but) what are the *critical contingencies* of the market which most affect a firm.

- *What are the best portraying factors of the external business environment?*
  (Dominant factor = importance)
- *What critical contingencies of the market which most affect a firm?*
  (Dominant factor = Impact)

The "critical contingencies" referred above are not the same thing as "critical factors" *(contingencies ≠ factors). Critical contingencies* are described by Boxall and Purcell (2000) as the inputs of greater importance for one specific BEAP. The *critical factors* refer to the type of information collected at the level of business ecosystems/industries, which determines the level of openness, competitiveness, and so, of attractiveness of the industry. This clarification is made here to solve any misunderstanding. The critical contingencies entail then all the most important factors, regardless of the segments, which on the company/manager´s eyes may affect the most the firm, whether general factors only (on projects classifiable as pure BEAP) and critical factors (on projects classifiable as hybrid projects).

David Cotton, when proposed in his book the use of importance, impact and time, despite not labelling it objectively "criteria", neglected though stepping forward with a solution on how to measure them, or how to apply them in a systematic way. This aspect is of extremely relevance for the companies to be able to put them into practice, when designing a BEAP. Regardless of a perspective (universal or relativistic) of the BEAP, without scales the factors are not assessed, and without such factor´s auditing it is not possibility to build an analytical framework focused on objective data (Cotton, 2012). In this sense we propose the use of a simplistic way for the utilizations of such criteria. An identical scale per criterion, with measurement of different attributes.

The measurement units applied to these criteria allows a practical exercise of the decision-making, as to the choice of factors, and the effective exploitation of the rational model. In this case, the model could adopt a plethora of possibilities, as the manager/strategist/consultant may objectively decide what to analyze and what to not analyze. Hence, below is distinguished between Universalist and Relativist BEAPs:

Table 1. BEAP design: Scale/Measurement Units for the Criteria

Measurement	Criteria		
Criterion	1	2	3
Description	importance	impact	time
Number of levels	4	4	4
Descriptor	Critical (C) Important (I) Unimportant (Ui) Unknown/undefined (U)	High (H) Medium (M) Low (L) Null (N)	Long-term (LT)> 5 y Medium-t. (MT) (>1 <5 y) Short-term (ST)(< 1 year) Instantaneous (I) (Just now)

Source: Own elaboration

a) Universalist BEAPs

The figure below presents five models of factor selection according to the criteria above discussed, and variables positioning (as dominant or secondary). The models emphasize different ways of selecting factors, accounting *inclusivity* and *partial selectivity*.

Figure 4a. Universalist representation of factor´s analysis

Criterion	Diagrammatic representation
Dominant: Importance	*Time (T)* 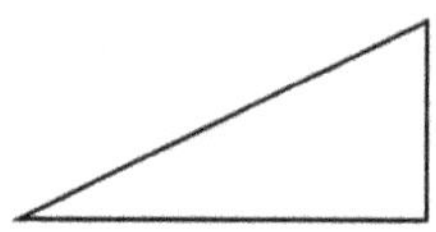 *Impact (Ia)* ***Importance (Io)***
Model 1 (inclusive)	*T = {I, ST, MT, LT}* 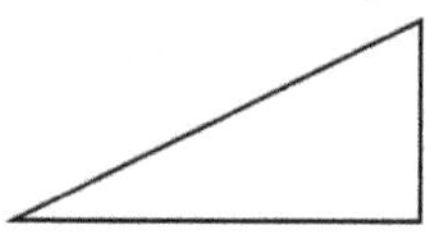 *T = {H, M, L, N}* ***Io=*** *(C ∩ I}*
Model 2 (time exclusive – long-term effect factors)	*T = {I, ST, MT}* 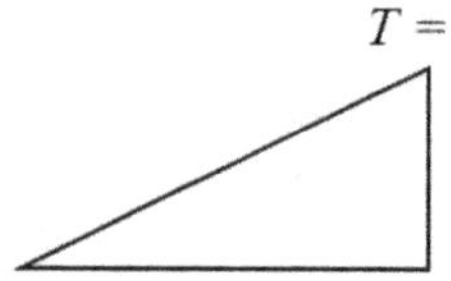

Figure 4b.
Source: Own elaboration

	Ia= {H, M, L, N} **Io=** *(C ∩ I}*
Model 3 (impact exclusive – low impact exclusions)	*T = {I, ST, MT, LT}* 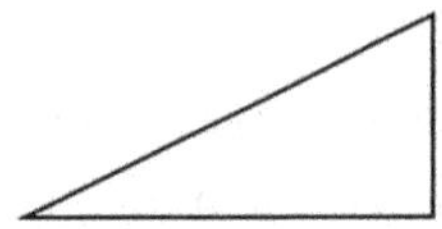 *Ia = {H, M}* **Io=** *(C ∩ I}*
Model 4 (time selective)	*T = {I, ST}* 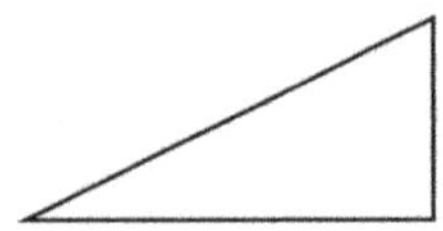 *Ia = {H, M, L, N}* **Io=** *(C ∩ I}*
Model 5 (impact selective)	*T = {I, ST, MT, LT}* 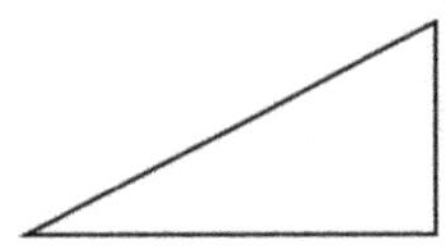 *Ia = {H};* *or Ia = {H;M}* **Io=** *(C ∩ I}*

In this sense, deciding what to analyze and not in BEAP, begins with a seminal decision. Having *importance* as a dominant criterion, then the decision is regarding these models what decisions of factor selection to take, prior the analyzability procedure. A plethora of rational options are though opened here. For instance, all models consider a scenario of lower restrictions of resource to the conduction of the project. Let us say, the analysts has time and space to adopt a model 1 (inclusive). Then this could be 1represented as:

$Io_{(model\ 1)} = n\ (x_1;\ x_2,\ x_3,\ x_4....,\ x_n),$

Each *x,* refers to variable, as a factor to be analyzed, whenever it is observed its existence (x>0). So, x_I entails a decision,

$x_1 = \sum(c) \subseteq Io,$

In which, *c* identifies to the number of combinations or options (of selection for future analysis). Naturally, if the dominant variable (Io) is expressed as null (x=0) or not observed in a relevant status (i.e. *unimportant* or *unknown*), than x is a variable that does not belong to this model of analyzability ($x_I \notin I_{o\ (model1)}$), so

$x1 \not\subset I_{o\,(model1)} = \{x_1; x_2, x_3, x_4 ..., x_n\}$

And commutatively

$I_{o\,(model1)} \not\supset x_{1,}\ if\, x>0$

However, considering $x_1 \subseteq Io$, then model 1 allows the adoption of one or more of twenty-four combinations *(c)* of factor selection, according to the perception of measurement defined per criteria, and willingness to pursue a certain line of investigation.

The potential combinations within model 1 are multiple. Focusing on a dominant variable (io) rated as "critical" a set of 12 possible combinations are,

x_1 = (Critical U High U Long-term); x_2 =(Critical U High U Medium-term);

x_3 = (Critical U High U Short-Term); x_4 = (Critical U High U Instantaneous);

x_5 = (Critical U Medium U Long-Term); x_6 = (Critical U Medium U Medium-term);

x_7 = (Critical U Medium U Short-Term); x_8 = (Critical U Medium U Instantaneous);

x_9 = (Critical U Low U Long-Term); x_{10} = (Critical U Low U Medium-Term);

x_{11} = (Critical U Low U Short-Term); x_{12} = (Critical U Low U Instantaneous);

While the "important"-rated (in Io) combinations are,

X_{13} = (Important U High U Long-term); x_{14} =(Important U High U Medium-term);

x_{15} = (Important l U High U Short-Term); x_{16} = (Important U High U Instantaneous);

x_{17} = (Important U Medium U Long-Term); x_{18} = (Important U Medium U Medium-term);

x_{19} = (Important l U Medium U Short-Term); x_{20} = (Important U Medium U Instantaneous);

x_{21}= (Important U Low U Long-Term); x_{22} = (Important U Low U Medium-Term);

x_{123} = (Important U Low U Short-Term); x_{24} = (Critical U Low U Instantaneous);

This means that a specific project (BEAP) which pursues a macro analysis (MEEA) line of investigation that is Universalist (i.e. *Io*, as dominant criteria) than has varied possibilities of analysis, since multiple rational strategic decisions are available, regarding the combination of criteria to include and exclude from the analytical procedure, assuming that the decision-maker aims at maximize the economic value of his/her decision.

Such strategic decisions, as to the utilization of criteria, or modelling of factor selection, is obviously influenced by the individual perception of the decision-maker as to the positioning of a factor on the scales (1-4) per each measurement unit *(Io; Ia; T)*. Thus, rational models of factor analysis entails naturally two (2) attributes: researcher *bias* and *error*, ought not to be disregarded at this stage.

b) Relativist BEAPs

The relativistic approach being symmetrical implies the shift of importance for the impact, being the latest the dominant variable, as exemplified on the table below. Likewise, 5 models of factor analysis emphasize inclusivity and partial selectivity (of one of the secondary variables) at a at time, such as, on the Universalist approach.

Figure 5. Relativistic representation of factor´s analysis
Source: Own elaboration

Criterion	Diagrammatic representation
Dominant: Impact	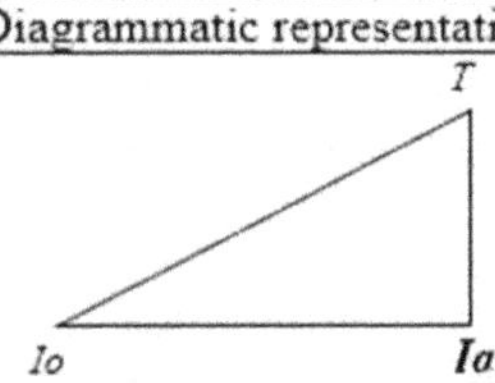
Model 6: Inclusive	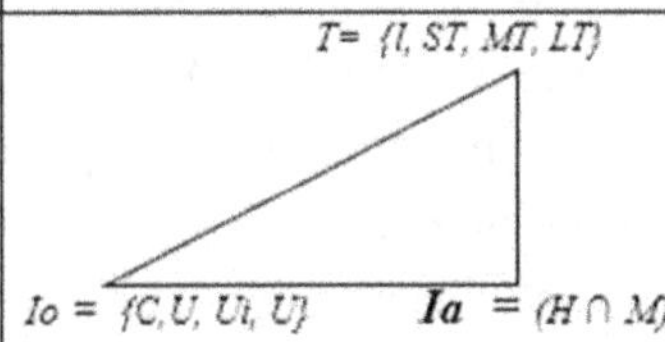
Model 7 (Time exclusive – long-term effect factors)	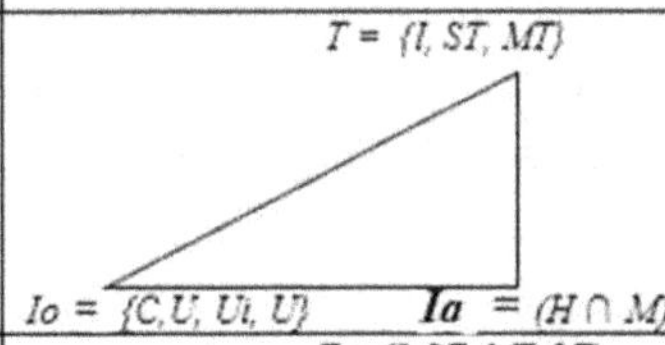
Model 8 (importance exclusive – low importance exclusions)	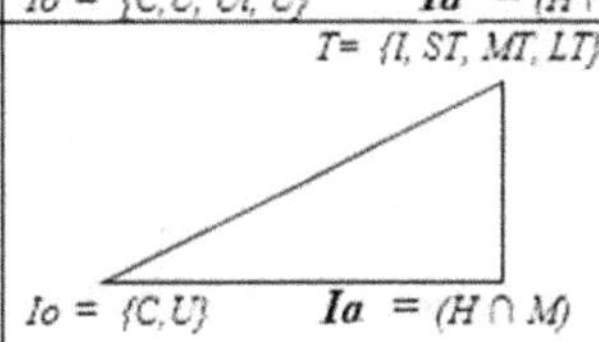
Model 9 (time selective)	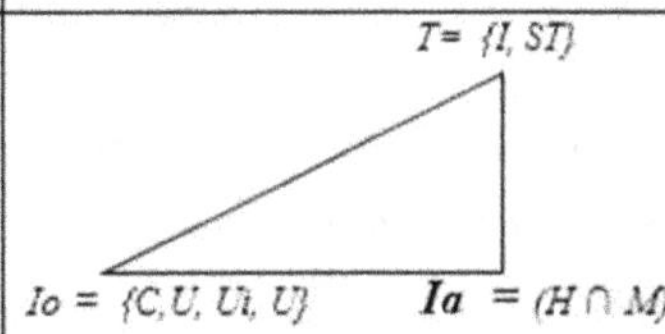
Model 10 (importance selective)	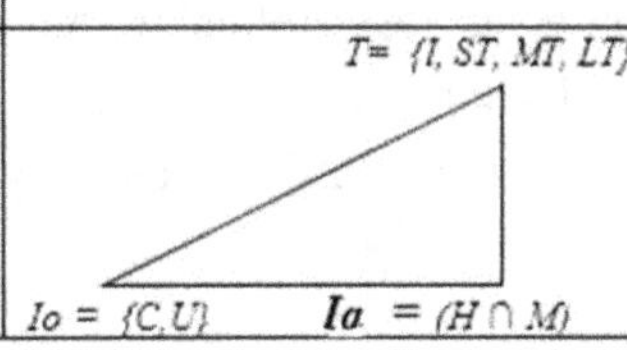

The focus on criteria, as explored on this section uncovers a clear gap in strategy literature related with business environment analysis, as the vast majority of textbooks currently utilization in instruction on business schools and tertiary education programs, neglect a decisive part of the job, i.e. *factor selection*.

Here, it is intended to shed some light on how may a company take rational decision as to selection of what to focus on when analyzing a business environment and ecosystem, since the three (3) criteria here draw are applicable to both the general environment (and macro analysis) and the industry environment (an micro analysis). This was a fundamental aspect, determining the success of any analyzability project, so far, seemingly overlooked by strategy theorists. Most academics accept almost unanimously accept the *Strategic Decision Making Process* (pictured below) but oversimplifying with regard to the strategy formulation, the importance of "scanning" the business environments and auditing the compliance or adaptability of the firm to it (Wheelen and Hunger, 1987).

Figure 6. Dominant paradigm: strategic decision making process
Source: Wheelen and Hunger (1987)

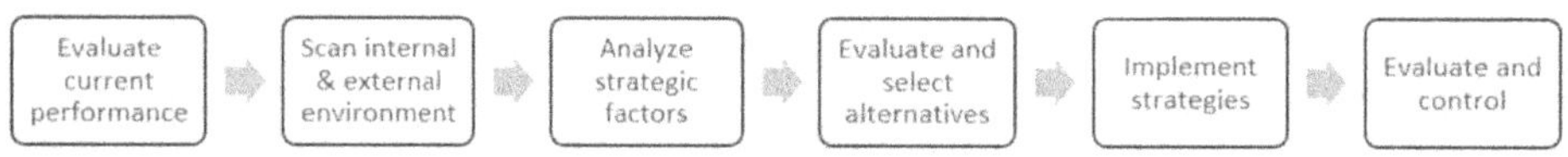

Hence, this dominant reasoning imposed by the resource-based theorists in the last decades, in which, the firm´s resources and capabilities´ (R&Cs) development ought to a high(est) accountability of the firm, have gradually grown into a devaluing of the markets, and subsequently, overlooking market´s conditioning of the strategic action of a firm. On the book "*Contemporary Strategy Analysis*", Robert Grant, which exhibits likewise an application for *Strategic Analysis,* as shown in this figure above, also corroborates such reasoning paying limited attention to (the sloppiness of scholars towards) business environment analysis. In fact, on chapter 4, gathers a collection of studies demonstrating the corroboration of multiple authors as to the limited industry effects on firm´s profitability, using the return on assets (ROA) as the gauge of value (Rumelt, 1991; McGahan and Porter, 1997; Hawawini et al., 2003; Roquebert et al, 1996). Recalling the definition of strategic management process, it is proposed in this book, an alternative perspective towards the strategic management of the firm, giving a rather balanced attention to the both interfaces of strategy with the environment, the *internal interface* (firm-strategy) and the *external interface* (business environment – strategy), so that companies may take wiser strategic decisions in the future. Hence, we advocate the balancing of the industrial-organization (IO) model with the resource-base model.

Strategic Management Process is the full set of commitments, decisions, and actions firms take to achieve strategic competitiveness and earn-above average returns (Hitt, Ireland and Hoskinsson, 2019, p. 6)

For the sake of clarity, let me emphasize that on external interface of strategy, when referred to "business environment", such idea refers to what is outside the firm´s realm (on the detached view) which corresponds to the idea of external business environment on the circumvented view.

The alternative procedure here suggested for recasting the strategic formulation and the strategic controls functions, aims at breaking with the preconception or dogma that EBEs are "something" that may be grasped by a "scan" through the selection of factors (that constitute an opportunity or threat), and the subsequent analysis of those factors is simply a reductive narrative, which may lead to strategic drift in the markets, i.e. rigid organizations unable to cope with change, specially fast paced and/or disruptive one. Firstly, scanning is one of several analysis typologies available, something that is explored on the next section of this chapter. Secondly, factor selection is not a binary decision of whether constitutes an opportunity or a threat. As discussed above, since a rational model of strategic decision-making, entails the adoption of a philosophical position within the continuum of the analyzability paradigms. Furthermore, factor selection, in order to maximize its utility, as to an effective accomplishment of goals and/or effective usage of resources, ought to take into consideration the criteria of analyzability above, from which, the firm may define beforehand, what type of criteria have a better fit to their own interests or research purpose.

The alternative strategic analysis process suggested on the figure above systematizes the external business environment analysis, beginning with a setting of the criteria to circumscribe the type of information required in order to select the segments and factors to focus on, and subsequent to collect data, crunching it, and profiling the EBE plus its interface with the firm.

This alternative *Strategic Analysis & Decision process (SADP)* is centered on the general environment, or the Layer 1, in a circumvented vision of the markets, as described in chapter 4. The layers´ interactionism bring though together the stratified ontology of the universe under analysis (macro and micro) and emphasize the existence of a dual *tier* of projects. One may recall, an organization may decide to conduct not simply a pure project of a market x or an industry Y, but instead, execute a hybrid project, with extended complexity but accounting both tiers. Furthermore, it is worth to mention that both tiers are complementary, and hybrid versions of a BEAPs, may consider the interchangeable use of data within and across tiers and segments.

Figure 7. Alternative strategic analysis & decision process (SADP)
Source: Own elaboration

1. Evaluation of Performance

+

2.1. External Business Environment Analysis	*2.2. Internal Business Environment Analysis*
Criteria setting —→ Segments and Factor's selection → Choice of Analysis type → Data gathering & analysis → BE profiling → Measurement and evaluation of performance	*(Resources & Capabilities, Goals and Vision)*

+

3. Formulation of Strategic Change Options (Set Course of Action)

+

1. Strategy Implementation

+

2. Suitability, Acceptability & Feasibility's (SFA) Evaluation

+

3. After-Action Review

Taken as an example, one segment ("political environment") may shape the national landscape by implementing public policies centered on a particular domain (categorizable as a sub-segment). "Sustainable policies", can be here given as an example, as governments focus their attention on the discussion of particular topics, taken as factors, and propose a bill for further legislation over relevant topics such as pollution, energy consumption, renewable efforts, green production, environmental-friendly products or hydric resources. Those can be analyzed then as separate pieces of data on the sub-segment. The same happens across tiers, since a piece of information may be of great utility for multiple types of analysis, with tier reciprocity being mutually influential/ed, on a downwards and upwards way. In this case, a general factor might be relevant for comprehending the dynamics of the industry competition and structure (e.g. *competition barrier/s imposed to foreign trade*). Such a particular political and legislative combined action (factor) on the general environment has the power to influence the transactional industries which rely on inward/outward trade of goods. Also, a critical factor on the industry, for example the implementation of a best practice (e.g. shifting to a green portfolio of products) from an incumbent (critical factor) may generate a chain reaction of competitors imitation strategies, industry best-practices resolution by professional associations, or even the regulation (general factor) of the production chain by the legislator.

In example above, of general factors influence on the industry, it is clear that national policies regarding entry/competition/exit barriers, may shape the acceptance of foreign goods, limits to inward trade, or quotas to multinational enterprises (MNE) establishment, and contribute for the general political landscape/segment. Yet, at the industry-level, to analyze an essential component of the industry structure (i.e. the entry barriers) this requires the gathering of information from the upper tier (MEEA) competition policies, and its articulation with industry-level barriers (e.g. on licensing; technical standards; capital requirements, collusion or anti-trust) and firm-level or individual competitor´s barriers (e.g. market share; innovation capital; deterrence maneuvering or preemption to resources).

CHANGING EVENTS AND ANALYSIS-RELATED PHASES AND ACTIVITIES

The macro analysis of the external business environment (EBE), mostly focused (as a hybrid project) or totally focused (pure project) on the general environment, shall assume in principle that all projects are different.

On the previous section it is mentioned that markets are dynamics, so an iteration cannot reflect a blind standardized, copying a successful recipe from a previous BEAP (project), as all changes occurred overtime ought to be accounted at present, even though, the philosophical stance toward analyzability is identical, and the goals/objectives are the same and the *locus* is also the same.

Actually, a BEAP might adopt different analytical procedures, as dissimilar typologies of analyzability, using multiple phased of the EBE analysis. One may assert that those *typologies* are complementary (Systemic Thinking), and in that sense, they are *parts* of a BEAP. Opposing to the prior is claim that the goals/objectives which shape the research purpose, have the strength to determine the nature of the BEAP, thus, the choice of the path about to the EBE analysis becomes a teleological argument build on the reason.

Here, such discussion, of whether EBE analysis is better exercised through a *Teleological Thinking* or a *Systemic Thinking* is a problematic here ignored as the book is not centered on the meanders of the philosophies of analysis, being therefore irrelevant in my conception for the apprenticeship of the strategic managerial practices of EBE observation.

Yet, on a simple clarification may be provided, these two philosophies (Teleological and Systemic Thinking) entails two (2) divergent streams of thought. On one side, is the underpinning of one single choice, as a best-fit. As shown in the figure below, the company chooses to either execute a type of project (A; or B; or C, or D). Analysis is considered a chosen "path" for achieving the goals, and envisions the overlapping of types of analysis, as being a choice for complementary analysis, as third projects with to be furthermore conducted with a concurrent nature, which can be pursued or not, and are resource-consuming adding complementary value, but requiring multiple endeavors for reaching the same goals. A line of though mainly holistic. Such corporate thinking, contrasts with the ones advocating towards the conduction of BEAPs by building blocks, i.e. the heuristics, as analysis is instead a "process". Analysis is not a path for the latter ones, but a complex task requiring the implementation of a serial set of sub-activities (parts of the BEAP), in which, a stepwise procedure requires the implementation of different and sequential analytical procedures.

Figure 8. Teleological Vs Systemic Thinking
Source: Own elaboration

Teleological Thinking	Systemic thinking
Type A, or Type B, or Type C, or Type D	Type A *(step 1)* → Type B *(step 2)* → → Type C *(step 3)* → Type D *(step 4)*
(4 separate BEAPs)	(1 single project)

To visualize the fundamental differences of those streams of thought, the figure above represents on the left-hand side the assertion of *autonomy* of the analysis momenta, so independent projects *(= x* number of *BEAPs*), while the box on the right-hand side represents *association*, as phases of a single project (=1 BEAP). Yet, regardless of what one tends to believe, either on the *teleological thinking* (i.e. analysis as path) or on *etapic thinking* (analysis as a process), this section will describe all types or parts of analysis.

Hence, there are five (5) types of BEAPs, or parts of EBE analysis:

- Inspecting
- Scanning
- Monitoring
- Forecasting
- Assessing

The table below shows the main attributions of each type/part of EBE analysis.

Table 2. Types or phases of EBE analysis

Type	Focus	Time	Markets	Job	Actions required
Inspect… Or Update…	Main features and profile	On-Demand Occasional Frequent/For Updateness	All	Map the main factors and grasp the profile Comprehend major national/regional risks/opportunities Explore the nature of those factors, context and historical background and evolution *(research + analysis)*	Set goals and resources (constrain/allocation) Define segments, factors and criteria for the analysis Gather and treat data Transform it into information and strategic intelligence
Scan…	All early signals of environmental change	Occasional (one point in time) Casuistic choice of time (at need/strategic decision)	Medium/ High volatility	Search Data collection Interpretation of meaning *(research + analysis)*	Identify if early signals of environmental change Grasp early patterns and formation of trends
Monitor…	Just on important trends	Occasional (one point in time) Casuistic choice of time (at need/strategic decision)	Medium/ High volatility	Search Data collection Interpretation of meaning Strategic decision (of the events to track) Early-assessment of the impact of trends *(research + analysis)*	Follow the evolution of signals, track changes, and identify most critical trends emerging Identify the most important stakeholders affected by market evolution
Forecast…	Projection of impact (of important trends)	Occasional (one point in time) Dependent on Monitoring	Medium/ High volatility	Scenario Thinking of possible directions on the EBE (Future Thinking) and impact on the firm (Strategic Thinking)	Design the scenario-planning processes and instruments/methods to be used Build Scenarios: *Base Scenarios*; *Normative Scenarios*; Dystopian scenarios; *Critical scenarios* and *Utopian Scenarios* Distinguishing *Trends* from *Fads* Identification of *Wild cards* (events creating discontinuities in the development curve) Evaluate the learning from multiple scenario-making
Assess…	Implications of trends	Occasional (one point in time) Dependent on Forecasting	Medium/ High volatility	Scenario-based appraisal: specify the implications of the understanding of future scenarios (i.e. *Scenario evaluation*)	Comprehend the effects of change Determine the relevance of the implications of those effects for the competitive positioning of a firm Design of options for strategic optimization Understand the complex relationships among *uncertainties*, *objectives* and *strategic options*,

Source: Own elaboration

Environmental *Inspecting* refers to an initial contact with a market, local or foreign/host, for instance, in case of a startup establishment, or as to the need for probing data with for the internationalization of a business. This implies a collection of substantial data from multiple segments, since it is assumed the analyst and/or the company possessed until that stage, a low or null connection with the observed reality, and low knowledge about it, in most cases the reduced extent of knowledge is experiential market knowledge solely. It may explain several moments of observation and extraction of data, hence it is also me be recognized, not solely, as a first data collected from the EBE, but also, their updating on a later stage.

Inspecting one or multiple business environments may than be triggered by intrinsic motivations, managerial intention, desire, hubris, or a real one-off opportunity for partnering with a local player. Hence, the range of analysis possibilities is very wide and is initially recommended to start off with a general and updated reporting scheme as a single reporting solution get first familiarized with. One may encounter low-efficiency/volatility to high, and availability and trustworthiness of the sources to vary in an identical way.

Environmental *Scanning* is an analytical procedure centered on the identification of early signals of change and on the recognition of new forming *trends*. It configures a market research of those newer events, and the subsequent analysis of its shape and direction, being a feature of novelty with a ascending or descending patterning, or reconfiguration or renewal of prior phenomena. It implies the possession of a baseline of market knowledge to determine whatever is different from the world as perceived it before. This type of projects are of great importance in high volatility markets. Consequently, to design of a *scanning system* for a stable environment seems inappropriate, excessive and a resource-waste applicable to an activity with low utility for the future competitiveness of the firm, since the information (factors) analyzed contain incomplete data, ambiguous and far from the firm likely capability to connect it. Here, the notion of *business environment scanning system (BESS)* refers to a set of systematic processes for the spotting of early-stage maneuvers prior the recognition of effective change. Thus, this type of projects occur, as a rule of thumb, not on a programmed basis, but are more sporadic and dispersed in time, since their purpose is to analyze some extent of novelty intruding in the market.

Generally these are projects involving fuzziness and complexity and require in-depth analysis, in which consultants, intend a make sense from data outputs, and anticipate possible scenarios for its dissemination. In this context, the usage of ICT mechanism are powerful, as means of accelerated collection, especially as, information has to be cherry-picked, opening the door for faster and more abundant inputs to be scanned, as potential opportunities/threats.

Actually, any type/part of analysis intends at remove the blurriness and create new knowledge, as a way of eliminating *threats* at the general environment, and creating *opportunities*. The parts collaborate (under a logic of systemic thinking) for reducing VUCA. Here the notion of threat corresponds to a condition (at the business environment) with a negative effect that may deviate or hinder the firm from reaching its goals and/or gaining strategic competitiveness. On the contrary, the opportunity, is a condition (at the business environment) with a positive effect at firm-level. The opportunity may not necessarily impact equally across the organizational ecology. However, the exploring of such condition, on an effective manner, may facilitate the reaching of goals, plus the gaining of strategic competitiveness and open horizons for further strategic actions.

The E*nvironmental Monitoring* is subsequent to the Scanning. One cannot conduct an environmental monitoring project without having gained a strategic awareness as to the existence of newer events constituting a potential threat/opportunity. As an example of a potential treat is delivered in the case-study below.

Definitely the business model of the case-firm (*Coupang*) combining AI-tech constitutes a threat for the giant *Amazon*. The company holds approximately ¼ of this ecommerce market in the country, which is one of the biggest and most competitive e-commerce markets in the world (the sixth largest) with a steady growth and annual revenue of US$80 billion in 2020, placed ahead of France and behind Germany where large players compete, as *NAVER Shopping; eBay Korea; 11st; Wemakeprice*; *TMON*.

From the reading of this case, it may be deduced that an exercise of timely recognition of the early signals of threats and opportunities on the environmental scanning phase is a critical one. *Monitoring* gives then continuity to this work as the firm intends at predict the implication of these (most critical) events, which are already on their way, yet centered on the most hazardous or beneficial ones (e.g. the consolidation of players as *Coupang;* due to its efficient delivery system powered by AI-tech).

In this way, *monitoring* requires the following of the evolution of particular sets of events which are of high relevance, as per se or interacting with others occurrences/events and trends, have the ability to disrupt the environment´s status quo, with underlying effect/s on the firm. Thus, those events are the ones with critical or high importance and high impact corresponding to the BEAPs´ Model 3 or Model 8, as presented in the previous section. The job of analyst/s on those projects is to follow the trail of data, decode it and comprehend their meaning.

However, scanning is based on open-research as to detection of signals and comprehension of their attributes, while the monitoring entails a close-research centered on critical factors. The latter has more clear objectives defined, as to the following of most significant events, and trace the evolution of those phenomena in scope, pace and direction of its diffusion, aiming at generate critical maps as to the converge of potential risks/opportunities into real ones.

Both typologies (Scanning and Monitoring) require, for their effective exercise, an initial identification of the most important stakeholders, their position and reputation, for addressing their needs. Here, the notion of stakeholder encompasses all affected by the performance of the project and firm, whether being internal or external stakeholders, organizational stakeholders, capital market stakeholders (including the firm´s stockholders), or product market stakeholders (e.g. customers, suppliers; competitors).

Moreover, Scanning and Monitoring are intrinsically connected to change. As addressed at the chapter 3 (*3.1 Introduction to Business Environments*), the two type of observable events are the fads and wildcards, with the latter being most significant for the monitoring phase, due to its potential to create long-lasting change with inherent risks and opportunities. In turn, black swans, maintaining its status, means that they were unable to be revealed into something predictable to occur.

Hence, analysis function can be broken down into multiple sub-activities:

- discovery;
- anticipation,
- identification;
- observation;
- analysis;
- conclusion;
- action.

The discovery refers to the uncovering of potential black swans. The anticipation encompasses the ability to imagine and visualize patterns of motion within the business environment and detecting emerging events. Such ability (to picture a new phenomenon) is what distinguishes wild cards from black swans.

Thus, whenever the latter is idealized by a company, loses consequently the unpredictability status and becomes either a wildcard or not depending on its disruptive potential.

The identification may be easily confused with the anticipation. While anticipation entails a future thinking exercise for imagining the future, the identification is a observational exercise of the present, in which the analyst spots an (already) existing fairly new event. The action is the use of market information gained from the exposure to new events, to apply it into future business strategy plans.

The assumptions made about these type of changes are, as follows:

1. The Analyst cannot observe predict them all, nor observe the whole universe

Due to a human bounded rationality, as an individual limitation of the amount of information of that we can mentally process, plus considering furthermore that the whole information is likely not to be available or not totally at our disposal when needed, decisions as to the analytical path over an EBE leading to the planning of a full BEAP, are embedded on what is called *satisficing*. Here, satisficing is decision pattern, in which, the Analyst purposively chooses a course of action most satisfactory under certain circumstances, which is believed to deliver results good enough to achieve the project´s goals (Boddy, 2017).

2. *Black Swans* are events not to be analyzed

This means that, if a Black Swan cannot be predicted, consequently thus cannot be analyzed, being out of the scope of all the type of sub-activities of the analysis function.

3. Once predicted, no longer a Black Swan anymore

Regardless of dimension and impact of a new phenomenon, whenever is idealized by generative instruments or identified on EBEs, then lost the non-cognoscible status, won´t be able to recover it ever again, and its believed randomness disappears, as firms may begin to study its nature, regardless of the likelihood of its occurrence.

4. Wild cards are consequential

Acknowledging an event and categorizing as a wild card, brings an implicit label of seriousness, as the event carries an accentuated degree of motion, shaking the status quo, hence being disruptive, and its elevation to a tier of high seriousness, as their effects are often large and cover multiple quadrants of society, this means that the firm ought to be in a state of alertness and prepared to the analysis of such event along the different phases of analyzability, as described above.

5. *Fads* are good to know, but are not the focus

If you record the description of the five phases of EBE analysis, you remember, that the impact of an event determines the choice of where to place attention on. Fads are short-termed and inconsequent phenomena, leaving no footprints as the expectations or habits, hence, something to be "the" locus of the analyst´s attention.

Consequently, as to the morphology of the most relevant ones (black swans and wild cards) one may claim that each has a triad of morphological attributes:

(i) Black Swans:
1. Unimaginable
2. Unpredictable
3. Impossible to occur

While,

(ii) Wild Cards:
1. Imagined
2. Predictable
3. Likely or Unlikely

The sum of these two types of events, brings us to setting of the sub-phases of the analyzability function, represented in a workflow below:

Figure 9. Analyzability: sub-functions
Source: Own elaboration

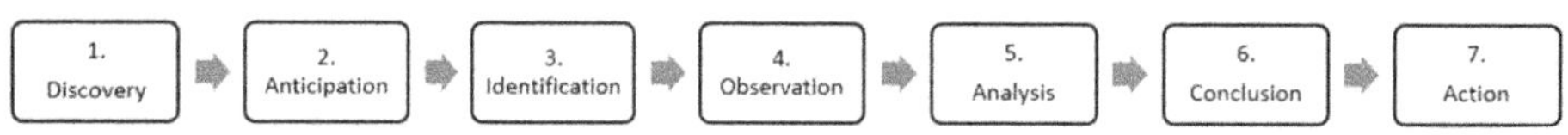

Looking at the activities involved on the analyzability function, it certainly resembles the phases of the scientific method (i.e. ask a question; test hypothesis; exam the results and draw conclusions), but blended with the project management tool of the *PDCA* cycle (Plan-Do-Check-Act), as an extended version of this tool applicable specifically for Business Environment Analysis Projects (BEAP´s).

The Forecasting phase entails an analytic procedure, in which, general focus research questions and market-data are tested. Hence, on the Environmental *Forecasting* phase, consultants assume the role of "pure analysts" cross-manipulating multiple sets of data records collected on an earlier part. The job of the analyst shifts partially then, from a blending of research and analysis, to mostly (or solely) qual and quants data manipulation. From the firm´s records of units of data, the analyst develops projections one might denominate as *scenarios* (Schoemaker, 1993; Bradfield et al. 2005).

Under the assumption of being normative instead of utopic, scenarios are assumed to be feasible, suitable (and likely, acceptable) predictions. Scenarios are outputs of human (re)thinking that exist associated to the domain of strategic planning for over fifty (50) years now, firmly rooted on the military field. Nonetheless, its origins go back to the Old Greece´s time in which, the philosophical though re-thinks the future, as in the case of *Plato* envisioning an ideal (scenario) for a society (a "republic"), constituting an embryonic form of scenario-thinking, as the philosopher conceives a new mental model for a supreme political governance system. These cognitive and simulative exercises, future-oriented, and weighting multiple options, fall under what Bradfield et al. (2005) denominated as the groundwork for *scenario building* and *scenario planning,* nowadays widely utilized in the Strategic Management (SM) domain.

As stated by Lindgren and Bandhold (2009), strategic planning is a powerful tool, thus used for many large organizations, for anticipating and managing change at the business environment level and at industry level. They are therefore the trigger for the formulation of ideas and judgements of value about the upcoming context of the business environment (i.e. *future thinking*) as a mediator of strategic action and innovativeness. Thus, a chain of constructs are leveraged by scenario planning on a serial way or as a chain.

Figure 10. Environmental forecasting
Source: Own elaboration

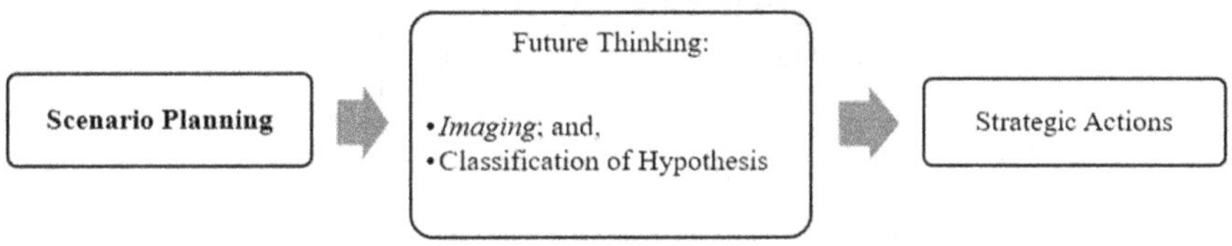

Scenario planning encompasses invariably the generation of ideas to be mapped as the number of future options (imaging), to be accounted as hypothesis, regarding the likelihood of resemblance to the universe on a near or far future. This activity (imaging) is associated with a larger process of *scenario thinking*.

Such options are visualized as possible future hypothesis of how the universe may look like and are assumed to be potentially concurrent scenarios previously idealized (imaging), about the continued evolution (or trend) of the change of a (critical/impactful) event.

For example, in this chapter´s case (Coupang), an early identification of a signal of utilization of AI-tools by a competitor on delivery systems to the consumer, could be considered as an input of information triggered a strategic action. Such strategic action could entail multiple options, such as, to the variable of "time" to predict the extent (of time) that would take to *Coupang Corp.* or other player/competitor to fully implement the business model of a 24h delivery system nationwide, and/or the expected time of dissemination on the consumers´ side, from early to late adopters.

The applicability of scenario planning comprises then the cross-observation of two interconnected dimensions of *scenario thinking* and future planning, both representing the conception of the future (i.e. future *thinking).* A project of Environmental Forecasting may apply a cognitive toolbox for the mental conception and drawing of how the EBE may look like (*Scenario Thinking*), and how the organization may be shaped like (*Strategic Thinking).*

Hence, the formulation of future hypothesis is externally-focused (i.e. *Future Environment Thinking*) while the classification of scenarios is internally-focused on the best interests of the firm (i.e. *Future Strategic Thinking*). The first, comprises the mapping of "dramas" or worse-case-scenarios, multiple futures, different types of uncertainty, actors, systems, kinesis or moves. The latter, the mapping the possibility of existence of visions, life-cycle, resources, jamming/bottlenecking processes, and paradoxes; and consequently, interpret the type of risk inherent to such future options considering the context of the firm. For instance, the multiple futures colliding with the vision or with the organizational moral-ethical system. On section 5.5. *Models of Analyzability* a particular set of Situational Analysis Models are focus on comprehending this fit of the firm to a future scenario.

Scenario thinking comprises building scenarios based on the projections of impact based idealized future outcomes, which implies cross-checking the impact of these future universe dimensions into the organizational sphere, as to: (i) the corporate vision; (ii) resource and capability´s (R&C) ownership; (iii) collusion with strategic goals; (iv) time horizon, pace and life-cycles; and, (v) factor´s control shift. The latter, is also denominated as the to a reflection on "jamming", as a third principle of strategic thinking related to the mapping of what is the radar of control and out of the span of control in that future scenario.

Table 3. Environmental Forecasting: philosophical principles of scenario planning

<table>
<tr><th>Instrument</th><th>Philosophies Principles</th><th>Methodologies</th></tr>
<tr><td rowspan="7">Scenario Thinking</td><td>Principle 1 – Get a toolbox (identification from emergent trends, potential issues</td><td rowspan="14">• media-based methods
• interview-based methods
• timeline-based methods
• generative, intuitive methods
• actor-oriented methods
• consequence-focused methods
• systems methods</td></tr>
<tr><td>Principle 2 – Handle brain with care</td></tr>
<tr><td>Principle 3 – Think in dramas</td></tr>
<tr><td>Principle 4 – Think in futures</td></tr>
<tr><td>Principle 5 – Think in uncertainty</td></tr>
<tr><td>Principle 6 – Think in systems</td></tr>
<tr><td>Principle 7 – Think in actors and moves</td></tr>
<tr><td rowspan="7">Strategic Thinking</td><td>Principle 1 – Think in paradoxes</td></tr>
<tr><td>Principle 2 – Think in visions</td></tr>
<tr><td>Principle 3 – Think in jamming</td></tr>
<tr><td>Principle 4 – Think in time</td></tr>
<tr><td>Principle 5 – Think in resources</td></tr>
<tr><td>Principle 6 – Think in lifecycles</td></tr>
<tr><td>Principle 7 – Think in experiments and bets</td></tr>
</table>

Source: Lindgren and Bandhold (2009)

The categories of methodologies addressed above in the figure encompass a myriad of analytical options.

The Media-Based Methods encompass the utilization of varied assortment of methods, such as *media scanning*; *automated media watch*; *targeted Internet search; netography*; nomination of *trend-tracker groups*; *keyword analysis* as a sub-type of targeted Internet search or *narrative/thematic* or *content analysis*.

Interview-Based Methods might be quite insightful on the collection of qual data, as the *Delphi studies or surveys; opinion pools; long range data; focus groups; executive and/or expert panels; guruing.* Moreover, on time-line based method (e.g. *archetypal development patterns; trend extrapolation through time series analysis; Multivariate analysis and multivariate time series analysis; analogies; Kondratieff´s long wave*, as to long cycle´s prediction; *S-curve analysis*; or *paradigm shifts*).

The generative methods comprehend *brainstorming, intuitive timeline construction*; *headlines and posters; imaging; future history; paradoxes.*

Actor-oriented methods comprise actor analysis/competitor analysis; competitor watch; and, value-chain analysis.

The Consequence-focused Methods entail *issue management* (as a combined method accounting trend watch with actor analysis); *single-impact analysis (SIM)* focused a dominant factor, as the assessment of a certain technological advancement; *consequence tree*; *future event production* (a combination of brainstorming with consequence trees to image multiple events occurring in a chain reaction; or a *probability effects*, as self-judgement of the extent of the predicted effect, often measured in a scale 0-100.

The category of System Methods comprise more pure EBE analysis of *complexity and uncertainty analysis (CUA)*; *cross-impact matrix analysis (CIM); Causal mapping/causal-loop diagrams*; *four-field analysis*; or (complex) *system analysis* and *systems modelling* (Lindgreen and Bandhold, 2009).

Environmental Assessments are then inevitably dependent on the work developed on the Forecasting side and henceforth based on scenario-based appraisal deriving from the earlier part. Its focus is the specification of the implications of change, for the understanding of future scenarios. Thus, this assessment phase comprehends firstly, an observation of effects of change. Secondly, the understanding of the relation of uncertainty (according to factors selected) with strategic goals, in order to infer potential strategic options (i.e. *uncertainty x objectives x options*).

The combination of those three dimensions, uncertainty – objectives – options will dictate the real routes available for a rational decision-making as options for a future redirection of the firm, at a given place and time, thus, for its strategic (re)formulation, under a likely logic of strategic optimization, in which decision are taken under a rational model.

Hence, the assessment of whether trends constitutes a real threat or opportunity is determinant for the competitive implications of the firm, which the strategic reformulation aims at assume a control of. Forecasting is not enough.

Forecasting, despite being likewise a pure analytical exercise aims at open horizons and produce new information and insights while real useful information supporting the decision-makers as to the strategic planning contexts occur in this latter part (Assessment).

In this sense, it may be inferred that the types of Business Environments shows that on the two analysis-centered parts (Environmental Forecasting and Environmental Assessment), the BEAP is subdivided into multiple sub-projects, corresponding each to the analysis of multiple future scenarios (Sc_x) accounting each scenario a set of factors (F_n), possibly varying (Δ) among the simulative exercises of the other scenarios.

$$BEAP(x) = \{Sc_1, Sc_2, Sc_{3,}, Sc_n\}; S(x) = \sum \Delta(F_n)$$

Thus, each sub-project *S(x)* ought to account the derivate of each function ($f'(x) = \ldots$) as to the $F_{n.}$ Here, the measure of the rate of variation, represented as $y = f(x)$,

$$f'(x) = df/dx$$

In which, the function *(f)* in relation to the variable *(x),* equivalent to a factor´s *parameter*, may be accounted on a quadric manner (Dinçer, 2004). Firstly, the variation of a trait, or separate components to the sub-factor/factor. Secondly, the sub-factor to the factor. Thirdly, th the factor (or sub) to the sub-segment (or segment). Finally, the sub-segment to the segment. Recalling the example given in section *4.5. ("Elements of the EBE")* as a national government may take action to introduce further sustainable policies, the analysis of the bill at firm-level, as a new BEAP, could take with varying contours. So, on simple example, let us say the company X define for the BEAP, as a general goal, the "understand of the impact of changes caused by that government´s bill", as unfolded below.

Table 4. Example of an event (environmental) and cascading the EBEA

Segment	Sub-segment	Factor	Sub-factor	Component
POL	Sustainable policies (POL1)	*N* changes brought by new the bill on renewable energies (POL1.F1)	Changes on renewable energy production for industries (POL.F1.SF1)	Fossil dependency or (POL.F1.SF1. C1)
				machine/unit efficiency (POL.F1.SF1. C1)
			Changes on renewable energy production for industries (POL1.F1.SF2)	Subsidization of Installed capacity (POL.F1.SF2. C1)
				Taxation of green-shift asset (POL.F1.SF2. C2)

Source: Own elaboration

Here, in this case the segment corresponds to the political landscape, as the dominant area of research and analysis, the sub-segment to the sub-field of sustainable policies, the factor selected is bill of industries towards renewable energies, and the likely sub-factors could energy consumption, and energy production. The function could descend even to the singular trait (of renewable energy consumption or production, such as, installed capacity or seasonality (energy production); and, fossil dependency or machine/unit efficiency (energy consumption) among other traits, in which, the ratio of variations may account each proposed change in the governmental proposal, as a function to be measured against of the elements of analyzability above.

SOURCES OF DATA

Considering the three initial types or parts of analyzability (Inspecting; Scanning and Monitoring), and regardless of whether the BEAP philosophical position (more or less universalist) a question which imposes itself, at least in frequent in my students is: *Where may I collect data from?*

Naturally, companies utilize a wide variate of materials, as sources of data, to comprehend the general environment (Hitt, Ireland and Hoskinsson, 2019), as follows:

- Public and private-sectored sources
- Official and non-official sources
- Inside the organization (across, subsidiaries, divisions, departments, projects, centers, and teams)
- Using above-the-line and below-the-line sources
- Through applied research content (e.g. journal articles; research books) and/or basic research content (e.g. business publications; technical reports)
- Gathering descriptive, opinion-based sources and media
- Materials available as printed and digital materials (including audio/video podcasts)

- Background exemplifying materials (Critical or typical cases)
- Secondary data, confirmatory/triangulative, ratios and indexes

As the number of available sources is so vast nowadays, we decided to make a short selection of them. However, one shall notice that, the list below comprises solely "sources" as places where you extract you data from. There is also a numerous possibilities as to the choice of market intelligence tools, to support organizations administrating their BE data storage, crunching, manipulation and transformation into strategic information or BI. These tool we address them though on the next section.

A suggestion of sources aims at cover these type of sources (as bullet-pointed above,), reflecting not solely such diversity, but also opening the spectrum of multiple types of data. The sources shown in the table below are an example, of likely the most known, reputed, and commonly used by large organizations.

Table 5. Examples of sources of market data

Data Provider (Type of Institution)	Denomination (Data Provider/Brooker)	Access to (URL)
Private firm (Business Data)	Bloomberg	https://www.bloomberg.com/professional/expertise/data-and-operations/
Private firm (Business ethics and risk data)	BERI (Business Environment and Risk Intelligence)	https://beri.com/
Public Organization (International Organization)	Central Intelligence Agency (the World Factbook)	https://www.cia.gov/the-world-factbook/
Private firm (Market Intelligence)	Dun and Bradstreet	https://www.dnb.com/
Private firm (Market Intelligence)	Euromonitor	https://www.euromonitor.com/
Public Organization (International Organization)	European Central Bank (ECB)	https://www.ecb.europa.eu/stats/html/index.en.html https://sdw.ecb.europa.eu/
Public (Statistical Office)	Eurostat	https://ec.europa.eu/eurostat/data/database
Private (Foundation)	Heritage	https://www.heritage.org/index/explore
Private (Market Intelligence)	IHS Markit	https://ihsmarkit.com/products/global-industry-forecasts-analysis.html
Public (International Organization)	International Monetary Fund (IMF)	https://www.imf.org/en/Data
Public – International Organization	International Trade Centre (ITC)	https://www.intracen.org/itc/market-info-tools/trade-statistics/
Private firm (Marke Intelligence)	Marketline	https://www.marketline.com/
Private firm (Market Intelligence)	Mintel Reports	https://reports.mintel.com/homepages/guest/
Private firm (Market Intelligence)	Mordor Intelligence	https://www.mordorintelligence.com/
Private Firm (Global media and audience data)	Nielsen	https://www.nielsen.com/us/en/

continues on following page

Table 5. Continued

Data Provider (Type of Institution)	Denomination (Data Provider/Brooker)	Access to (URL)
Private Firm (Global media and audience data)	Observatory of Economic Complexity (OEC)	https://atlas.media.mit.edu/en/resources/data/
Public – (International Organization)	Organisation for Economic Co-operation and Development (OECD)	https://data.oecd.org/
Powered by Euromonitor	Passport	https://www.euromonitor.com/our-expertise/passport
Private Firm (Global media and audience data)	Proquest	https://www.proquest.com/products-services/culturegrams.html
Private (Market and consumer data)	Statista	https://www.statista.com/
Private	The Economist - Intelligence Unit	http://www.eiu.com/home.aspx
Public – (International Organization)	United Nations Educational, Scientific and Cultural Organization (UNESCO)	https://en.unesco.org/gem-report/statistics
Public (Statistical Office)	US National Databases	http://stat.unido.org/?_ga=2.202675607.709573973.1518083199-1039022964.1518083199
Public – (International Organization)	World Bank (WB)	https://databank.worldbank.org/data/home.aspx
Public – (International Organization)	World Trade Organization (WTO)	https://www.wto.org/english/res_e/res_e.htm
Public – (International research program)	World Values Survey (WVS)	https://www.worldvaluessurvey.org/WVSContents.jsp

Source: Own elaboration

From the figure above, you can really tell the existence of an infinity of sources to where one may collect data from. My recommendation, especially for BEAPs that are *Environmental Inspections* is to prioritize the options of full reporting. Since the market knowledge of a focal country/region is likely limited, their requirements of data are high and time-consuming, in order to gather it and transform into BI. So quicker is the "full service" where profiling is already delivered in a plate to the analyst.

Marketline is one of those cases, the company offers detailed market reports at different tiers, as complete profiles developed at country, industry, regional/city and company-levels, including case-studies. Relevant for the pure EBEs analysis circumscribed to general environment tier are their "*PESTLE country analysis report*" something to elaborate on section *5.5. ("Models of Analyzability")*, as *Marketline* applies one of those models (i.e. PESTLE).

Statista is also a great resource at your disposal, with an assortment of statistics, reports, outlooks, infographics and special services for companies, as *customized research and analysis projects*. Here, these consultancy on projects (BEAPs) are circumscribed to the Inspection, Scanning and Monitoring, as the type of projects involve a higher component of market research and data than pure in-house analysis. When looking for a complete report for a quick profiling, they have two types, "*Country Reports*" and "*Politics and Society Reports*". Moreover, one may find also industry-level or company-specific reports, and others such as, digital, consumer, trends and brand reports. Quite interesting, especially for micro and small companies, might be one of their tools, the "*Business Plan Export*", which allows the modelling of a business plan, on a business-to-consumer (B2C) perspective towards the digital and consumer markets.

Useful is also the *IHS Markit* national risk assessments. In fact, *IHS Markit* is more than that, since they are broad data providers allowing you to compare several sorts of data benchmarks (e.g. size, risk, or rank) and furthermore collect a infinity of industry data on industry and company performance, demand drives and growth opportunities and so forth, having a breadth of intervention on three areas of business: *economics, engineering* and *sustainability* intelligence data.

The Heritage Foundation makes available country-level data, particularly useful, among other tools, for its Index of Economic Freedom, which accounts four dimensions of market evaluation: *Rule of law; Government size; Regulatory Efficiency*; and, *Open Markets*. From those dimensions you may extract comparative design, as to the current *index* plus the *trend* (upward, downward or stabilized). These dimensions evaluate the performance on *Property Rights*; *Judicial Effectiveness* and *Government Integrity* (on the dimension Rule of Law); plus *Tax Burden; Government Spending*; and *Fiscal Health* (on Government Size), and the *Trade Freedom; Investment Freedom* and *Financial Freedom* of the market (on the Open Markets dimension). The search for data is free and it also allows you to create your own comparison chart between nations.

The Observatory of Economic Complexity (OEC) offers also country reports (such as Heritage and others market commercial and business data providers). Interesting on OEC above all, are the two rankings, the Economic Complexity Index (ECI) and the Product Complexity Index, which measure the knowledge intensity of a country or a product. Here, an option for Economic Complexity Legacy Indexes (ECLI) and the Product Complexity Legacy Indexes (PCLI) provides also specific ECI and PCI values, which are estimated directly from matrices summarizing the geography of economic activity. They utilize a statistical law (the Principle of Relatedness) for the calculation of *relatedness*, as a measure of similarity and compatibility between an economy and an activity. Also their visual tools on country data offer greats representation of trade fluxes (exports and imports). Simple to picture it, especially when using tree maps, or stacked graphs. Some data may be downloaded and moreover get access to a Premium account which requires a membership. This grant you access to additional tools as the Trend Explorer, full Bulk Downloads, Data Explorer and Regional Profiles.

The *International Trade Centre (ITC)*, as a development agency founded by the joint effort of the United Nations (UN) with the World Trade Organization (WTO) has a mission of of supporting of SME´s internationalization. Thus, ITC provides market access information and analysis tools with trade statistics on industry trading for export development. Among other tools, they have developed the *trade map*, with a free utilization (until a 2-digit level) covering 220 countries and over 5300 product categories. The trade map compiles stats on the domains of, alternative markets, export performance, international demand and the role of competitors. At tariff-line level monthly and quarterly trade data is also available.

OECD makes available a wide variety of hasty data insights using data visualizations tools. One may access also to a large data warehouse *(OECD.Stat)*, run queries, download or contrive data. One may also stay updated through their statistical newsletters. Here, data insights are country specific though allowing comparisons and trend lines. You might plot on twelve (12) domains of interest (or societal segments): *Agriculture; Development; Economy; Education; Energy; Environment; Finance; Government; Health; Innovation and Technology; Jobs*; and *Society*. Here, different stats can be juggled over sixty (60) different factors, such as, *household accounts; prices*; and, *productivity* (on the segment *Economy*);

educational attainment; international student assessment (PISA); or *youth and labour market* (on the segment *Education*); monetary aggregates; interest rates; and, conversion rates (or on the segment *Finance*).

Another fantastic tools for exploring data on the demographic segment is *Proquest Culturegrams*. They provide a rich and powerful database with national information sub-divided by region/province and factor categories as *people*; *customs and courtesies*; and, *lifestyle*. So, more general demographic data, may be found under the ribbon people, with data on factors as, *population; language; religion; general attributes;* or *personal appearance*. Other specific data encompass, *greetings; gestures; visiting* and *eating* related data, regarding the customs. Also, data about *family; housing; dating; marriage; diet; recreation; and art*, as a part of lifestyle data.

Complementary to the Proquest Culturegrams, The *World Values Survey (WVS)* provides a more scientific and broad perspective of demographic and socio-cultural aspects. The WWS is a scientific program and an international network of social research, developing critical insights on human behaviour worldwide, inclusively used by governments and media. They run cross-national surveys with a broad thematic scope covering fields, such as, Sociology, Political Science, International Relations, Economics, Public Health, Demography, Anthropology, or Social Psychology. Here, data addresses three types of factors: *values, beliefs* and *norms*, allowing EBE, to answer questions (related to the goals of your BEAP) on problematics as *economic development, democratization, religion, gender equality*, or *social capital*.

However, the above discussion at a glance of the potential utility of these sources, combining multiple attributes for the analyst´s utilization (e.g. key insights, data visualizations, trends, outlooks, reports, infographics, databases; surveys and so forth) is just a quick overview of the potential of analyzability, in terms of of the breadth and depth of data available out there.

The purpose of bringing those sources was to familiarize the most incautious with existence of multiple sources, in which a huge diversity of tools/instruments and with dissimilar types of data. Perhaps, one may explore them in good time either on the need or the willingness to know more about them.

BE INTELLIGENCE TOOLS

Market intelligence tools are essentially intelligence applications, in which, the business intelligence (BI) software is a significant part of. Instead, of great repositories of data with semi-sophisticated applications as we had in the past, ICT allowed with the advent of Internet, and most especially with the web 2.0, interoperability and democratization of the logic of user-generated content. A second economy emerged along the business digitalization path, as business moved increasingly to web-based channels and competition shifted considerably in many industries to an online environment with competition becoming digital.

Hence, data become crucial element of information, empowering digital players with digital assets. In this context data analytics also became a seminal instrument at the firm´s disposal for administering digital assets. BI software became also a tool useful for web discovery; web analytics; connectivity/automatization of processes; and, consumer and competitor´s prediction.

In this section, attention is given, not to the comprehension of the usage of those systems in BE analyzability, hence I will refrain from elaborating here more on this issue, as chapter 6 "*Systems Analyzability, Analytics and Empowering Business Intelligence (BI)*" is dedicated to it.

The reason for bringing a section of BI tools is, on the sequence of the section of sources of data (in previous section) for EBE analysis, for complementing it with relevant applications which enable the firm through their administration and transformation into resourceful bundles of informational assets, for taking future valuable strategic decisions and achieve high returns. Undoubtedly, computer-assisted data analysis is simpler, faster and accounts a myriad of possibilities which manually we could not take advantage of.

I remember, a few years ago, a postgraduate student with over 200 documents in hands to manipulate intended to analyze them manually. Of course, I could foresee him struggling to complete the tasks with such an overwhelming amount of data to cope with. The reality is, one simple analytical task, as for example, to generate a *word cloud* or a *word crunch* map from qual raw data, takes only a fraction of a second for the computer to run the query, to be processed internally, and generate the data output of a word cloud using a typical computer-assisted qual data analysis (CAQDA) software. To the student the task to be handled manually would take weeks (perhaps, months) to get completed. Moreover, the software surely delivers error-free results, while the likelihood of a researcher error is substantially higher.

Hence, on this section I will draw a few notes, and share a few ideas on market BI software. So, the utility of those tools is to support (not solely the storage) but the sense-making of the data accumulated data over time. Companies have nowadays two (2) types of options as to those applications: (i) *Full-Stack Business Intelligence Tools*; and, (ii) Data *Visualization Tools*. The first (full-stack BI tools) have advantage to ensure consistency of format across the firm, as operational reports are build, typically to the front-line staff, with an identical structure, facilitating its alignment and comprehension. The second category of BI tools (data visualization) replaced the traditional rows and columns table presentations with dominantly graphical pictures and charts, ideal for early-stage analysis (e.g. heatmaps; or scatter plots).

The BI tools come with advantages such, application platform interface (API), mobile capabilities, data discovery, or standard and ad-hoc reports. A list of the most common and satisfactory tools, according to the *trScore* (measuring research frequency by prospective buyers) is delivered by *TrustRadius* and presented below.

Table 6. Intelligence tools: examples

Tool	Type	*trScore*[1]
SAP Analytics Cloud	Visualization	8,5
Google Data Studio	Visualization	8,4
Tableau Desktop	Visualization	8,4
Microsoft Power BI	Visualization	8,4
Google Charts	Visualization	8,4
TIBCO Spotfire	Visualization	8,3
Sisense	Full-stack	8,2
Board	Full-stack	8,0
IBM Cognos Analytics	Full-stack	7,9
Dundas BI	Full-stack	7,5
MicroStrategy Analytics	Full-stack	7,5

Source: Trust Radius (online)

Using those BI tools the company may combine its utilization with other tools, from other interdisciplinary domains, such as, *web analytics; search engine optimization (SEO); sales enablement software; customer relationship management (CRM),* or *Enterprise resource planning (ERP),* since one of the capabilities of these BI tools is precisely interface (API). For instance, on Web analytics tools, the ones with highest rate of satisfaction on *trScore* are *Chartbeat* (9,2)*, Parse.ly* (8,8); *Google Analytics* (8,7); *Google Analytics 360* (8,6) and *Adobe Analytics* (8,3); while on sales enablement software are, *Bloomfire* (9,4), *Lead 411* (9,4), *Gong.io* (9,2), *Chorus.ai* (8,8) and *Drift* (8.0) (Trust Radius, online).

Another relevant type of tools is competitive analysis, which may be sub-categorized as a part of web discovery/analytics. Those tools are then specialized on tracking in web, analyzing, and learning from their competitors' strategies and strengths and weaknesses to outsmart them. Thus, competitor analysis tools trace numerous types of factors as prices, earnings, culture, customer practices, brands, technology, or distribution, through the discovery of dispersed data and crunching of it (i.e. *digital footprints*) of their peers. This data from competitive hints (e.g. toolbar data; panel data; ISP network data; benchmarks from vendors; self-reported data) or even from *data fumes,* the latter generated by other parties, which were left online for the company´s benefit as a (positive) externality. Some of the most popular ones are *Quick Search; Wappalyzer; BuiltWith; WooRank; Google AdWords Keyword Planner; SEMrush; SpyFu; Owletter; SimilarWeb; or Followewonk* (Talkwalker, online). Here, I shall draw the reader´s attention to the problematic of using *data fumes*, with regard to big data analytics, as indirect records generated from original data records, from which they were deduced from. Some researchers on the field of information systems warn for the likelihood of bias, high risk of error, hence the fallibility of the results which may be obtained when such data units are incorporated on BEAPs (Thatcher, 2014).

MODELS OF ANALIZABILITY

Surely, for every single BEAP an analyst may consider to create its own model (of analyzability) applicable to the particular context and in conformity to the specifics of the project´s nature and goals. However, the array of existing models for supporting the analysis function, on data searches and manipulation offers immense possibilities and may facilitate the work. Hence, this section is an essential component for facilitating the EBEA.

Regardless, of the philosophical assumptions followed and/or willingness to set your own model of analyzability, here you have contact with different solutions for dissipating the likely fuzziness one may encounter on a BEAP. These tools travel all the way down through the projects´ phases, from design until an after action review, and aim at support the analyst in multiple tasks, such as, planning the phases (of the project); setting goals; selecting the dimensions of analysis (segments, factors and criteria), prioritize by criteria; collecting data; or even, report the results.

The Affect Infusion Model (AIM)

A study on human aspirations conducted on Tesco´s employees in UK, by Lynda Gratton, has shown that individual behaviour is shaped by contextual *immediate* and *wider elements*, as the job, organization and environment. In this context, the experiment of Forgas and George (2001) on social psychology supported the prior, postulating that the particular ability of an individual to process information and make wise judgements is also influenced by the interplaying *features* of the (internal/external) environment, *the target features, judge features and situation features*.

One may ask at this stage,

Why to start this section (on models of analyzability) by presenting this model (AIM)?

Or, what may I learn from the social psychology domain which may be useful for analyzing a business environment?

It is crucial before immersing to other more hand-on models, to have a clear idea on how the context affects our perception of the reality. Here, the issue is, the analyst is a part of the context. He/She is not a part of the *locus* of analysis (the external environment); however, is a part of that contextual scheme of analyzability. So, *what distinguishes the environment from the context?*

The environment identifies object to be analyzed (as the "what"…), while the context answers to the way the task of analysis is being performed (as the how…). Thus, the AIM model is quite insightful, as being aware of the context influence on information processing, judgements and decision-making, then the analyst may take it into account for taking more wise decisions, striving to follow the *rational model* of strategic decision-making.

Forgas and George´s (2001) *Affect Infusion Model (AIM)* elucidates on the pervasive influence of the affective stats or moods of a person and how it influences the individual capacity to process and discern information and make judgments.

The model offers four (4) perspectives on how decision-makers make social judgments and subsequently take decisions. One may recall that on chapter 4 (section 4.5. *Elements of analyzability*) is identified four main strategic decisional outputs (*rational; administrative; political* and *garbage-can*), as the level of internal uncertainty (*agreement*) surrounding the decision-makers level of conflictuality on the theme, interplays with the external uncertainty (of the business environment) on the outcome of such decision.

Although it was not explored the context of decision-making, and here Forgas and George´s AIM model asserts that decisions are taken accounting the association of three (3) components: the goal (or the *judgmental target*); the context (or *judgmental situation*) and the perception of the decision-maker (or *judge*).

The interplay of the *target features* (i.e. *complexity; familiarity*; and, *typicality*); plus the *judge features* (i.e. *personal relevance* for the decision; *motivational goals*; *affective state*; and, *cognitive capacity*) and the *situational features* (i.e. further *need for accuracy*; *availability of criteria* of information; and *social desirability*) will dictate an output of low or high infusion strategies taken to decide. The low infusion strategies are reconstructive approaches of the EBE context, either through a conventional search and stereotyping which narrows the scope and limiting the possibilities of informational gains, or due to the judge´s own limitations as due to a cognitive inability to take the search task and/or due to a temporary emotional condition inhibiting to perform at the desirable minimum standard. The first corresponds to the *direct access strategy* and the second to motivated *process strategy* for judging organizational issues and taking further decisions.

The higher infusion strategies, reveal, as to the *heuristic processing strategy,* a partial/open search for information, in which the affect seems to be information, and there is an ability to "connect the" dots as to the needs. Data is collected in a heuristic manner, even mechanized and with no intention to serve as its best, or uplift, the quality of the decisional outcome. On the other hand, on the *substantive process-*

ing strategy, the analyst conducts a full (open) search, as to the context of a BEAP, in connection to the objectives to be set or to their accomplishment, with lower affective bias and lower cognitive inabilities.

Figure 11. Affect infusion model (information processing and strategic decision making)
Source: Forgas and George (2001)

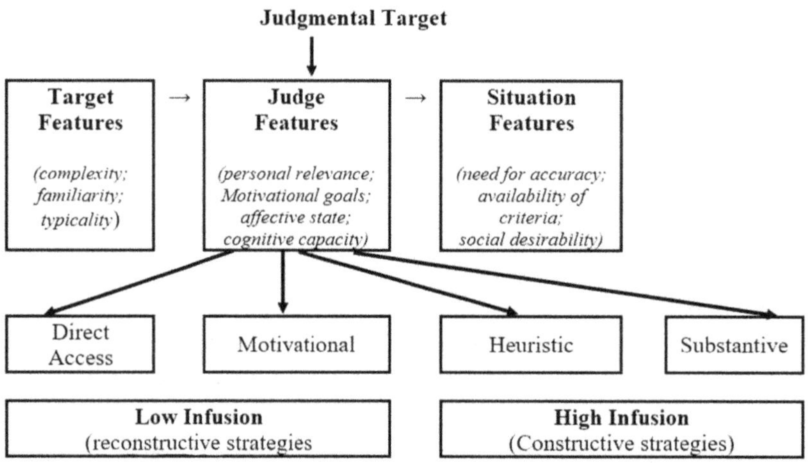

Hence, needless is to say that *contexts* are the fog surrounding the information processing, which in turn blurring our judgments. Unsurprisingly, under atypical and stressful circumstances the context may bias furthermore the perception of the *situation features* above presented. For instance, the processing of any message who´s been yelled at which could well be a reality faced by colleague or a manager; or the processing of information by whom suffered a recent loss of a family member have, in both cases, certainly consequences on the ability to comprehend the message or data, likely twisting them. Hence, these examples point towards motivational processing strategies, or short cut judgments through direct access strategies, as temporary inability, or even trauma, resulting into deviate understandings of the reality; and moreover, to deviating modes of (impatient) collection or screening of data, tendency to stereotype or subscribe to first-impressions or earlier judgments, as a *halo effect* or *contrast effect*.

Such contexts, just tops up on the fact that a part of the individual behaviour at work is routinized, based on prior experiences, habits, precedent and unconscious scripts, as not all tasks are so satisfactory, enthusiastic or require the same amount of criticality or imaginative activity. This models just shows that the individual´s ability to process data may vary emotionally-wise, altering perceptions, feelings, opinions, judgments, choices, commitments, and the timing for the performance of a task.

This model was brought here initially to make an analyst more aware of the state of mind´s influence of its ability to balance emotions and reasons and take rational decisions. Easily, a bad mood may compromise a task, such as, setting goals in a project management office´s (PMO) meeting, and alter a decisional model, instead into a garbage-can or a political model.

GROW Model (or, Sir John Whitmore Model)

On section 2.3. *Strategic Planning and Strategy Controlling* was discussed the different types of goals (e.g. directional vs. specific; stated vs. owned) and disclosed as to the challenging of setting the right goals for the project, the idea of SMART goals.

In this regard, I was bringing here as a first model, *Sir John Whitmore Model* (also known as the *GROW model*) as an useful check point to assist the analyst determining the best goals for a project and isolating the non-complying or most doubtful ones for further discussion with the managers.

Table 7. Goals setting: Grow Model or Sir John Whitmore Model

Goal	Reality	Options	Will
(for succeeding)	(adversity- barriers against goals)	(breakthrough insights)	(actions and timeframe)
What do I want	*Where are you now?*	*What could you do?*	*What will you do?*

Source: Performance Consultants (2021)

An initial idea to take from the above is that is designed to be self-coaching model, to support the design and execution of a project from A to Z. The analyst is invited to think critically what does his/her company want to accomplish with the project, and what are the obstacles in the reality for its accomplishing. Thus, suggests an exercise of reflection of:

(i) Gap between current reality and envisioned reality
(ii) (Formal) barriers or (informal/indirect) obstacles to the goal´s attainment

Furthermore, on the "options" phase, it is suggested to determine beforehand and on daily basis the options or routes to be followed, self-questioning on a daily basis its effectiveness and likelihood to be improved by more imaginative and adequate solutions. The author is appealing here clearly to the utilization of *generative environmental forecasting (or intuitive forecasting)*, prior the beginning of the project, as a preparatory work of setting activities and accountabilities to be conducted during the project, using likely tools as brainstorming or intuitive timeline construction for:

(iii) Mapping of activities and accountabilities of the project
(iv) the identification of the actions.

This implies also an on-going accompanying of the activities (research+ analysis) and results for constant self-evaluation. The "will" phase refers to the measurement of actions, as a controlling process, as to the accomplishment on time of those actions and further reporting. The GROW may be used as a holistic tool, reminding the analyst of the phases and tasks to be taken, to stay sharp on its control.

However, I would like to emphasize from the model, the aspect of checking a goal is likely well drawn or not. Here this model, suggests the observation of a check list of features, corresponding to three mnemonics:

4. SMART (**S**pecific; **M**easurable; **A**ttainable; **R**ealistic; **T**ime-phased)
5. PURE (**P**ositively stated; **U**nderstood; **R**elevant; **E**thical)
6. CLEAR (**C**hallenging; **L**egal; **E**nvironmentally sound; **A**greed; **R**ecorded)

Checking cumulatively those features will tell the analyst whether may be well drawn or not. For instance, as to the compliance with the law and the business ethical practices in the country/industry; or even if the goal is relevant for the company (vision; business goals) and if its design is sound and challenging for the company and whom is involved in the project. Moreover, communicate them to the consultants/analysts participating in the project is essential, such as their acceptance, of tasks and responsibilities, written down to docs to be archived and used as elements confirming the existing accountabilities.

I would recommend though a tool for the self-organization, as to the checking of goals´ (g_n) resilience, for the definition of what the author calls "the right goal". A check list of goal´s pre-assessment was drawn for that purpose.

Figure 12. GROW model: the right goal (check list)
Source: Own elaboration

1. Goal´s setting												
	Goals	Description										
	Goal 1 (G1)											
	Goal 2 (G2)											
	Goal 3 (G3)											
	…											
	…											
1. Goal´s Pre-assessment												
		G1	G2	G3	G4	G5	G6	G7	G8	G9	G10	Notes
SMART	Specific											
	Measurable											
	Attainable											
	Realistic											
	Time-phased											
PURE	Positively-stated											
	Understood											
	Relevant											
	Ethical											
CLEAR	Challenging											
	Legal											
	Environmentally-sound											
	Agreed											
	Recorded											
Sub-Total (of deficiencies): *sum of crosses (X) per goal*												

As Krogerus and Tschäppeler (2017, p. 22) recommend, *keep it simple, stupid!* (KISS). As clear is the goal written down, easier is it to pre-assess it on these 14 components, in which, this check-list document above may be of great utility, articulated with some appended "notes" justifying the rating of each component per goal.

The Eisenhower Matrix

Another useful model, as to the design stage of the BEAP, is the *Eisenhower Matrix.* This is a decision making model for assisting one making effective decisions. It is applicable to BEAPs either if *importance* or *impact* are the dominant variable. Thus, the model supports the design of goals across the continuum of paradigms, from the philosophical stance of Universalism to Relativism), accepting then market-centric and firm-centered approaches (as addressed on section 5.1. *Criteria setting and factor´s selection*). In fact, the model is useful for filtering what to analyze and what not to focus on, as it offers a perspective on how to rank your factor´s selection.

Indeed, the *Eisenhower Matrix* is a supporting tools for compartmentalize ideas/perceptions and establish priorities. The models defines two (2) axis, *importance* and *urgency*, as two other criteria already defined above for factor selection of what to analyze, according to the goals of the project.

Figure 13. Eisenhower matrix (EM)
Source: Krogerus and Tschäppeler (2017)

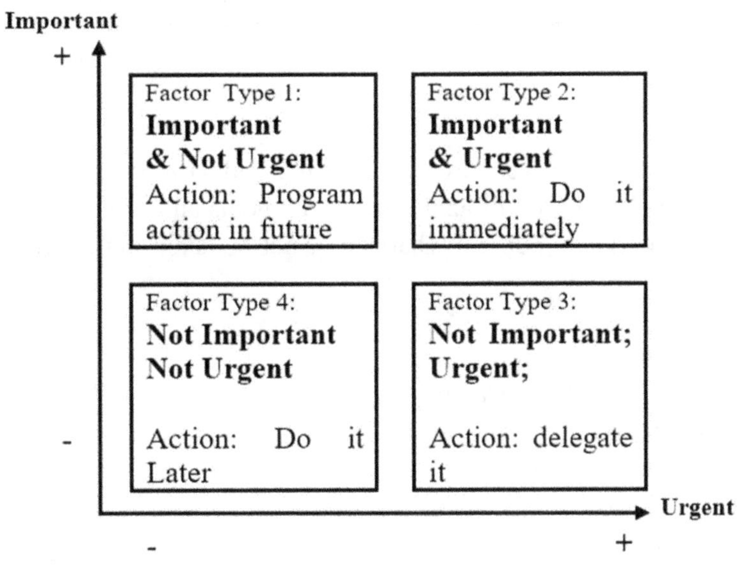

In case, a project is a market-centric, with the domain criterion of analysis being *importance,* in which, the impact on a firm or group of firm is less relevant to establish, the "urgent" factors are the ones associated in criteria time horizon. However, David Cotton´s time horizon criterion is associated to duration of the effect (instantaneous, short, medium or long effects), while Eisenhower´s matrix refers to timely necessity to focus on such factors. In this sense, all 24 models of analyzability drawn on section 5.1 focused on critical and important factors may be applied to the context of urgency/non-urgency. Nevertheless, this model is quite interesting in defining which factors to choose, as it prioritizes the urgency of their collection. In this sense, regardless of the importance model 1 to 24 to adopt, the ranking of the factors by adopting this matrix for their distinction, may facilitate the decision-making as to what factors to incorporate and not. The same with the decisions.

Figure 14. Using Eisenhower matrix: rank goals and/or factors
Source: Own elaboration

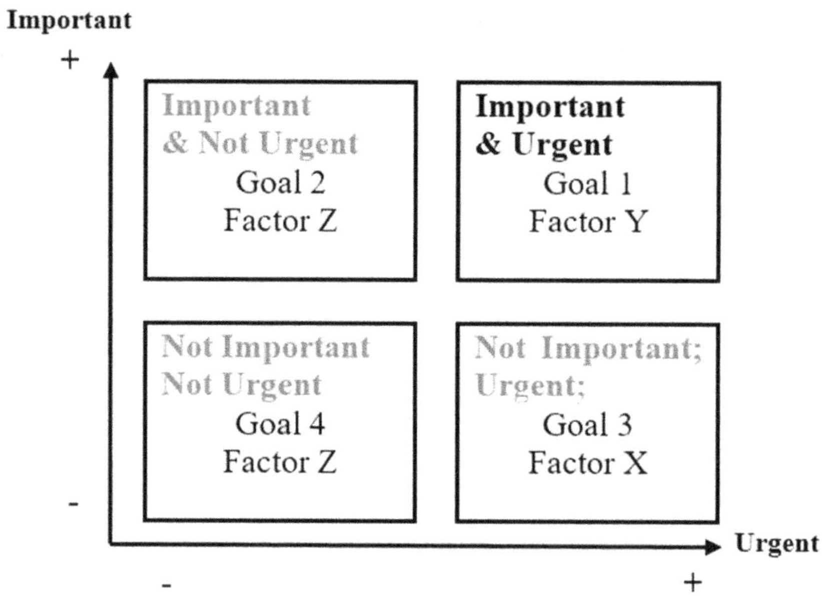

Looking at the figure above whenever the company is focused on applying an Universalist philosophy, with importance as dominant criterion of analysis, to rank goals and/or factor on a logic order, prioritizing them, as based on the ranking define what can or not be taken in the project. A typical ranking would be, as follows:

1st - Factor Type 2: Important and Urgent
2nd - Factor Type 1: Important and Not Urgent
3rd - Factor Type 3: Not Important and Urgent
4th – Factor 4: Not Important and Not Urgent

Naturally, the BEAPs may prioritize importance and urgency, as something relevant to the profiling of the EBEs and which data is required there from. This is the case of goals which require compliance to *wild cards* occurring at the EBE. These type of environmental changes are disruptive in nature forcing the mandatory adherence to, normally coming with a deadline to be taken. Wild cards are therefore considered to be influential drivers of change and are normally associated with events on policy or regulatory affairs. These drivers of change have so an inner capacity to trigger further changes inside of the firm, as they force managers to take corporate actions and further investments (More, et al., 2015).

Thus, this is the case in the European Union of the new General Data Protection Regulation (GDPR). This new law, which came to force in May-2018, imposed new directives to be obeyed by European firms as to the information provided to online services as to the storage of data of personal users.

Nonetheless, the typology of the project requirements (goals) may take the analysts to prioritize/rank goals differently, and subsequently the type of factor to be used. You may note, this model offers simply a referential framework for the setting of goals and choosing factors.

One may also ask about the impact criterion. This matrix does not account impact, as it cross-observed only two variables, and plots them in x and y axes. Nevertheless, it is recommend here, as to the vertical line of the model´s diagram, corresponding to the y-axis (importance) to replace it by the impact criterion, as your dominant one for analyzability. The results you will get are alike:

1st - Factor Type 2: Impactful and Urgent
2nd - Factor Type 1: Impactful and Not Urgent
3rd - Factor Type 3: Not Impactful and Urgent
4th – Factor 4: Impactful and Not Urgent

In this way, if a BEAP is considering to, let´s say, scan environmental changes with high impact, the analyst would naturally exclude the 3rd and 4th options. Moreover, whether to focus again on urgent decision/goals or not depends solely on the typology of the project and goal´s set for it.

The PEST Framework (and Variations)

A seminal type of models of analyzability are the *situational analysis* ones. The PEST fits into this category and their utility is to provide an overview of *locus* for the better comprehension of the universe under analysis (or getting a "better picture" of it). Thus, they are also termed as a sense-*making technique.*

The earliest reference to this model (PEST) is traced five decades ago, as the first utilization is linked to Francis J. Aguilar´s (1967) book "*Scanning the business environment*"). This book suggested a systematized way of observing the outer reality surrounding a firm, in order to understand the overall picture of how their reality is like, and moreover to comprehend their contained attributes (designated above as "factors") which may constitute a threatening or hazardous event entailing risk for the firm, or on the other hand, its condition may be a favorable one, possibly being materializable as a potential new competitive advantage or a new business opportunity.

Aguilar (1967) claimed the importance of identifying the key external factors that may affect the organization, or its future strategy and/or its operations/projects. The author suggested the mapping of those factors within four (4) major domains, as sub-parts of the external business environment, which we also labeled on the previous chapter as *segments*. The segments suggested were:

- Political: (observation of the situation of the) *governmental influence*
- Economic: (observation of the situation of the) *economic conditions and global scenarios*
- Social: (observation of the situation of) *demographics and cultural traits*
- Technological: (observation of the situation of) the *impacting technology on competition*

The origin version of this framework comes naturally from the combination of the first letters of the four segments. These segments, were as a matter of fact, already used in section 4.5. (*Elements of analyzability*) when presenting Yüksel´s (2012) suggestion of *sub-segmentation* of the EBE.

Aguilar´s analysis of the *political segment* aimed at cover the factors related to the governmental influence in society. For the *economic segment* aimed at determine the main economic conditions at a certain moment in time and place, and the macroeconomic scenarios of the global economy which might affect the company in the future. On the *social segment* the attention is placed on the examination of factors for gaining insightful data on the social profiling of companies and citizens, population and demographics´ tipification, gathering of habits and cultural traits and trends. As to the technological segment information the focus is on the examination of data which may affect favorably or negatively a market.

Below is suggested an extended version from the original framework (PEST) with 64 suggestions of factors for one selection.

Table 8. Potential factors for EBEA

P segment	E segment	S segment	T segment
Conflicts	Annual growth rate	Advertising means and media	Automation level and automotive capacity (techniques, processes, soft/hardware
Foreign investment policies	Business establishment (and administration) costs	Brand and product preferences	Computer calculation power/ speed
Foreign Pressures	CPI[2]	Buying access and consumer patterns	Cybersecurity (skills, systems and intel)
Government´s rotation and stability	Currency fluctuation	Digitalization payment methods	Greening technologies and eco/ environment-friendly products
Government leadership	Disposable income	Demographics	Internet connectivity, coverage
(adherence to) International Conventions/ Agreements/Policies	Foreign exchange rate	Education level, PISA results and University world rankings	NPD[3] and product innovations¸ and strategic/business and process innovations
Labour and employment policies	GDP and GNP[4]	Ethics, moral, and business relations and etiquette issues	Microchipping advancements
Local administration and decentralization policies (including over insular regions/ islands and off-shores)	General taxation to privates and companies	Ethnicity/ies	Patents and Licensing
Lobbying	Local/Foreign economic trends	Historical background	Research and development expenditure
Membership/affiliation to International Organizations	Inflation rate	Lifestyle	Restrictions to tech implementation (policies/laws)
Monetary policies	Interest rates	Health	Robotization and IoT
Political system	Personal Business savings rate	Mother tongue and attitude/ proficiency on foreign languages	Security in cryptography
Political Parties	Public debt (central/local administration)	Religion/s (dominant/ minorities)	Societal digitalization of public process
Regional relations and cooperation with neighbor countries	Taxation changes	Roles models in society	Trending technological advancements
Regulatory bodies and agencies	Trade deficits or surplus	Safety/security, delinquency and criminality issues (physical/ digital)	Technological development
Territorial boundaries and administrative organization of land/air/water		Sentiment on local, ecological and handicraft products	Three D (3D) technologies
Trading policies	Trade tariffs	Socio-cultural main values	Utilization level of social media and online shopping
Taxation policies	Unemployment level	Minorities and Women in workforce and senior management	Wireless charging

Source: Own elaboration

Despite, the PEST upsurge in the subsequent decades of its original conception, this framework evolved to multiple variations, as descendent frameworks, in which, different authors have decided to modify the 4 original segments, according to their perception of what is critical information, either merging two or segments into one single segment (e.g. administrative; legal and political landscapes); or withholding segments and thus disregarding the utility of the information about a particular set of data, suggesting alternative models of EBEA which included, excluded or blended segments, as follows:

- DEEPLIST: Demographic, Economic, Ecological, Political, Legal, Informational, Social and Technological
- ETPS: Economic, Technical, Political, and Social
- *PESTLE or PESTEL:* Political, Economic, Sociological, Technological, Legal and Environmental
- *PESTLIED:* Political, Economic, Socio-Cultural, Technological, Legal, International, Environmental, Demographic
- EPISTELS: Environment, Political, Informative, Social, Technological, Economic, Legal and Spiritual
- PESTILE – Political, Economic, Sociological, Technological, International, Legal and Environmental
- *STEPE or STEEPLE:* Social, Technological, Economic, Environmental, Political, Legal and Ethical
- *SLEPT:* Socio-Cultural, Legal, Economic, Political, Technological
- STEER: Socio-cultural, Technological, Economic, Ecological, and Regulatory

Furthermore, it shall be clarified that an explicitly defined tipification of the options for analyzability (EBEA), on a local/regional, national or global scale, the LoNGPESTLE is the name of the tool commonly designated as, the tool often utilized by multinationals combining these differences tiers of analysis, whether their BEAPs adopt such terminology or not.

Nonetheless, is another model, the *Decision Making Trial and Evaluation Laboratory (DEMATEL)* to introduce the idea of *tier distancing* of the EBEs, dividing EBEs into *far* distant (meta-regional and global) and *near* distant ones (local, regional and national).

Figure 15. General environment: far and near BEs
Source: Own elaboration

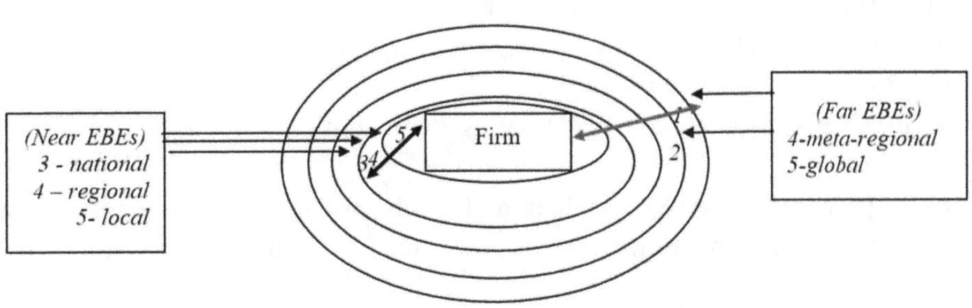

Source: Own elaboration

The tier distancing (far) identifies the closest point´s distancing to the firm. For far environments, the closest point is given by tier 4, equivalent to meta-regional EBEAs. On near environments the tier 5 (local environments) are the closest one. Hence, discerning the classification far from near, is a simple binary one, identical to the notion of local and foreign markets, in which, local corresponds to tiers 3, 4 and 5 (as represented in the figure above) while the foreign/host-markets of a early-internationalizing firm is given by tiers 4 and 5.

The Decision-Making Trial and Evaluation Laboratory (DEMATEL)

The model was originally developed in 1972 by the *Science and Human Affairs Program* of the *Battelle Memorial Institute* (Geneva – Switzerland). Firstly, I shall clarify that the acronym *DEMATEL,* despite the resemblances with PESTEL *it is not a pure* EBE situational analysis model, as all variations of PEST above exhibited. Instead, is a multi-criteria decisional analysis (MCDA) apparatus, for rational decision-making; and is applied with the purpose of determining the EBE´s factors one ought to focus into.

It is developed on the original assumption that (assumption no. 1) "impact" is a dominant criterion, and consequently the DEMATEL consists of a systematic approach for deciding on optimal factor´s selection; hence not being an actual method to be adopted per se as a full situational model of analyzability. It aims at determine factorial interdependencies and independencies and identify the most impactful factors for the firm´s strategy, which justify a decision of cautious reflection on.

Hence, the DEMATEL configures itself as, not à concurrent but, a complementary model, which structure is supported in fact on the structure of the PESTEL. Yüksel (2012) integrates it, assuming that (assumption no. 2), those six (6) segments (P; E; S; T; E; L) are the major segments of the EBEs. Secondly, this method sets a systematic process, with an alternative logic to the one presented in section 5.1. about David Cotton´s *criteria*, as the selection of segments, sub-segments, factors, sub-factors and parameters of analyzability, given rather attention the influence of a factor (i) on another (j).

The intra-factor relations are modelled in the DEMATEL through the usage of two (2) techniques: (i) *Analytic Hierarchy Process (AHP)*; and, (ii) Analytic Network Process *(ANP)*; and, the model follows eight (8) steps:

Step 1: Choice of factors and hierarchic structure of the PESTEL analysis
Step 2: Mapping the potential interdependences between PESTEL factors
Step 3: Determine local weights (lw) of independent factors
Step 4: Visualize the inner dependences using a digraph
Step 5: Calculating the interdependent weights using the ANP
Step 6: Determining the PESTEL sub-factors weights by the AHP
Step 7: Determining the global weights (gw)
Step 8: Evaluate PESTEL sub-factors and calculating the macro environment level

At the end of the process (on step 8), a scale of real numbers with a measurement unit and transitivity, as bullet-pointed below, exhibiting a direct correspondence to the current aims of the BEAP.

- $0.80 \leq$ macro environment level ≤ 1.00: The macro environment is highly supportive of the company's current aims.

- $0.60 \leq$ macro environment level< 0.80: The macro environment is good for the company's current aims.
- $0.40 \leq$ macro environment level< 0.60: The macro environment is moderate for the company's aims.
- $0,00 \leq$ macro environment level< 0.40: The macro environment is not supportive of the company's aims.

This has the advantage of, when crossing the plotted data per factor across multiple EBEs, to benefit from the utilization of the comparative design, which allows the analyst to facilitate broader data for better business decision-making.

The usage of the Analytic Hierarchy Process (AHP) implies the determination of the interdependences, obtained through the calculation of the average matrix, given by this equation:

$$a_{ij} = \frac{1}{H} \sum_{K=1}^{H} x_{ij}^{k}$$

Here, a third assumption is built on the likelihood of two distinct factors contain multiple parameters each (p_n). The analyst is supposed to consider the relation between factors i and j $(i \rightarrow j)$, but also the direct relation of parameters ($p_n i \rightarrow p_n j$). I would emphasize as to the application of this method, or others alike, the plotting of the data outputs related to the regression of aspects of covariance and collinearity, which the model seems to overlook, as the analysis is seemingly unidirectional (not considering $(j \rightarrow i;$ $i \rightarrow j$ *and* $j \rightarrow i;$ *or* $\Delta(x \rightarrow y))$.

However, the logic suggested is, to rate with an integer (from a $\mathbb{Z}$, ranging from 0 to 4) the degree to which, the analyst perceives that one (independent) factor (i) influences another factor (j).

$4 \leq \text{Rate (f)} \geq 0$

The higher values indicate a greater influence. Thus, X_{ij} represents this direct relation. For $i=j$ the diagonal elements are set to a zero value, as a null representation of influence. X_1, X_2,, X_3,……X_H are the matrices from H opinions/perceptions, from n number of analysts, or other respondents delegated from the prior ones.

In short, $X_{n\,(I,\,j)} = 0$, represents a statement of independency of factors, as an absence of a direct relation between factors. However, this is not the same of the non-linearity of the variables´ relation. Let us say, given by the function below, for any set of $i \rightarrow j$ testable relations until k pairs, the geometrical representation of the such is given by the y-intersect (associated to the j factor), with the i factor plotted as a $x=0$.

$f = (X_1\, \beta_1, X2\, \beta_2, X_3\, \beta_3, \ldots, X_k\, \beta)$

Hence, a team of analysts can share the role of analyzing jointly the interrelation of two (or more factors) through an iteration exercise ran n times, accounting the multiple perceptions/opinions from $H = n$, building a composite average matrix: $(A = [a_{ij}])$; and, determine at the end that the parameters of the derivatives may match, whenever they are identical (in i and j), or may not match.

However, the analyst may finding independencies, once the parameters (p_n) are different (between $i \rightarrow j$).

$j \not\subset i$; or (fully different - option 1),

This happens when the parameters i and j are, as follows,

$i = \{u, v, w\}$; and, $j = \{x, y, z\}$

Or,

$i = \{u, v, x\}$ and $j = \{u, w^2\}$

$i = \{u, v, x\}$ and $j = \{u, \sqrt{vx}\}$

Another possibility is simply
$j_{(pn)} \notin i$ (exclusion of a parameter – option 2)
In this case, considering the set of parameters contained in i and j,

$i = \{u, v, w, x, y, z\}$; and, $j = \{u, x, z, \phi, æ, å\}$

Not all parameters are contained in the notation of both sets of And B, regardless of the parameter types ($\mathbb{R}$, $\mathbb{Z}$, or $\mathbb{N}$).

The full association of factors, $(A_{(n)}=1)$ and partial $(A_{(n)}<1)$, depends on the full matching of parameters, given by the notation,

$A_{(i)} \cap B_{(j)}$

$i = \{u, v, w, x, y, z\} \cap j = \{u, z, \phi, æ, å\} = \{x, z\}$

Hence,

$A \cap B = B \cap A = \{x: x \in A \text{ and } x \in B)$

Here $(x:)$, is described as a hypothetical parameter symbolizing the applicability to any factor. The direct relation between factors may be then theoretically modelled as,

$y = (\beta 0 + \beta_1 x);$

Or, as to the case of using simulative values,

$\hat{y} = (X_1 \beta_1, X2 \beta_2, X_3 \beta_3, \ldots, X_k \beta) + \varepsilon$

The function ($\hat{y}$) represents the prediction of the variable´s (i→j) direct relation, considering the residuals (ε), in which the latter is accounted for the extent of bias or error of the analyst with a confidence interval (CI) and prediction interval (PI) definable casuistically per project, in which, the CI (or α) is normally given by $\alpha = .95$. For instance the probability (p) of the occurrence can be defined considering the extent of impact (e.g. financial rebounds) notated as a $p < .05$, with the optimal risk (free of losses) on the scenario of no faults, with the factor holding $p=0$.

However, based on Saaty´s (1986) it is also suggested the alternative usage of an Analytic Network Process (ANP), in which, the independence of factors, implies a pairwise evaluation of them. In this case, the *impact* (on the firm) loses a dominant position as a criterion, being replaced by the inner "importance", as this scholar suggest the adoption of a rating system with a scale 1 to 9, as follows, $\mathbb{Z}(i))\ \{1, 3, 5,, 7, 9\}$, in which the factors are judged separately, considering, naturally, the mathematical principle of transitivity determining that, $1 \leq \mathbb{Z} \geq 9)$.

Table 9. Saaty´s (1996) Scale for Independent factor´s rating and selection

Scale	Measurement (of importance)	Explanation
1	Equal (baseline)	Equally relevant as others
3	Moderate	Experience and judgement slightly in favor (over another)
5	Strong	Experience and judgement strongly in favor (over another)
7	Very strong	Strongly favored demonstrable in practice
9	Absolute	Importance over others – (Highest possible order)

Source: Yüksel (2012)

The factor selection among the network, implies the prioritization of the importance of factors, as highest the rating (from 1-9) the highest the order of importance. The 9th tiers assumes a theoretically fundamental importance, as the highest order, regardless of the pre-tested/initial data demonstrate the opposite, as its configures a set of information which has to be included in the BEAP. The level 7 corresponds to the highest order of factors, demonstrated in practice by the relevance of the figures on the pre-test/sampling of data collected, configuring likely a changing factor on the EBE requiring further monitoring, forecasting and evaluation. To avoid bias, this authors suggest to conduct the rating only once and do not attempt to repeat it just for the sake of improvement of the rating system.

Steeple Matrix

This model promoted by Cotton (2012), is identical to other variations of Aguilar´s situational analysis frameworks (i.e. the PEST). However, the STEEPLE matrix, distinguishes itself from the others, firstly due to the breadth of segments under consideration: Social, Technological, Economical, Environmental, Political, Legal, and Ethical, and secondly, with the rational factorial selection based on three criteria (importance, impact and time horizon) as presented on section 5.1.

In this way, whenever adopting it, I would suggest, as an alternative to the DEMATEL´s ANP with a 9-units scale of importance, the considering of these three criteria above, using the following scale:

The scale is an ordinal one, applicable to the measurement of perceptions, as applicable here, in which, were are rated according to the analyst insight. Hence, the scale, call also be adapted, extended or shrunk according to own needs, or transferred into a typical Likert scale of 5, 7 or 9 points or even a Stapel scale accounting furthermore negative and symmetric perceptions.

Table 10. STEEPLE matrix´s scale and measurement units

Measurement	Impact	Importance	Time Horizon
Type:	Itemized rating scale (IRS)	Itemized rating scale (IRS)	Itemized rating scale (IRS)
Range:	4	4	3
Tiers	High (H) Medium (M) Low (L)	Critical (C) Important (I) Unimportant (Ui) Unknown (Un)	Long-term (LT)> 5 years Medium-Term (MT) (>1 <5 years) Short-term (ST)(< 1 year) Instantaneous (I) (Just now)

Source: Own elaboration

It is allow the crossed applicability to multiple EBEs, under a BEAP comparative design of multiple markets´ analysis project.

The matrix might be built on sample spreadsheet gathering the following components: *segments; factors; raw data; criteria; classification* and further notes, as exemplified below.

Figure 16. Steeple matrix's spreadsheet

STEEPLE Matrix

Date: Dd/mmm/hhhh
Type: Scanning
Markets: (1) - Denmark
Analyst: XPTO

Segment	Sub-segment	Factor	Parameter	Data		Classification			Factor		Notes
				Observed	Variation	Impact	Importance	Time horizon	Score	Rating	
S	S1	F1 F2	Pn Pn								
	S2	F3 F4	Pn Pn			H M L	C I Ui Un	LT MT ST I			
T											
E											
E											
P											
L											
E											

Date: Dd/mmm/hhhh
Type: Scanning
Markets: (1) - Denmark
Analyst: XPTO

Seg.	Sub-seg.	Factor	Parameter	Data		Classification			Factor		Notes
				Observed	Homologous Variation	Impact	Importance	Time horizon	Score	Rating	
Soc	S1. Standards of living	S1.1. Human Development Index	P1 Ratio	.923	-	L	I	LT	-	-	-
Tech		T1. Mobile penetration	P1. Ratio P2. Units of possession P3. Per 100 habitants	1.51	+.019	L	Ui	LT			
Econ	E1. general macro indicators	E1.1.Inflation rate E1.2. Unemployment	P1. Ratio P1. Ratio	0,5 0.062	-.2857 +.1698	L M	Ui I	MT MT	…	…	…
Environ											
Pol	P1. Governance indicators	P1.1.Regulatory qual and control of corruption P1.2. Quality of Democracy	P1. Ratio	92,31 8,85	- -	H H	C I	LT LT	…	…	…
Leg	L1. Business laws	L1.1. Establishment (time to open a new firm)	P1. In number of days) P.2. exclusion of property registration	4	-	L	I	ST			

The matrix above, was, divided in two, the first exhibits a common template and the second with exemplified semi-filled up (national) information about a single market.

As to projects with multiple markets, then the STEEPLE matrix may be adapted slightly to accommodate such changes, including n columns/rows for information such as:

- Listing of n countries
- Include meta-regional and regional information
- Cross-observational of geographical spread data
- Co-occurrence of phenomena (as qual factors)
- Etc.

On the matrix you may observe as well additionally two (2) extra columns corresponding to the components of *factor score (FS)* and *factor rating (FR)*. The FS (score), has nothing to do with the quants raw data obtained from external sources, as ratios or indexes, as the *Better Life Index; Corruption Perception Index; Global Competitiveness Index; Human Development Index*, and many others, which deliver quantitative data outputs. Those are mere external indexes.

For the analysts, such type of figures are, in many cases, significant to follow the progression of them as leading measures for the future, however there are not the FS. The latter score, is an internal score resulting from the internal evaluation of each specific factor, on a given time of conduction of a BEAP. Thus, iterations to the BEAP, means new classification and new scores, ought to be considered as been in constant change, hence the analyst takes a proactive stance renewing a past appraisal.

An FS can be calculated through 3 steps shown below, while the FS rating may be done after getting the FS scores.

Figure 17. Factor selection (FS) scores´ calculation
Source: Own elaboration

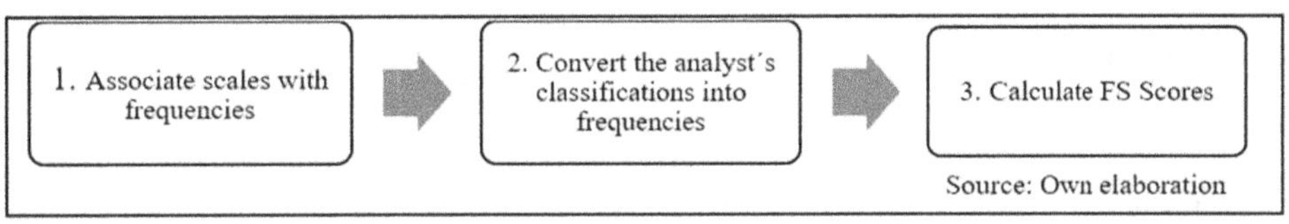

To obtain the FS, the analyst is required to transform the classification of the factors, according to the scale in use, with numbers (scores), making a correspondence to a degree of value (from 0 to 1) equivalent to, in descriptive statistics, to the relative frequency *(f)* of the data in your sample, either being simples cases or categories of data.

The scales of the three major criteria (*impact; importance*; and *time horizon*) are itemized rating scales, which are a subset of ordinal scales. This means, by knowing the scale we are able to determine the range, plus rank the order, or the position of the items, which identify their characteristics. However, because itemized rating scales are not numerical scales, they do not assign a quantitative value to each position (item), as for different projects the value can vary. See the example below comparing the different value assigned to the scale between three different BEAPs (called "project 1"; "project 2"; and, "project 3").

Project 1:

- <u>Impact (*Ia*) criterion´s scale</u>: High, Medium, Low
- <u>Value assigned to the scale:</u>
    - *High* impact – 1
    - *Medium* impact – 0,6
    - *Low* impact – 0,4

Figure 18. Project 1: Exemplified use of criteria and scale/s
Source: Own elaboration

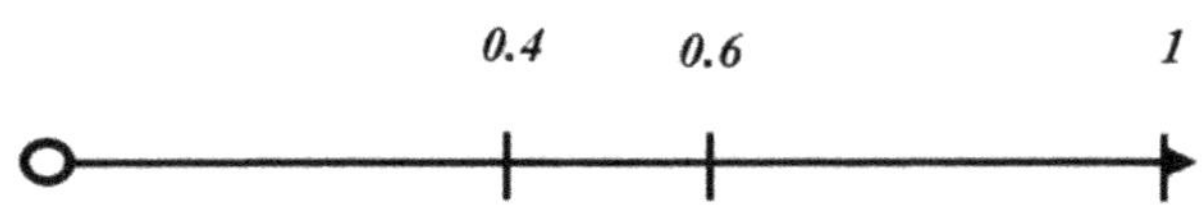

Project 2:

- <u>Impact (*Ia*) criterion´s scale</u>: Very High; High; Medium, Low; Very Low; Null impact
- <u>Value assigned to the scale:</u>
    - *Full* impact - 10
    - *Very High* impact – 9
    - *High* impact – 7
    - *Medium* impact – 5
    - *Low* impact – 4
    - *Very Low* impact – 1
    - *Null* impact - 0

Figure 19. Project 2: Exemplified use of criteria and scale/s
Source: Own elaboration

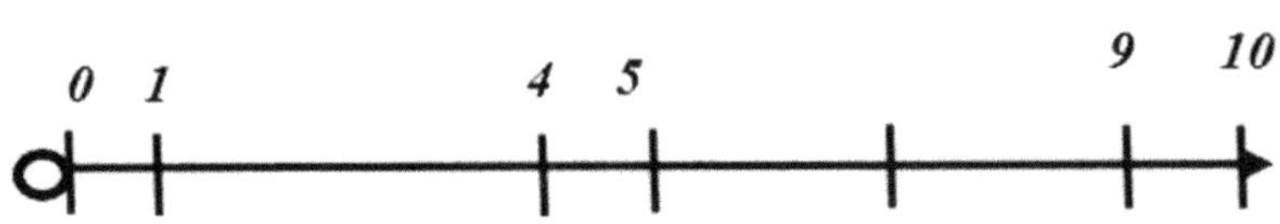

Project 3:

- <u>Impact (*Ia*) criterion´s scale</u>: Very High; High; Medium, Low; Very Low; Null impact
- <u>Value assigned to the scale:</u>
    - *Full* impact - 100

- *Very High* impact – 0,75
- *High* impact – 60
- *Medium* impact – 45
- *Low* impact – 30
- *Very Low* impact – 15
- *Null* impact – 0

Figure 20. Project 3: Exemplified use of criteria and scale/s
Source: Own elaboration

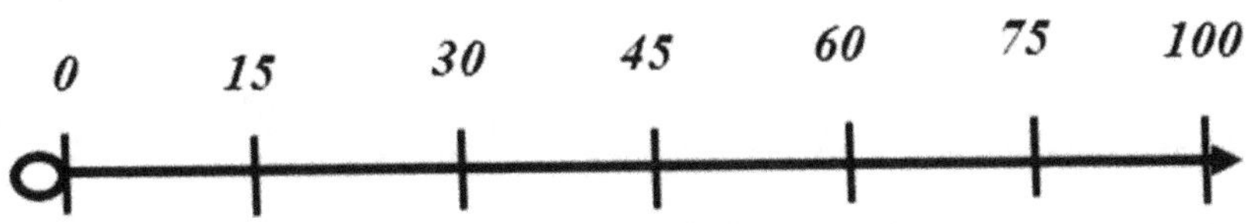

It can be interpreted, by looking at the scales in the three projects, the *high impact* is valued differently by different project, as dissimilar circumstances lead to a perception of an unlike extent of worth.

This scales could even be designed and applied by a same person, working on different BEAPs. The important is, analysts will rate differently the factors in the EBEs. In this example, the same classification "high impact" is rated, respectively, as a *1* (in project 1); as a *0,7* (in project 2) and 0,6 (in project 3).

This is another concern for the analyst when attempting to run any descriptive statistics measures (of central tendency or dispersion) as a mean. One cannot extract any direct quants from the results got from different team-members as to the classifications of the itemized scale, as the answers are merely positional or ordinal, not expressing the intensity or degree or worth of the judgement. This cannot simple be done, otherwise, the results are, decision-wise, absolutely meaningless.

An ordinal scale (as the IRS) needs to be transformed always into a numerical one (an interval scale or ratio scale) in order to be processed quantitatively. This can of course be seen as an extra step requiring time, but certainly paying of later on. The great advantage of such procedure is, whenever treating an enormous amount of data, it simplifies the factor´s selection for further phases of (e.g. forecasting) by using a mechanism of filtering those factors. Actually, this allows the usage of any spreadsheet for data visualization and analysis such as MSFT Excel, to manipulate in, a much simpler manner, the processing of those figures on a computer, facilitating the factor selection afterwards, not anchored solely on semantic judgements of the scale with a single qualitative nature.

One could also ask, *why not to apply directly the numerical scale instead?* The answer is similar to the reasoning given on the previous paragraph. If with ordinal scales one cannot have quantitative force of numbers, by opposition, just with an interval scale one loses the power of the words, i.e. the meaning of what one wants to classify in the EBE´s factors. Such an approach to industry research is equivalent to an academic research project to a *sequential exploratory* one (Saunders, Lewis and Thornhill, 2019).

So, once you are done with the association of scales with frequencies (step 1), for obtaining the FS scores; then, the conversion of the classifications given to each factor need to be converted into a number stating the judgment of quantitative worth of factor per criteria.

Figure 21. Factors selection´s (FS) scores: A "sequential exploratory" reasoning in practice
Source: Own elaboration

Here, I will be using a simple conversion scheme (as an example), in which, the extent of variations is equal across tiers.

Table 11. Example of Conversion of Criteria into Factor Scores (FS)

Factor	Conversion			Classification		
	Importance (Io)	**Impact (Ia)**	**T**	**Ia**	**Io**	**T**
Eco1 (inflation)	Critical → 1 Important → .75 Unimportant – .5 Unknown → .25	High → 1 Medium → .66 Low → 0.33	Long- → 1 Medium → .75 Short → .5 Instantaneous → .25	M	I	M
Frequency (f)	-	-	-	0,66	.75	.75

Source: Own elaboration

One may ask, so *how´s the factor score calculated by converting scales into frequencies)?* We have so far been through the first step (association of scales with frequencies), so now the next step is to convert the classifications of criteria, according to the scale (IRS), into the respective frequencies; and subsequently, to sum the frequencies of the three criteria, since the FS score, is a general score of internal ratio weighting the relative value of the criteria. So, one can argue that,

$$FS(f) = \sum(Io + Ia + T)$$

Hence, the FS score for the factor ECO1 with an equal relative weight across criteria is,

$$FS_{(ECO1)} = \sum(0,66 + 0,75 + 0,75) = \underline{2,16}$$

When using unequal *relative weight (rw)* between criteria, the calculation of the FS score changes slightly. For instance, in a BEAP where the criterion "impact" on the firm´s activity is weighted 4/5 of the whole accountabilities (as the analyst used a firm-centered model of analyzability), and considering that the other criteria remain equal (10% each), then the calculation shifts,

$$FS(f) = \sum[(Ia \,.\, (rwIa) / (Ia+Io+T) + (Io \,.\underline{(rwIo)}) / (Ia+Io+T) + (T \,.\, \underline{(rw\ T)}) / (Ia + Io + T)]$$

$$\Leftrightarrow FS(f) = \sum[(Ia \times .01) + (I \times .8) + (T \times .1)]$$

So, in the example above, applicable to the *ECO1 - inflation rate* and according to the classification given to each criterion and its underlying conversion (*Ia=M=0,66; Io=I =0,75; and, T=M=0,75*) then the *FS = 0,678*, as demonstrated below:

$$ECO1_{(FS)} = \sum[(Ia \times 0{,}8) + (Io \times 0.1) + (T \times 0.1)] \Leftrightarrow$$

$$ECO1_{(FS)} = [(0{,}66 \times 0{,}8) + (0{,}75 \times 0.1) + (0{,}75 \times 0.1)] \Leftrightarrow$$

$$ECO1_{(FS)} = (0{,}528 + 0{,}075 + 0{,}075) \Leftrightarrow$$

$$FS_{(ECO1)} = \underline{0{,}678}$$

Having plotted the full range of FS scores, then its arrangement in an ranked order, according the scores, allows to take a likely fairly confident as to the factors to include and not on a next part of the BEAP.

SWOT Analysis Framework

The SWOT is another neoclassic framework which fits into the category of "situational analysis" tools. It not a pure situational analysis tool as the PEST, but a framework to be utilized as a complementary apparatus for diagnosing a firm´s fit to a market context. Thus, it is categorized as a *Hybrid Situational Analysis Framework (HSAF)*, cross-observing the firm and the market/s.

Accordingly, the SWOT does not explore directly the elements of analyzability (i.e. segments and factors) as the PEST or the DEMATEL do. Moreover, the SWOT does not lay eyes directly on the collection of data about those elements. It is rather an analytical centric procedure to be conducted after the collection phase, where data is gathered by a *Pure Situational Analysis Framework (PSAF),* such as the PEST.

As the acronym clearly tells, it explores Strengths, Weakness, Opportunities and Threats, deriving from the preliminary collection and interpretation of data, for a sense-making purpose. It is, in this way, a sense-giving framework with its utility residing on the contextualization of the observed external universe against the internal realm of the firm (analysis of IE vs. EE).

As it crosses both proxies (IE= firm; outer/external environment=markets) of the strategy function, it is then a framework which aims at deliver a critical contribution about the existing information obtained from the recent manipulation of external data and transform it into strategic information, as business intelligence inputs, generated from the cross-observation of the two strategy interfaces.

The SWOT it is fashioned on the assumption that the "impact" on the firm (as a criterion of EBE analysis), is the most relevant part of analysis to be explored. Moreover, it is sensitive to mutations on the external environment, as it aims at understand, based on the current state of the firm and the EBE, what are the panorama of preparedness of the firm, called referred in strategy books, as to the state of strategic awareness and strategic agility. The first (awareness) reflecting the extent of theoretical preparedness based on the learning from the EBE. The latter (agility) referring to the degree of adaptation to comply with the dynamics or VUCA.

Consequently, the four (4) components (the S-W-O-T) of analysis of the model are all, as aspects of analyzability, focused solely on the intertwining of IE/EE (i.e. the *firm-environment interrelation),* accounting the underlying dimensions of interdependencies and interactions, reflecting such immersion into "impact" as the dominant variable and the most fundamental criterion of EBEA. The general aim of this framework is to sustain the firm amidst all the changes, whether observed externally on the markets or internally, within the organization.

This original design of this tool from the 1950s, is credited to, a triadic origin, *Albert Humphrey* from Stanford University; but also, *George Albert Smith Jr.* and *C. Roland Christensen* from Harvard Business School (HBS); and finally, *Kenneth Andrews* also from HBS (Friesner 2011).

The four components are described below:

Strength (S): The positive characteristic possessed by a firm, constituting a strategic advantage over the competitors.

Strengths can derive from tangible and intangible assets, and occur isolated or jointly through the combined interaction of multiple resources and capabilities. The sources of these strategic advantages vary, such as, aesthetics; brand recognition; economies of density; know-how; intelectual property; reputation; trade secrets and so forth. An example, of a distinctive feature constituting a strength is *Pandora´s* product innovation. Pandora is a Danish jewelry manufacturer, recognized nowadays internationally for allowing the customer´s self-personalization of the final product, from a wider variety of components and at an affordable price.

Weakness (W): An internal characteristic that restrains the firm from gaining a strategic advantage over competitors.

The weaknesses are the symmetric position of the strengths. In that sense, who possesses them over others is more competitive and reaps the benefits of such preparedness to the EBEs, whether in a short or long-run. A characteristic which is, distributed across firms in a market and balanced in the degree of their possession then it becomes a parity.

The strengths and weaknesses are summarizable as an internal state of the capacity of firm to comply with the outer conditions faced at as certain moment in time. This can be interpreted as the inner potential "worth" of a firm likely to be exploited in the context of market competition. Opportunities and threats are a measure of potential external value to be explored against other players, according the extent of S´s and W´s developed, but also, according to the micro environment context not here covered in the book, as the absolute comparative advantage of a country, the relative comparative advantage of the industry in a market X and combined interaction of other factors, called a "Diamond" framework, as the factor conditions; demand; strategy, structure and culture; and, degree of national rivalry (Porter, 1980)[5].

Opportunity (O): Favorable/lucrative condition of the market for the firm to yield higher profits

Threat (T): Hostile condition of the market which can be dangerous for the business.

A threat can result from changes in regulation (e.g. trade barriers; customs and monetary policies), newer technologies, disruptive products (or processes or business models) or even spurious products, direct confrontational maneuvers of a competitor, new entrants in the markets, harsh and/or unexpected natural conditions, rapid switch in demand habits, fluctuation in interests rates, or fiscal policies.

Nowadays, the SWOT, became a widespread technique used by managers for decision-making even when reflecting on problems that are fully internal issues for an organization, but in this case, configuring a perception of a particular "innerness" and "outerness" for the manager´s point of view; as the problematic, case or solution involves multiple parts all being inside of the firm (as teams or units; projects; departments; divisions; or subsidiaries).

Despite some scholars term it a "responsibility", to know the S-W-O-T´s, the SWOT is essentially a tool at the manager's disposal, the ones accountable for the effective fulfillment of strategic goals, efficient administration of resources and compliance with the vision, mission and values of the firm.

Hence, managers applied it widely for keeping their business on the right track, being this tool, a pure analytical procedure from which one may extract insights from the analyst´s work to develop more rational strategic frameworks, and consequently, more likely to be effective and successful for the future of businesses and corporations.

The SWOT analysis accounts two (2) major elements:

1. The mapping of the SWOT conditions
2. The visualization (the SWOT Analysis Matrix)

For mapping the SWOT conditions, the analyst is recommended to follow these steps:

1. *Factors´ gathering and classification by the degree of effect/intensity*, as to the criterion "impact":

Table 12. Factors gathering and classification by impact

Criterion´s classification	Factors	
	Description	**Relevant Data (attesting the classification)**
High	F1 -.... F2 - ... F3 - ...	... ...
Medium	F1 -.... F2 - ... F3 - ...	... ...
Low	F1 -.... F2 - ... F3 - ...	... ...

Source: Own elaboration

2. *Classify the factors* by *nature of impact* (*Positive* or *Negative*) in addition to the degree of (High, Medium or Low impact) and nature impact:

Table 13. Factors by nature (Positive or Negative) and degree (High, Medium or Low) of impact

Criterion´s classification	Factors			
	Description	**Positive**	**Negative**	**Relevant Data (attesting the classification)**
High	F1 -.... ✔ F2 - ... ✔ F3 - ... ✔	Whether H+	Or, H-	... ...
Medium	F1 -.... ✔ F2 - ... ✔ F3 - ... ✔	Whether M+	Or, M-	... ...
Low	F1 -.... X F2 - ... X F3 - ... X	Whether L+	Or, L-	... ...

Source: Own elaboration

3. *Divide the factors into lists of O&Ts for maximization and minimization:*

Table 14. Division of factors into O&Ts

Classification	Upper Max. Opportunities	Mezzo Max. Opportunities	Upper min. Threats	Mezzo min. Threats
H+(O´s)	List of H+ (Factor 1; Factor 2; Factor 3; Factor n)	---	---	---
M+ (O´s)	---	List of M+ (Factor 1; Factor 2; Factor 3; Factor n)	---	---
H- (Ts)	---	---	List of H- (Factor 1; Factor 2; Factor 3; Factor n)	---
M- (T´s)	---	---	---	List of M- (Factor 1; Factor 2; Factor 3; Factor n)

Source: Own elaboration

Here, the *maximization* targets the factors which the analyst considered to have a positive impact and represent an opportunity to the focal firm, while the *minimization* focus on the factors with negative impact and negative impact likely to be a threat.

Furthermore, as one may observe in the table above, the analyst is recommended to separate the list of factors representing O&Ts, by intensity or degree of the effect (High and Medium), generating two separate positive lists and two negative lists. The positive ones are the factors constituting *upper opportunities (H+)* and *mezzo opportunities (M+)* for maximization. The negative factors may be likewise separated into *upper threats (H-)* and *mezzo threats (M-)* for minimization.

The rationale of the analysis is to separate the wheat from the chaff, what is good (O´s) and bad (T´s) news and discern also the intensity of their effect, so there is a clear output of the SWOT mapping for the benefit of the operational or strategic decision-making and for the future strategic formulation.

Hence, the job of the analyst at this stage is, to rank factors by intensity plus nature and associate those with a possible action, determining what are the ones requiring further work of maximization and minimization. This constitutes a clear input for another model (i.e. TOWS).

Summarizing then the ideas of maximization and minimization above, those can be represented as:

Max(O) = (Upper Max + Mezzo Max) ⇔

Max(O) = Sum (H+ and M+)

And,

Min(S) = (Upper Min + Mezzo Min) ⇔

Min (S) = Sum(H- and M-)

Now one might repeat these steps above (1, 2 and 3), but applying them to Strengths and Weaknesses (SW´s) analysis.

This means to identify for the internal factors, exactly as for the externals, the ones with a degree of impact (high, medium or low) which may affect a future performance, and then divide them by nature (positive and negative) and finally constitute separate lists of S&W´s for maximization of S´s and minimization of W´s. This requires from the analyst to observe, enquire and determine from a multiplicity of aspects within the organizational realm, what are the ones constituting S-W-O-Ts from A to Z. For instance, considering the design of the vision and mission; the setting of goals; the type of organizational structure; the model of governance and international coordination of subsidiaries and divisions; the organizational culture; the resources owned; the capabilities acquired/built; the human capital´s worth; the products/services attributes; systems, processes and/or physical and digital infrastructures and placing, and so forth. There is a tone of information to be collected internally, equivalently complex and broad as in the case as the data collected about the EBEs.

So then, may you generate a *SWOT Analysis Matrix*, which may represents a visual mapping of different angles of the context in which the firm is embedded in:

a) A summary of major S-W-O-T´s (i.e. H+ and H-´s)
b) Or, summary of mezzo issues (i.e. M+; and M-s)
c) Or, a correlative matrix (H+´s and H-´s and their M´s implications, and vice-versa)

A SWOT is a subsidiary tool complementary to others, providing EBE`s prior data collection (e.g. PEST or the DEMATEL). It is not a pure situational analysis framework focused on the external business environment, but a hybrid situational analysis tool for comprehending the interrelation of the internal and external environment, and especially to diagnose the extent of preparedness of the firm against a particular market context, physical or digital. So, all these options of matrices which one may generate hold a significant relative utility/value.

Hence these visualizations can be combined in meetings and professional presentations. As a rule of thumb, at first, is important to keep it simple. Exhibit initially (and discuss it) the major SWOTs with the upper issues to maximize and minimize. Subsequently, immerse into correlations, to comprehend the domino effects of a single factor on others, whether H´s or M´s (or even L´s; if your analysis wishes to go more in-depth). Finally, look into the factors with medium (and/or low) influence and comprehend how isolated their effects are.

In fact, the SWOT is a tool with a dual functionality for "kick-starting" the strategy, as it be explored simultaneously as an input and output. As an input the SWOT is a more informal practice, while as an output a more formalized one.

One company may use it as an internal data collection instrument (input perspective), in which, the role of analyst is to gather several teams from a range of functions and levels in your organization and apply *generative methods* (e.g. brainstorming) for obtaining new insights about relevant S-W-O-Ts.

The utility of the SWOT here is to build a list of ideas about where this organization currently stands. Every time a SWOT is brought to the discussion and signaled as a Strength, Weakness, Opportunity, or Threat, the analyst ought to write it down in the respective part of the grid. Recording of these sessions is recommended so the whirlwind of unstructured ideas can always be revisited latter on, and transferred to different formats and documents.

However, one company may also use it as formal output of information to be presented to the manager or other decision-maker (e.g. a client). The explanation of the SWOT as an output was on the previous page more emphasized, as the SWOT is rather seen as a process (for generating such output).

Many organizations also use it in both ways on a regular basis, blending inputs and outputs, namely using the outputs of a previous BEAP, namely the SWOT Analysis Matrix, as a starting point of discussion, in which the previous findings are used to comprehend the deviations of the analysis to the current reality and trigger new insights also into actionable strategy.

It is relevant to emphasize that discussion is organization-wide, not just top-level centered, which is normally a myth, as strategy matters are reserved to senior managers. Under such logic, the analyst is challenged to adopt a most large approach possible, inclusive of all organizational-stakeholders. More discussable is whether freelancers, outsourcers and suppliers ought to participate on such exercises. My understanding of this is, the product-market stakeholders hold different interest and conflicts of interest which may bias and confound their participation on the generation of new meaningful insights for the design of a new deliberate strategy.

TOWS Matrix

Commonly confused with the SWOT, the TOWS is not a misuse of the acronym SWOT, but is actually a complementary tool of situational analysis for the development of strategic options (Weihrich, 1982).

The TOWS links the information provided by the SWOT analysis (as an interrelation analysis of two separate environments - internal and external) with the domain of strategy formulation, providing a set of scenarios for a design of a Mintzberg *deliberate strategy,* which is formulated as a desirable one but not realized, or a non-implemented strategy.

The model was invented by the American scholar *Henry Weihrich* and published on a seminal article "*The TOWS matrix—A tool for situational analysis*" presenting firms with a solution against SWOTs. The framework is arguable by some as a defensive apparatus and criticized by others as a limited tool for shielding the hurdles of the environment. Nonetheless, the TOWS matrix bring undoubtedly a next layer of analysis over the SWOT, hence being complementarily of the latter provided a far better picture of the competition´s context then simply using the SWOT.

Weihrich (1982) raises several questions about to maximize and minimize external effects, drawing up thesis upon the following four (4) scenarios:

- *SOs (Strength and Opportunities)*
- *STs (Strengths and Threats)*
- *WOs (Weakness and Opportunities)*
- *WT (Weakness and Threats)*

The reflection upon internal and external conditions, as positive or negative conditionings of future strategic behaviour/positioning, is this an impacting criterion on the firm´s future success (business strategy) direction and future destiny (vision/corporate strategy).

Consequently, the *Weihrichian* research focused on how to transform S-W-O-Ts, as separate insights, into combinations of scenarios with distinct settings, which require an equivalent distinct actionable approach, or a specific strategy, targeting the specifics of the context (SOs; STs; WOs; and/or, WTs).

The great virtue of the TOWS matrix (see below), is the unravelling of a triad of strategic options (or "organizational needs") to further account and map:

1 – A double minimization need (of W´s & T´s – or WTs)
2 - A double maximization need (of S´s & O´s – or SOs)
3 - A hybrid minimization/maximization need (S´s & T´s, and W´s & O´s – or STs and WOs)

Table 15. TOWS matrix

		External	
Internal		Opportunities (O)	Threats
	Strengths (S)	SOs: 1. 2. 3. *n*	STs: 1. 2. 3. *n*
	Needs:	(SOs): Double Maximization	(STs): Hybrid max/min
	Strategies:	*SOs: Maxi-Maxi Strategy*	STs: *Maxi-Mini Strategy*
	Weaknesses (W)	WOs: 1. 2. 3. *n*	WTs: 1. 2. 3. *n*
	Needs:	(WO): Hybrid min/max	WTs: Double Minimization
	Strategies:	(WO): *Mini-Maxi Strategy*	*Mini-Mini Strategy*

Source: Adapted from Chaffey (2021)

The TOWS matrix appeals to a direct resolution of internal-external conformities and conflicts, as organizational needs of maximization and minimization, as described in the SWOT framework are here transferred into concrete recommended strategies (Warren Lynch, 2020).

Each type of need is associated with a strategy:

1. Double maximization (SOs) → *Maxi-maxi strategy*
2. Double minimization (WTs) → *Mini-Mini strategy*
3. Hybrids:
    a. STs → *Maxi- Mini Strategy*
    b. WOs → *Mini-Maxi Strategy*

The maxi-maxi strategies are the ones which utilize own strengths to maximize opportunities (Warren Lynch, 2020). The mini-mini strategies aim at minimize weaknesses and avoid threats, regardless of the origin of the T´s are internal debilities (W´s) or not.

The maxi-mini strategies are the ones focused on utilizing own strengths to avoid or prevent the effects of a threat. The mini-maxi strategies are the minimize weaknesses but taking advantage of opportunities. Inevitably, I will draw some lines about the theory of constraints (TOC) below as a systematic approach for solving contexts of S&T; or W&Os.

The Theory of Constraints (TOC)

Dr. Eliyahu M. Goldratt was an educator, scientist and philosopher whom created the TOC, an overall framework for helping organizations to apply a systematic approach to change, by focusing on their weaknesses for use them as a leverage point to create practical solutions. Thus, the principles of the TOC are useful for solving organizational situational contexts of WT and WOs, which means applicable to Mini-Mini Strategies and Mini-Maxi strategies.

The TOC framework draws attention on the improvement of processes within a system. The theory acknowledges that the past construction of the system had a logical purpose; however, action can be taken to deal with improvements at any part of the system. Those are what we labelled as weaknesses at the SWOT and TOWS.

The model obeys to five (5) major principles. Firstly, the constraint is a limitative to growth or development of the system, also termed often as *a bottleneck*. Secondly, such limitations restrain the firms from achieving their goals. Thirdly, the best way to tackle a limitation is uncover and solve it. Fourth, a system cannot produce more than the output of the weakest links. So, the focus ought to be on major constraints first, which we termed as weaknesses of negative high impact (H-) for upper minimization (whether through mini-mini or mini-maxi strategies, as seen on the TOWS matrix).

Fifth, the limitations in system caused by the weakness links are a structural problem but also a risk for the fulfillment of the remaining activities in a processes, whenever they are linked in a workflow in a serial manner. In this sense, *parallel activities* are likely to be less constrained than *serial activities*.

Hence, Goldratt (1990) proposes a stepwise process for minimizing those weaknesses. Such managing of constraints obeys to five (5) steps:

1. Identify the system´s constraints
2. Decide (how to deal with the constraints)
3. Subordination
4. Elevate the system (increase capacity)
5. Go back to step 1 (if constraint changes, or a new constraint arises)

I would had a sixth step of continuous improvement, as such management of weaknesses is a continuous improvement or never-ending process.

The first step with the SWOT is done by mapping and registering the weakness in the grid of the matrix. The second, a rather delicate one, involves a reflection of options, likely shared by multiple stakeholders and accounting how the maneuvers taken affect the rest of the system. As stated by Goldratt (1990), the resolution of constraints will be supplied by the non-constraints, so firm´s shall consider a smart and most effective way of solving the weaknesses without over-consuming the remaining resources. The third step involves the adjustment of the whole system. Limitations are a consequence of the direct impact on the system. Then, modifications to a constraint, to solve its limitations imply modification in other parts of the system also affected by the actions taken to solve the constraint. The authors of the model recommends then the circumscription of the limiting impact, since the system performance is sealed and subjugated by the constraints as a bottleneck. Fourth, focus on other side constraints deriving from the resolution of the original one, in order to keep increase the capacity of the system, normally those are transferred from the shop floor to policy constraints. Fifth, exactly due to the latter, go back to step 1 and identify the nature of lateral constraints, as the policy constraints, deriving from the existence of many internal organizational rules.

SOAR Framework

Another frequent tool used by industry practitioners is the Strengths, Opportunities, Aspirations and Results (SOAR) framework (see below) which is a tool mostly centered on the internal environment, provides an extent of internal consistency between the environment and effectiveness of the firm as to the achievement of their goals.

Figure 22. SOAR framework
Source: Own elaboration

Positive Impact Drives	Outcomes
Internal drives: Strengths →	Aspirations
External drives: Opportunities:	Results:

Source: Own elaboration

The advantages recognized on the SOAR is its simplicity, facilitating the understanding and the utilization of it.

Furthermore, is centered on the strategic effectiveness of the firm (aspirations and goals), and so may be a tempting tool for a quick presentation of outputs of strategic performance management endeavors regarding the evaluation/diagnosis of the business performance at a certain moment. Furthermore, it articulates results with future direction (vision) which may be a simplistic explanatory model to non-strategists.

Despite its simplicity, seen as an advantage, on the other hand, the major drawbacks are lack of further theoretical foundations due to its simplicity, the disregard of the external environment in great extent (i.e. threats) and the moreover the disregarding of the whole limitations that the firm may encounter, as factors of great importance to consider and work on are precisely the ones with high impact of negative nature (H-), whether W or Ts. In this sense, excludes from the strategic thinking process, the double minimization needs (WTs) and the hybrid ones (ST; WO) which are connected with three types of possible strategic actions to minimize constraints and take advantage of opportunities: the mini-mini strategies; maxi-mini strategies; and mini-maxi strategies.

Strengths, Challenges, Options, Responses, and Effectiveness (SCORE) Analysis

Pinpointing substantial critiques to the SWOT, the model argues that the latter lacks on measurability and stimulates isolated actions (as a one-off analysis), arguing furthermore that companies have difficulties to repeat its utilization, specially linking the results from an earlier BEAP to a current one (Graves, 2006).

Consequently, it recommends a rethinking of the SWOT, arguable with a simplistic background, and a subsequent shift to a SCORE Assessment, as follows:

Figure 23. SWOT vs. SCORE
Source: Graves (2006)

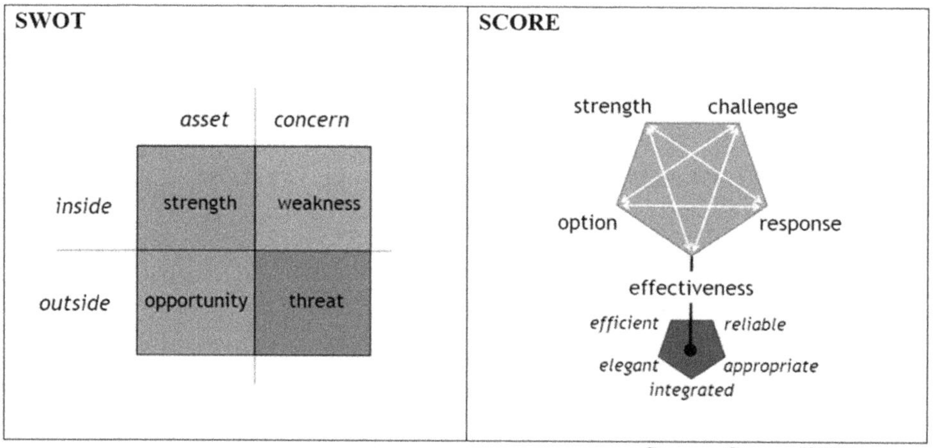

Source: Graves (2006)

Tom Graves asserts that the SCORE is a more robust analytical framework. Its virtues (against the SWOT) are the enhancing of the methodology with subsequent quantitative measurement and the applicability of the model to more complex contexts. Furthermore is exalted the comparative power of the SCORE for conducting multiple iterations of an original BEAP, thus, offering a roadmap for taking informed business decisions with a rather more consistent utilization of this tool.

The dimensions of the model account the following deliverables. As to the organizational *strengths*, the SCORE refers to the set of capabilities on a positively distinctive level from its competitors. The *challenges* refer to a prioritized roadmap of events with acknowledged change and constituting some sort of risk. *Options* are the strategic scenarios to be analyzed and take a decision as to a certain path, encompassing a risk trade-off between the utility of the compromise made about a decision, against other possible options. The *responses* accounts a response to specific risk scenarios as to the scope and type of pro/re-action and to the specifics of the business case. The *effectiveness* is the performance measured as to the impact of the project and integration of its outcomes on different strategic business units.

The measurability of the SCORE implies the development by the analyst of multiple scales with ranges between continua, as follows:

(i) Strength – response; Response – strength
(ii) Strength – effectiveness; Effectiveness – strength
(iii) Challenge – option; Option – challenge
(iv) Challenge – effectiveness; Effectiveness – challenge
(v) Option – response; Response - option

The measurement units have a dual directionality and the position of the rating range between the poles above (from i to v), not as simply binary choice but with an interval of options. The rationale is, the crossing of the outputs, as to the geometrical drawing of hexagonal lines of a virtual object, united the dots (or ratings) which determine the vectorial position with more or less incidence, over variables such as the efficiency; reliability; elegance; appropriateness; and integration.

Telescopic Observations (TO) Framework

The *Telescopic Observation (TO)*, fashioned by Panagiotou and van Wijnen (2005), appears as a natural response to the limitations of the SWOT, as these scholars criticized the vagueness and oversimplified methodology.

However, the simplification of environment analysis methods, such as the SWOT, is also pinpointed by other authors, asserting to be a great risk, as the superficial listing of data outputs is dangerous for strategic decision-making (Pickton and Wright, 1998).

It is certainly to be agreed with these authors on the latter, and hence, the methodology here developed in this book as to the improvement of the SWOT, which opens two (2) different sub-tools with a stepwise approach and comprising both the aspects of mapping and visualization, is a consequence of this criticism that I do also subscribe to as well. Hence, in its original form the over simplistic SWOT analysis matrix relies on a market structure, in which, six decades ago, dynamics and evolutionary patterns made them to become quite different. Undoubtedly, markets were before far more stable than business is nowadays and frameworks developed on the field of business strategy at that time had consequently a lower demand in sophistication.

Definitely, the SWOT relied largely on the free will and ability of the analyst to conduct further research to solve the omissions and inconsistencies of data as a result of the generalization of the information and (somehow sloppiness of the) analytical process. That is precisely why in this book such tool is refined into a deeper endeavor (as a" *Detailed SWOT*"), yet not attempting to solve in total the structural debilities of the model, but solely, bringing a remedy for a more contemporary usage.

Hence, the diagnostic power of a situational analysis tool is dependent on the ability to provide a clear holistic picture, and through a perspective that matters for the organization (Baker, 2000). However, in the vast majority of the cases, both due to scholarly and practitioner´s error, the SWOT is applied under the *organizational perspective*, not the market perspective (or the *customer perspective*). Consequently, firm develop analysis based on environmental diagnosis or scans which assessments of its own view, since is the perspective of analysts/consultant´s team that is shown. But, their view, reflecting an organizational perspective lacks on inputs from the customer-base.

In essence, I must agree with marketers on this regard, as one of the best ways to comprehend what a customer wants is simply to explore his/her thoughts and wishes about the company´s brands, goods or services. An analysis should be reversed, according to Baker (2000), and I do corroborate with such thesis. Perhaps, better said, mixed, accounting both an organizational and customer perspective, and abandon the single traditional self-enquiry path with wrong general focus research questions (GFRQs) like, *What are we good at?*; or, *What are our limitations?*

Instead, give room to the market to reflect about the organization: *What do I (dis)like in the organization?; How could the product be better?; How would I be more satisfied?; What would make me more pleased with?; What makes a great customer experience?;* and so forth.

The attempts to develop holistic models of environment assessment seem an incomplete portrait of a distant reality, as the models developed so far, fail to fully attain such inclusive perspective. This assertion is valid to all models (e.g. the SWOT, PEST, or the DEMATEL). Invariably, these models attempt to build a system-based framework, as a methodological referential focused on environment assessment; however, disregarding as to the system´s architecture the sharing of the responsibility of the data with other stakeholders; and, moreover, the inclusion of other non-system tools, as generative, media-based or interview-based methods.

Scholars, have worked with time on the improvement of the venerable framework of SWOT, developing SWOT-based strategies, as descending models, exactly the same way as happened with the PEST.

Multiple descending theories from the SWOT arose with a multiplicity of variations, such as, the SOAR replacing weaknesses and Threats by aspirations and results, as swiftly represented above, or the WOTSUP with the inclusion of Under Planning or the SOFT (with "faults" replacing the weaknesses), the SCORE (Strengths, Challenges, Options, Responses, and Effectiveness) analysis offering a two-step approach pre and post action for a continuous improvement or the SOFT technique attempting to broaden the scope of the threats in SWOT. The author claims that facts are considered in SWOT simply as value negative events, by opposition with Opportunities as potential value positive events (Shadfar, 2013; Panagiotou, 2003). This scholar perceives the EBEs, as to the general environment, into two (2) sub-tiers:

1. The *reality*, as the portrait of a particular EBE, as a sum of factors illustrating it, after an inferential thinking process of the analyst. This presupposes the existence of a single reality at a time.
2. The *facts*, as the full assortment of events to be mapped and analyzed, contain potentially value (positive, negative or neutral) as a single type of effect (or typology of impact) they may generate on a firm, whether deliberate or not.

Others descending models assumed a significant popularity and importance, such as, the Jay Barney´s (1996) VRIO framework, pillared on Penrosian foundations, focused on the internal environment analysis of resources and capabilities instead of actually depicting the connection internal-external environments. This model opened, as a matter of facts, doors for resource-based theorists as *David Teece, Gary Pisano, Amy Shuen* and, *Kathleen M. Eisenhardt and Jeffrey A. Martin*, on a new theorization line about the importance of developing dynamic capabilities (DC),, giving origin to the now trending DC framework, with two major streams of thought (The Teecian and Eisenhardtian) (Teece, Pisano and Shuen, 1997; Eisenhardt and Martin, 2000).

In this context, the Telescopic Observation seemed an attempt to a more ambitious and integrative answer to the complex requirements of the organization to grasp the business environmental conditions and dynamics of change.

The authors had the courage to break the ties with some of the previous conceptions as to the analysis as a process. For instance, abandoned the assumption of data that needed to be manipulated as a "funnel", rejecting the logic of a procedure based on the sequence of "collect", "screen" and "filter" environmental variables. Secondly, their structure is based on, an ample objective, purely holistic, to scan an organization and bring distant objects into focus. Thirdly, these scholars balance two criteria (importance and impact) as they equate the relative weight of the criteria for the eligibility of a factor to be included in a BEAP. This opposes clearly to the SWOT-based strategies which are impact-centered.

The Telescopic Observations (TO) provide a systematic approach comprised of a process with four (4) steps:

(1) a full-scale internal situational analysis (to determine their current position)
(2) Evaluation of findings (from step1)
(3) Formulation and implementation of strategies specific, measurable, attainable, realistic, and time-bound (SMART) strategies
(4) Performance monitoring and determination of corrective action as required.

These steps have the virtue to link the analysis of the business environmental with the strategic formulation and strategy controls. Moreover, connect general environment and industry environment. Despite such linkages with the strategic planning and strategic performance management, the model centers itself mostly on environment analysis, cross-observing twenty-two (22) dimensions of internal and external analyzability, from which, the analyst may select general factors and industry factors, as follows (Panagiotou and van Wijnen, 2005, pp. 162-163):

T – Technological advancements
E – Economic considerations
L - Legal and Regulatory requirements
E – Ecological and Environmental issues
S – Sociological trends
C – Competition
O – Organizational culture
P – Portfolio analysis
I – International issues
C - Cost efficiencies and cost structures
O – Organizational core-competences and capabilities
B – Buyers
S - Suppliers
E – Electronic commerce
R – Resource audit (including capital structure)
V – Value system
A – Alliances, Joint-ventures and other types of partnerships/networks)
T - Total Quality Management

I – Industry Key factors for success
O – Organizational Structure
N – New Entrants
S – Substitute Products and Services

The initial idea that certainly has crossed your mind is, this is a hybrid model, crossing the external general environment with the external industry environment, which in turn, has many pros and cons.

The matrix of the TO Strategic Framework combines several models therein, as the PESTILE analysis, the SWOT analysis, the TOWS strategies and Porter´s Five forces of competition. A downside is at first the excessive focus on the company, falling into the organizational perspective again, as other models did.

Moreover, the blending of criteria (importance and impact) it is not clarified as to the applicable scale, measurement units, transitivity principles, and what it constitutes the eligibility for factor selection or exclusion.

The analyst may consider it as a directional model, in which these specifics are left to the free arbitrage, despite the pros and cons, as the risk of saturating or burning out the analyst with modeling aspects instead of real analytics.

As I have introduced here this model as a potential adopting model in an organization, with multiple virtues but also at the end so drawbacks, I have at last to clarify the following: the model is holistic, not fully holistic, is broad but does not cover (and does not intent to) all the problematics one may encounter in the business world. For instance, does not aim at spot particularly environmental change aspects (e.g. fads, or wild cards). Likewise, holism related to a large scope of environmental analysis. Definitely the model is broad in dimensions of analysis (i.e. 22 units) but sparse as to the accomodation of techniques of lateral models (or even recommendations of them) for determining selecting factors, and their further classification (as SWOTs) and pursuing strategies (TOWS).

Breadth is obviously an enemy to depth, which means is utopic to believe on a full coverage of all aspects of medium and high concern (importance and impact on the firm) and to a very high depth of analysis.

This model is broad, holistic, with a large scope, what scarce in information on how to get there, thus relies largely on the skills and knowledge of the analyst (and the whole firm and external informants) to extract the best and most of relevant data units, from example, determine the most concerning international major issues, or conduct spot the problems with the current product´s portfolio or map the capabilities of the firm.

As to the depth, any experienced Strategist and/or Marketeer would ascertain a gap on multiple components of analyzability. For instance, just reflecting upon the question *what does "competition" entails*?, would open some holes in the model. Some dimensions concur already with this dimension ("competition"), as the authors refer to "new entrants" or "substitute products"; "suppliers"; or "buyers", but one may naturally criticize the choice of the dimensions, and/or the neglecting of sub-dimensions of analyzability. Furthermore, is clear the overlooking of critical information for the whole industry analysis, as the segments, a crucial part of the Segmentation, Targeting and Positioning (STP) analysis, which is core for this dimension. The same with Strategic Groups as the identification of clusters of similar strategic positions is also key for modern competition.

However, the reader may recall that this book is essentially about pure external business environment analysis, not about industry analysis, so looking uniquely at the general environment tier, then the TO framework is not so much on the lens of the critique. Nevertheless, the analyst at to each specific endeavor (or BEAP) may determine in advance if the focus is a far or near business environment, the perspective of analyzability (customer or organizational) and the philosophical stance whether universalist or relativist to make it more clear to him/herself and the team the circumscription of the project.

TAIDA Model

We have discussed in chapter one, the role of instincts on environment attentiveness and how innate that is to human beings. We saw that this implies a constant state of awareness about the immediate surrounding, and cumulatively, the observation of the natural and social elements that compose the standing reality.

As to the organizational realm the behavior is identical (as depicted on section 5.2. *Types of External Business Environment Analysis*); however organizations employ a more structured observation, comprised of a surveillance system combining five (5) types of measures, termed as "phases", due to their complementarity and sequential logic of adoption for gaining insightful information about a business environment.

The first phase, if one may recall, is the *inspection,* typically a one-off project to build original and a more basic understanding of the market´s functioning rules, its dynamics, "the chess board" players, agents, and the configuration of the competition´s arena and the firm´s positioning. The *scanning* attempting to spot new events and trends, while the forecasting focuses on a sub-set of events with an emergent trend evolving and sounding the alarm of strategic thinkers for reflect on future strategic responses to them. On the assessment phase, the changing patterns studied in previous phases, as to their evolution, formation of trends are analyzed as to their embeddedness on present environmental features as they turn into mainstream events.

The TAIDA is a specific tool for developing projects with particular emphasis on the environment forecasting phase. It is a scenario planning framework. Here, the notion of *scenario planning* is an analytical procedure based on self-generated cognitive options.

One may well, relate the role of the analyst/strategic thinker, focused on future thinking towards the control of paradigm shift of new events/trends, with the role of leader focused on altering the current paradigms, whether under a logic of creative of effective leadership thinking. Here, the analyst conceives new contrived thoughts, which expands into more sophisticated and clearer ideas about how the future might look like. Those latter ones are the hypothesis of how the world might resemble (future hypothesis).

The first step (hypothesis formulation), in general, results from the application of generative methods for idealizing the upcoming reality, which is designated as a process of *future thinking*. From there, the analyst (or team) then crosses these multiple virtualizations of the possible paths to classify the likelihood of their realization. This means to separate the hypothesis more likely to become a true reality, from the ones that are a mere idealization of it. Two dimensions are used on the second step of classification of the hypothesis, a likelihood dimension and an impact dimension.

The analyst aims at this stage to comprehend what are the future hypothesis constituting a *normative scenario*, a *utopian scenario* and a *critical scenario* and a non-critical one. A scenario-planning matrix for classifying future hypothesis is presented below.

Scenario classification allows, as observed on the matrix, to separate the real scenarios (*normative* and *alternative* ones) from the delusional construction of fictional scenarios which are unlikely to occur. This classification is beneficial as it accentuates that the engagement of a firm on forecasting and foresight activities to anticipate the future or explore future states, and their inherent challenges and opportunities allows them to pre-empt and shape the business environments (i.e. *corporate foresight*)

(Semke and Tiberius, 2020). Of particular relevance are the *strategic foresight* activities, as the ones dedicated to the gain of strategic intelligence about the future, and furthermore foster strategic flexibility and rationality to the decision-making process.

Figure 24. Scenario planning matrix: Classification of future hypothesis
Source: Own elaboration

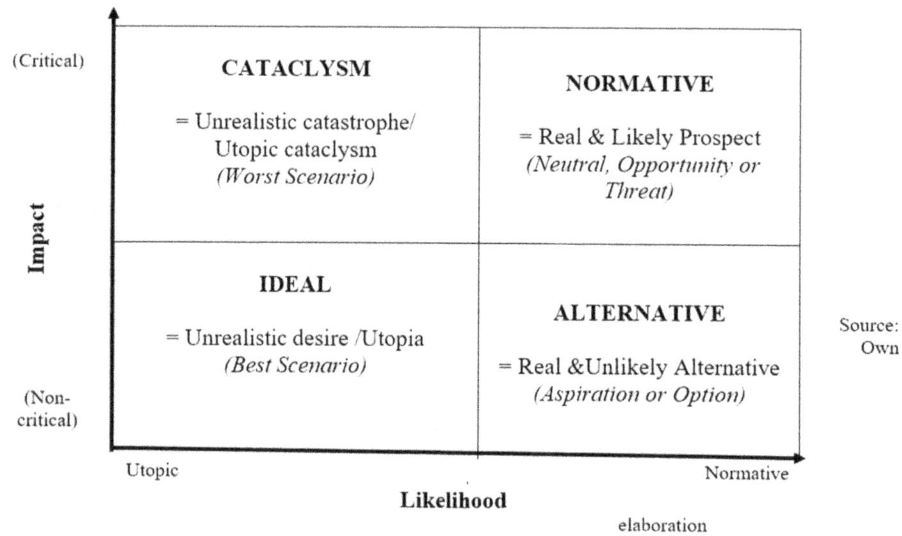

Since they are taken with a null likelihood, utopian scenarios of utopic cases of cataclysms, unrealistic events of worst-case-possible occurrences, though even if their impact is classified as being critical and pointing towards a large value-destructive hypothesis, they are irrelevant and consequently they are not a real threat for the managers, as their insolubility (or simple sterility of solutions by the firm) is not accompanied by a real need for its resolution in any time in the future. Subsequently, they are also frequently undermined by the professionals on the field of risk management as to their triadic role of identification, analysis and documentation of risks to business operations and profitability expectations.

The ideal scenario above, fitting also a quadrant of a utopic scenario but a non-critical one, is arguably a symmetrical of the utopian critical (i.e. the *cataclysm*). The reader may believe at this stage that an investment of resources towards the construction of scenarios, which implies a partial allocation towards the identification of utopian scenarios, is a bad use of organizational resources.

At first glance, the analyst might believe that yes, it is a waste of resources. This assumption is especially applicable to experienced analysts, with a RBV background or influenced by it. For instance, the analysts whom have already applied the Grant´s (2016) framework for appraising resources and capabilities may be mistaken to judge the data (list of utopic ideas) as "superfluous" strengths of intangible resources (alias, information). However, I would remind that the use of resources that are "superfluous strengths", as creative/contrived data, may constitute not solely a weighting item to be equated as a hypothesis for scenario planning, but also, seen as an information asset deriving from the interpretation of market research inputs, which use can be furthermore applied in multiple contexts. For instance, that data may inspire product designers in their new conceptions; or support industrial designers to picture fabrication alternatives and solutions; or yield new ideas for marketers´ development of a new campaigns, advertisements, content or a new way of reaching a target audience; or enlighten a new type of risk to be mapped for risk managers; or simply, endow strategist with more experience in applying scenario planning tools.

In this context of environment forecasting, the TAIDA´s process is composed of five (5) steps (Lindgreen and Bandhold, 2009):

- *Tracking,*
- *Analyzing*
- *Imaging*
- *Deciding*
- *Acting*

The steps occur in a serial manner, equivalent to the different phases of external environment analysis. The model adopting a series of endeavors on a serial manner, starts with the *tracking. This* initial step aims to find any changes at the EBE and early signs of whether those changes contain potential threats or opportunities. The *analysis* is the subsequent step focused on the manipulation of inputs of data from its interpretation. The aim is to decode their symbology and from there derive possible scenarios of impact on the firm and strategic actions to be taken. The *imaging* is a cognitive exercise of constructing an idea about the future, identifying possibilities and generating visions of what is desired, and subsequently, sharpening those initial ideas a fuzzy thoughts into a clearer image of what a future scenario might look like.

Hence it is here advocated, amidst not referred by the authors of the TAIDA model, that the imaging may contain two (2) underlying steps: *formulation* (conception of a thought/idea) and *conceptualization* (refining of its edges and removing of fuzziness). The fourth set, deciding, is the judging of multiple sets of information and identification of choices and strategies. The last step, the *acting* it refers to the initial deeds and follow up actions.

Another noticeable feature of the model is that, it does not start on the environmental forecasting´s phase, as the tracking is a step where the analyst is focused on finding changes, discovering patterns, trends, threats and opportunities. Moreover, to get an in-depth understanding of them and discover their interplay. This step is equivalent to Hitt, Ireland and Hoskinsson´s (2019) notion of environmental scanning (an earlier phase of analysis than forecasting as discussed in section 5.2.).

The virtue of the model is that it spreads across phases, gathering multiple analysis procedures into a single BEAP, stimulating the firm to go all the way through all phases, as the need for allocation of resources to a project is done all at once and shared across the TAIDA process instead of casuistically set per each new project. Moreover, it stays solely on the general environment being scenario planning and assessment tool which allows the immersion into depth, by opposition to SWOT, SOAR, TOWS, TO or SORF analysis.

The Cage Distance Framework

This is a framework with a clear comparative design. Actually, its architecture is built in such a way which one cannot apply it without at least the instrumentalization of two separate countries, as it is particularly suitable for comparing one country against another (1:1 logic). Thus, this is a model thought to assist organizations who require the mapping of cross-border differences (Ghemawat, 2001).

The model highlights the fact that borders still matter, as distance constitutes a significant barrier to competition. Thus, a traditional country portfolio analysis is advocated to be insufficient, needing to be tempered with the evaluation of multiple dimensions of distance, as to their probable impact on risks and opportunities in foreign markets. The model does not intend to subjugate the gravity theory of trade flows, which in turn, advocate a positive relationship between economic size and foreign trade and a negative relationship with distance and trade. On the other hand, is anchored on the empirical results as *Jeffrey Frankel* and *Andrew Rose*, as to the likelihood of distance variables to affect trade volumes.

Hence, distance is here classified it in terms of cultural, administrative, geographic, and economic distance between countries and its denomination is an abbreviation of these four dimensions of distance.

The CAGE can be particularly useful whenever a company is deciding in which direction to expand into a particular foreign country. However it takes as an initial assumption that an internationalization´s decision is based on a prior assessment of an own portfolio of products and their market positioning, as to their current status ones and possibility for their renewing their condition in the future, both products and markets.

Consequently, the firm is expected to have weighted, in advance, the pros and cons of a certain strategic action and the decision has been taken under a rational model. I would emphasize here the utility of the framework developed by *Iggor Ansoff* for such assessment, known as the *Ansoff´s Matrix.* On the latter, four (4) major options are delivered and represented as quadrants (i.e. *market penetration*; *market development*; *product development;* and *diversification*). Hence, at this stage a company willing to apply a CACE has likely taken a business strategy decision with preference to the extension of current number of markets (market development).

The main goal of the model is to analyze the probable impact of distance on a particular industry for organizations engaged in global businesses, considering the four segments above (i.e. cultural, administrative, geographic and economic distance). Herein, Pankaj Ghemawatt recommends the cross-observation of factors between observed countries, in complementarity to geographical distance, such as, language; religion; race; or social norms (cultural distance); colony-colonizer links; currencies; trading arrangements; social norms (administrative distance); and, income; plus, distribution-channel quality (economic factors) (Ghemawat, 2001).

Moreover, the author of the model suggests the registering of the highlights of distance (+) and proximity (-), as exemplified in the figure below.

Table 16. CAGE framework

	C	*A*	*G*	*E*
Contexts increasing the distance (+)	- Differences: i) language ii) ethnicity iii) religion iv) social norms - Lack of social networks	- Absence of monetary or political association - Political hostilities - Weak legal and financial institutions	1. Lack of common borders 2. Physical remoteness 3. Climate differences	4. Different consumer incomes 5. Difference of costs and resources[6]

Source: Ghemawat, 2001

This scholar claims though that industries most highly affected by cultural distance are the ones on economic sectors that span across communication, national identity; and/or carrying country-specific quality assumptions (e.g. TV/radio; or food/food services). Moreover the industries most affected on the administrative distance are the ones more exposed to the governments views as staples (e.g. the utilities´ sector). On the geographical distance the most affected industries are the ones, in which, the nature of the product or its perceived value, or the connectivity and communication is essential. This is the case of fresh food, cement, or even financial services. Finally, the economic distance makes some industries more sensitive to it, leveraged exposed to household income on business-to-consumer (B2C) sectors and labour intensive sectors (e.g. automobile; or garment/apparel).

Consequently, Ghemawat´s (2001) article "distance still matters" rates the *industry sensitivity* to distance, concluding that some industries are *more sensitive* and other *less sensitive* to each type of distance dimensions. This can be of special useful as an initial check-point, i.e. determining the likelihood of encountering higher barriers and potentially being exposed to higher risk of losses. For instance, on cultural distance the linguistic ties seems to make food companies more sensitive to distance (e.g. cereals, meat, and other miscellaneous edible products including tobacco), but less sensitive cork and wood products, photographic apparatus, optical goods and road vehicles. On the administrative distance as to the preferential trading agreements observed are coffee, tea, sugar, honey electricity, gold and textiles (and less sensitive, footwear, furniture, travel goods and sanitary products). On geographic distance, physical remoteness makes companies more sensitive on electricity, gas, live animals, paperboard; while less sensitive are for example the industries of coffee, tea, cocoa, species, telecommunications and photographic apparatuses. As to the economic distance more sensitive is to wealth differences activities related to meat, iron/steel and manufactured fertilizers and less sensitive are coffee, tea, animal oils and fats, power-generated machinery, office machines and data-processed equipment.

The comparative design is here an enemy of a phronetic study. The analyst is expected to have collected in in-depth data on equal variables in both studies countries before engagement into a cross-observation of them and subsequently choosing the most impactful ones to include in the model´s representation. Hence, this procedure may be time-consuming and a costly one, however, also of enormous utility comprehending country specifications and their meaning when compared means. This brings intel not attained with single country studies Final note to emphasize that the preconception that distancing was something negative has been most recently softened by the Uppsala School of thought (or U-model), which more recent studies in the context of Swedish multinational companies demonstrated that distancing is not always a retraction factor. The studies of Nordman and Tolstoy (2014) on 314 Swedish SMEs with higher sensitivity to uncertainty and risk-taking (which lead to high *psychic distancing*), were actually the ones who developed larger effort on developing market-specific capabilities and transformed psychic distance barriers into further learning which enabled international business´ adaptation (Abrantes, 2020).

5.6 INDEXES, RATIOS, AND BENCHMARKING

Here, I would add quickly a distinction of them. An *index* refer to an event to be observed on multiple units (several locus and time) (e.g. the person´s body mass). Thus, indexes are variable in nature and allow the monitoring of their performance.

Indexes have a variety of measurement possibilities according to the method of the calculation. Herein, the notion of *benchmark* refers to the multiple indicative values collected within the same index, which allows for comparisons and furthermore, the diagnosis of the direction taken by a certain variable, based on the evolution of the performance outputs, or temporary progression values.

The *ratio*, similar to an index, is more limited in output possibilities. However, is also not dependent on previous figures (benchmarks) to have a context of analyzability, as they are tied to absolute frequencies (F=1), ranging the units of observation, as indicator of relative frequency (f) varies between 0 and 1.

Both, indexes and ratios, due to their quantitative properties shall be recognized an excellent profiling and comparative apparatus which on the analysis of EBEs contribute to uncertainty reduction, and furthermore reduction of bias and error in further analysis and future decisions.

Here, there´s a list of possible indexes/ratios, as an example, of possible variables accounted on a pipeline of observation within your BEAP:

Certainly, other macroeconomic indicators can be tested, furthermore, against the ones indicated on the table. For example, Mügge (2015) suggests indicators like, *public deficits*; *inflation*; *unemployment ratios; public expenditure;* overall *taxation*; *private consumption*; *interest rates; private savings* or *investments*.

However, whenever a BEAP requires one to go deeper into data collection some of the indexes above divide itself on multiple options of sub-indexes.

As to economic landscape, the study of the Heritage Foundation on economic freedom (or, the IEF) contains multiple indicators within four (4) dimensions (Miller, Kim, & Roberts, 2021; Abrantes, 2018):

1. Rules of Law:
    a. Intellectual property;
    b. Judicial effectiveness;
    c. Government integrity.
2. Government Size:
    a. Tax burden;
    b. Government spending;
    c. Fiscal health.
3. Regulatory Efficiency:
    a. Business freedom;
    b. Labour freedom;
    c. Monetary freedom.
4. Market Openness
    a. Trade freedom;
    b. Investment Freedom;
    c. Financial Freedom.

Moreover, as to economic transformation (i.e. IET), the BTI Transform Index as a project resulting from the regional collaboration over 300 experts, allowed the measurement of, not just one IET indicator, but fourteen (14) indicators divided by seven (7) criteria. These encompass variables related to *economic performance*, *competition policy*, *property rights*; *social security* and *compensation*; *equality of opportunities*; and, *sustainability*, such as, Level of Socioeconomic Development; Organization of the Market and Competition; Monetary and Fiscal Stability; Private Property; or Welfare Regime (BTI, online).

Table 17. Examples of indexes/ratios for a BEAP

Index/Ratio´s Designation	Area of intervention
Balance of Trade (BoT)	International trade fluxes
Business Ethics National Index (BENI)	Sector´s formal business ethics
Consumer Price Index (CoPI)	Evolution of Good´s prices
Corruption Perception index (CPI)	(all major forms of) Corruption
Democracy Index (DI)	Global average/national data
Economic Complexity Index (ECI)	Knowledge Intensity of a country
Environmental Performance Index	Compliance to Environmental SDGs
Ethics Index Score (EIS)	Societal ethical conduct
Gender Development Index (GDI)	Gender gaps in human development
Global Cybersecurity index (GSI)	National commitment to cybersecurity at global-level
Global Competitiveness Index (GCI)	Macro/microeconomic foundations of national competitiveness
Global Entrepreneurship Index (GEI)	Entrepreneurial activity of business ecosystems
Global Health Security Index (GHSI)	Vulnerability to biological risks
Global Food Security Index (GFSI)	Measures affordability, availability and quality and safety of goods
Global Tourism Index	Measurement of national factors of attractiveness to develop business related to this industry (hospitality/traveling/tourism)
Gross Domestic Product (GDP)	Value added by the production of goods/services
Human Development Index (HDI)	Overall achievements on education, life expectancy and standard of living
ICT Diffusion index (ICTDI)	Access, connectivity and policies
Index of Economic Freedom (IEF)	Multiple factors, related to, Policies, Regulation and Market Openness
Index of Economic Transformation (IET)	National economic evolution on 14 indicators
Index of Political Transformation (IPT)	Change in Political Climate
Operations Risk Index (ORI)	Ease of the business climate
Political Stability Index (PSI)	Stability of Politics and Governance issues
Political Risk Index (PRI)	(National) Risk
Producer Price Index (PPI)	Average changes in selling prices
Product Complexity Index (PCI)	Knowledge Intensity of a product
Regional Entrepreneurship and Development Index (REDI)	Measurement of regional entrepreneurship
Rule of Law Index (RLI)	Adherence to the rule of law in practice
Transnationality index (TNI)	Firm-level´s international business (commitment)
Women Peace and Security Index (WPSI)	Draws on women's inclusion, justice, and security

Source: Own elaboration

Moreover, the BTI measures, within the political landscape, the extent of Political Transformation, including furthermore 18 indicators, such as, *Stateness*; *Political Participation*; *Rule of Law*; *Stability of Democratic Institutions*; *Political and Social Integration*.

Therein, the Rule of Law, taken by the RLI, exams in practice eight other sub-factors: *constraints on government powers*; *absence of corruption*; *open government*; *fundamental rights*; *order and security*; *regulatory enforcement*; *civil justice*; and, *criminal justice*.

Other examples of breadth and cascading of a general index into others is the BERI or the GEI. The BERI run a three-times per year "Country Risk Assessment" combining 15 criteria that measure the country's business environment from 0 (*"unacceptable"* conditions) to 4 (*"superior"* conditions), over 50 countries. Those criteria are divided into four (4) *ratings*:

1. Political Risk Index (PRI);
2. Operations Risk Index (ORI);
3. Combined Score CS)
4. Remittance and Repatriation Factor (RRF)

The image below provides an example of real BERI scores, applied to a European country (Germany), for the year 2020.

Figure 25. BERI country ratings - Example for Germany, year 2020
Source: Own elaboration

	Combined Score	Political Risk Index	Operations Risk Index	Remittance and Repatriation Factor
2013	68	64	63	77
2014	70	64	64	81
2015	68	62	64	79
2016	66	57	63	77
2017	67	53	69	78
2018	64	50	66	77
2019	59	47	60	69
Present	53	45	54	61
+1 Year	54	43	56	63
+5 Years	59	48	60	68

The objective of the PRI is to measure social political changes while the ORI is to gauge the business operations climate (BERI, online). The *R* factor measures the risk that affects the access to foreign exchange and remittances of profits and repatriation of capital in a convertible currency. Hence, the R factor estimates the country's capacity and willingness for private foreign companies to:

1. Convert profits and capital in the local currency to foreign exchange and transfer the funds;
2. Have access to convertible currency to import components, equipment, and raw materials.

The "interpretation of the ratings" in the user guide is quite useful as it contain the rubric and descriptors for evaluating the benchmarks. You ought to note that both PRI and ORI have a similar scale and transitivity of the meaning of the scores. Here is below shown the ORI´s "guidelines on risk" for the interpretation of the ORI rating above in the table about Germany:

700 – 100 scores – Indicates a *"Stable Environment"*.

Note: Score typical of an advanced industrialized economy. Generally, the problems for foreign businesses are offset by the country's efficiency; market opportunities; financial system; and, advanced infrastructure.

55-69 scores - Indicates a *"Moderate-risk country"* with complications in day-to-day operations.

Note: Usually the political structure is sufficiently stable to permit consistent operations (without serious disruption). The country may assist a dynamic economic expansion, often accompanied by the potential for attractive profits.

40-54 scores – Indicate a *"High risk for foreign-owned businesses"*.

Note: Only special situations should be considered, e.g., scarce raw materials or unusual profit potential.

0-39 scores – Indicates an *"Unacceptable"*

Note: The status of national risks establishes intolerable conditions for establishing foreign-owned businesses.

In this case, the ORI benchmark on "present" *(Y2020)*, indicate, contrarily, to what it could be expected a high-risk for foreign-owned business, as the country was affected by a slowdown of business activity, due to economic implications of Covid-19 linger. The comprehension of these ratings shall be revised (and interpreted) by the reading of the "outlook" section.

For further exploring of all indexes (namely the guideline on risk), the sub-indices and criteria; the measurement rules; the scales; the benchmarks per time (year; 5-year or 10-year conditions); or even, to comprehend/interpret the results, is suggested, furthermore, the articulation of the specific country reports acquired from BERI, S.A. with *the User Guide* of the *Business Risk* Service (BRS).

The GEI measures annually the "health" of entrepreneurship ecosystems over 135 countries and ranks them against each other. This provides a picture of how a country performs, both domestically and internationally.

The Global Entrepreneurship and Development Institute (GEDI) accounts on the collection of data the entrepreneurial *abilities*; *attitudes*, and *aspirations* of the local population and then weight these against the social-economic "infrastructure". This is pulled up to a subsequent measure of performance of the health of regional ecosystems. Based on Sternberg´s (2009) study on the causes and effects of regional entrepreneurship, the REDI condenses fourteen (14) indicators, crossing the "regional start-up activities" (as, education, capital, knowledge-transfer, cultural norms and values, industry and macro-economic trends) with "regional attributes" (as the supporting mechanisms, institutions, infrastructure, labor, capital, organizational ecology per industry and location factors).

With regard to ethics, the BENI is a reference of the measurement of formal business ethics´ activity. It is consisted of seven (7) distinct dimensions: academia; business; social or ethical investment; business ethics organizations; government; social activist groups; the media.

Within digital infrastructure, the Global Cybersecurity Index (GCI) is a reference for the measuring of the commitment of countries to global cybersecurity. The International Telecommunication Union (ITU) monitors cybersecurity in a broad range of national applications, across industries and sectors, to comprehend the country's level of development and engagement towards five (5) pillars assessed in this index: (i) Legal Measures, (ii) Technical Measures, (iii) Organizational Measures, (iv) Capacity Development, and (v) Cooperation – and then aggregated into an overall score.

As to the physical infrastructure, the European Environmental Agency (EEA) had developed a set of one-hundred and twenty two (122) indicators monitoring the environmental landscape on 13 environmental topics (i.e. Air pollution; Biodiversity – Ecosystems; Climate change adaptation; Climate change mitigation; Energy; Environment and health; Industry; Land use; Resource efficiency and waste; Soil; Sustainability transitions; Transport; Water and marine environment). The EEA monitors through the following classification (EEA, online):

- *Descriptive* indicators (Type A)
- *Performance* indicators (Type B)
- *Efficiency* indicators (Type C)
- *Policy effectiveness indicators* (Type D)
- *Total welfare indicators* (Type E)

These indicators respond at specific objectives per category, as follows:

(i) Type A: To comprehend, *what is happening?*
(ii) Type B: To understand the actions, *does it matter? Are we reaching targets?*
(iii) Type C: To grasp evolution associated with the actions, *are we improving?*
(iv) Type D: To determine how positive is evolution: *Are the measures working?*
(v) *Type E: To evaluate in general, are we better off?*

A final index here described from the broad list above is the HDI. Especially for the BEAPs, which aim at portray, on a host-market, some specific data requirements (e.g. human capital or purchasing power of a potential customer-base), this index is especially relevant. Furthermore, this can be accentuated by the industry itself, since for the businesses selling directly to the consumer (B2C), this index can be even more appealing. The HDI is composed of three (3) sub-indexes, the Education Index (EI); the Life Expectancy Index (LEI) and Gross National Income (GNI).

$$HDI = \sum \mu \, (EI + LFI + GNI)$$

Or,

$$HDI = \sum \underline{(EI + LFI + GNI) / N}$$

This index (HDI), is focused on measuring three (3) dimensions, corresponding each to one sub-index. The dimension of "long and healthy life" matched the LEI (index) naturally focused on data of life expectancy at birth, while the knowledge dimension corresponded to the EI. On the "knowledge" dimension, the index (EI) is obtained by the simple arithmetic function of expected (*e*) number of years of schooling against the subtracted number of effective or real (*r*) years *in school on average per citizen:*

$$(EI_{(mean)} = e(\mu)/r(\mu)).$$

The third dimension ("decent standard of living") in which the GNI, as an index, fits into, describe the income per capita.

LEARNING OUTCOMES

- The scope of analyzability and the analysis function
- The criteria of factor´s selection
- The relation of BEAP´s goals, philosophy of analysis and criteria

- The types or phases of EBE analysis: inspecting, scanning, monitoring, forecasting and evaluation
- Comprehending the differences between market data, information, organizational knowledge and market intelligence
- BEAPs and the source of data and intelligence tools
- Understand the use of the models
- Recognize the importance of benchmarks, and the use of indicators, indexes and ratios as secondary data

CASE: COUPANG CORP

Coupang is a "rocket deliver" in South Korea. Mr. *Bom Kim* (an American-Korean graduate from Harvard) founded the company in 2010. *Coupang* sells a variety of goods online on the website www.coupang.com within the consumer discretionary sector.

Their products, sold and delivered throughout Korea, range from apparel, cosmetics, electronics, footwear, food products, furniture, toys, and so forth,, becoming the largest online retailer in country adopting Artificial Intelligence (AI)-driven tools, harnessing a vast number of warehouses (a main unit placed at the city of *Daegu* an several hubs), and being the third-largest employer in country, even despite the allegations of employees´ stress or burnout.

Naturally, one may wonder how being a native has helped him Mr. Kim to build in South Korea an e-commerce giant. However that does not seem to be the reason behind the great success. *Coupang* offers their customers something clearly distinctive (and unmatched) on their services: *convenience* and *speed*, which it is marketed exceptionally. Despite selling online products on a variety of items/ different products categories, *Coupang* guarantees nonetheless a fast-delivery, as a unique selling proposition (USP), with all orders being are treated and delivered within 24 hours in 99,3% of the cases.

The singularity of their business model combines AI advanced technology with operational efficiency applied to their delivery system, which culminates in an almost instant delivery. In fact, AI-skills on proprietary algorithms seems the secret of efficient logistics processes, accounting volumetric staking/ groupage per lorry, precise ordering of delivery combined with a precise route delineation.

Coupang Corp. raised in 2018 a sum of 2B USD from *SoftBank's Vision Fund* in result of 9B USD´s valuation. In Mar-2021 went public in the *New York Stock Exchange (NYSE)* being the most value private-held startup in the country with a real net worth of worth of 5,7B USD, and the biggest U.S. listing of an Asian company since Alibaba in 2014 (Forbes, online; MIT Technology Review, online).

CHAPTER HIGHLIGHTS

- BE events and factors of analyzability (selection and criteria)
- EBEA´s philosophical perspectives: universalism vs. relativism
- Typologies of analyzability: System-thinking and teleological thinking
- The 5 parts of the EBEA: from inspection to assessment
- The dominance of business environment scanning systems (BESS)
- Future thinking and scenario-making: typologies and methods
- Models of EBEA (e.g. the Cage; Dematel; Steeple; or the Telescopic Observation)

- Sources of data for EBEA and intelligence tools
- Indexes, ratios and benchmarks

CONCLUSION

In this chapter a sequential order of topics were naturally tied up together. Firstly, addressing the three (3) main criteria of factor´s selection. Here, the philosophical aspects of analyzability along the continuum of paradigm was also discussed, as the BEAP may vary substantial according to purpose of the analysis.

Afterwards, were depicted the types (or phases) of analysis and described their utility. Multiple concepts on environmental change were either introduced or revisited. Afterwards, a broad range of sources of data and intelligence tools were also listed and we ended the chapter was a section on models of analyzability exploring a dozen of situational analysis tools (i.e. Eisenhower Matrix; PEST; SWOT; TOWS; GROW; CAGE; SOAR; TOC; TO; AIM; STEEPLE; and DEMATEL) centered on the comprehension of the external environment and in some cases its relations with the micro tier (the industry) and the focal firm.

Moreover, quick reference was made in some of those models to other tools, due to their interdependence. Thus, we brought to the light some ideas encompassed on the Ansoff Matrix, the SORF, the U-model, Lewin´s 3 steps model (U-C-F) or Kotter´s 6-step change. Many other tools could be naturally considered in either pure or hybrid situational analysis studies. For instance, Geer Hofstede´s 6-D model, of great utility for the analysis of distances, which was precisely the last model revised (i.e. CAGE). The mapping of the average results using the 6-D or other alike tool of cultural mapping elevates the use of this comparative tool using quants a mechanism of data triangulation for confirmatory purposes.

Many other models could be included in this chapter, since a BEAP may account a multiplicity of other instruments to be brought in the pipeline of analyzability, whether with an internal, external or hybrid-focus. I took furthermore the liberty of adding a few more tips, over three dozens of extra strategic analysis models used both in the academia and business world, as follows:

- The 5 Fs of competition
- the 7S framework
- the AAA Global Strategy Framework
- the ADDING value scorecard
- the BHESC framework
- the Balance Scorecard (BSC)
- the Benchmarking Model
- the BCG portfolio matrix
- the Bowman´s clock
- the Blue Ocean Strategy (BOS)
- the Canvas Framework
- the Change kaleidoscope
- the Cultural tiles;
- the Cultural web;
- the DCAL (Digital competition augmented learning model)
- The Double Diamond model
- the Diamond Framework

- the DuPont Method
- the ERPG
- the Environment turbulence level (ETL) assessment
- the Internal/External (I/E) matrix
- the Framework for Competitive Analysis (FCA)
- the GCAM (for capability diffusion across M-forms)
- the Grand Strategy Matrix
- the Grant´s taxonomy;
- the product life cycle (PLC);
- the MCDA (Multi-criteria decision analysis)
- the Monte Carlo simulation;
- the Objectives and key-results (OKR) model;
- the OLI framework
- the Perceptual mapping (of product positioning);
- the Performance Evaluation Matrix (PEM);
- the Performance Measurement Matrix (PMM);
- the Quantitative Strategic Planning Matrix (QSPM);
- the Strategic Position and Action Evaluation (SPACE) matrix;
- the Tableau the Board;
- the Trompenaars 7 dimensions model;
- the Stopford and Wells
- the Strategy Maps (a core tool of the Balanced Scorecard, above referred);
- the Strategic Success Paradigm (SSP);
- the Suitability, Feasibility and Acceptability (FSA) analysis
- the Optimal Strategic Performance-positioning (OSPP) matrix
- the Value Chain (VC) analysis
- the VRIO/N;

Due to natural, limitations of the scope of book, I have refrain myself from elaborating a little bit about them. However those are unavoidable models to refer to in the context of Strategic Management and specifically Business Environment Analyzability. I leave it, at this stage, at your criteria and curiosity, to do the further exploring of these and other tools.

Nevertheless, I shall recommend you, upon need or curiosity (again) to explore all the other theories referred in the book (excluded from this list above) (e.g. Ansoff Matrix; Kotter´s 8-stage model; the Eisenhower matrix; and so forth).

Moreover, as the BEAP is intrinsically related to two other close domains (i.e. Project Management and Decision-Making), thus, some other tools (over two dozens) are added as well, on these rather specific two areas, as suggestions for your further search and reading as complementary tools for the analysis of the Business Environment on both interfaces (internal/external) with the firm´s strategy:

Again, many other recommendations of models could be added here in these two domains as well (Project Management and Decision Making), whether for supporting pure internal or external BE analysis or supporting the design of the project (BEAP) or its administration.

Furthermore, it is recommended, the articulation of these tools at each project with relevant *indexes* and *ratios*.

Table 18. Other useful models for business environment analysis (BEA)

Tool	BE	Applicability
- The Appreciative Inquiry (AI) model	EE or IE	Build organizational vision; align direction, and/or generate innovation
- The Belbin & Bono´s Role-playing model	EE or IE	Determining the strengths of an individual or team for project effectiveness
- The Cognitive Dissonance model	EE or IE	Identify potential (individual) tensions (behavior vs. beliefs) and/or conflicts
- The Drexlet/Sibbet team performance model	IE	Predict the stages involved in both creating and sustaining teams
- The Energy Model	IE	Determine resource expenditure per expected output
- The Feedback Box & Analysis	EE or IE	Classification of types of criticism per individual or team/unit
- The Gant Chart	EE or IE	Visualization of the activities´ timetables in a single diagram
- The ICOM model	IE	Drawing of general terms for the organization of a project
- The Ishikawa diagram	IE	Outline the different steps in a process
- The Johari Window	EE or IE	Self-awareness for interpersonal relations
- The Pareto principle/chart	EE and IE	To identify opportunities related to Root Cause Corrective Action (RCCA)
- the Maslow pyramid	EE and IE	Mapping of needs
- The Maylor´s 4-D model	IE	Project´s structuring
- The Pert chart/diagram	IE	Planning of serial tasks in a project
- The Prisoner´s dilemma	EE and IE	Access the outcomes of decisions
- the Project Portfolio Matrix	IE	Define growth and market share
- The Result Optimization model	EE and IE	Determine feasibility
- The Rubber Band model	EE and IE	Choice between 2 real options
- the Rumsfeld matrix	EE and IE	Anticipate (the degree of) uncertainty

REFERENCES

Abrantes, B. F. (2020). Are Neoclassic Internationalization Models Enduring? A Case-Review of the Uppsala Paradigm. *SAGE Open*, *10*(2). doi:10.1177/2158244020932535

Abrantes, B. F. (2018) The internationalization paradigm and dynamic capabilities of Portuguese firms: contributions from case studies in the metallurgical and metal-mechanic sectors. *Repositório do ISCTE.* http://hdl.handle.net/10071/16556

AgnolettoJ. (2020) *Project Assurance Fundamentals.* PricewaterhouseCoopers. https://www.pwc.com.au/assurance/internal-audit/Project-Fundamentals-Slides.pdf

Aguilar, F. J. (1967). *Scanning the business environment.* McMillan.

Amit, R., & Zott, C. (2015). Crafting business architecture: The antecedents of business model design. *Strategic Entrepreneurship Journal*, *9*(4), 331–350. doi:10.1002ej.1200

Andersen, P. (2013). *Performance management: A handbook for small business banks and microfinance institutions.* Practical Action Publishing. doi:10.3362/9781780447926

Arrow, K. J. (1956). The Role of Securities in the Optimal Allocation of Risk Bearing. *The Review of Economic Studies, 31*(2), 91–96. doi:10.2307/2296188

Bakos, J. Y. (1991). A strategic analysis of electronic marketplaces. *Management Information Systems Quarterly, 15*(3), 295–310. doi:10.2307/249641

Barker, J. R. (1993). Tightening the iron cage: Concertive control in self-managing teams. *Administrative Science Quarterly, 38*(3), 408–437. doi:10.2307/2393374

Barney, J. B. (1996). The resource-based theory of the firm. *Organization Science, 7*(5), 469–469. doi:10.1287/orsc.7.5.469

Beer, M., Voelpel, S. C., Leibold, M., & Tekie, E. D. (2005). Strategic management as organizational learning: Developing fit and alignment through a disciplined process. *Long Range Planning, 38*(5), 445–465. doi:10.1016/j.lrp.2005.04.008

Bennis, W., & Nanus, B. (1985). *Leaders: The strategies for taking charge*. Harp & Row.

Biron, B., & McDowell, E. (2021) Inside the wild and tumultuous history of Toys R Us, a once beloved children's brand that just closed its last 2 stores in the US. *Business Insider*. https://www.businessinsider.com/the-tumultuous-history-of-toys-r-us-photos-2020-8?r=US&IR=T

Blacker, F. (1995). Knowledge, knowledge work and organization: An overview and interpretations. *Organization Studies, 15*(6), 1021–1046. doi:10.1177/017084069501600605

Blok, V. (2019). Xenophon's philosophy of management. *Handbook of Philosophy of Management*, 1-19. Bloomberg Coupang Corp. https://www.bloomberg.com/profile/company/COUPAZ:KS

Bloomberg. (2022) *Data and Operations.* Bloomberg Professional Services. https://www.bloomberg.com/professional/expertise/data-and-operations/

Boddy. (2020). *Management: Using practice and theory to develop skill, (8th ed.).* Harlow – UK: Pearson Education Limited.

Bosch-Rekveldt, M., Jongkind, Y., Mooi, H., Bakker, H., & Verbraeck, A. (2011). Grasping project complexity in large engineering projects: The TOE (Technical, Organizational and Environmental) framework. *International Journal of Project Management, 29*(6), 728–739. doi:10.1016/j.ijproman.2010.07.008

Boxall, P., & Purcell, J. (2000). Strategic human resource management: Where have we come from and where should we be going? *International Journal of Management Reviews, 2*(2), 183–203. doi:10.1111/1468-2370.00037

Bradfield, R., Wright, G., Burt, G., Cairns, G., & Heijden, K. (2005). The origins and evolution of scenario techniques in long range business planning. *Futures, 37*(8), 795–812. doi:10.1016/j.futures.2005.01.003

Brouthers, L. E., Gao, Y., & Napshin, S. (2014). *Keiretsu centrality: Profits and profit stability: A power dependence perspective.* CORE.

CaseCoach. (2021). The The Top-10 Strategy Consulting Firms Compared. *Case Coach.* https://casecoach.com/b/the-top-10-strategy-consulting-firms-compared/

Central Intelligence Agency. (n.d.). *The World Factbook*. CIA. https://www.cia.gov/the-world-factbook/

Chaffey, D. (2021). SWOT analysis template examples. *Smart Insights*. https://www.smartinsights.com/marketplace-analysis/swot-analysis/swot-analysis/

Chandler, A. D. (1962). *Structure and strategy*. Harvard University Press.

Chao, G. T., & Moon, H. (2005). The cultural mosaic: A meta-theory to understand the complexity of culture. *The Journal of Applied Psychology*, *90*(6), 1128–1140. doi:10.1037/0021-9010.90.6.1128 PMID:16316269

Chesbrough, H. (2010). Business model innovation: Opportunities and barriers. *Long Range Planning*, *43*(2/3), 354–363. doi:10.1016/j.lrp.2009.07.010

Cisco. (n.d.). *Acquisitions by year*. Cisco. https://www.cisco.com/c/en/us/about/corporate-strategy-office/acquisitions/acquisitions-list-years.html

Cohen, M. D., March, J. G., & Olsen, J. P. (1972). A garbage can model of organizational choice. *Administrative Science Quarterly*, *17*(1), 1–25. doi:10.2307/2392088

Cotton, D. (2010). *The Business Strategy Toolkit*. Gloucestershire: UK: Management Books 2000.

Debreu, G. (1959). *Theory of value*. Wiley.

Dinçer, Ö. (2004). *Stratejik yönetim ve işletme politikası*. Beta Yayınları.

Dun and Bradstreet. (2021) *Our analytics*. DNB. https://www.dnb.com/

Duke, L., & Birkinshaw, L. (2011). *The rise and fall of Nokia*. Think at London Business School Magazine. https://publishing.london.edu/cases/the-rise-and-fall-of-nokia/

Dunning, J., & Kim, C. (2007). The Cultural Roots of Guanxi: An Exploratory Study. *World Economy*, *30*(2), 329–341. doi:10.1111/j.1467-9701.2007.00885.x

Economist Intelligence Unit. (2005). *Business 2010: embracing the challenge of change*. Economist Intelligence Unit: London, U.K. EEA (online) About EEA indicators. Available at: https://www.eea.europa.eu/data-and-maps/indicators/#c0=30&c12-operator=or&b_start=0

Euromonitor International. (2021). Explore insights. EI. https://www.euromonitor.com/

European Central Bank. (2022). Statistics. ECB. https://www.ecb.europa.eu/stats/html/index.en.html

Eisenhardt, K. M., & Martin, J. A. (2000). Dynamic capabilities: What are they? *Strategic Management Journal*, *21*(10-11), 1105–1121. doi:10.1002/1097-0266(200010/11)21:10/11<1105::AID-SMJ133>3.0.CO;2-E

Erikson, R. S., & Tedin, K. L. (2003). *American Public Opinion* (6th ed.). Longman.

EU. (2020). EU data protection rules. *Europea*. https://ec.europa.eu/info/priorities/justice-and-fundamental-rights/data-protection/2018-reform-eudata-protection-rules/eu-data-protection-rules_en#documents

Eur-Lex. (2016). Regulation (EU) 2016/679 of the European Parliament and the Council of 27 April 2016, *Official Journal of the European Union, L119/1*. https://eurlex.europa.eu/legal-content/EN/TXT/PDF/?uri=CELEX:02016R0679-20160504&from=EN

Fenwick. (2020) Coronavirus Impact on M&A and Other Strategic Corporate Transactions. *Fenwick.* https://www.fenwick.com/insights/publications/coronavirus-impact-on-m-a-and-other-strategic-corporate-transactions

Fischer, B., Lago, U., & Li, F. (2015) *The Haier Road to Growth.* Strategy + Business. https://www.strategy-business.com/article/00323.

Forgas, J. P., & George, J. M. (2001). Affective influences on judgments and behavior in organizations: An information processing perspective. *Organizational Behavior and Human Decision Processes*, *86*(1), 3–34. doi:10.1006/obhd.2001.2971

Friesner, T. (2011). History of SWOT analysis. *Marketing Teacher, 2000-2010.* https://www.researchgate.net/publication/288958760_History_of_swot_analysis/citations

Friedman, V. J., & Antal, A. B. (2005). Negotiating reality: A theory of action approach to intercultural competence. *Management Learning*, *36*(1), 69–86. doi:10.1177/1350507605049904

Gartner Inc. (2021). *Gartner Forecasts Worldwide IT Spending to Reach $4 Trillion in 2021.* Garter Inc. https://www.gartner.com/en/newsroom/press-releases/2021-04-07-gartner-forecasts-worldwide-it-spending-to-reach-4-trillion-in-2021

Geiss, C., Geiss, S. (2009) *An introduction to probability theory*. Jyväskylän yliopisto.

Ghemawat, P. (2001). Distance still matters. *Harvard Business Review*, *79*(8), 137–147. PMID:11550630

Goldratt, E. M. (1990). *Theory of constraints.* Croton-on-Hudson: North River.

Grant, R. M. (2021). *Contemporary strategy analysis.* John Wiley & Sons.

Graves, T. (2006). *An introduction to SCORE: Beyond SWOT analysis: strategy, capability, and effectiveness*. https://documen.site/download/introduction-to-score-tetradian-consulting_pdf

Grundy, T. (2006). Rethinking and reinventing Michael Porter's five forces model. *Strategic Change*, *15*(5), 213–229. doi:10.1002/jsc.764

Gürkan, E. (2012). The efficacy of Ottoman counter-intelligence in the 16th century. *Acta Orientalia (København)*, *65*(1), 1–38. doi:10.1556/AOrient.65.2012.1.1

Hansen, C. (2020). Daoism. *The Stanford Encyclopedia of Philosophy (Spring 2020 Edition),* Edward N. Zalta (ed.). https://plato.stanford.edu/archives/spr2020/entries/daoism/

Hawawini, G., Subramanian, V., & Verdin, P. (2003). Is performance driven by industry-or firm-specific factors? A new look at the evidence. *Strategic Management Journal*, *24*(1), 1–16. doi:10.1002mj.278

Hitt, M. A., Ireland, R. D., & Hoskisson, R. E. (2016). *Strategic management: Concepts and cases: Competitiveness and globalization*. Cengage Learning.

Markit, I. H. S. (2021) *Economics and country risks.* IHS Market. https://ihsmarkit.com/products/global-industry-forecasts-analysis.html

International Trade Centre. (n.d.). International trade statistics 2001-2020. ITC. https://www.intracen.org/itc/market-info-tools/trade-statistics/

Krogerus, M., & Tschäppeler, R. (2017). *The Decision Book: Fifty models for strategic thinking (New Edition).* Profile Books.

Lynch, R. (2009). *Strategic management.* Pearson Education Limited.

Lynch, R., & Cross, K. (1991). *Measure Up! Yardstick for Continuous Improvement.* Blackwell.

Lindgren, M., & Bandhold, H. (2009). *Scenario Planning.* Palgrave MacMillan.

McGahan, A. M., & Porter, M. E. (1997). How much does industry matter, really? *Strategic Management Journal, 18*(S1), 15–30. doi:10.1002/(SICI)1097-0266(199707)18:1+<15::AID-SMJ916>3.0.CO;2-1

Miller, T., Kim, A. B., & Roberts, J. M. (2021). *Index of Economic Freedom.* Heritage Foundation. MA. https://www.heritage.org/index/pdf/2021/book/index_2021.pdf

MIT Technology Review. (2021). *Tech policy: This company delivers packages faster than Amazon, but workers pay the price.* MIT. https://www.technologyreview.com/2021/06/09/1025884/coupang-amazon-labor-costs-worker-death/

Moon, H. C., Rugman, A. M., & Verbeke, A. (1998). A generalized double diamond approach to the global competitiveness of Korea and Singapore. *International Business Review, 7*(2), 135–150. doi:10.1016/S0969-5931(98)00002-X

Nielsen. (2021). Insights. Nielsen. https://www.nielsen.com/us/en/

Nordman, E. R., & Tolstoy, D. (2014). Does relationship psychic distance matter for the learning processes of internationalizing SMEs? *International Business Review, 23*(1), 30–37. doi:10.1016/j.ibusrev.2013.08.010

Ohmae, K. (1982). *The Mind of the strategist: The Art of Japanese Business.* McGraw-Hill Observatory of Economic Complexity (OEC) Data. https://atlas.media.mit.edu/en/resources/data/

Organisation for Economic Co-operation and Development (n.d.). *Data.* OECD. https://data.oecd.org/

Euro Monitor. (n.d.). *How passport helps.* EM. https://www.euromonitor.com/our-expertise/passport

Project Management Institute. (n.d.). *What is Project Management?* PMI. https://www.pmi.org/about/learn-about-pmi/what-is-project-management

Proquest. (2022). Culture Grams. Proquest. https://www.proquest.com/products-services/culturegrams.html

Panagiotou, G., & van Wijnen, R. (2005). The "telescopic observations" framework: An attainable strategic tool. *Marketing Intelligence & Planning, 23*(2), 155–171. doi:10.1108/02634500510589912

Performance Consultants. (2021). *What is the GROW Model?* Performance Consultants. https://www.performanceconsultants.com/grow-model

Pickton, D. W., & Wright, S. (1998). What's SWOT in strategic analysis? *Strategic Change, 7*(1), 101–109. doi:10.1002/(SICI)1099-1697(199803/04)7:2<101::AID-JSC332>3.0.CO;2-6

Porter, M. E. (1979). How Competitive Forces Shape Strategy. *Harvard Business Review, 57*(2), 137–145. PMID:18271320

Porter, M. E. (1980). *Competitive Strategy*. Free Press.

Porter, M. E. (1997). How much does industry really matter? *Strategic Management Journal, 18*(S1), 15–30. doi:10.1002/(SICI)1097-0266(199707)18:1+<15::AID-SMJ916>3.0.CO;2-1

Roquebert, J. A., Phillips, R. L., & Westfall, P. A. (1996). Markets Vs. Management: What drives profitability? *Strategic Management Journal, 17*(8), 653–664. doi:10.1002/(SICI)1097-0266(199610)17:8<653::AID-SMJ840>3.0.CO;2-O

Rumelt, R. P. (1991). How much does industry matter? *Strategic Management Journal, 12*(3), 167–185. doi:10.1002mj.4250120302

Rugman, A., & Cruz, J. (1993). The "double diamond" model of international competitiveness: The Canadian experience. *MIR. Management International Review*, 17–39.

Saaty, T. L., & Takizawa, M. (1986). Dependence and independence: From linear hierarchies to nonlinear networks. *European Journal of Operational Research, 26*(2), 229–237. doi:10.1016/0377-2217(86)90184-0

Shadfar, S. (2013). Application of SORF Analysis in Formulating Businesses Strategies. *International SAMANM Journal of Marketing and Management, 1*(2), 96–102.

Schoemaker, P. (1993). Multiple scenario development: Its conceptual and behavioral foundation. *Strategic Management Journal, 14*(3), 193–213. doi:10.1002mj.4250140304

Sternberg, R. J. (2009). The nature of creativity. *The Essential Sternberg: Essays on intelligence, psychology and education*, 103-118.

Teece, D. J., Pisano, G., & Shuen, A. (1997). Dynamic capabilities and strategic management. *Strategic Management Journal, 18*(7), 509–533. doi:10.1002/(SICI)1097-0266(199708)18:7<509::AID-SMJ882>3.0.CO;2-Z

Thatcher, J. (2014). Big data, big questions| Living on fumes: Digital footprints, data fumes, and the limitations of spatial big data. *International Journal of Communication, 8*(19), 1765–1783.

United Nations Educational, Scientific and Cultural Organization. (n.d.). *Reports*. UNESCO. https://en.unesco.org/gem-report/statistics

Wheelen, T. L., & Hunger, J. D. (1987). Using the strategic audit. *S.A.M. Advanced Management Journal, 52*(1), 4–27.

Weihrich, H. (1982). The TOWS matrix—A tool for situational analysis. *Long Range Planning, 15*(2), 54–66. doi:10.1016/0024-6301(82)90120-0

World Bank. (2022). *Databank*. World Bank. https://databank.worldbank.org/data/home.aspx

World Trade Organization. (n.d.). *Documents and resources*. WTO. https://www.wto.org/english/res_e/res_e.htm

World Values Survey. (n.d.). *Findings and insights*. WVS. https://www.worldvaluessurvey.org/WVSContents.jsp

Yüksel, I. (2012). Developing a multi-criteria decision making model for PESTEL analysis. *International Journal of Business and Management*, *7*(24), 52–66. doi:10.5539/ijbm.v7n24p52

ENDNOTES

1 The *trScores* were obtained *TrustRadius* on the 10th of Sep-21.

2 Consumer Price Index (CPI)

3 New Product Development (NPD)

4 Gross Domestic Product (GDP) and Gross National Product (GNP)

5 It is recommended a few readings surrounding the re-thinking of competitive positioning of the firm and particularly questioning the (single-country) national context (also known as, the comparative position/advantage) and the emerge by the critics of *M.E. Porter* of the so-called "Double Diamond" model of international competitiveness. Here, I would advise, in particular, the reading of the scholarly contributions of, *Rugman and Cruz (1993)*; *Moon, Rugman and Verbeke (1998)* and *Grundy (2006)* (full references available at "Read More" at the end of the chapter).

6 e.g., financial, human and natural resources

Chapter 6
Systems Analyzability, Analytics, and Business Intelligence

ABSTRACT

This chapter focuses on the influence of information and communication technologies (ICT) in strategic communication and market research. One addresses, among others, the role of computer-based information systems (IS) and IS management in contemporary businesses; the intelligence cycle and the types and categories of IS and their utility to operational and strategic activities of a firm. Furthermore, it discusses the increasing digitalization of societies, and therein, the challenges of digital business communication and business digitalization. Seminal aspects are here uncovered with this regard, as the copiousness and overdependence of data analytics, the phenomenon of big data, the concentration of economic agents over platforms, the use of web-based value chains, and the shift to "reintermediation."

INTRODUCTION

Reflecting on the direction of an external business environment analysis (EBEA) function may assume on a given organization, a focal Business Environment Analysis Project (BEAP) is here recommended to be fashioned on the light of the considerations on the previous chapters regarding the assumptions with regard to Philosophy of Analyzability (PoA) and the previous goals´ set for the project, whether as a one-off enterprise or as an endeavor with some continuity. In addition, a reflection about, before the conducting an analysis procedure, has the virtue of approximating the company with its strategy, revisiting previous strategic choices and hence deepening a critical sense as to the choice of EBEA´s factors (aka, *factor´s selection*), as discussed in chapter four.

This implies equating more consciously the types of analysis, the instruments to adopt and other underlying resources to be allocated to (the question of what´s and where to); in sum, a higher degree of awareness about the task and most likely a better comprehension of the screened events (as fads; trends; or wild cards). As asserted by Boddy (2017, p. 379) "*the way a firm communicates with the exterior shapes*

DOI: 10.4018/978-1-6684-5543-2.ch006

indelibly the type and pace of data collection". This is indeed a universal law for corporate governance and real management practice. It is key for the success of the capture of external information, both the relation with the markets (as addressed on chapter *2. Organizational Management and Strategic Behaviour*) and the means used to gather such information. The latter one is what this chapter is all about, as it looks into the information and communication technologies a firm needs to be equipped with, and the business architecture systems to be set in place for conducting one external analysis.

An organization is *per se* a large system, trapped on a continuous cycle of value-addition, the iteration of the processes entail a constant review of *inputs*, *transformation* and *outputs*. This systemic principle is applicable to all types of organizations, whether being a public company, stated owed or private-held, and regardless of the sector and location. Herein, the societal technological advancements play a decisive role adding value to business models, processes, products and services.

Surely, Information Systems (IS) exist already for a few centuries; however is undeniable their drastic evolution in the last two or three decades due to the appearance of new technologies and impact on the business realm.

ORGANIZATIONAL´S COMMUNICATION AND THE INFORMATION SYSTEMS

It is recognized though that at different stages of the business activities, with more or less sophistication, functions as planning, organization and controlling existed long ago in craftwork, family-ventures and industrial enterprises, regardless of the technological acumen.

For ages, the management of business ventures, even in the Hellenic notion of *Xenophon´*s household/property management, encompassed endeavors like, the control of costs with materials or staff (inputs); the execution of production timetables and delivery of schedules (transformation), and price registering; or verification of the customer´s satisfaction (outputs). However, technology shaped our modern world, including the operationalization of strategy-related tasks.

One could then ask: So, *what´s the role of computer-based information systems and Information System´s (IS) management?* In an organization, the role of technology is a whole disruption from the fashioning and unfolding a company´s strategy until the most quotidian activities; herein, contributed furthermore to the evolution of the analysis function as to the screening of the whole market´s ecosystem; well, technology is everything nowadays!

Now, try to picture "technology" in the strategy domain. The bulk of this sub-system´s dynamics and its intra-stakeholders´ exchange content are intangible (assets). The core "locus" of observation of an EBEA is, the intangible external resources at one´s disposal (i.e. *data*). Available as separate or combined units of data, then computer-based IS has, at first place, the virtue of accessing large quantities of data in a short period of time and facilitating their manipulation in significantly in a more organized and swift manner, making the, sometimes, heavy burden of making sense of data a much more efficient processes, and also clearly more insightful. Arguably, also a much more amusing one!

Analysts face almost exclusively the need to collect different typologies of data (quants and/or qual), in different formats (audio and visual; many times written in plain text; or delivered in numeric tables). Often, one receives unstructured data (e.g. standard reports), or structured but with different formats (and using different scales of measurement of the same phenomenon), and often requiring the contriving of data variables which builds on the hand-picking of particular sub-units of data across datasets. This job is to uncover *patterns* of information, as follows:

(i) Identify *strategic possibilities* (as opportunities, to the focal firm/project),
(ii) Find *potential risks* (as threats).

Needless to say, the creation of a common language and rules specifying the format in which data could be send and received electronically (aka, *Internet*), opened a myriad of communication possibilities and intra-device connectivity to be explored maximize operational but also strategic horizons. The sections below explore some of those considerations.

THE INTELLIGENCE CYCLE AND IS MANAGEMENT

Data refers to a broad range of recorded descriptions of objects, events, activities or transactions transferable in multiple formats. One might summarize it as raw units of unanalyzed facts, figures or events.

Subsequently, *information* can be assume though in two ways. Firstly, as a describing element of the first (data) accompanying it storage and transference, which is also an unanalyzed unit or *factum*, as the data itself. This is for instance, the information travelling about the type of a file, its size or version. It accounts furthermore all the general information of the document and personal information of authorship, security, and other details. Also, the status of availability on a network, virtual machine´s origin and/or server fault position of storage.

Secondly, information refers also to the utility of the separate analysis of each record, or cross-observation of a set. This implies the judgement of the analyst, as to three dimensions of data: *significance* (or meaning); *utility* to a certain context, and perception of *urgency*. The output of such interpretation of these dimensions, yields new insights, i.e. *information*.

Hence, *information systems management* refers to the administration of IS infrastructures engaged with the Internet, were different elements as people, processes, hardware and software are administrated within four (4) sets of activities: *planning*; *acquisition*; *development;* and, *utilization*.

In this sense, computer-based IS´s gather inputs of data, which transform into outputs of information. The data transformation process implies unavoidably the organization´s allocation of people and the design of processes. The latter is introduced into the IS, using the hardware apparatus and according to the software rules and organizational processes in place. The purpose of this series of stages of the (data) transformation process, also called *intelligence cycle*, is to produce friendly or threatening intelligence, as outputs of knowledge to secure the firm and its assets (Smith and Brooks, 2012). Typically, their administration is in charge of an Information Security Operations Center (ISOC) is as the facility in charge of monitoring, and defending enterprise ISs.

Figure 1. Intelligence cycle (IC)
Source: Own elaboration

Data → information → Intelligence

This intelligence cycle is a process aiming to produce meaningful outputs of a higher-order of information´s utility by its transformation into knowledge units (*intelligence*) with a strategic value for the business unit or the whole organization or, deriving from the processing, crunching and dissemination of original data and information.

Unstructured data might derive from sources like, conversations, e-mails, graphs, images, memos, movies, news, reports, spreadsheets, text, videos, or web pages (Negash, 2004). *Structured data* is originated from subsequent data mining (DM), into information and from on-line analytic processing (OLAP), insights from data warehousing (DW) typically provided by ISOCs or from enterprise resource planning systems (ERP). Thus, the IS´s oriented particularly towards the formation of business intelligence (BI) are defined as *business intelligence systems (BIS)*.

BI systems combine data gathering, data storage, and knowledge management with analytical tools to present complex internal and competitive information to planners and decision makers (Negash, 2004, p. 178)

Consequently, these type of IS´s (BIS), in general assume the form of a *Managerial IS* or E*xecutive IS*, rather than *operational IS* (definitions addressed on the next section) being also termed as *Computer-Based Business Intelligence Systems (CBBIS)*. They are powerful tools, namely for the administration of multiple projects (BEAPs) or programs, as they assist in strategic and operational decision-making elucidating companies in multiple areas, for instance, in customer relations; business activities and performance; implementation of specific projects/operations; or managing the reporting of BI (Willen, 2002).

MANAGERIAL AND OPERATIONAL INFORMATION SYSTEMS

A distinction should be made between Operational IS and non-Operational IS (Negash and Gray, 2008). The first, typically presented in the form of *Transactional Processing Systems (TPS)*, *Process Control Systems (PCS)* or *Office Automation Systems (OAS)* mine micro-units of information at the shop or factory floor and yield operational intelligence. A PCS may be then defined as a system that monitors and controls variables that describe the state of physical process (e.g. temperature; pressure/flow; time/speed, etc.) while a OAS combine several systems to create, process, store and distribute information (e.g. e-mails; word processing templates; or spreadsheets).

At the non-operational side, this category is termed as *Managerial Informations Systems (MIS)*. Here, two typical sub-sets are the *Executive IS (EIS),* which draw data from the prior to gain strategic insights (e.g. prediction of outputs of financial investments) or the *Decision Support Systems (DSS)* to plot the consequences of alternative before actually taking a decision. The latter (DSSs) are particularly useful for Strategy Consultants/Analysts.

Making a distinction of those MIS typologies, the EISs are tailored for senior managers and are configured for an easy-to-access experience, with timely relevant information, instead of detailed one. The DSSs, also labelled as *knowledge management systems (KMS)*, not solely allow the storage and transference of knowledge, but also the assessment of real options, as they are particularly suitable for the calculation of the outcomes of normative scenarios, as the analysts dig into the understanding of the likely consequences of alternative actions. Commonly they integrate a model of the situation (*model-driven DSS*), and its data derives from information obtained from internal or partnered operational systems. Often, DSS/KMS are concentrated in a single point, a portal accessible to employees as a source of multiple types of information.

In sum, MISs provide managers with information for decision-making, to increase the chance of their decisions adding value to businesses. Hence, "good information" is critical for increasing both the confidence of taking good decisions and secondly building on accurate and updated information-base (Boddy, 2017).

However, the rationale of the IS architecture, as to the infrastructure design and accessibility to information units is intrinsically dependent on the corporate mindset. Tambe et al. (2012) argue that modern ISs are the ones able to timely respond to the changes in business environment. For instance, actively tracking customer behaviour, with the inputs of new data records allowing the company to use the information effectively on a value-creating manner; thus, optimizing products or processes or strategically modifying business goals. These authors claim that decentralized external networks, involving customers, suppliers and other partners, are likely to be more effective in response to external information requirements, namely in context of more subtle change. Their "complementarities model", asserts that decentralized networks, open to external information and anchored on *self-managed teams* and *cross-enterprise training* allows the faster and more efficient absorption of information.

An example of the success of this openness to cross-enterprise MIS systems is Walmart´s *Vendor Managed Inventory (VMI) system.* This retail giant in USA literally allowed its suppliers to manage their inventory by sending shop floor data to centralized datasets of stock inventories guaranteeing items in stock nearly at all times and with a more cost-effective administration, as vendors started to self-administrate, electronically, the inventory of their goods, leaving Walmart with a higher focus on warehouse-shop distribution of goods. Hence, Walmart released itself from the costly and difficult task of controlling own inventories, namely the over-costs with regard to overstocking and additional payment for storage and the inherent bullwhip effect. On the other side, the VMI system allowed gains of efficiency on the suppliers´ side, as Procter & Gamble, which managed to adopt disseminate cross-docking practices as their distributors started to unload directly at stores instead of distribution centers (Skubana, 2020).

This example of the VMI system uncovers though a phenomenon, Henry Chesbrough designated as the *open innovation paradigm*. Here, a new computer-based IS providing inflows/outflows of data to be transformed into meaningful information, has subsequently generated knowledge gains, allowing the companies engaged in the same external network to achieve win-win efficiency outputs, creating real economic value (Chesbrough, 2003). Thus, in a context of commercial stability, purposive inflows and outflows of knowledge create stimuli for the acceleration of cross-enterprise innovation. The MIS was, naturally, at the epicenter of such process-innovation, efficiency gains and performance amelioration.

However, as an opposite example is, the creation by Xerox Corp. of the Palo Alto Research Center (PARC). Despite the many successful research achievements of PARC, namely developing strong capabilities on vacuum tube technology at a lower cost and best quality, a self-centered vision of a lab providing the "*architecture of information*" for the corporation did seem to pay off (Chesbrough, 2003, p. 2). The PARC has accomplished important societal discoveries, namely for the personal computer´s industry, as the graphical user interface, the bit-mapped screen or the E*thernet* networking protocol and others on laser printing. However, if PARC´s research created enormous economic value for society, little was the appropriation made of that same value or any indirect benefits for the whole corporation. In sum, highly advanced systems created on PARC did not allow the parent company to appropriate almost any value of it.

One questions is to be raised: *What went wrong?* The case of Xerox shows us that PARC was far from ineffective, or managers far from being unreasonable individuals. As some researchers abandoned PARC and started up new companies. Moreover, Apple or Microsoft later on commercialized some of those technologies. Therefore, Xerox market´s dominance with a verticalized model left at some point these upstarters with no competitive or financial alternative than to be rather creative on modelling their business framework, since to compete by deep vertical integration was not a viable option for those small entrepreneurs. However, some of those startups managed to prosper (e.g. as 3Com or Adobe) (Chesbrough, 2003). This scholar concluded then that failure was caused by the way the innovation process was managed. PARC managed innovation 100% internally, fitting the so-called *Closed Innovation paradigm*, as the corporation sought to achieve new discoveries and market them all by themselves, due to their strong skills and spreading across the value chain.

However, the lesson to be taken is, internally generated knowledge is incomplete, thus management systems as the DSS/KMS, if internally focused within an information locked-in, are condemned to obsolesce in the near future. Secondly, others might have a tremendous contribution, since scientific knowledge and particularly technological advancements are appearing at a fast rhythm and generated worldwide, from all corners on earth. Moreover, the rationale of external innovation being owned by third parties and seen as a "competitor", something like, this was "not invented here", refers to a mindset of exclusion of new ideas from the pipeline of data inputs, which is constitutes a hazard for the future.

EXTERNAL COMMUNICATION PARADIGMS AND METHODS

On the previous section, we have addressed the Chesbrough´s innovation paradigms and two (2) examples of success and failure associated with OI and CI models. The first case, Walmart´s VMI system, regarded as a reference of best practices of process innovation. The system leveraged benefits for the corporation and other external partners, due to the data flow´s optimization, manifested in the securing of products in shelf all year long without stock ruptures, and inherent reduction of costs with the management of distribution centers and inventory control. The second case, a likely bolder project, the Xerox´s "PARC" revealed to be more a "PARC problem", as the information seemed to be locked-in. Despite the non-breaching of data inside-out, from employees to competitors, and furthermore, the corporation´s market dominance (and positive results), the exclusion of external partners and the adoption of a solo-playing mode of competition, dictated the inability in the long run to manage their own innovations and appropriate significant value from them.

Tambe et al.´s (2012) complementarities model, stressed that the system sat in place for the administration of information is key to business performance. These authors, advocating the OI paradigm, argued that external information systems are a determinant of faster product development and higher productivity. The rationale being, the company does not hold necessarily, all the time, all the skills, and cooperation is an essential dimension of competition, including with direct competitors (*co-opetition*).

These scholars assume that a modern MIS, externally oriented, is like a rocket-shooting element from attaining of higher-productivity levels. They stress the importance of the *decentralization* of systems (i.e. self-managed teams and cross-training) and an *external focus* as to the collection of data (e.g. benchmarking) and with the gathering of skills (i.e. recruitment and formation of best project teams).

Hence, recognizing then, that the Internet changes the relation with other agents in the market, is half way through to admit a second part, that is, electronic systems change the interaction. Thus, business practices and models have necessarily to change as well. This is applicable also to the way we collect data and analyze the industries, namely the role of each agent inside the markets.

This first step towards a digital change is changing the corporate mindset, from the traditional delivery of products towards "customer participation". This implies a reinvention of business, in which, the customer is considered, not solely the buyer, from whom is imperative to acknowledge the needs and habits, but also envisioned as a business partner in value-addition to the market.

An example of a successful story of a shift in strategic thinking, is the lesson given by the *Lego Group* in Denmark. Lego is the biggest toy manufacturer in the world, but recently seems to have gained a unique competitive advantage with "customer involvement" (Critical Mass, 2021). At the industry-environment tier, *Lego* initiated a project back in 2011 targeting the demand-side, i.e. *Lego Ideas*.

Grant Owens, Chief Strategy Officer (CSO) asserted that the key for their performance and current growth was partially the shift from the interaction with the customer, changing from the traditional idea of "customer" to being a "contributor". Acknowledging that online interaction with customers may be impersonal, and to gain trust on the digital channels is a challenge for all organizations, *Lego* decided to invest not merely on "customer experience" but to create a community in which fans were empowered to submit ideas and concepts for new products. Moreover, the thousands of ideas received yearly from their customers, are given full attention, internally, by their officials, as to the evaluation of the feasibility of the concept into production and commercial potential. Thus, they have began to jointly explore ideas for new product development with their customers. Whenever an idea is approved and goes to production, becoming a Lego set, the customer receives 1% of the total net sales and ten (10) complimentary sets of his/her Lego idea.

Paal Smith-Meyer, head of the *Lego New Business Group* asserts that customers have great ideas, and more than transcending short-term earnings commercializing them, *Lego Group* is investing on loyalty (Critical Mass, 2021). This is in line with Boddy´s (2017) assertion about how to succeed in e-marketplaces and/or with e-business models. The advent of Internet is not a technological challenge. It is much more that, it is a people´s challenge to recalibrate attitudes and skills, to be aligned with the evolution of society, and people´s ideas, vision and lifestyle.

Undoubtedly, the Internet affects all the organizational activities, enabling new ways of doing business; however, to get to the stage were Lego is nowadays, business organizations seem to follow a stage-like process, increasing from phase to phase the skills and commitment in the way they use the Internet:

<u>Stage 1</u> (Information): websites with an informative purpose about the company´s businesses and products.

<u>Stage 2</u> (Interaction): Options are provided (e.g. product/service´s availability and timing) and at best the supplier may agree (manually) on a purchasing order.

<u>Stage 3</u> (Transaction): Automatic enabling of the purchasing order.

<u>Stage 4</u> (Integration): Link of internal systems with website. Here, orders are automatically accepted and feedforward to the internal operating system to be further treated.

<u>Stage 5</u> (Transformation): Internal and external systems across the value network are linked, including customers to product design and engagement with online communities

Naturally, *Lego Ideas* is more than a simple, micro-level project, of external business environment analysis, centered upon the surveying of customer's habits, needs, expectations or wishes. Being at an advanced stage of their digitization process, truly reaping the benefits of the second economy, the company is an open innovator investing on digital-development towards their approximation to the customer-base and building a broader audience.

Indeed, initiatives, as *Lego Ideas*, for raising customer intimacy, are a mechanism for consolidating in the future the loyalty to the products and brand. It can be argued that this company is investing on *co-creation*, as the joint creation of value with other network actors (inclusively their customers) (Boddy, 2017). Truth is, firstly they are creating competitive advantages based on direct customer involvement, by commercializing their customer's ideas. Here, they seem to have incorporated clearly Robert Metcalf thoughts as to the importance of scale in networks. A former researcher/engineer at Xerox at PARC, and co-inventor of the Ethernet (as described in a previous section of the chapter), the willingness of the project (*Lego Ideas*) is to attract new customers as "contributors":

$$NV = (\sum u_{(x)})^2$$

The Metcalf´s law argues that *network value* (NV) increases with the squared number of *users* (u) connected to the network (*x*). Moreover, the logic of co-creation and customer involvement, it accounts also a dimension of indirect customer involvement, termed as *User Generated Content (UGC)*. The UGC comprehends the visual or audio material that users create and place online instead of the brand owner or the company itself.

Here, Lego embraces a rather sophisticated snowballing approach towards self-generated online content. Foreseeing it as a tiny fraction of customer involvement, their attention is placed on "hooking" the most enthusiast customers with new constant ideas (as "*piercing the veil*", here using their own metaphor) (Critical Mass, online). Hence, *Lego* has managed though to create a wave of new independent, self-denominated, "Lego artists" or "Brick artists" using social platforms as Instagram or Youtube, as means of UGC communication of Lego-themed content to the masses. Those enthusiasts became their indirect "spokesmen" to more indifferent audiences, "recruiting" online new "fans". Artists as, *Adnan Lotia, Dante Dentoni, Ekow Nimako, Nathan Sawaya, Rebecca Grimm* or *Tiago Catarino*, have millions of visualizations, followers and subscribers of their content, which is posted professionally on a regular basis.

Definitely, computer-based information system are key on business development. Hence, they are also key to analysts as to the data collection within the scope of a BEAP, functioning as rich data resource conveyers at one´s disposal. However, those systems, which can be, furthermore powered by artificial intelligence technology, are in broader sense as a larger source of competitive advantage for a firm, with implication on the overall business strategy and future returns. Thus, IS utility goes much beyond the examples of *Walmart´*s VMI project (see section 6.3) or the latter case of *Lego´*s customer involvement. These systems supporting both differentiation and cost-leadership strategies, allow for internal changes on computer-aided activities, for instance, on automated manufacturing, stock control and inventory cutting, customer´s hypertargeting, treatment of online orders or customer delivery.

Companies are then challenged at a more advanced stage of digitalization to administrate a myriad of digital assets. Here comes the quest for integration, sharing, and efficient cross-utilization of these assets accumulated from multiple sources. This entails multiple-sourced data, for instance, stored at a customer relationship management (CRM) system, or at an enterprise resource planning (ERP) system or at a knowledge management (KM) portal. You may recall, in section 6.3. *Managerial and Operational Information Systems (IS),* we have addressed the different typology of those systems. Here the challenge is to develop meta-systems able to absorb data from the remaining ones, to administrate global skills and assets and accelerate organizational learning.

However, many companies worldwide did not manage to ride the wave of digital transformation (DX) as the two leading companies addressed in this chapter (Lego or Walmart). Many companies have not reached an advanced stage of Internet usage, as *integration* or even *transformation*. This means lagging behind and wandering around phases as *information*, *interaction* or *transaction*.

The digital transformation challenge is in theory quite simple (i.e. the reinvention of the supply chains), yet hard in practical terms its application in business, as technological upgrading is directly connected to customer relations. Upgrading digital technologies may lead to downgrading or decline of proximity in commercial relations.

However, as a starting point, companies need surely, to adapt their value chains to become more digitally competitive. Here, the notion of digital competitiveness is intrinsically dependent on three (3) factors:

a. Knowledge
b. Technology
c. Future Readiness

Knowledge requirements encompass both explicit (know-about) and implicit (know-how) types, which is necessary to discover, understand and build new technology (IMD, 2021). Sub-factors as talent, training, formal educational background, and the scientific concentration staff should be taken into account as knowledge-formation aspects. *Technology*, as the overall context affecting technological development, including sub-factors as regulatory framework, capital investments and scope of technologies. The *future readiness* refers to the preparedness to exploit digital transformation.

Despite the asymmetries between regions and countries with regard to the IT infrastructure and societal digitalization, progresses are felt in digital investments worldwide, namely in Eastern Asia (also accompanied by Western Europe) with a clear upward transformation tendency, visible on investments in specific technological domains as, DevOps and Robotics. This opposes to the American companies´ downward trend. However, the coronavirus pandemic has though spurred worldwide the adoption of digital solutions, as referred before.

According to Gartner Inc. (2021), the overall IT spending on the areas of data center systems; enterprise software; devices; it services; and, communication services, has grown by 8,4% in 2021 reached the four trillion dollar (4T USD) mark, and they have also forecasted a growth in 2022 of 5.5% in comparison with this year.

Undoubtedly, the digital transformation in on the march, as companies are pushing themselves towards more advanced stages of Internet utilization, hence working on the optimization of their digital supply chains.

However, one of the biggest challenges brought by the advent of Internet, if not the toughest, is the change in the relations, *company-customer*. In more mature-stages of digitalization, where the company expects from an institutional client more than repurchasing, the technological issues of trust on digital purchasing (easier to manage), sums to the relational aspects of customer of *trust* (as *trustworthiness* or *relationship-building*), tied to other issues as, *customer involvement, customer intimacy*, or *customer loyalty*. This is applicable to both business models (B2B and B2C).

Anchored on electronic systems, web-based business models, as *e-commerce* (selling goods or services online), or *e-businesses* (integration of business processes from supplier to customer) or even, digital business *platforms* (DBP), as the concentration of multiple agents and technology on a hub, provide in all cases the ability to accelerate the digital transformation of the firm. I would say, solving the issues deriving from the technological pillar of digital competitiveness is the less complex part of the equation, even though, one might consider it an overwhelming task. Technological adaptation allows the company to proceed with a transactional approach toward online businesses. The challenge is to transform a *transactional* supply chain into a *collaborative* one.

Undoubtedly, the Internet allowed a flexibilization of the supply chains, as e-commerce/e-business are allowed to cut in number of activities/agents from the manufacturer to the consumer, a phenomenon known as *disintermediation.* Wholesalers, might, on the Internet, leapfrog the phases of the supply chain and simply bypass their partners. Actually, this led to a whole new e-commerce model (i.e. *Drop Shipping*) popularized in USA, and quickly spreading all over the world, with the intermediation of platforms (DBPs) (e.g. *Shopify* or *Wix*) allowing a seller, with an almost incipient investment, to trade goods from point-to-point, origin to destiny, avoiding other intermediaries.

However, as demonstrated on the case of *Lego Group*, long tailed supply chains are not, necessarily, inefficient, neither an obstruction to cost-efficiencies, long-term business prosperity and wealth. Here, it should be introduced the notion of *reintermediation.*

The benefits of disintermediation are, in short, the reduction of transaction costs, and the quick expansion of local presence to international coverage. These advantages are acknowledged as essential in early stages of the digitalization of business (e.g. *interaction* or *transaction*) where the company is takes steps to learn further about digital business architectures and operability in such business environments.

The *reintermediation* is quite the opposite. It is the purposive creation of new intermediaries between customers and suppliers by providing new services (e.g. product evaluation). Hence, examples of reintermediation, as product evaluation, or purchase/experience rating, are the most primeval trials, or simplest endeavors of reintermediation. Those deliver limited added value, with regard to customer involvement or intimacy. The co-creation may be said to exist though, as customer as stimulated to provide sporadic inputs, with limited direct interaction with the firm. Hence, these simplistic tools, contribute likewise, to a lower degree of appropriation of value by the firm.

The case of Lego is a paradigmatic one of success on extended reintermediation. The company approximates the customers with its structure (direct customer involvement); and approximates customers with other customers, and customers with the community (indirect customer intimacy). Moreover, the direct customer involvement, not only "instrumentalized" the customer as the gatekeeper of ideas (as inputs of information) but also allows it co-operation in primary activities with the first line of creative staff (product designers), and finally shares a "slice of the pie" with symbolic profit distribution and courtesy gifts. Despite investing less on UGC then it creates the conditions for feed-forwarding UGC-development and proliferation of above and below the line communication from their customers to their customers (and potential target customers) without their direct intervention, but building on present interaction and loyalty to a future better position and extended customer base.

BIG DATA ANALYTICS AND TRUST

The notion of *Big Data* (BD), which emerged in the 90s, is more than a mere expression in vogue in the beginning of the 21st century. It refers to the amount of data greater than the capacity of what a computer could process or store, nor their analytics performed by a standard software, regardless of its configuration (Abrantes and Ostergaard, 2021).

A question to be raised is, *How (and why) is BD relevant for a Business Environment Analysis Project (BEAP)?* Firstly, BD has expanded drastically the horizons of analyzability, as the ability of the firm, to collect large amounts of data, greater than the capacity of a computer to manipulate it. Secondly, the benefits of larger cloud storage on datacenters, entail a larger comprehension of the meaning of data as a whole. Larger units of data gathered together, unravel patterns of information than smaller samples would not be able to do. With BD, scale brings precision, compensating the previous inaccuracies of sampling, being the company less dependent on forecasting skills and scenario planning (Abrantes and Ostergaard, 2021). Thirdly, the BD analytics may crunch now a large number of data sets with a gigantic number of data records. This is possible through a BD software, as *Apache Hadoop; Apache Spark*; *Zoho Analytics*; *MongoDB* or *Xplenty.*

Consequently, the enhanced digitalization of societies and businesses brought an underlying dimension of *datafication*. Data became central, and from analyzing online data to entering into *data surveillance* (*dataism*) concerns it was a short step. Dataism came almost naturally as an attempt, to expand the mere prediction of future events, as companies strived to also control the outputs of data (namely the individual behaviour). Moreover, companies wanted to be able to determine or constrain the free (and likely) informed choices of the consumer, shaping individual decisions on their favor.

Consequently, the dataism in the business world was materialized into specific endeavors to comprehend cross-sectional patterns of data, for instance, across regions and segments for modifying product features and optimizing product portfolios. Also, for micro or *hypertargeting* the consumer through the tracking of digital footprints left online by his/her past navigation. The analysis of navigation patterns, as *digital footprints*, plus the utilization of shared (and reposted) personal content (often without personal data-owner´s permission), and the use of byproducts from the utilization of the further analysis of navigation (*data fumes*), equipped in general many companies with digital information assets unattainable before.

Hence, hypertargeting became a phenomenon of automated selection of visualizations, as alternatives of visualization are predetermined for the user. Hence, hypertargeting implies, as to the advertising of product/service, the ability to control the options of the consumer. Subsequently its future choices (*market discrimination*) and purchase trends (*product discrimination*).

Moreover, this allowed companies, especially, marketing and advertising agencies, to furthermore, develop content specifically for the type of navigation exhibited by the digital footprints (*hypertargeting*). This made emerge an alleged differentiation as to price-offers, according to individual profiles (*price discrimination*) and complying with the marketing strategy for optimizing the sales of particular products with higher gains (*price steering*).

All these concerns made emerge a growing negative opinion and sentiment about BD (*ant-dataism)*. Consequently, the European Union decided to legislate on data protection, issuing on May-26th 2018 the General Data Protection Regulation (GDPR) setting the principles of personal data protection, such as, the *right to erasure* and the *right to be forgotten;* moreover, setting the compliance rules for European firms, preventive of data breaches and misuse of data (Abrantes and Venkataraman, 2022; Abrantes and Ostergaard, 2021). As these ethical concerns are real challenges, for professionals more directly exposed to data. This is especially the case of Consults/Analysts, whom run EBE analysis, as the job is all about data collection and analytics during and after the duration of the BEAP.

The recommendation here left is, to be particularly sensitive to these ethical issues and be informed about the applicable legal framework (*Regulation – EU 2016/679*) and consult the Data Protection Officer (DPO) of your client and/or of your company. Furthermore, read the EU guidelines and ultimately, in case of a specific doubt, or conflict of interest, contact the European Data Protection Supervisor (EDPS) (Abrantes and Venkataraman, 2022; EU, 2020; EDPS, online; Eur-Lex, 2016).

LEARNING OUTCOMES

- Levels and types of computer-based information-systems
- Intelligence cycle: Data, information and knowledge
- *Henry Chesbrough´*s innovation paradigms
- Digital transformation: Knowledge, technology and future preparedness
- Reinvention of the supply chains: Disintermediation and Reintermediation
- Big Data: Analytics, GDPR, digital footprints and consumer sentiment

CASE: LEGO GOUP

Back in 2011 *Lego Group* launched a bold project (*Lego Ideas*) with the purpose of developing new products based on community-based ideas.

Customers and enthusiasts were encouraged to submit new ideas to a platform (ideas.lego.com) and become a Lego Designer. Furthermore, encouraged to vote on others fans´ ideas, and participating in other blog contests and activities.

According to Paal Smith-Meyer, Head of the *Lego New Business,* this has proven to be a successful formula, as he argues,

"our fans and consumers have proved time after time that they have great ideas that can lead to products. We see this as an investment in the future rather than for immediate sales gain".

As explained by Grant Owens, Global Chief Strategy Officer at Critical Mass, a Digital Experience Design & Marketing Agency partnered with Lego, this giant toy manufacturer has managed to create a unique and "seemingly unfair" advantage in the their industry. The advantage is a singular digital "*customer involvement*".

Lego´s model followed for customer involvement is simple, empower customers to express their passion for their products, and suggest the freely the type of products they would like to play with in the future.

All suggestions from customers submitted to *Lego Ideas* are visible for peer-evaluation by other customers in the same blog. Whenever an idea reaches a 10-thousand supporters mark, is assessed in terms of feasibility by the company´s product and industrial designers and is given full consideration for production. External ideas, receive an equivalent treatment as any other internal one, generated from a product design team.

A proprietary process is used to capture the customer´s "voice" following six (6) tenets:

(I) Winning with Customer Involvement;
(II) Don't Settle for User-Generated Content (UGC)
(III) Listen and Respond
(IV) *Make Them* [customers] *Part of the Company*
(V) Customers Won't Invent Your Future
(VI) Start A.S.A.P.

Furthermore, Lego decided to reward their customers´ involvement, as a virtual business partnership, where the customer resembles a freelance designer. If an idea gets an approved and goes into production, becoming an official Lego set, for omnichannel distribution, the customer receives 1% of the total net sales and 10 complimentary sets of that Lego idea. *Grant Owens* claims that there´s still a lot more to be done though to involve customers and capture the "Lego Magic". (Critical Mass, 2017)

CHAPTER HIGHLIGHTS

- Information systems (IS) and elements of a computer-based IS
- The evolutionary stages of adoption of the Internet
- The intelligence cycle and IS management
- Types of Managerial/Operational IS
- Factors of Digital Competitiveness
- External communication paradigms (OI/CI)
- Platforms and network value (Metcalf´s Law)
- Disintermediation/reintermediation processes in web-based value chains
- Challenges of Big Data Analytics

CONCLUSION

In this chapter, we have addressed the utility of computer-based information systems (IS) and its emergence with the advent of Internet.

We described also the "intelligence cycle", as a linear approach towards the transformation of data into knowledge. Furthermore, one saw the notion of *digital competitiveness* and its intertwining with the intelligence cycle. Herein, *knowledge-possession* is considered one of the three factors, together with *technology* and *future readiness,* for the digital business success. The latter factor (readiness) was discussed its connection to the Organizational Strategy. In sum, digital competiveness (and inherently success) is demonstrated to be equally dependent on the managerial capabilities of (strategic agility), such as, two other factors, knowledge and technology.

Lego Group is the case explored in this chapter, presented as an example of strategic agility. Companies in more advanced stages of digitalization (as Lego), acknowledge that one of the biggest challenges of online business models is the relation with the client. Hence, *trust- building* and *customer loyalty* are seminal aspects to be managed efficiently, and the Lego´s model of customer involvement seems to behold a successful formula.

Apart from the factors of digital competitiveness and the underlying challenges of digital business architectures, we have also zoomed-in the specific issues of Big Data (BD), and BD analytics. In the meanwhile, it was also addressed: the stages of adoption of the Internet; the different types of managerial and operational IS; open innovation; the external communication paradigms; and also, the importance of collaborative approaches (versus transactional ones) on web-based supply chains. We have discussed here multiple concepts as, the *network value* (Robert Metcalf´s law), UGCs, and *disintermediation* and *reintermediation*.

REFERENCES

Abrantes, B. F., & Venkataraman, A. (2022). Environment kinesis and organizational adaptability: Effects of EU's General Data Protection Regulation on the Danish software industry. *International Journal of Learning and Change*, *14*(1), 22–45. doi:10.1504/IJLC.2022.119516

Abrantes, B. F. & Ostergaard, K. (2021) Digital footprint wrangling: are analytics used for better or worse? A concurrent mixed methods research on the commercial (ab)use of dataveillance. *Journal of Marketing Analytics*, *10*(2022), 187-202. https://doi.org/ doi:10.1057/s41270-021-00144-5

Boddy, D. (2020). *Management: Using practice and theory to develop skill* (8th ed.). Pearson Education Limited.

Chesbrough, H. (2010). Business model innovation: Opportunities and barriers. *Long Range Planning*, *43*(2/3), 354–363. doi:10.1016/j.lrp.2009.07.010

Critical Mass. (2021). To be the best, be like Lego. *Critical Mass*. https://www.criticalmass.com/think/detail/to-be-the-best-be-like-lego

EU. (2020). *EU data protection rules*. EU. https://ec.europa.eu/info/priorities/justice-and-fundamental-rights/data-protection/2018-reform-eudata-protection-rules/eu-data-protection-rules_en#documents

European Data Protection Supervisor (EDPS). (n.d.). *The History of the General Data Protection Regulation*. Europea. https://edps.europa.eu/data-protection/data-protection/legislation/history-general-data

Eur-Lex. (2016). Regulation (EU) 2016/679 of the European Parliament and the Council of 27 April 2016. *Official Journal of the European Union, L119/1*. https://eurlex.europa.eu/legal-content/EN/TXT/PDF/?uri=CELEX:02016R0679-20160504&from=EN

IMD. (2021). *China and US pursuing markedly different digital transformations*. IMD. https://www.imd.org/news/updates/China-US-pursuing-markedly-different-but-equally-competitive-digital-transformations-WCC/

Negash, S., & Gray, P. (2008). Business intelligence. In *Handbook on decision support systems 2* (pp. 175–193). Springer. doi:10.1007/978-3-540-48716-6_9

Negash, S. (2004). Business Intelligence. *Communications of the Association for Information Systems*, *13*(15). doi:10.17705/1CAIS.01315

Schumpeter, J. A. (1942). *Capitalism, socialism and democracy*. Harper and Brothers.

Skubana (2020). *Walmart Supply Chain [2021]: Why It Continues To Dominate*. Skubana. https://www.skubana.com/blog/walmart-leading-way

Smith, C., & Brooks, D. J. (2012). *Security science: The theory and practice of security*. Butterworth-Heinemann.

Willen, C. (2002). Airborne Opportunities. *Intelligent Enterprise*, *5*(2), 11–12.

Section 2

Business Environment Analysis Projects (BEAP)

Chapter 7
Managing a Business Environment Analysis Project (BEAP)

ABSTRACT

Approximating itself to project management theory, this chapter contextualizes the BEAP into the multiple types of project contexts and characteristics. Considerations are made as to the project design, regarding the project brief´s components and the constraints about the project´s approval in the context of the portfolio´s pipeline and management requirements. It considers furthermore the 5C´s influencing the project environment and the project structuring, from the simple input-out model, passing through the ICOM, 4-D, the MODest and the 7-S framework. Furthermore, it centers attention in the project´s architecture and on the alignment to the organization, considering seminal aspects as organizational culture; structure and business processes). The phases of project, the structure and roles of each project´s element, and cascades the project´s "architectures" (or systems) into processes and their underlying project/corporate nexus.

INTRODUCTION

Are you considering to an initiate as analysis procedure of the business environment (BE)? Unavoidably, the fashioning of a work "arrangement" out of the boundaries of a department, as to formal responsibility, resources allocation (assets) and chain of command, it definitely qualifies for the epithet of a "project".

Before entering into the three (3) sub-sections of the chapter on the project management around the Business Environment analysis one might start with a simply but essential definition - Project management (OM). For *Biff Baker, project management* is defined it as, "*the planning, organizing, directing and controlling of company resources for relatively short-term objective that has been established to complete specific goals and objectives.*" (Baker, 2018, p. 10). Looking at this definition, you might certainly recognize in the four (4) features of this definition (plan; organize; direct; control) a similarity

DOI: 10.4018/978-1-6684-5543-2.ch007

with enterprise-level management, as the definition resembles the POLC cycle addressed in the part one of the book.

Using in this chapter some borrowed conceptions and frameworks from Project Management (PM) theory, hopefully, this chapter will support your understanding of what it requires to undertake a Business Environment Analysis Project (BEAP) and what it entails from the idea to its completion.

To retain in the first place about PM is, most theorists in the field consider your Business Environment Analysis Project (BEAP) as, a one-off project, which they denominate as a *first-timer*.

What does it mean, my project is a first-timer?

A dominant trace of projects (including the environment analyzability ones) is, each (project) is unique. It assumes contours of a one-time endeavor; so, a rule of thumb is, mostly are first-timers. Scholars denominate projects in this way, when the projects have unique tasks, in comparison with the referential of previous projects in the same firm, accounting a dyad of singular features (Maylor, 2010):

(i) a high-*variety* of processes
(ii) and, with a low *volume* of tasks

Hence, as BEAPs are critical mass information seekers, the project requires, more than any other type of project, a meaningful understanding of the context and scope and a criterious definition of goals and methods. A BEAP requires than more critical sense in the project design phase than other more simplistic and fairly routinized/mechanized work, typical of batch or mass production/service development projects that imply re-use of project principles and ideas and iteration of processes. So in BEAPs, as in any first-timer, projects teams are expected to immerse into rather reflective exercises with several grey zones of unknown tangibility, such as, process metrics (as tools´ calibration or activities completion), or performance metrics (of progression or results).

PROJECT ENVIRONMENT: CONTEXT, STRUCTURES AND FRAMEWORKS

The starting point for managing a whole project from A to Z entails *ex ante* some degree of commitment and preparatory endeavors. Basically, the project begins with someone´s ideation before its execution. Thus, one will need to develop a set of documents establishing the scope and preparing it for being communicated to organizational-stakeholders with decisional power to approve or reject it. Hence, reporting and review of its execution are naturally subsequent tasks after the preparation phase.

The most essential documents one needs to prepare are:

(i) *the project brief*;
(ii) the *project chart*;
(iii) the *project scope statement*; and,
(iv) the *project management plan.*

In this chapter it will be given broad attention to the project brief due to its importance on the project design stage and connection to project environment.

Any project of environment analyzability can be triggered by an initial reflection about its purpose and the definition of the aims and objectives not the minutiae, but the general draft of a higher-order of objectives that justifies the realization of such BEAP. Nonetheless, project-owners/managers cannot detach themselves from the corporate direction and planning. Such, exercise would be selfish and/or naïve. The objectives of any project ought to be perpetually aligned to the vision, mission, and strategic and financial goals established at each division or business unit level, namely as to the portfolio priorities.

Such compliance of project with the company, is an alignment of organizational and micro-organizational interests, in which, such "micro-fit" makes a project a contributory endeavor to the strategic milestones. Hence, project-proposals have an inner ability and responsibility, to be designed in such a manner, that their alignment is accounted as a key-determinant for the increase of the chances of success in the future, in terms of project execution (or approval); and subsequently increase the likelihood of accomplishment of goals; and further learning, which are two cumulatively essential component (alias, project success and project learning) for the subsequent triumph of the remaining upper goals established for the overall business portfolio and for the (type, pace and direction of) growth of the corporation.

As a particular sub-group of projects, *first-timers* observe typically an inverse relationship between two characteristics (*volume* and *variety*). In addition, it would be useful to underline, beforehand, the thesis of continuity of first-timers. Despite, each project is a separate and unique project, in chapter 4, we referred to the different Types (or Parts) of BEAPs, a chain of analysis (from original business environmental inspection until environmental assessment), due to their distinctive purpose. This means that, a new project is separate from the others but shall retain memory for the learning gained from previous ones, that is not only essential for the success of the project, but also, before that, for its execution.

On Project Management´s theory, this sequence of descending types of analysis are denominated as "*as... but´*s". Here, the phases of Environmental Monitoring, Environment Forecasting and Environment Assessment of projects are consequently, "as... but´s" as well. They deriving from original Environment Inspection or Environment Scanning projects, which were concluded in an earlier moment in time.

As...but is not a repetitive environment analysis operation, but a new descending type of projects with a high degree of commonality in the process of analyzability; yet the "final product" delivered, i.e. the project outcome is utterly different. Both, project typologies (first-timers and as...buts) are, working together as parts for a common organizational goal of uncertainty and risk-reduction.

Although, one may explore further these project categories and characteristics in the next session (*7.2. Project Architecture*), in which, building on prior literature of Business Architecture (BA), we elaborate on the importance of system design, as a heuristic approach for developing the specifics of these type of projects (BEAP), as to the cascading of the whole project, conceived as a system, into further subsystems, and therein, into multiple processes and activities per process.

Indeed, strategizing the contours of a project is the job that begins with the fashioning of the guidelines, the position, and the means for its execution, in order to achieve the highest competitive advantage and at best value possible (Maylor, 2010). Hence, the design of a project is undoubtedly a challenging task, and comprehending the context surrounding its feasibility and success is key for achieving the latter. This chapter begins with the most holistic aspects surrounding the *Project Environment*, which in turn, are critical for success.

As a micro-enterprise replicated from a focal organization, *projects* inherit the aforementioned notion of "system" and furthermore inherit the typical vision dominating PM for many years of oversimplification of the project design. The dominant paradigm in most organizations was to conceive projects as basic designs, following the *input-output model* (Maylor, 2010).

According to this model, regarding the context of what any project is able to appropriate (in terms of value) is thoroughly influenced by the set of *constraints* and the possible set of mechanisms to be utilized, to make the project executable and its output the most favorable. The *inputs* correspond to the combination of the required resources (needs) and the additional expectations of desired resources (ambition), to satisfy a need (output). This conversion process inputs-output is mediated by a dyadic set of constraints, the internal triangle of constraints (time; quality; and cost) and external constraints (as PEST). Then, the simplified lens of this model, termed in PM as the *ICOM model*, as to the administration of cycles that convert realized inputs into output, for managing a whole project seems, however, short as a framework for attaining these objectives aforementioned.

Secondly, resources are finite assets, hence tightly administrated due to its scarcity. In most organizations, this comes at the expense, in a simple assumed rule, that sparse means have to be managed to its optimization, as they are costly to acquire/develop, or difficult to locate/preempt.

Consequently, the execution of a particular project is decided by its selection among a pool of other concurrent proposals. The firm´s constraints in terms of resources (e.g. talent, network or finance) dictates that projects cannot be pursued all at once (*ad libitum*). Sparse asset possession determines that multiple ideas have to compete for imposing itself against others in terms of importance, urgency and potential merit/performance; hence for being authorized within the pipeline of eligible projects to be pursued.

As any other project, this means that Business Environment Analysis Projects (BEAP), as the one category fitting into the nature of this book (and amply discussed until this stage), require a prior internal approval of the ideas regarding the type of work to be conducted, and further approval as to the budgetary conditions for its execution. Even for its preliminary structuring by the project manager, before its initiation.

In this context, grasping (and reporting) the project environment is of extreme importance to clarify the inner competition and value-potential, and at the same time, to reduce the complexity surrounding both internal and external impacting factors (e.g. the resources to be committed to the design). Here the organizational setup that defines the internal project environment is linked, inescapably to the external business environment (EBE) (addressed in chapters 3 and 4) and the EBE´s plays a decisive role in the fashioning of any project.

The EBE conditions and inherent dynamics of change, cumulatively occurring at multiple dimensions (i.e. market, industry, firm and consumer levels), set often the projects in harsh contexts dragging them for the pursuing of further sophisticated constellations in terms of (variety) of scope as to the project designs. For instance, all firms, in general, strain to innovate and reap the benefits of the value-added to the market. This means rushing to explore the ability to generate novelty in the same product categories, or in similar processes of fabrication, or eventually creating a business model that sets them aside/above competition. Furthermore, all firms not only funnel into the same "destinies" (types) of innovation, but also normally follow an evolutionary logic, starting by exploring the simplest ideas and then spiral them into a more complex scope. Not to forget also other external constrains, beyond the competition agents´ action, as the political and legal frameworks, the economic systems, or the technological advancements. Altogether, they shape the ability of the firms to modify their own value networks, modifying the behaviour towards (product) life cycle´s management.

Indeed, the project´s morphology is a by-product of the combination of organizational environment and EBEs´ pressures. From its start, face a scrutiny over the initial proposal. *Project proposals*, are reports aimed to be internally communicated to senior managers (and assessed by them at the strategic apex of the firm), being typically encapsulated in single documents. Such documents, express the *brief* of the proposal. Thus, the brief is a most relevant document that describes the nature of the work to be undertaken, which in turn, may determine the likelihood of the approval of the project and the extent of the resources to be released to it.

On the other hand, the brief will compete with peer proposals and furthermore, competes with the strategic options of the company and its availability of internal resources. It may sound bizarre to use the word "competition" in this context, but senior managers have the responsibility, among others, of managing their *portfolio* of operations. *Portfolio management* entails then the set of activities and responsibilities related to the selection, prioritizing and controlling of the execution of programmes and projects, which are more directly in line with the corporate and business objectives, considering their likelihood of successful delivery.

Despite, several are the companies (specially micro and small firms) which do not keep track of ongoing activities and operations, it is recommended that managers maintain *aggregate resource plans* for having under control their knowledge about the set of running new projects (first-timers) and repetitive operations (as "as ... but´s" or "painting by numbers" projects). This is not just to know number of projects but also to acknowledge their realities (Maylor, 2010). To determine, in first place, whether the execution of the project is feasible or not is key for the effectiveness of the operatives and projects success. Resources (people as any equipment or machinery) have a finite capacity, and the monitoring of overall design capacity and production capacity of the firm (e.g. an assembly line) are essential capabilities to possess to be able to administer a portfolio.

Portfolio management corresponds to the selection, prioritization and controlling of an organization's programmes and projects, in line with its strategic objectives and capacity to deliver. The goal is to balance the implementation of change initiatives and the maintenance of business-as-usual, while optimizing return on investment. Future project managers developing preliminary work, acting as Project Designers, are recommended to incorporate into the internal reporting manuscript (i.e. *brief*), in a summarized way, the main aspects surrounding the project environment.

Similar to any project with a dissimilar nature, whether focused on internal aspects of the firm (e.g. a financial audit) or external within the realm of the markets (e.g. a civil engineering project), this type of report, the brief, ought to consider, furthermore, the five (5) categories of factors that influence the project environment of the BEAP. These (5) types of factors represent the set of events with an impact on the project that shape the circumstantialism it has to deal with. They are a number of challenges to be mapped to ascertain the degree of difficulty (or *complexity),* which in turn, determines the completion of tasks and overall successful conclusion (*completeness).*

Moreover, might account the factors, including any barriers (e.g. of accessibility or performance) affecting the *competitiveness of the* project-launching and on-going developments. They could be also extraordinary events, concerning, the *context* or, herein, to the *customer-focus*, as natural conditions, or imitating/deterrence maneuvers from other organizations or even other divisions of a focal corporation. The latter situation typically happens when companies whom achieved a certain degree of maturity of their business diversification, consequently have adapted their divisional structures into competitive multidivisional forms (or competitive m –forms).

Indeed, project designer/s are summoned to be critical thinkers in preliminary stage, not solely to be able to control the present set of circumstances expected to shape the product quick off, but also, making an exercise of reflection, in advance, about future developments and broad scope of their impact in the project and the organization. This implies, in summary, taking seriously into account these five (5) major categories of factors that shape the project environment (i.e. *complexity; completeness; competitiveness; context, customer-focus*).

Known in PM as the *5-C´s*, these elements describing the surrounding environmental conditions, encompass on the first *C* (complexity), the (description of the) level of expected difficulty to be experienced in the project. Such "difficulty" entails the overall opposition (barriers) to its implementation, execution and/or conclusion. Within those barriers may be considered the technical challenges of the (project) since the formulation of the original idea/concept; market standards; the resource-requirement versus resource-shortages (e.g. skills; or technology); the on-going maneuvers of the focal firm´s competitors and the deterrence endeavors faced by all the potential and direct competitors within the same segment or strategic group.

Completeness, refers to the extent of outputs likely (to be) generated. In this factor, whenever the project is destined to a client (inclusively as internal one), the completeness may be taken, especially as a selling argument (or proposition) against other competing projects. This implies the materialization of the objectives into end requirements, as to the cascading of these objectives into a set of products (and by-products), services, and determining the likelihood of integrating them (products/services) into further sellable solutions. The competitiveness refers to the number of competing organizations to deliver the same type of output, regardless of whether other competitors are already taken pioneering or imitation efforts. The context refers to the combination of external general influences in which the project is taking place. The customer-focus refers to expectations build around the outcomes of the project, in relation to its objectives, and the likelihood of their achievement (e.g. new standards of requirements of products/services).

Probably, a question must hover your thoughts: *Is the company part of the internal or external Project Environment*? Seemingly, projects are independent structures, with its own internal logic of functioning (and chain of command), with owned resources, goals and systems. Subsequently, one may be deceivingly misguided to suppose that projects are independent structural configurations from the organizations they belong to. However, as micro-enterprises dependent on the latter, they are embedded into their firm´s reality, even being empowered for a (semi)autonomous course of action.

Hence, project´s existence (or "life", a concept explored below) is defined by/inside the organization, customarily by organizational-stakeholders with ample decisional power (from middle to senior managers) whom are not directly participating in the project execution. Often, approval ascends also to stockholders´ assemblies. Thus, the direction of the "ship" (the organization) equates and determines the whole project, from its approval, morphology, execution, length, renewal or subsequent iterations of the original first-timer.

Consequently, any conjectures about the firm being either a part of the internal or external environment of the project are clearly discernable. Only the universe outside of the whole organization´s borders is what it constitutes the *External Project Environment (EPE)* and everything within these thresholds, living inside of the organization, is part of the *Internal Project Environment (IPE)*. Projects hold though as to the internal environment (IPE) a double tier of internal factors. One inner sphere with inner project-specific characteristics (e.g. the idea/concept; assumptions; mindset; strategy; structure; culture; methods; and so forth), which interacts with an outer sphere of other intra-organizational factors (e.g. type/number of decision-makers; available talent; access to technology; organizational culture; corporate policies; long-term strategies, and so forth). The external project environment (EPE) accounts the external societal segments. For example, the MIT´s designed PEST segments (i.e. the Political; Economic; Social; and Technological; among others, discussed in chapters four and five). These offer a reality that surrounds the companies in the markets where they present themselves. Cumulatively, EPE´s intertwine with the internal project environment circumstances, the IPE´s, providing the context of multiple factors to deal with, as a BEAP manager.

Yet, projects are not just about something one sketches and then stores it inside of a drawer. Saying that, until now, one may assume that the focus of this chapter has been to conceive a project´s foundation and propose it, using an adequate reporting instrument (the brief) to communicate a proposal to the decision-maker/s determining its likelihood of approval. Hence, this entailed to look at the project environment as the seminal set of events (factors) shaping the likelihood of its successful execution. Less attention has then be placed on project goals. The reason is, goals´ setting, is already something I have dedicated some space, in chapter two (in section 2.3) when elaborating on the themes of Strategic Planning and Controlling. Projects are equally susceptible of applying such SM theoretical background (of planning and controlling), as they are a spin-offed micro intrapreneurial realities deriving from the "mother" structure, i.e. the focal firm.

My initial thoughts as to the unravelling of the technicalities regarding the preparations and organizational endeavors of the project were to convey some guidelines of what to account to set the foundations of a project proposal. However, projects preliminary conception leads subsequently to an execution in case of approval that obeys to a *Darwinian*-like natural life cycle, as projects are like micro organizational structures, though with a particularity (distinctive for their organizations), i.e. they are established to born, grow, mature and die. Hence, they follow a phased approach, typical to other life cycles in the organization, as the products or the processes´ life cycles.

Therefore, once you compromise to it, you need to do it by carrying on all the activities throughout those phases until the project "dies" (successfully, hopefully) with its completion. Those phases refer to the *Definition*; the *Design* of processes; the *Delivery* of the project; and the further *Development* of the currently adopted processes (Maylor, 2010). Project management theorists labeled this sequential phased approach as the *4-D Model*.

Table 1. Project life cycle: phases

No.	Description	Focus
D1	Project´s definition	*What is it about?* *What is to be done?* *Why is to be done?*
D2	Project Design	*How it will activities[1] will be carried out?* *Who is involved?* *What´s his/her role in the structure?* *What resources (and how) are utilized?* *What´s the timeline (including start and finish time)?*
D3	Project Execution	*What/how, activities should be daily monitored?* *What/how, do we solve (emergent/bottlenecking) constraints?* *How´s the decisions, report and workflow like?*
D4	Develop the processes	*What/how processes to be monitored?* *What instruments/techniques of processes´ measurement?* *How can we improve the processes for the future?*

Source: Maylor (2010)

Companies are recommended to follow this framework, since the 4-D is structuring and subsequently contributory to better performance outputs. Perhaps, you have (most likely), from the scanning of this table above, realized already what is this first phase (D1 - definition) about. The D1 encompasses all precursory work before initiating any operational activities of the project (execution). Whenever the project fits into the typology of a BEAP, the definition phase (D1) refers to all the activities one takes before jumping into the initial contacts with source providers, or any initial searches, towards the collect of market data.

In the D1, is all about gathering information and writing it down about the following:

- Motivations (or reasons for existence)
- Intentions (about you foresee it being conducted)
- Paths/trajectories (both alternatives; and opportunities plus threats)

It is in the D1´s phase that the idea-generator, as the person whom conceives initially the project, carries out several endeavors, in an attempt, to transform its idea into a materializable product to be communicated (and "sold" internally to potential decision-makers) and likely make it into reality. Among those actions, to create a "productizible" solution with the potential to be recognized as a feasible and acceptable one, are these following preparatory actions:

(i) Gather and evaluate opinions and suggestions for the improvement of the project´s concept;
(ii) Creating a coalition among organizational-stakeholders (and possibly the external entities involved in the value chain of the firm and/or external partners);
(iii) Explore the availability of resources to the project;
(iv) Negotiating about partaking roles in the project;
(v) Prepare the necessary documents for the communication of the project and its future administration.

The *project brief* is a seminal document elaborated at this phase. However, if the Definition phase entails the description of what the project is and its rationale, a brief cannot be elaborated, merely, based on the mapping of the project environment circumstances (5 C´s). To put on paper the project´s settings and illustrate it in general one needs to do something more. The owner of the project proposal presenting the brief is required to demonstrate the prerequisites for its implementation, such as, the goals, the target group, the strategy, or the disbursable resources and the period of their consumption or expenditure.

In this context, is recommended the use of holistic framework capable of covering several aspects of the definition, both for the self-structuring reasons, but also, for making clear the purpose of the project, whenever it needs to be communicated to others parties. Here, the *McKinsey´s and Co.´s 7-S Framework,* has the virtue of fulfilling such expectations. This management model, developed by *Robert H. Waterman Jr.*, *Thomas J. Peters* and *Julien R. Phillips*, allows the structuring of the project around seven (7) pillars (Waterman, Peters and Phillips, 1980).

From Alfred Chandler´s association of strategy and structure, mentioned in chapter two, they have gone beyond such interrelation to expose that organizational changes towards substantive positive performance "*... is really the relationship between structure, strategy, systems, style, skills, staff, and something we call superordinate goals.*". (Waterman, Peters and Phillips, 1980, p. 17). These authors have labelled their model as the *7-S Framework*. The original idea of the model is that organizational effectiveness, here replicated to the project realm, stems from the interaction of these seven (7) factors effectiveness.

However, perceived as a key concern for managers, effectiveness is difficulty to manage, as it is not solely dependent on the skills or technology, but also dependent on the shared set of values built around business, which belong the "higher order" values or aspirations (i.e. the superordinate goals). *What does this mean (effectiveness is hard-to-manage)?* Although, strategic and operational effectiveness represent a set of value drivers pointing towards higher-gains; however, at the same time, stockholders seem to place rather attention on the primary goal of the company, which is the concern placed to the returns on the invested capital on the short-term (or present), the attaining of above-average returns, and the maximization of profit. This constitutes, in turn, a managerial (ethical) dilemma of better management versus better results, as a silent conflict of stakeholders' interests plus time horizon interests. Others scholars refer to this superordinate values as the stakeholder´s thinking (Maylor, 2010).

Yet, leaving aside these theoretical issues about the 7-S framework, as they are concerns of the domain of Strategic Management not pertinent to the construction of the characteristics of the definition´s phase (D1), I would rather emphasize here merely the utility of its replication due to its suitability to this phase. Thus, borrowing the structure of the 7-S can facilitate the task (of organization + presentation) a more simplified job. Hence, this framework can work as an initial tool for wrapping up the major features of the project and presenting them in a more systematic and clear manner. Surely, the requirements of structuring and communication of the project´s definition may certainly vary from an organization to another.

The table above summarizes, thus, the type of information to be casuistically administrated as to their communication to others. However, it is advisable the articulation of the prior in this phase (D1) with another relevant tool that may present clearly the complexity of the project, such as, the *Technical, Organizational and Environmental (TOE) Framework*; or the M*ODest framework (*Bosch-Rekveldt, 2011; Maylor, Vidgen and Carver, 2008).

The M*ODest framework,* as it was the first to be developed and is a dominant model of managerial complexity *(*Maylor, Vidgen and Carver, 2008). It is based on five (5) parameters of complexity: *mission; organization; delivery; stakeholders*; and *team*, which in the original empirical study these researchers tested across industries in the context of the defense, regional transports and telecommunications sectors. The TOE framework cascaded the classification from five (5) categories of complexity features of the project to three (3) categories, which are breakdown into fourteen (14) other sub-categories as represented here in this orthogonal tree.

Table 2. Utility of the 7-S for the project definition phase (D1)

Factor	Description
Strategy	Anticipation of external business environment features (and changes) Project objectives and underlying plans (as means to achieve the first)
Structure	Determining the governance and roles´ distribution
Systems	The set of formal and informal procedures requiring design and monitoring
Staff	The internal selection and further recruitment, training programmes, pay scales and appraisal instruments
Skills	Technical and managerial attributes required
Style	Desired culture of cooperation and interaction, comprised of a set of symbolic and relational patterns of behaviour (role-model - of best practices)
Stakeholders	The individuals and groups with interests in the projects and their distinctive assumptions[2] about the progression and outcome

Source: Waterman, Peters and Phillips (1980)

Figure 1. TOE Framework: Sub-categories representation
Source: Own elaboration

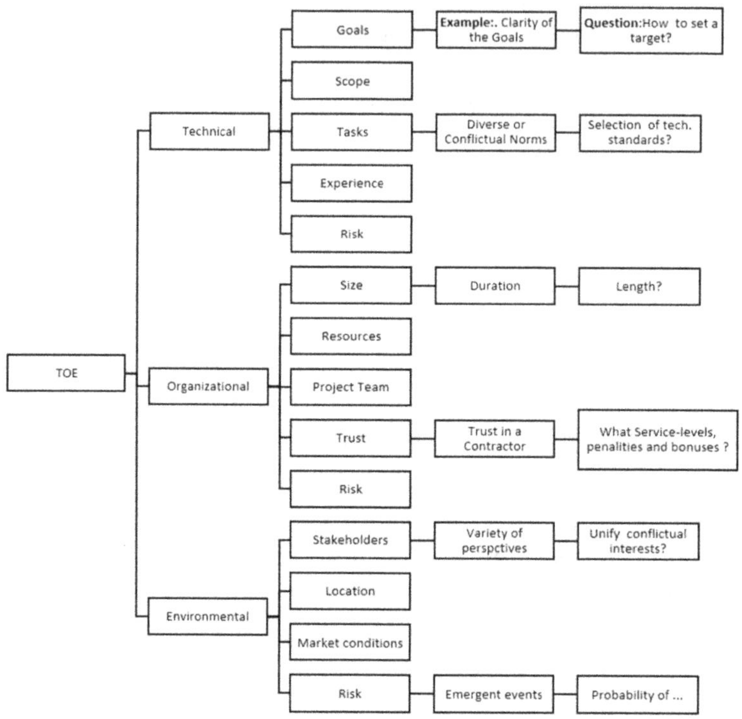

The diagram above represents the elements of complexity (T-O-E), cascaded into the 14 sub-categories, with examples of specific challenges of complexity accompanied at the right-hand side by an equivalent question to every exemplified issue. For instance, the degree of trust as to the hiring of a consultant, outsource or contractor, which triggers a need for establishing service level agreement (SLA) clauses. Those are a contractual baseline of minimum or target performance, often accompanied by a measurement of achievement of those SLAs (and inherent deviation ratios), whether positive or negative, and respective terms indexed to those deviation (bonuses or penalties). This is just an example of the project´s inherent complexity. Bosch-Rekveldt et al. (2011) set in the article a list of fifty (50) typical complexity elements faced in engineering projects. The reader is recommended the revisiting of this article, especially while defining the BEAP (and/or if less accustomed with this task), since this list of complexities may be inspirational for the reflection about the problematic, sometimes unclear, to support your identification of the specific ones applicable to a focal context.

The design stage (D2), which will determine the execution (D3) it ought to establish a roadmap for the direction of the operations and their architectural specifics. This answer to the question:

What needs to be equated in the project´s operation´s system?

This entails looking into a set of five (5) aspects: *capacity; materials; scheduling; standards;* and, *control* (Sprague, 2007). The *capacity* refers to the ability to deliver an output, in which, a given limitation resides in the resource in the shortest supply. The materials as the inflow of resources or stock of inventory needed to perform a task. BEAPs are however a category of projects not usually constrained by materials since they deal mostly with intangibles. However, *materials* are closed tied with capital investment, hence to cash flows disposal, as working capital stocks. The quest for short storage in time and space considering its relative weight of the cost of goods sold (COGS) or even obsolescence issues and extraordinary losses with inventory pushes companies (and projects) to generally administer stocks in a lighter manner. For instance, preferring *just-in-time* (JIT) inventory systems, in which the purchasing of goods is matched with the need in time only when is required its usage in production.

The *scheduling* is a task encompassing the coordinated allocation of available resources by time and place. This starts from the pool of team members´ working time to other physical or resources, as software or other equipment, or even the utilization of metered-charged services or premium ones. The *control* are the processes for monitoring the planning (for capacity, scheduling and inventory). This is something delivered by a project quality assurance framework. This latter issue, such as the *standards* (about the quality or work performance), I will elaborate further on those aspects in chapter *9 Project Quality*.

The development stage (D4) is arguably the most important along the 4-D for the future of the organization. It refers to after-action review of the whole project processes, delivery and its performance. The bottom line is, project managers need to be able to convert the project learning into potential transferable knowledge and convert it effectively into collective learning to the company. Otherwise, the project is completed but the company keeps no memory of the happening and takes no lesson from it. This phenomenon designated in project management as the *hedgehog syndrome* constitutes an immense hidden risk for the future of the organization´s business, which may lead to a very high price to pay for mistakes made in management at project-level (Maylor, 2010). The reason for this label (hedgehog syndrome), I believe is easily recognizable. Hedgehogs have unsuspected encounters with cars on the road every day. Such inevitable confront is almost a *(Jacques de) La Palisse´s* utterly obvious truth; as long as we will keep having cars and hedgehogs. The reason is hedgehogs do not learn with previous mistakes crossing roads repeatedly and falling into the same hazard. In short, there is no amendment of the behaviour according to the risk, as it happens many times in the organization´s realm. A hedgehog syndrome deriving from a lack of post-projects review and consequently endowment of the organization with further information/knowledge. Feedback to the organization is essential for learning, otherwise, knowledge is simply lost, and this comes at a high expense. On section 7.3., when addressing the role of the project management office, I do elaborate shortly on the key-activities to ensure that project learning becomes a systematized into as explicit knowledge asset gains (or organizational learning).

PROJECT ARCHITECTURE

We live in an unprecedented world dominated by systems (Boddy, 2017). The quest for societal control of the unpredictability of external factors surrounding human living in general, since our ancestral *Homo Sapiens* period, placed humankind into an evolving path of experiential learning overtime challenging our original beliefs, myths and fears. Indeed, such intra-generational memory, retaining earlier societal conquests, leveraged by explicit knowledge-gains, new human skills, and most particularly, enhanced by technological/scientific advancements have shaped profoundly whom we are and how we live nowadays.

This world of "systems" as our way of living, is a self-inflicted social regime that we managed to build around as a "fortress" and gently call it *society*. Modern societies, many of them innovation-centric or tertiary-based economies, are anchored on digital technologies as an engine for the uprise of their (second) economy (Abrantes and Ostergaard, 2020; Abrantes, 2020a, 2020b). These phenomena could not naturally exist without an individual evolution fueling this collective evolution (or rather transformation). Primeval knowledge transformed into more sophisticated one, and materialized into a more civilized living, is a by-product of the "hominization" process of the ancestral *Homos Emotionallis*, typically biased by perceptions and error prone, towards a current *Homos Economicus* more sophisticated in rationality, ability to take informed decision, and create wealth.

As architects and engineers of such world, we are surrounded by a myriad of systems ensuring such predictability, removing randomness in external events, and ensuring that behaviour on the multiple quadrants of the individual/collective action is safeguarded. As systems unfold in multiple roles, they function as our gatekeepers, holding a role of accessibility, mobility and security of the parts.

Beyond the project´s sphere, many aspects of living in societies constitute also a system (e.g. consumption; art/intellectual enrichment; production and work or simply socialization) being determined by an overall structure and (typically routinized) processes and procedures, that are interdependent and occurring in a stepwise manner. Herein, underlying to the conception of a system is the logic of *gates*. Being a dominant paradigm, the existence of a gate logic in projects will take us to revisit along this section the role of *stage-gates* in project architecture (Edwards et al., 2019; Cooper, 2010).

One surely recognize, if not all, most of those parts, shaping the way of doing things, conveyed in multiple forms (e.g. laws; hierarchies; protocols, regulations; guidelines; instructions; standards; (best) practices; software/hardware tools; workflows; and so forth). Literally, everyone and everything is an object or an agent of a part of the system.

Organizations are without exception a mezzo-level (most) relevant part of the system. They also benefit from controlling activities to ensure *predictability* in their course of action. This requires internal *consistency* across all elements of the organization for an effective administration of their challenges, capable of contributing to its stability, development and prosperity. These consistency challenges are common primary responsibility of several domains. For instance, the operations management (OM), which at first, needs to connect at all times with other parts of the company to be able to produce and deliver goods or services at a predetermined output standard. Also, middle managers whom monitor the operational indicators of progression (and the outputs of performance) and link them with the strategic goals. Nonetheless, these are dependent beforehand on the intervention of the Strategist whom designs the specifics of the intertwining between the linking activities that ensure internal consistency.

Such design belongs to the realm of Business Architecture (BA). Here, causal links across functional areas and organizational-stakeholders, ensure that organizational systems are configured, and set in place accordingly, to respond to the internal challenges (e.g. goals set; or the resources limitation) and external challenges (e.g. natural mutations in the external business environment; or defined by the preempting/deterring action of the competitors).

Projects are like the reproduction at a nanoscale of the characteristics of the organization they belong to. Some authors have termed as *micro-enterprises*, and so they require an equivalent project architecture, as a design for their success, namely for the reaching of its goals (Whittle and Myrick, 2016).

Projects conceived as micro-organizations are like sub-systems, and this section is here placed for exploring precisely how to structure them (in the sequence of the initials ideas on project environment laid out in the previous section). Thus, I would recall first, that the "success" of strategic - addressed in chapter 2 *(Organizational Management and Strategic Behaviour*) - is straightly linked to the operations (i.e. activities; responsibilities; and, decisions). The effectiveness of these interrelations, often referred to (below) as *architectures*, is argued, to be dictated not only by the overall business plan, but also, dependent on the ability to derive specific plans with inner consistency across organizational elements, which one might denominate as strategic fit. The same assumption is established to the management of a project as micro-enterprise – the quest for *enterprise-project fit* and *inner project fit*.

Hence, we reintroduce the notion of *Organizational Levers* (L_n), with regard to *Organizational* and *Strategic fit,* as the most seminal interrelations of the system. In this sense, these interrelations explain the elements associated in between; consequently, one wants to, initially, consider these links when attempting to design the specifics of a project. These L_n represent the principles that ensure an *internal compatibility* among all its organizational elements (or project ones), and the *external compatibility* with the EBE; so that firms may, ultimately, succeed as to the achievement of its business goals (Beer et al. 2005; Abrantes and Venkataraman, 2022).

A cumulative fit between parts *(Fit* $=L_1$*:*L_4*)* was argued as crucial to avoid the negative effects of the external context in the firm, represented by the categories of traits 1 to 4 (i.e. V-U-C-A) and furthermore ensure, an internal connectivity between organizational parts and a (rational) causality within their interrelation (Beer et al. 2005; Abrantes and Venkataraman, 2022).

We recall here the eight (8) elementary organizational parts: *vision; goals; strategy; structure; culture; capabilities*; *systems/processes*; and, *behaviour;* plus the four (4) organizational levers of internal compatibility (Abrantes and Venkataraman, 2022):

- L1: Business Strategy → Internal Business Environment
- L2: Organizational Capabilities → Business Strategy
- L3: Organizational Design → Leadership behaviour
- L4: Organizational Culture → Organizational Capabilities

Naturally, the enterprise-project fit corresponds, on the point of view of the project, to an external environment. As a project becomes alive, for the project leader and the team, their vision of the positioning of the firm to the project is modified. The firm switches from being the internal environment (IE), in a relative positioning assumed to the strategy function, to become a first layer of the *project external environment (PEE).* Fundamentally, this occurs because, from the perspective of the project leader, the focal entity ("the project") is the threshold, thus the external environment holds only two tiers for project-teams (i.e. the whole firm and its markets). The *project general environment (PGE)* corresponds to the markets, and therein, the *project firm environment (PFE)* to the whole context inside of the organization.

The underlying rational decisions about the project (the what´s; who's; how´s; where´s; and, why´s), as to setting of these system principles, is embedded in the governance and constitute the 1st – inner – layer of the PEE. Projects adhere to the *modus operandis* one may relate to, ensuring the connectivity and causality needed between the whole enterprise and the project, and ultimately, reducing the uncertainty at the PFE-level. This *modus operandis,* it refers to what two (2) scholars (*Ralph Whittle* and *Conrad Myrick)*, termed as the *Corporate Nexus.*

The notion of *Corporate Nexus* entails the set of essential links that unite the enterprise to form a harmonious whole (i.e. the firm as a *system*) (Whittle and Myrick, 2016). Here, the set of processes, with each *process* conceived as a chain of predetermined and sequential activities, reveals itself as the unitary composing elements of the transformative system of the firm (to add value to the market), seminal to the business success. Thus, the rationale behind corporate nexus is to create "high-achievers", in which, organizations are capable of managing, wisely and on a balanced manner, the *effectiveness* (of their goals) with the *efficiency* (of the resources) allocated to those activities. Here, the nexus resides in the rational decisions leading to simultaneously *High Efficiency* and *High Effectiveness.*

Figure 2. The project external environment (PEE)
Source: Own elaboration

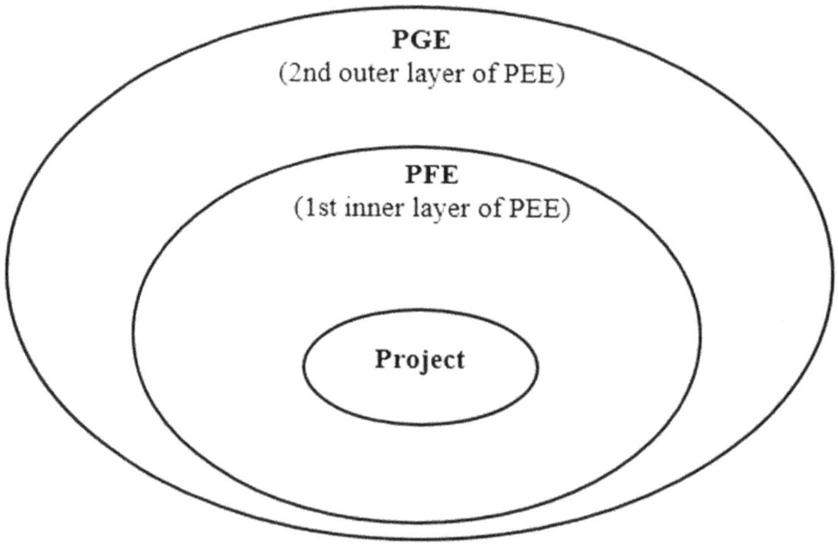

Figure 3. Rationale of the corporate nexus
Source: Own elaboration

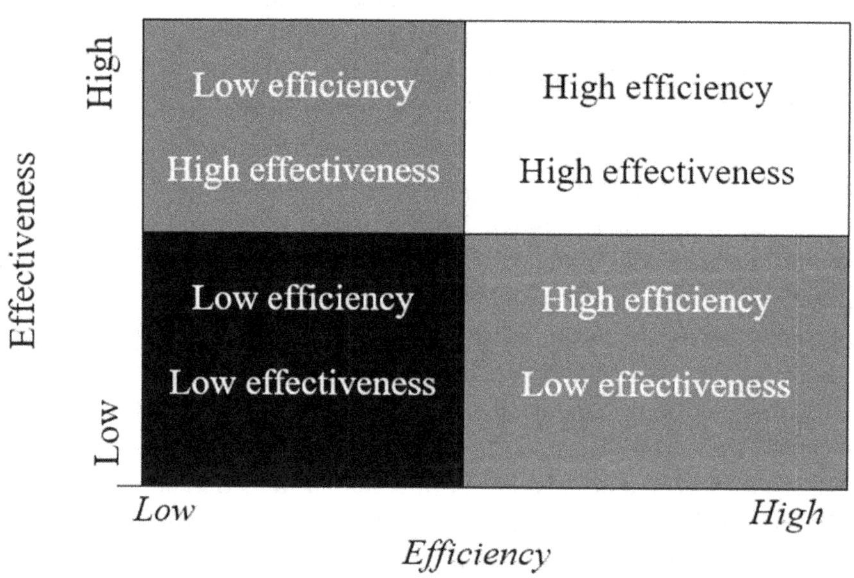

Hence, sound results or high-achievements do not simply appear out from the sky. Their achievement requires a holistic view to create an initial understanding of what the corporate center of gravity is (and should be), encompassing the key aspects of: (i) leadership (thus, an ability to inspire and motivate the team/s); (ii) the modelling of proper enterprise and project architectures; and, (iii) and a lucid out of the box thinking (*clear thinking*), as to the linkage of strategic goals, business operations and strategic results (Whittle and Myrick, 2016).

With regard to projects, as micro structural configurations, inside of the organizations that replicate the structural configurations of the firm, it is required a managerial capacity to understand that "context matters", as the intertwining of internal and external factors being a mediator of success (Boddy, 2017). *Clear thinking* means to comprehend the importance of the context and to acknowledge such factum before taking any action.

Moreover, clear thinking encompasses a sense of awareness to the tormenting fact, that the surrounding context, i.e. the business ecosystem – where firms compete on, molds the thoughts, ideas, methods/practice and the results of any organization. Hence, the "clear thinker" acknowledges that the context affects inherently his/her area of responsibility and takes it firmly as an assumption. Clear thinkers respond dualistically (to efficiency and effectiveness), as the corporate nexus aforementioned, which relies on an ambidextrous approach (i.e. internal/external), as shown on the diagrammatic representation of the pyramidal model below:

Figure 4. The performance pyramid framework
Source: Lynch and Cross (1991)

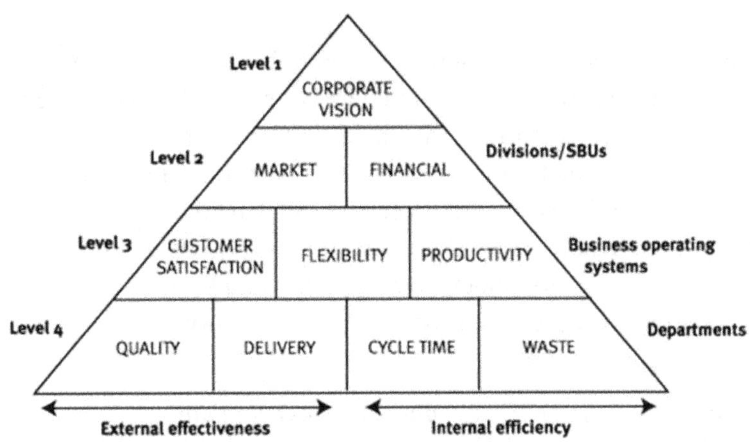

This "*Performance Pyramid Framework*" model shows the link between strategy-design and day-to-day operations (or strategy execution). Also labelled as the "SMART pyramid", the achievement of the corporate vision is cascaded down through a number of levels (level 1 to 4), for the achievement of the corporate objectives.

According to this model, the goal´s accomplishment is related to the ability of the firm to function in a disciplined way across all levels. Such discipline corresponds to the focus on the courses of action to reach simultaneously the duality of objectives towards effectiveness/efficiency targets. This requires a synchronized effort of the whole organizational-stakeholders to cooperate as an orchestra playing together on the multiple tiers (senior, middle and line management), not merely linking but critically associating the interests of corporate governance actors´ vision; with the business divisions; departments and work centers´ operations.

Lynch and Cross (1991), argue in the "SMART model" above that the *effectiveness* of strategic goal´s accomplishment is dependent on the quality and outward/outbound logistics´ processes, while the *efficiency* on the waste and cycle time[3]. Altogether, this contributes to better systems of customer satisfaction and productivity.

However, the most fundamental aspect of the model refers to the design of the system. In the middle of the pyramid it can be identified the business operating systems, denominated the *central plexus*[4] for the firm´s success (Lynch and Cross, 1991). One will revisit (and define) this concept (central plexus) below in this chapter. However, one may say so far, that the corporate nexus is the "brain" acting like the center of gravity that establishes how everything happens, while the central plexus is the "heart" where the action happens[5].

Hence, an enterprise architecture is all what this is about, the design and the monitoring of execution of the whole system. Hence, as shown in the diagram above, one might adopt preferably a more flexible configuration, for the benefit of its competitive implications (as to the market positioning and ease of innovation-launching) and as to the benefit of the performance consequences (as to financial returns). Such flexibility is something also discussed below as to the importance of creating *adaptive* and *integrative* business architectures (BAs).

In short, a clear thinker means, the individual that feels the need to careful and constantly observe the context, as explored in the achievement-related pyramid (Lynch and Cross, 1991). In other words, the clear thinker is an adopter of (what is here drawn as) the *Factor-Decision-Context (F-D-C) Model,* as represented below.

Here, the initial problematization or review question refers to the *F*, taken as an independent variable brought to the table to take action upon *D*, the dependent variable requiring the formulation of the decision. Yet, the sum of factors, are though mediated by *C* the context, as outer events from the span of control of the real-manager, which initial assumptions about the importance of the context and its knowledgeability are crucial and lead to the avoidance of remedial solutions (as careless replication of formulas from the past applicable to similar contexts). Surely, clear thinkers, as high-achieving individuals, develop a sense of curiosity about every context, and seek more information, exploring the circumstances and search for evidence about the confronting reality.

Figure 5. The factor- decision- context (FDC) model of clear thinking
Source: Own elaboration

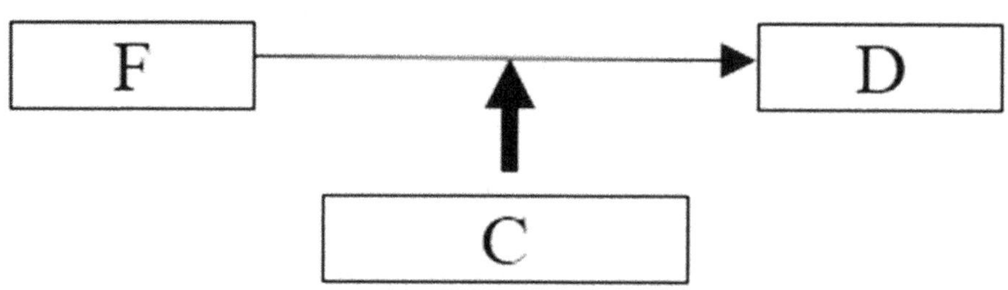

In short, the corporate nexus represents the formal relations between the organizational parts, deliberately set in disciplined terms, as a manifestation of the corporate strategy for achieving high results and above-average returns (a.a.r). In this sense, the reader may argue that the a.a.r.´s are, in fact, a measure of success (or a strategic performance indicator) of the business external fit to the markets (and such statement is certainly correct!); thus, the corporate nexus sets the path for the accomplishment of the a.a.r´s being dependent on the internal fitness of parts (level 1-4). The corporate nexus expresses on these linkages across levels, the ability to design, engineer and maintain a transformational system of value-addition.

Conversely, the logic of *stage-gate* aforementioned seems to be used counterproductively. Despite, it emphasizes a link between project design and execution for reducing uncertainty while focusing on the best practices of project controls; however, its application, seems to be hampering five (5) out six (6) of external effectiveness and internal efficiency aspects of the SMART pyramid in two (2) different levels of the system:

- Level 3 (flexibility; productivity)
- Level 4 (Quality; Cycle Time; and, Waste)

According to Becker (2006) and Edwards et al (2019), one may identify three (3) major points of criticism in the use of stage-gates: *rigidity* (fixed mindset); *myopia* (not context-based); and, *under emphasis on value* (by contrast with an over emphasis on the structure). Before we move into a discussion of what these three (3) major aspects mean and comprehend why they garnered such a wide criticism, let us firstly understand the stage-gate logic.

A Stage-Gate® system consists of a series of sequential stages of which a project goes through preceded by a sequence of identical number of gate controls, as quality check points in favor ("go") or against ("kill") the investment decision points in the process (Cooper, 2010). Hence, the stage-gate is, in its original form (full version) is an idea-to-launch process or an idea to launch system with five (5) stages: *discovery/scoping; business the business case; development; testing; launching* (Cooper, 2008; Cooper and Edgett, 2008). The stages had a corresponding gate: *idea screening* (a quick preliminary investigation and scoping of the project); *second screen* (a project reevaluation); *go to development* (rigorous readiness check - as lab-tests; in-house tests; or alpha tests) as the final gate before killing the project – usually staffed by senior managers; *go to test* (as a market pretest/test or trial sell); and, *go to launch* (final door before operations start-up and subsequent commercialization).

Traditionally, the stage-gate followed a "single stage-and-gate process" as a one size-fits all project architecture. Yet, its fashioning was suitable for more complex development projects. Nonetheless, in the vast majority of the cases, companies held a much large number of simpler projects[6] that did not require such a tight gate system. In practice, project teams in these smaller projects learnt to circumvent those gates (Cooper, 2010). This raised a dilemma of over resource-allocation to project development when the bulk of projects were less demanding that led to the streamlining additional version of the stage-gate *XPress* (for moderate-risks projects) and Lite for lower-risk projects including internal sales force requests (Cooper, 2010). The seminal difference of the full stage-gate to the *XPress* resided in the reduction of the number of gates to two gates. The Gate 3 making a check on Stages 1 and 2 while Gate 5 controlling the Stages 3 and 4. Likewise, the difference of the full stage-gate to *Lite* implied the reduction of gates to a single Gate 3, in which, a final decision of senior managers to "go to development" or kill the project before entering into operations and before higher financial commitment.

Despite the noteworthy evolution of the gate system, the stage-gate kept on receiving, not an antagonism but, an opposition as to its current adoption, channeled mostly to the three major critics above indicated (*rigidity not-context-based;* and, *under emphasis on value).*

Firstly, the claim of rigidity of the system and it fixed mindset referred to the requisite of formal reviewing and the need for higher level of approval from senior management (particularly noticed in Gate 3) (Edwards et al., 2019). This represents an opportunity loss to manage projects in a more flexibly manner, namely the missed opportunity to focus rather on detecting on-going market changes and tech-innovations instead of over-controlling the processes. These authors, supported by others, as Svejvig and Andersen (2015) or Sethi and Iqbal, (2002) argued on favor of more responsive and adaptive project architectures to surrounding reality. The major consequence of such rigidity is, that the inattentiveness to the markets dynamics will make it difficult later on to alter the course of action of the project (CoA)[7] (Svejvig and Andersen, 2015; Sethi and Iqbal, 2002).

Secondly (myopic/not-contextualized), one-size certainly does not fit all project typologies and dimensions, nor the multiple research and development requirements; and the streamlining of the full version of the stage-gate seems insufficient to cope with the diversity of projects (Edwards et al, 2019). Moreover, there are different processes to deal with the contingencies of a project and different processes to handle uncertainty in the innovation-launching/diffusion processes.

Thirdly, the over emphasis on the project design rather than value leads to projects being: too structured; and, to financially-constrained. The stage-gate logic makes the system to become too controlling and too burocratic, with multiple quality check points, checklists and excessive paperwork in general (Becker, 2006).

It is evident that the stage-gate has evolved with time. The different versions of the system have been streamlined to handle: (i) multiple project sizes; (ii) various development complexities; and, (iii) divergent approaches towards risk-perception/risk-tåking. Moreover, iterative experimentation loops have been added to the stage-gate to enable the teams to learn and consequently alter, both the project´s direction and the design of new products/services. But it remains still time-consuming, time wasting and pillared on burocratic procedures which restrict the learning opportunities around the project (Cooper, 2010, 2008; Edwards et al., 2019).

The emergence of a hybrid model emerged as a solution to solve these issues above (Edwards et al., 2019). According to Karlström and Runeson (2006) the application of Agile methods to the stage-gate system would provide a powerful toolbox for micro-planning, day-to-day work control and progress reporting. Furthermore, the agile approach to stage-gate constituted more than an approximation to the software industry or a research opportunity, as highlighted by Cooper and Sommer (2016) in terms of its benefits on faster and more responsive execution. With origin on the research of Sommer et al (2015), who coined it as the *Agile-Stage-Gate (ASG)* model, this hybrid model aimed to solve the limitations of, linear product-developments processes (including the traditional Stage-Gate process) - who could not support iterative cycles (assuming projects as first-timers) - and the absence of external collaboration particularly needed as to the intertwining with the customer-base).

Hence, *agility* ought to be considered, with regard to project management, as to the development of new products in a manufacturing firm, to one´s ability to modify the project plan and actively involve customer in the development process (Conforto et al., 2016). Thus, the ASG model entails the use of *agile sprints* and *feedback loops* (Edwards, et al., 2019). The agile sprints corresponds to a short, time-boxed period, in which, scrum teams conduct a set of assignments while the feedback loops encompasses the constant feedback to customer built into each of the stages of the project.

Inevitably, the ASG is a key element of project design for the building of a more effective/efficient corporate nexus, which is, in turn, is operatively and strategically dependent on program design and the overall enterprise business architecture (BA). Considering the larger, the agility of the program and enterprise functions inherently as the *central plexus* for the designing and execution of a focal project, as to:

a. The functionality of each architecture, or sub-system;
b. The iteration of the project and adaptability to meta-enterprises (including feedback loops);
c. The evolution of the architecture in time.

Herein, the meta-enterprise comprises the larger system than the organization itself. For instance, a merger or acquisition's integration architecture; or a *zaibatsu* network (as addressed in chapter 2); a joint venture; or any other type of cross-enterprise cooperative body, as a consortium, a group of professional associations (e.g. federations or unions), or a research network.

Indeed, at this stage, one might raise a couple of reasonable questions:

So, What´s Enterprise or Business Architecture (BA) after all?

Why is it (BA) important or necessary in the context of a BEAP?

Before delivering a definition of Business Architecture, (BA) is important to stress, that one of the motives for its establishment is, precisely, related to the Business Environment´s constraints (as presented further below in this chapter). BA allows firms to unite two (2) fundamental sides of organizational strategy:

(i) The formulation (or strategic design);
(ii) The implementation (or strategic execution).

Often, those two dimensions seem distant from each other. Despite being fundamental, the activities of Strategic Planning and Strategic Controls (as addressed in chapter 2) are for many scholars indivisible in thesis but separate universes, as a common practice in most firms. Yet, both are part of the role of the strategist (and strategy departments´ accountability), regarding the job of Strategic Performance Management (SPM), i.e. to measure whether the corporate´s vision and objectives are actually met by business on-track measurable results.

BA is what actually bridges the company´s strategy with the subsequent realization of its goals. A North-American digital strategy-consulting firm (*STA Group)* explains it nicely. BA bridges the "where the business really is" with "where we want to go" and "what truly takes to get here" without the costly risk of trial-by-error (STA Group, 2021). Unfortunately, this is still the dominant paradigm in our times. According to Hughes (2021), 70% of all organizational change management initiatives fail. Consequently, as firms compete today on an e-age where markets hold VUCA traits, the risk of failure by failure, identically to inaction or unpreparedness is a very high price to pay.

Now, digging into the first question (above), *Business Architecture (BA)* refers to the basic precept for uniting and integrating all of the "architectures" as parts of the system (or subsystems) of the enterprise in a formal and disciplined manner (Whittle and Myrick, 2016). This logic closely tied to the aspect of functionality, as one of the architectural goals above mentioned. Besides the *architectures* (or subsystems), business architectures are also comprised of *workflows* (or processes) and *events* (or activities). However, these scholars provide a far more clear definition:

"An enterprise business architecture defines the enterprise value streams and their relationships to all external entities and other enterprise value streams and the events that trigger instantiation. It is a definition of what the enterprise must produce to satisfy its customers, compete in a market, deal with its suppliers, sustain operations and care for its employees" (2003, p. 4)

It must be emphasized also in this definition the notion of *value stream*, as the end-to-end collection of activities that creates a result for a "customer," whether it is the ultimate customer or an internal "end user".

The concept of Business Architecture derives naturally from the parent concepts of *Business Model* (and *Business Model Design).*

Firstly, a *Business Model* describes the interdependent activities performed by a focal firm and its partners and the mechanisms of interrelation established across them (Amit and Zott, 2015, pp. 331-332). As described in simple terms, is "*the way your business is run*" (Economist Intelligence Unit, 2005). A *Business Model Design* is,

"the conceptualization of a boundary-spanning activity system that includes the mechanisms that connect these interdependent activities and the identification of the party that carries out each of the activities within the system"

However, these Business Models to be effective in goal´s accomplishment, they require a preliminary reflection about their shape and their initial sketching (i.e. a *Business Model Design*).

The *Business Model Design* is a general outlining of activities, as arrangements to be provisioned in the future Business Model. The *Business Architecture* comprises the detailed description of the all activities´ linkages per business process deriving from the Business Model Design, and the whole set of business processes per each subsystem for the whole "architectures". The Business Model is the output a holistic approach to business development (i.e. (*Systems Thinking*). The connection of those three concepts is show below:

Putting it all together, *Business Model Design* is focused on "design themes" and its realized *Business Models* are subsequently focused on the on-going activities of the firms. The Business Architecture is all about system´s design and monitoring.

Figure 6. Business model design & architecture
Source: Own elaboration

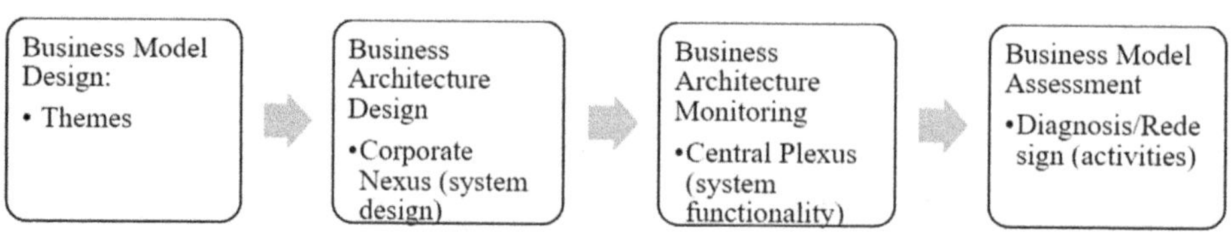

Source: Own elaboration

Looking at the focus of the Business Model Design, i.e. "*design themes*" and the focus of Business Architectures (the system´s parts) they make them clearly distinguishable. The *design themes* are the main areas of orchestration of the business. These themes are directional in nature and connect the *elements* of the model:

Element 1: The content (of business offering)
Element 2: The organizational structure (and its structural configuration)
Element 3: The governance (of the corporation)

The Business Architecture on the other hand, is centered on the design of the linkages (as the corporate nexus) and on the monitoring of the functionality, adaptability and evolution (i.e. the central plexus). Enterprise business architecture works as a hub-and-spoke model of disciplined central connections of the whole sub-systems, with a triadic typology of architectures (Whittle and Myrick, 2016):

- Organizational and strategic architectures
- Security architectures
- IT architectures.

As to the second question ("*Why is it important or necessary in the context of a BEAP?*") the why is anchored on the earlier explanation of the three (3) major architectural goals: the system´s functionality; adaptability; and, evolution. Those have already set, most likely, the tone for the importance/need of BAs.

Moreover, one may remember the discussion above about "*context matters*" and the importance of its recognition, termed as *clear thinking*. In fact, it was also represented the F-D-C model for clear thinking in which the context is considered a mediator of effective business models and their ability to seize opportunities, deal with barriers and innovate (Chesbrough, 2010).

For scholars as Zott and Amitt (2007, 2008), the exercising of clear thinking helps on the building of an organizational capability (aka, *context awareness*), which is a part of one of the four (4) business model *antecedents:*

- the setting of organizational *goals;*
- recognition of the t*emplates* for seizing opportunities and innovation;
- to have a profound understanding of stakeholder *activities;*
- grasp the *environmental constraints.*

Context awareness entails an ability of the manager to picture the internal and external compatibility of the organizational strategy to prepare the firm to keep being, or becoming, both, organizationally and strategically fit. This (contextual awareness) is particular important, as the firm may face the adversity of the dynamics of the markets (namely the e-markets), and a very high degree of rivalry deriving from internal/direct/indirect/potential competition. For instance, the internal competitors for the same resources or market position. Also, the direct competitors within the segment or the indirect competitors across segments, from other related industries, or from the same strategic groups. Finally, the potential competitors from upstream/downstream agents in the same value network and other firms willing to innovate in the same market or acquire positions in the same value network.

The importance of Business Architecture is directly related to the success of the projects (BEAP). As shown in the discussion in this section, the effectiveness of the goals towards market research, market bundling data outputs and building insightful business intelligence for the analysis of Business Environments, do not appear to come, solely, from the skills of the Consultants/Analysts, as to the understanding of Business Environment-related theories, or state-of-the-art models of External Business Environment Analysis.

The formation of a project and the nomination of the project management is actually a micro-enterprise, identical to the firm itself. Projects being a spin-off of the organization (and of its intrapreneurial ability), retain in general the fundamental attributions of the firm´s DNA on the root of the project´s foundations. Among them are the major characteristics, such as, structural configuration, culture, capabilities, systems, vision, goals, strategy and a particular project behaviour. In this sense, the tenets of organizational success are mirrored in this tenets of the project´s success.

Needless is to say that the internal tenets of success (as goals´ setting; resources allocation and careful strategic design) are equally important as the external tenets (of market research), to the effectiveness of this type of micro-enterprise. Thus, the design of BEAP ought to consider as key, the definition of long-term goals, resources allocation and careful strategic design. The design of the *themes* where the project intervenes on, it requires on a second stage the deepening of these themes into criterious project architectures.

The utility of project architecture is identical to the business architecture, as it shrinks the gap between strategy design and the strategy execution. Similarly, it requires the design of the corporate nexus and the creation of the central plexus. Identifying the "architectures" or subsystems of the project is a prerequisite, since these sub-systems need to be accounted in their number and mapped further in scope.

Each "architecture" ought to be cascaded into the several processes. For instance, the design of a project of market research on the utilities sector by an oil and gas company centered on the exploring of extractive potential of the subsoil of a market X, needs to identify beforehand the multiple sub-systems to be considered when executing the project (e.g. drilling; geological/seismic assessment; partnering; or procurement, among others). Thus, breaking down one sub-system (e.g. drilling) into multiple processes for the hypothetical project design, we would well end up designing processes related to directional drilling; deep-water drilling; or hydraulic fracturing. Thus, putting together the associated activities of each of processes related to the drilling architecture entails also to grasp the connectivity of each singular activity and its causality inside the processes and across the system.

Furthermore, business/project architecture is an imperative as the advent of Internet fueled a global revolution in computing and communications online, with new ways of doing businesses being shaped every day in all industries worldwide. Consequently, there is a number of phenomenal opportunities for those whom are audacious, but also have the vision and creativity to innovate. This requires undoubtedly the internal alignment of strategy, structure, systems and resources.

Moreover, an entrepreneur or small family business may in this age (or Second Economy) of a digitalized world, aspire naturally to become the next mega-enterprise, such as *Amazon, Coupang, Taobao* or *Uber*. However, one may need to be aware that those modern mega-enterprises are building integrated and adaptive architectures, constituting a new corporate nexus, where the linkages are purely web-based. Remember here the example of *Lego Group* (in chapter 5) on the new supplier-customer linkages on the customer involvement process, focused on activities beyond UGC towards business co-creation/development. This is the recommendation left for any contemporary businesses (and its programmes and projects). Follow the BA sapiency and results of these successful digital native firms.

Indeed, such bold new enterprises are not building static business architecture skeletons or binding by the rules of the large firms of the pre-digital age. For them, the latter are as business "dinosaurs" trapped in the past. Accordingly, the ideas of these non-fully digital firms are imprisoned by their path knowledge. Consequently, their limited horizons and creativity leads most of them to build default solutions, commonly adopted as safety nets whenever no alternative arises. This is called *path dependency* and the default solutions are the outcome of core-rigidities in terms of their competences.

On the contrary, bold business architectures are rather flexible (than rigid defensive "castles"), allowing modern firms to take agile business modifications according to new strategic directions, as *adaptive architectures*. Furthermore, they are developing architectures that can have the potential to evolve. They quickly adapt to the social and technological modifications in time, but also adapt functionally (i.e. *integrated architectures*) as they are capable of evolving in a predictive way, operating holistically, designing a corporate nexus with a central plexus that works in favor of business, not as a "silver bullet" but like a "golden spike" (Whittle and Myrick, 2016).

However, (let´s say) the major drawback of *project architecture* as a replication of the business architecture principles to a project, particularly as to its applicability to Business Environment Analysis Project (BEAP), is the need to conduct a serious strategic analysis of the enterprise. Such strategic analysis, as preparatory condition for the project is made before attempting to initiate the *project design*; and, subsequently the *project architecture*, or even, immerse into the *project execution*. This consumes time and resources. Thus project´s expenditure starts normally before the project even starts to get executed. That is totally right! The good news is, preparatory endeavors pay off, as the strategic analysis prior any attempt to design a new project enhance the project´s results, providing a clear competitive advantage in terms of the comprehension of the potential value streams and consequently improving stakeholder value. Another attenuating factor or further good news is, acting as a project designer, exactly a business model designer, you can borrow ideas from other companies. It is actually a commonplace to draw inspiration from others, by observing existing firms, or other workflows of organizing activities and exchanges, and moreover, talking to, mentors, managers and colleagues who might be able to offer further advice (Snihur and Zott, 2015).

The purpose of enterprise strategic analysis is to build ground knowledge for a future project design/architecture. Hence, it is suggested here on this analytical exercise to account the following:

a. Built a holistic model of the business, summarizing and representing the major organizational parts: vision; objectives; strategy; structure;
b. Support the summarized representation of the business model with viable and synthetized information
c. Put aside internal politics and functional silos mentality, and so, consider the influence of the business strategic roadmap with the project vision and objectives.

These recommendations for building an enterprise/strategic roadmap may equip project designer/s and decision-makers with the necessary internal information to build a better project design solution. As a final note, is relevant to stress that a "good design solution" reflects two (2) major features: the balancing of competing demands and an open discussion of stakeholders´ tensions. The *balancing* of competing demands referring to the ability to elect the needs and expectations across all users, while the open/creative and critical reflection about the multiple *tensions* of multiple stakeholders covering the set of competing logics, needs and goals.

PROJECT ALIGNMENT TO THE ORGANIZATION

Every organization is unique in their assets, transformative activities and outputs (David and David, 2017). Such heterogeneity reflects a unique *culture* making every entity a distinctive configuration with an unrepeatable DNA. This entails a specific way of breathing and living the internal ambience, activities and interactions with the remaining (external) business environment. Organizational-stakeholders adhere and socialize to it and can freely get detached from it (Friedman and Antal, 2005).

The structuring of the firm and its strategic planning endeavors go, as seen before, side-by-side. Hence, we dedicate here a section to the projects´ structure. However, companies are also irremediably influenced by the the inner traits of corporate culture that shape the company´s behaviour. These somehow invisible traits are displayed in a mirror of *cultural products,* as the characteristics that carve corporate cultures and that can be defined as the explicit and tacit assumptions or understandings commonly held by the members of the organization (Phillips and Sackman, 2000).

These (cultural) products encompass an assortment of habits, espoused norms and artifacts that profiles the hidden dimensions of the firm, but uncover its essence. I would label it the "invisible hand of culture", may times disregarded by senior management. For instance, the set of values, beliefs, rituals, myths, languages, rites, ceremonies or symbols. These products are the ones conveyed to the younger members of the "clan" by other types of (narrative-based) cultural products, as stories, folktales, metaphors or heroes/heroines descriptions (Trice and Beyer, 1984). Those products are, according to Chao and Moon (2005) a *cultural mosaic* of the firm. For these scholars the mosaic is though built on the backstage by each individual who composes the mosaic, and representing on of its units (or a *tile*).

Each *cultural tile* brings to the mosaic the assumptions and beliefs about the national cultural of an individual, as bundles of demographic, geographic and associative characteristics of all staff. The demographic characteristics as the physical and social inheritances (e.g. gender or ethnicity). These demographical characteristics intermingle with the natural and manmade physical features (or geographical) (e.g. temperature, climate or topography) and with the associative ones (e.g. profession; religion; and, avocations).

As Makay et al (2020) puts it, culture is a key-component carving the three main elements of the organizational: the *relationships*; the *structure* and the *processes;* thus, (culture) it could not be disregarded at this part of the book.

Such influence is directly exercised upon the relations established within the corporate hub and across other more distant organizational units, but also, prompting the way to do things since the conception of plans to the controlling of the inherent likelihood of success or failure. Projects face an identical circumstantialism, as they are embedded in the organization and replicate their culture to the micro-enterprise, if no changes are introduced in the project realm, with new blood, thinking or attitudes.

Hence, what is established for the firm as a structure feature can also be assumed in the project. Yet, this is a significantly large assumption of a homogeneous firm. That is not really the paradigm of we encounter in the business world, as many companies have, partially a structure which seems to row the boat in one direction and another into another direction. Some departments exceptionally agile, flexible, cooperative, proactive and with a forward-thinking mentality, while others more cloistered into their silos, less responsive, and committed to their own workspace and responsibilities.

Although, this all boils down to the element of relations, since intra-tile interactions are self-adjusted. The person has to, involuntarily, adapt to one-to-one relations and group interactions. This implies an adjustment to colleague's personalities and attitudes with whom he or she partakes work with. But also, adapt to other project members (e.g. from a project management office staff), and finally to the planning/organization/leading/controlling of project managers, manifested in the communication and command styles. Naturally, such self-adjusted behaviour to a working context one adheres to, or better said, one accepts to socialize in, this subsequently shapes the teams, departments and projects´ culture. *Relations* can represent, in this sense, a deviation to the dominant cultural matrix of the firm, challenging the established vision and values of the dominant paradigm.

Projects replicate the organization´s culture but also produce their own identity, as individuals (as project members) storm into projects from multiple functional areas, and withholding different perspectives, interests, priorities and even hidden agendas.

Regardless, of the extent of those differences being more or less notorious, as to the degree of personal twitching, professional conflictuality and to the amount of effort required to mutually adjust to a project structure; however, after the preparatory work on phase one (D1 - Definition), comes the actual structure´s formation. Needless to say, the project structure does not come "out of the blue", since at the initial project´s phase (D1), the project is initially conceived to be presented for internally approval, considering already a certain extent of needed resources and cost planning. This entails, of course, one preparatory effort of building a coalition of interests and building a pool of potential project members whom are likely to accept in the future to undertake some expected roles and responsibilities.

Based on Tuckman and Jensen´s (1977) theory as to the stages of team´s development, which are also applicable for any first-timer projects, with the scope of a Business Environment Analysis Project (BEAP), project teams go through five phases from the formation until their dissolution:

- Stage 1: Forming
- Stage 2: Storming
- Stage 3: Norming
- Stage 4: Performing
- Stage 5: Adjourning

The first (formation), begins at the phase one of the BEAP, considering the 4-D model (as addressed in the initial section of this chapter), and entails the recruitment and selection of individuals per functional and technical expertise, knowledge or skills. This forming phase continues along, with the approval of the project´s proposal, as the team begin to gather and to exchange the initial information. It is a moment where the different backgrounds are uncovered together with disparate points of view. The team does not really work as an orchestra, and the efforts are placed on organizing the group rather than achieving immediate effectiveness from a well-oiled group. Actually, the group effectiveness is the lowest.

However, with the allocation of resources and initial operative tasks, a team moves quickly into a stage 2 (*storming*), as the projects recently formed is start also a phase 2 (D2-design). Here, discussion and conflict as to the project architecture (i.e. processes and activities) and practices (i.e. frameworks; approaches; instruments; equipment; or standards) emerge, alongside with personality differences and it is a critical moment of often re-adjustment. In some cases, it cannot overcome this stage.

Once the team is able to accommodate personal and professional differences, by engaging into internal negotiation, ultimately accepting the others suggestion and managing to establish adequate ways of working together, the team moved into a stage 3 (*norming*). However, not all project teams are able to reach a system of *concertive control*. This phenomenon is what it allows ultimately the members of the team to accept each other differences and move forward in their discussions. Such acceptance, means undermining the *social forces* surrounding the social interaction (e.g. personal and professional motivations; personality differences; values, beliefs and divergences in the understanding of the word) and align on a superior common mission (Jønsson and Jeppesen, 2003).

According to Barker (1983), *concertive control* is not a entity to be imposed in top-down manner by the project manager. On the contrary, it results from the self-adjustment of individuals´ ideas, values and interpersonal relations, and from their joint ability to negotiate a consensus themselves.

At the norming stage, the team is working on the project´s phases D2 (*design*) and D3 (*delivery*). The ability to tackle the internally-generated uncertainty resulting from the conflict of interest among the team members and adopt an alternative decisional model (administrative or political), implies a stage of evolution in teamwork, in which, the members accept to jointly reach a best-decision (concerted). However, they acknowledge that such concertation, as a likely optimal technical solution for ones, is not necessarily a fully satisficing response for others, consequently, but converging to a point in the middle of confrontational ideas allows the project to move forward.

The specifics of the project architecture are entirely designed here in D2, and initiated the first operational tasks (D3). In the BEAP, this means to begin the contact with the entities, gathers of sources, contract the resources, negotiate access to information and prepare the mechanism of storage, plus the visualization tools for reporting.

At the stage 4 (*performing*) the team whom have organized the architectures in the norming phase is not reaping the benefits of their design work, as to the structure of processes and procedures, being now harvesting from the previous work. Operations should be running at a full speed (e.g. gathering data; building personalized datasets; working on dummy variable; building simulations; and so forth). The *adjourning*, as a final stage of the team´s lifecycle, refers to the disbanding either by an early abandoning of the project team typically still on norming of performing phases, or simply because of the completion of tasks. Some groups working on operative tasks tend to disband earlier than other members, which are involved on after-review of performing tasks, controlling and evaluation of project goals. Yet, such life cycle it may be repeated several times, considering each separate task within the project, which may require a call of the team members for its joint resolution (forming stage) and then going through all the stages of the same life cycle.

Until this stage of this section, we have dedicated rather attention in this section to the cultural fit of team members to the project to the company. The outlook of project´s structure linkage to the company´s structure was minimal. Exception to it was some brushstrokes about the project´s strategy and business strategy, when in section 7.1. I referred very briefly to the importance of Portfolio Management and the use of aggregated resource planning as a sanity check to avoid irrational project selection and losses.

However, it is inevitable to elaborate on the project structure whenever one wishes to understand its alignment to the company, whether the firm structure lands on the type of a *project-based organization (PBO)* or not.

First, it is important to distinguish two (2) concepts interchangeably used in section 7.1., which have not been defined yet. I am referring to the notion of *project* and *program*. A *project* is a "*temporary effort to create value through a unique product, service or result*" (PMI, online). This definition emphasis the three major properties of any project; they are *focused*; *temporary*; and *unique*. The focus is on the delivery of a task, product or result. Temporary because have a beginning and an end; and finally unique because it has not been performed before at the same exact time or place or resources, which means it has a certain degree of novelty associated to it.

A *program* is a group of related projects, including business-as-usual activities, managed together in a coordinated way, to ensure that the company reaches high-level of benefits, according to the previously set objectives (Morris, Jamieson and Shepherd, 2006). Hence, a programme is perceived as a framework for managing projects without having necessarily a clearly defined deliverable or a finite time horizon. To be highlighted are some benefits to the use of this programme management layer in an organization (Pellegrinelli, 1997):

1. Programmes provide a greater visibility of an individual project to senior management. As projects´ reporting focus on their specific goals, the programs´ reporting make a connection to the strategic performance of the firm by tracking the progress relative to competitors.
2. It allows a better prioritization of projects. Each project is instrumentalized as a chess piece, with a specific role, for the organization´s overall development.
3. Such prioritization leads to a more criterious allocation of resources where they critical or more useful/needed, even with funds already assigned to all of them. This means, more efficient and appropriate use of resources, which tend to be more productive and cost-effective in such a programme context.
4. Programmes approximate projects to businesses. They connect the project´s operations with business and market needs, and newly realized business strategies.
5. The latter leads to better planning and coordination; with inherent reduction of core functions and duplication of the incidence of backlogs.
6. Programmes make an explicit recognition of the interdependencies across projects, which is useful for setting interface management systems and/or their reengineering once inadequacies are identified in the project´s interface system.

Hence, programmes group independent projects under the protection of a big umbrella. Normally, this umbrella is a common theme (for these projects) and from the set of benefits above, companies tend to follow three (3) major reasons for establishing a portfolio program:

1. The existence in the company of distinct projects using a common or shared resource-base (e.g. skills);
2. When needed to develop a completely new systems, infrastructure or services;
3. To enhance existing functionality or service delivery.

Typically, the common denominator of these projects for their grouping is the need for joint coordination. In those cases, the simply arrangement of projects into a bundle is denominated of *portfolio programme*. Certainly, it can be claimed that the overall benefit of *programmes* is that they organize projects and their activities; thus the quest for portfolio grouping. Generally a panel of starting and/or on-going projects, even of dissimilar disciplines, or areas of intervention, require an upper entity (i.e. the Programme Manager) to arbitrate the successful execution of the whole (or part of) the running portfolio. Such coordination happens when the resources are shared across projects; or whenever the operations have interdependencies across them; or even when their joint action triggers advantages beyond operations´ performance or objectives´ accomplishment. These advantages are predictable intangible asset gains (*goodwill*) which can come in multiple formats, such as, reputation, network extension, economies of learning or intelectual capital gains.

Although, you want to acknowledge that different motives generate distinctive configurations of programme activities, as *portfolios, chains* or *networks*. The latter allows for interdependence or sharing of resources, which opposes to portfolios, or chains, which are independent or sequentially administrated (Maylor, 2010).

Figure 7. Projects grouping into programmes
Source: Own elaboration

Type	Role	Representation
Networks:	Shared activities or resources)	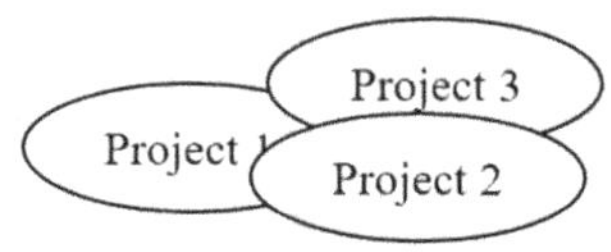
Portfolios:	Amalgamated of independent projects	
Chains:	Sequential/serial activities	

These three typologies of programmes with a design based on their utilitarian role, seemed to fit Pellegrinelli´s (1997) archetypes (i.e. *goal oriented*; *heartbeats;* and, *portfolios*), which he labelled of *program configurations*. To this scholar, programs might assist in attaining a higher organizational purpose of, operational utility; efficiency gains; and outputs accomplishment. The *portfolios are* relatively independent of one another but typically holding a common theme. The *heartbeats* focused on system improvements while the *goal oriented* enabling the management of initiatives outside the existing infrastructure or routine. Thus, if one consider a business environment analysis project (BEAP), it could fit into any of these archetypes.

Whether a company possesses or not this layer of programme management to support the structuring and improvement of project-specific (or business strategic) goals, certainly, during their lifetime, projects (including a BEAP) cannot live without other essential structuring parts. Those components are essentially the *project board*; the *project manager*; the *project management office*, and *project team(s),* usually composed of internally recruited members assigned most of them assigned to teams. In some cases, projects also hold a *technical advisory group* and a *project assurance* function. The latter is discussed in chapter 9 (*Project Quality*).

A senior executive often runs the project board being accompanied by a committee composed of senior representatives of the partners/suppliers and users. The senior user provides inputs from the side of whom will ultimately will be using the goods or services developed by the project. In a BEAP, could be mostly directly, in each division of the company, the Head of Strategy, Intelligence, Business Development or Marketing and their teams of experts (e.g. Market analysts; Business developers; or, Strategic planners). The senior supplier represent the side of the ones ultimately responsible for the delivery of the output/s of the project. Those could be a contractor, outsourcee and representatives of the internal organic unit responsible for the tenure.

The technical advisory group (TAG) are a highly skilled, and typically an external advisory and independent group of experts collaborating with the project board and manager, whenever the projects involve scientific research and the need for the application of Delphi methods requiring such an advisory panel for assessing the viability of goods/services, compounds or technologies. Moreover, such panel does not participate in operations (e.g. engineering; testing or prototyping), as their role is directive one, and restricted in their consultancy activities to the conveying of ad hoc advisory guidelines.

The project manager follows the on-going operations, coordinated all the activities, directly or indirectly until the final completion, ensuring its conclusion is done within the predetermined parameters, such as, within the scope and budget set in the project proposal´s brief and project design. This implies large scope of responsibility, demanding a problem-solving orientation and high degree of creativity, even though the project manager report to the project board, program manager and/or likely to other senior executives in the company.

Considering the latitude of the reporting, project managers often have at their disposal a *Project management office* (PMO) also called *Project support office* (PSO) assisting in large-scale and high-complexity projects, the completion of managerial tasks, including the preparation of reporting to/from the manager. In some cases, the role of the PMO is centralized in the figure of a programme management office.

PMO´s assuming many times the responsibility of being the "central nervous system" of the project managerial activities they are a central facility endowed with professionals with technical skills and knowledge on technical domains but also on project processes, working as back-end consultants and support staff. The PMO´s intervention may be categorized into six (6) different types of functions and responsibilities, or also designated PMO roles:

- Strategic design and communication;
- Resource and capabilities´ administration;
- Development of methodologies of work;
- Monitoring of activities and controlling of performance;
- Generalized multi (managerial) tasks;
- Conversion of project learning into organizational learning

A PMO is regularly composed of a heterogeneous team, carrying a multiplicity of tasks within an array of domains as, accountancy, economic-financial analysis, industrial/project design/architecture; project planning or software/system administration. Often, they are responsible for checking operational activities, running measurements, establishing standards (e.g. on health, security or performance) and other controlling tasks. They also prepare contracts, deal with all sort of paperwork and document the project´s activities. Moreover, they assist with resources allocation from procurement, purchasing, distribution or training. As to reporting purposes the PMO work, entails the progression of work and costs, for instance, related to overheads costs; information about the extent of execution or knowledge gains. Inevitably, their role implies also managing archives, assess risks, conducting audits and post-project reviews.

LEARNING OUTCOMES

- Internal and External Project Environment (IPE/EPE)
- Business Environment Analysis Project (BEAP): Features
- Types of BEAPs
- The 5 phases of the BEAP
- Project grouping, program-arrangement and project-based organizations (PBOs)
- Corporate nexus and central plexus in enterprise/project architecture
- Traditional stage-gate and the Agile-stage gate hybrid model
- The Project life-cycle (and the 4D´s)
- Project environment circumstances (5C´s)

EXERCISE: 4D & PROJECT LIFE CYCLE

In section 7.1 *Project Environment: Context, Structures and Frameworks* the text mentions the existence of the "4D". It is stated that firms summoned to follow this framework for better organizing the whole activities of the BEAP and subsequently due to inherent benefits in terms of performance outputs.

Considering the above, you are invited, firstly, to choose an organization of your choice, regardless of its size, typology and geographical of functional area or industry and so idealize a fictional project for that firm (e.g. the development of new product - or service; the redesign of a new package; or the opening of a new sales channel – as a website or store) and so use that chosen organization and fictional project in an exercise involving the application of the 4D.

Taking into consideration the table "project life cycle: phases" (in section 7.1.) and its four (4) phases (design, definition, execution and process-development), having a look again at the 13 refection questions covering the whole phases of the project life cycle and try to respond to each one of the them, in order to transform the idea you have generated into a wider project concept with a more clear mental model of all its entails from ideation to completion.

CHAPTER HIGHLIGHTS

- The project environment and typologies: "first-timer"; as…but; "paint by numbers"
- Know the essential docs: the project brief; the project chart; the project scope statement; and, the project management plan.
- Business and project architecture: clear thinking; corporate nexus; central plexus; stage-gates and other conceptions
- Project teams: stages of development
- From project design to post-action review: revisiting key frameworks and the 4D or the Performance Pyramid Framework (PPF)
- Stage-gate system: From the original Stage-Gate® to the variations (XPress and Lite) and the hybridization into the ASG model
- Project operation´s systems: revisiting the Technical, Organizational and Environmental (TOE) Framework; or the MODest framework

- Project´s grouping: using "programmes" (of portfolios, chains or networks)

CONCLUSION

The chapter addresses the common type of projects (*first-timer*; and, *as...but*) and most essential documents to account in a project a design, applicable also to a BEAP: the *project brief*; the *project chart; project scope statement*; and, the *project management plan*.

In relation the prior, also discusses the stages of project team-development, the difference between projects and programmes, and the role of PMOs and PSOs in each project and PBOs.

Moreover, it introduces the boundaries of the project environment and the two (inner and outer) tiers of the Project External Environment, together with seminal conceptions as *corporate nexus; central plexus; clear-thinking; stage-gates*; *enterprise-project fit* and *inner project fit*.

A few renowned frameworks are introduced in this chapter as well to assist one from the ideation phase passing through the execution phases until the post-action review of the project. For instance, the *4D*, the *7-S*, the *TOE*; the *Performance Pyramid*; the *FDC* or the *ASG hybrid model* are some of the tools here found.

REFERENCES

Abrantes, B. F. (2020a). Governance of academic laboratories and the capabilisation of higher education students. *International Journal of Management Education*, *14*(2), 135–158.

Abrantes, B. F. (2020b). Tech-innovation and spillovers on corporate-defensiveness: Evidence from the Lisbon startup ecosystem. *International Journal of Business Competition and Growth*, *7*(1), 68–100. doi:10.1504/IJBCG.2020.108439

Abrantes, B. F., & Venkataraman, A. (2022). Environment kinesis and organizational adaptability: Effects of EU's General Data Protection Regulation on the Danish software industry. *International Journal of Learning and Change*, *14*(1), 22–45. doi:10.1504/IJLC.2022.119516

Amit, R., & Zott, C. (2015). Crafting business architecture: The antecedents of business model design. *Strategic Entrepreneurship Journal*, *9*(4), 331–350. doi:10.1002ej.1200

Baker, B. (2018). Project quality management practice & theory. *American Journal of Management*, *18*(3), 10–17.

Barker, J. R. (1993). Tightening the iron cage: Concertive control in self-managing teams. *Administrative Science Quarterly*, *38*(3), 408–437. doi:10.2307/2393374

Beer, M., Voelpel, S. C., Leibold, M., & Tekie, E. D. (2005). Strategic management as organizational learning: Developing fit and alignment through a disciplined process. *Long Range Planning*, *38*(5), 445–465. doi:10.1016/j.lrp.2005.04.008

Boddy, D. (2020). *Management: Using practice and theory to develop skill* (8th ed.). Pearson Education Limited.

Bosch-Rekveldt, M., Jongkind, Y., Mooi, H., Bakker, H., & Verbraeck, A. (2011). Grasping project complexity in large engineering projects: The TOE (Technical, Organizational and Environmental) framework. *International Journal of Project Management*, *29*(6), 728–739. doi:10.1016/j.ijproman.2010.07.008

Chao, G. T., & Moon, H. (2005). The cultural mosaic: A meta-theory to understand the complexity of culture. *The Journal of Applied Psychology*, *90*(6), 1128–1140. doi:10.1037/0021-9010.90.6.1128 PMID:16316269

Chesbrough, H. (2010). Business model innovation: Opportunities and barriers. *Long Range Planning*, *43*(2/3), 354–363. doi:10.1016/j.lrp.2009.07.010

Conforto, E. C., Amaral, D. C., da Silva, S. L., Di Felippo, A., & Kamikawachi, D. S. L. (2016). The agility construct on project management theory. *International Journal of Project Management*, *34*(4), 660–674. doi:10.1016/j.ijproman.2016.01.007

Cooper, R. G. (2008). Perspective: The stage-gate® idea-to-launch process—update, what's new, and NexGen systems. *Journal of Product Innovation Management*, *25*(3), 213–232. doi:10.1111/j.1540-5885.2008.00296.x

Cooper, R. G. (2008). Perspective: The Stage-Gate® Idea-to-Launch Process—update, what's new, and NexGen systems. *Journal of Product Innovation Management*, *25*(3), 213–232. doi:10.1111/j.1540-5885.2008.00296.x

Cooper, R. G. (2010). The stage-gate product innovation system: from idea to launch. In *Encyclopedia of Technology and Innovation Management* (pp. 157–167). John Wiley & Sons Ltd.

Cooper, R. G., & Edgett, S. J. (2008). Maximizing productivity in product innovation. *Research Technology Management*, *51*(2), 47–58. doi:10.1080/08956308.2008.11657495

Cooper, R. G., & Sommer, A. F. (2016). Agile-Stage-Gate: New idea-to-launch method for manufactured new products is faster, more responsive. *Industrial Marketing Management*, *59*, 167–180. doi:10.1016/j.indmarman.2016.10.006

Economist Intelligence Unit. (2005). *Business 2010: embracing the challenge of change*. Economist Intelligence Unit: London, U.K.

Friedman, V. J., & Antal, A. B. (2005). Negotiating reality: A theory of action approach to intercultural competence. *Management Learning*, *36*(1), 69–86. doi:10.1177/1350507605049904

STA Group. (2021). *What is Business Architecture.* STA Group. https://www.stagrp.com/architecture/business-architecture/what-is-business-architecture/

Karlström, D., & Runeson, P. (2006). Integrating agile software development into stage-gate managed product development. *Empirical Software Engineering*, *11*(2), 203–225. doi:10.100710664-006-6402-8

Lynch, R., & Cross, K. (1991). *Measure Up! Yardstick for Continuous Improvement*. Blackwell.

Mackay, B., Arevuo, M., Mackay, D., & Meadows, M. (2020). *Strategy: Theory, practice, implementation*. Oxford University Press.

Maylor, H. (2010). *Project Management* (4th ed.). Pearson Education Limited.

Maylor, H., Vidgen, R., & Carver, S. (2008). Managerial complexity in project-based operations: A grounded model and its implications for practice. *Project Management Journal, 39*(1, suppl), S15–S26. doi:10.1002/pmj.20057

Morris, P. W., Jamieson, A., & Shepherd, M. M. (2006). Research updating the APM body of knowledge. International Journal of Project Management, 24(6), 461-473.

Pellegrinelli, S. (1997). Programme management: Organising project-based change. *International Journal of Project Management, 15*(3), 141–149. doi:10.1016/S0263-7863(96)00063-4

Performance Consultants. (2021). *What is the GROW Model?* PC. https://www.performanceconsultants.com/grow-model

Phillips, M. E., & Sackmann, S. A. (2002). Managing in an era of multiple cultures: Finding synergies instead of conflict. *Graziadio Business Review, 5*(4).1-11. https://gbr.pepperdine.edu/2010/08/managing-in-an-era-of-multiple-cultures/

Sethi, R., & Iqbal, Z. (2008). Stage-gate controls, learning failure, and adverse effect on novel new products. *Journal of Marketing, 72*(1), 118–134. doi:10.1509/jmkg.72.1.118

Snihur, Y., & Zott, C. (2015). Towards an institutional perspective on business model innovation: how entrepreneurs achieve robust business model design. *Working paper*, IESE Business School, Barcelona, Spain.

Sommer, A. F., Hedegaard, C., Dukovska-Popovska, I., & Steger-Jensen, K. (2015). Improved product development performance through Agile/Stage-Gate hybrids – The next-generation Stage-Gate process? *Research Technology Management, 58*(1), 34–45. doi:10.5437/08956308X5801236

Sprague, L. (2007). Evolution of the field of operations management. *Journal of Operations Management, 25*(2), 219–238. doi:10.1016/j.jom.2007.01.001

Svejvig, P., & Andersen, P. (2015). Rethinking project management: A structured literature review with a critical look at the brave new world. *International Journal of Project Management, 33*(2), 278–290. doi:10.1016/j.ijproman.2014.06.004

Trice, H. M., & Beyer, J. M. (1984). Studying organizational cultures through rites and ceremonials. *Academy of Management Review, 9*(4), 653–669. doi:10.2307/258488

Tuckman, B. W., & Jensen, M. A. C. (1977). Stages of small-group development revisited. *Group & Organization Studies, 2*(4), 419–427. doi:10.1177/105960117700200404

Waterman, R. H. Jr, Peters, T. J., & Phillips, J. R. (1980). Structure is not organization. *Business Horizons, 23*(3), 14–26. doi:10.1016/0007-6813(80)90027-0

Whittle, R., & Myrick, C. B. (2016). *Enterprise business architecture: The formal link between strategy and results*. CRC Press. doi:10.1201/9781420000207

Zott, C., & Amit, R. (2008). The fit between product market strategy and business model: Implications for firm performance. *Strategic Management Journal, 29*(1), 1–26. doi:10.1002mj.642

ENDNOTES

1 *The traditional activities to be carried out during the project life cycle (PrLC), specifically on phase D2, account five (5) types of operations: capacity; controls; materials; standards; and, scheduling.*

2 The *assumption* represents the accepted truth/s without a validated proof (or supposition) (Saunders, Lewis and Thornhill, 2019)

3 Scholars, as Svejvig and Andersen (2015) and Edwards et al. (2019), pinpoint as a major cause of inefficiencies in traditional project management methods the existence of *stage-gates.* They assert stage-gate are "time-consuming"; "time-wasting" and their application is embedded in routinized (and somehow myopic) "burocratic procedures". Yet, they recognized the importance of stage-gates in the project architecture to the reduction of uncertainty, but then, they suggest a more sophisticated application of gate systems.

4 One of epicentrum of the central plexus (in "Performance Pyramid Framework" - level 3) displayed above is the principle of "flexibility" of the enterprise/project architecture on level 3 (business operating systems). Concordantly, Edwards et al. (2019) criticized more recently the application of "stage-gates" for its rigidity and fixed mindset (and launched the discussion in favor of an "Agile-Stage-Gate Hybrid Model".

5 In chapter nine - "Project Quality Management (PQM)", the central plexus is again discussed in the context of Total Quality Management (TQM), to present the location ("Gemba") where the focus of operation´s improvement takes place, and the underlying processes (i.e. the "Go to Gemba" and "Gemba walk") associated with the Kaizen method.

6 In the case of Business Environment Analyzability Projects (BEAP) there´s likewise simpler development requirements.

7 Check in chapter ten ("Strategic Project Auditing") the discussion surrounding the Course of Action (CoA) around the diagnosis of project performance and strategic change options (SCOs).

Chapter 8
Business Environment Analysis Project´s (BEAP) Capabilities

ABSTRACT

Immersing into the resource-based view (RBV) and dynamic capabilities theory (DCT), the chapter emphasizes the importance of resource´s endowment function to any project, such as: (i) criterious asset´s deployment; and (ii) capability´s selection. Those are seminal to the approval of the project´s proposal among other portfolio candidates. One explores different views within the RBV and Human Capital Theory around larger conceptions (e.g., abilities; assets; capabilities; core-competences; resources; or skills) and their connection to market value in the form of individual/group´s worth and organizational capabilities and their inherent firm-specific advantages (FSA) transposed to the context of functional or ad hoc project teams. Seminal dynamic capabilities (DC) are brought to the light in the context of a business environment analysis project (BEAP), as the coordination; knowledge-utilization; or learning capability.

INTRODUCTION

For a project proposal to become a reality, as a micro-enterprise likely to be executed within the organizational sphere, the intrapreneur/s is/are required to begin a set of initiatives for building up a project design. This entails to come up with a *Project Brief* (as referred in the previous chapter), as an initial document for presenting internally a new idea/concept to the organization´s managers (Abrantes, 2018).

In this sense, building up such a reporting tool as a candidate of the project´s proposal to compete against others in an entrepreneurial pipeline and subsequently become a "member" of the company's portfolio, requires without any doubt a set of (entrepreneurial, managerial and leadership) capabilities to be able to envision from the general idea or concept a whole new project ´scope of activities, responsibilities, resources and time constraints(and opportunities), underlying to the set of goals, systems and structure, expected to be united around the future project.

DOI: 10.4018/978-1-6684-5543-2.ch008

Certainly, to be able to succeed in project execution the proposal ought to be, not solely aligned with the corporate direction (i.e. vision and mission) in terms of portfolio and growth options; and, capital allocation strategies, but also, portraying the whole project´s scope with a solid and coherent rationale as to its utility and likelihood of accomplishment. Three other documents are complementary to the project brief: the *project charter*; the *project scope statement*; and the *project management plan*, with the first (project charter) working as an elevator pitch of the project´s objectives, scope and responsibilities, as it describes in a short document entirely how the activities will be are carried out and by whom from the project team.

RESOURCES AND ASSETS: OWNERSHIP, ENDOWMENT AND DEPLOYMENT

Indeed, the design and planning phases of a project (i.e. BEAP) are invariably anchored upon the organizational capabilities apportioned to the project´s universe. The same happens also with the execution phase. To understand what a project´s scope entails, or what is required to; where the means are; and, how to divert them into the project, can be summarized in many times into large needs of multiple types of knowledge and different skills. Thus, one is required to hold a varied set of competences to ultimately deliver a strong project´s candidature.

According to some scholars as, Miner (2000) or Timmons and Spinelli (2004) there are four (4) major types of entrepreneurial skills required for being a business venture creator, as follows: to be an *Expert Idea-Generator*; a *Personal Achiever*; a *Real Manager*; and, an *Empathetic Supersalesperson* (Abrantes, 2018; Vega and Kidwell, 2007). This framework includes the context of the spin-offs of a business venture conceived inside of the organization (also known as *intraprise)* and moreover, the projects designed without triggering any intraprise but aiming to diversify existing portfolios (i.e. business units; programmes; and projects) by modifying product categories, processes and models, and adding a layer of innovativeness to the organization.

An idea-generator surely recognizes at an initial stage (i.e. *project design*) the need for a best use of his/her communication skills, such as, the ability to exert *influence* and move others to action, and so, build a coalition of expertise and interests. In other words, inspire its peers and/or business partners and attract them to actively (and loudly) advocate it and moreover participate therein by donating its time and skills. This involves definitely being able to identify Sales Champions and to nominate representatives and spokesmen which on the project´s behalf may spread its influence and diminish the friction of conflictual views/stances or opposition.

Although, Leadership Capabilities (namely, communication, motivation and influence) are also associated with Managerial Capabilities. Undoubtedly, ensuring of the attractiveness of the project is a focal point; however, the coordination of a set of motivations and skills, and other resources´ alignment to configure the activities requires from the project proposal´s owner to be likewise a Real-Manager able to negotiate with multiple parts, organize streams of work and its (best) practice, set the project´s structure, develop the "architectures" or systems and processes, and the mechanisms of controls of the operational progression and measurement of standards or target goals.

In this chapter, due to the seminal importance of the organizational resources and capabilities, as a cultural, human, informational and operational capital managerial basis for developing a Business Environment Analysis Project (BEAP), one enters here into the realm of the Resource-Based Theory (RBT).

Yet, one should be emphasized that regardless of the typology of resources and capabilities (R&Cs), the factors "ownership" and "utilization" of R&Cs are determinant for the development of a high degree of operational and managerial proficiencies (hence, routinization of processes). Thus, the reader is here presented with a chapter provided a brief introduction to RBT, focused on Cognitive and Managerial Capabilities in the first two (2) sections, and lastly covering the Dynamic Capabilities View (DCV). This latter set of first-order organizational capabilities, i.e. Dynamic Capabilities (DC) receives here ample attention, since is nowadays universally accepted by scholars in Global Strategic Management and other scientific domains as the most relevant type or Organizational Capabilities (OC) capable of influencing other OCs and DCs and so having direct implications on the competitive scope of the firm, and consequently on its ability to perform.

Setting the conceptual boundaries of *resources* and *capabilities*, and other related concepts as *assets*, *skills* or *abilities* is surely a decisive starting point to approach this section´s topic as clearly as possible. These concepts (resources, capabilities, assets, skills and abilities) are often interchangeably used and frequently give rise to misinterpretations. To avoid this picture, will begin by discerning them, hopefully making these conceptions discernable as I would like to dot the i´s and cross the t´s on these conceptualizations before moving forward.

First one should know, that there are many definitions for "resources". Here is highlighted one of the best known and least controversial ones that I also adhere to. *Resources* are stocks of available factors owned or controlled by a firm (Amit and Schoemaker, 1993). Everything that enters the spectrum of the company´s belongings can be taken as a resource. For example, a firm´s facilities; or capital (or debt); inventory; invoices; knowledge; machinery; patents; products; or software licenses. With a different outline, these resources above assume though multiple typologies.

How can we typify the Organizational Resources?

Organizational resources are categorizable into multiple sub-sets (as, physical, financial, human, legal, technological and informational resources), in which, the examples above may be arranged within those sub-categories. Making here a simple analogy, resources are categorizable like drawers of a wardrobe. Each drawer corresponds to a sub-type but then being an element composing the whole set of owned resources. Nevertheless, due to its morphology, resources may also be grouped classified as tangible or intangible ones. Hooley, Broderick and Möller (1998) discerned them with ease. *Tangible* resources can be heard, smelled, tasted and touched. The *intangible* resources live in the hearts and minds of people. In this sense, resources may be simultaneously scrutinized as to the tangibility and typology. For example, a tangible and, at the same time, a physical resource is a unit of stock in inventory stored at the warehouse of a given firm. An intangible, might be the individual knowledge about the operability of a machine or equipment or about a specific work instruction and its changes in time and market exceptions.

A conceptual distinction of resources and assets was offered by George S. Day separating them quite clearly. This scholar described *assets* as the effective endowed resources, which a manager allocates to a certain business unit or project. This definition, perceives the latter - assets - as the formal allocation of a resource to a unit or center of cost (i.e. the "endowment" process), which comes subsequently to the resource´s acquisition (ownership) and availability inside the organization. Thus, an asset can only exist with a prior acquisition (or initial development, instead) of a resource, being moreover dependent on its free-to-use status. Also it requires a decision of approval for its utilization by a manager to a given unit/

center (e.g. a BEAP). On the other hand, resources exists in a company by acquisition or development, regardless of its allocation or utilization.

PROJECT ARCHITECTURE

I suppose that you would agree, that a resource being kept without any use, as an *inactive* resource, is a waste of stock of availability factors in the firm. Their storage and accumulation does not generate any value *per se*. This could be the case, for instance, of an in-house developed resource, with an undetermined shape or with a vague scope that was not given any utility in the context of the company's business (i.e. an *amorphous resource*). Hence, the mere existence of inactive resources in the organization constitutes, as a matter of fact, a Competitive Disadvantage against peers, because its existence is superfluous, hence an inefficient use of resources, which in some cases, are complemented by (administration/maintenance) costs.

Consequently, as for a few decades scholars focused on the growth of the firm, and particularly on the resource-based of view (RBV), have come to a common understanding that the firm´s growth is dependent, not upon the "resource´s ownership" but, on the "resource´s applicability" in the context of daily business operations. Otherwise, "richer" firms in total number of accumulated resources, would naturally be also the ones with the highest profitability ratios. The table below shows however that performance outputs (e.g. revenue) is not that straightforwardly determined by resource ownership. The differences observed in the table below, in some of the world biggest companies, shows in the year 2019 the Fortune 500 ranking companies´ growth ratio (i.e. market capitalization), accounting the annual variations as to the earnings per share (EPS) against the annual revenue of the corporation.

As one can quickly infer from the table above is, that the cross-observation of results reveal discrepancies between EPS´ growth ranks and the annual revenue rank. But perhaps the most staggering shift in ranks was *Apple Inc.* (AAPL), which was knocked out of from the top spots in profits after a five-year reign (Fortune, 2020). Since 2017, the company oscillated between negative and positive growth, with significant variations in market cap, for instance, a change of 43,37% (2017) from the previous the year, or -13,34% (2018) and 72,59% (2019).

In general, such results corroborate the assertion above on (resource ownership vs asset´s deployment). Resource property is not a synonym for granted revenues and future wealth. Having said that, the link of resources to value for the resource-based theorists resides on two major points. Firstly in the distribution of assets (*resources´ endowment*) through an allocation of scarce resources to specific areas where they match the operative needs and corporate priorities (*asset´s deployment*). One may discern from the above, that asset´s deployment is far from being a task to be taken randomly neither on a lighthearted way.

Secondly, the link resources-value requires a dyadic use of these assets for an efficient administration and optimize the advantages deriving from their market potential. Such dyadic use is, at the tier of primary or transactional activities, and also at the tier of secondary activities corresponding to the technical support, advisory, managerial controls, and forecasting. The organizations of assets and its recombination and its full utilization combined with others yields proficiency gains at operational-level, such as, related to the routinization of tasks and further economies of learning, scale or scope creating direct and circumstantial value to markets which derive higher value appropriation as well, thus, higher economic rents or higher (and above-average) returns.

Table 1. Profits of the Fortune 500 companies in 2019

Rank	Company	Revenues Rank	(2019 - % growth in EPS
1	Cisco systems	63	12,950.0
2	Alleghany	351	2,166.8
3	Berkshire Hathaway	6	1,937.1
4	NRG Energy	324	1,832.2
5	Netapp	478	1,510.7
6	Altice USA	327	600.0
7	Cincinnati Financial	400	591.4
8	Becton Dickinson	187	556.7
9	Newmont	328	495.3
10	Davita	230	472.8
11	Cardinal Health	16	459.3
12	Jacobs Engineering Group	206	419.7
13	MGM Resorts International	249	379.0
14	Xerox Holdings	347	320.3
15	Jabil	121	269.4
16	Discovery	287	234.9
17	Oracle	82	230.0
18	Jetblue Airways	394	218.3
19	Eli lilly	145	184.0
20	Old Republic International	427	183.1
	Median (me)	-	**5.1**

Source: Fortune (2020)

1. Resources (ownership) → 2. Assets (endowment) → 3. Assets (deployment) → 4. Capabilities (abilities developed by asset´s utilization in firm´s activities) → 5. Competitive Advantages

The question that imposes at this stage is:

How do companies may deploy their assets to create Competitive Advantages?

Assets´ deployment is a determinant of the overall organizational success. The same happens at project-level. The impact of resource´s endowment and asset´s deployment on an individual project has an identical logic as to the whole portfolio (allocation).

Quantity does not dictate the output (success) in terms of accomplishment of goals or overcoming of the project environmental barriers. A satisficing approval of x units of a resource, with an efficient allocation and wise utilization is all together more decisive for the outcome of a project. Yet, without capabilities projects would be condemned to failure. So, capabilities are a prerequisite for success. All companies require some degree of cognition and sharp understanding of their surrounding reality by developing technical and managerial capabilities.

Likewise, projects designers need to stock up the right resources and hold a set of according prior capabilities (in the brain and body) to pursue such endeavor. Here, the term organizational *capabilities* refers to the set of *abilities* that allows the firm (and its project candidates) to plan, organize, lead, co-ordinate and manage the execution of a specific set of activities (Teece, et al. 1992).

In this sense, the completion of an activity is intrinsically dependent upon the bundle of tangible and intangible resources possessed (e.g. knowledge), and the skills or abilities to: (i) deploy assets together; (ii) to make them work together (iii) and, to create an efficient business process; which intertwined with task-specific execution abilities, facilitate the achievement of a desired end.

Prahalad and Hammel (1990) labeled the capabilities with higher contribution to added-value, as *core-competences*. These scholars considered that those are the ones to be possessed as they lead to unique firm-specific advantages (FSA), as they are likely to: (i) contribute positively and disproportionally to value; (ii) or, create efficiencies from which value is derived from; (iii) and, create opportunities for repositioning in current markets or entering new ones. Barton (1992) later on designated them as *core capabilities* and argued that they are pillared on four (4) dimensions: technical systems; managerial systems; skills and knowledge base; and, the values and norms. This scholar argues that they reflect the accumulated behaviours and beliefs which memory traces as leading to corporate success, hence being institutionalized and the danger for the corporation is to have them becoming "core-rigidities" as the organization may take for granted its value based on the past inprint in the corporate history. From the notion of core-competences, some authors have extended the horizon of capabilities to a upper level of them, which labeled as *dynamic capabilities (DC)*(Teece, Pisano and Shuen, 1997; Eisenhardt and Martin, 2000). To these authors, DCs are more important than the others (ordinary capabilities) stressing the importance of developing DCs within the organizations, as these first-order sets of capabilities are linked not solely to the formation of FSAs but also to the formation of long-term or sustainable competitive advantages (SCA), as they have the ability to reconfigure themselves, influence other OCs, in their reconfiguration or total renewal, and moreover, seizing new market opportunities, as described in the *Teecian* Dynamic Capabilities Framework (DCF) (Teece, 2010). Some examples of those dynamic capabilities are defined and described in the next section (*8.3. Dynamic Capabilities (DC) and the Project´s functions*) such as, the *knowledge-utilization capability*; *innovation capability*; *learning capability*; or the *marketing capability*).

In a nutshell, organizational capabilities derive from skills and competences of the individuals in an organization (Hooley, Broderick and Möller, 1998). They are brought-in or developed at individual level, but may be either locked-in such a lower tier (individual) or shared with others or even spread across the organization and systematized across units. In the latter case, this occurs whether the organization retains or not the object of learning for future memory. Thus, capabilities may exist, or co-exist as *individual*, *group* or *corporate capabilities*, respectively identifying individual, group/collective or organizational learning.

The transformation of resource into value is though considered by Human Capital (HC) theorists as a "black box" as these blame RBV scholars to overly focus on the competitiveness of the firm in general, i.e. the Firm-Specific Advantages (FSA), and so neglecting to explore the functional worth and the monetary worth of the individual units of human capital. This means to forget in each employee of the organization, as separate human resource, the individual attributions in terms of *Knowledge*, *Skills* and *Abilities* (KSA) that actually lead to the overall competitive gains (Abrantes, Preto and António, 2022; Kraaijenbrink et al., 2010). HC theorists argue then on the need of the firm´s managers (or programme and project managers) to focus their attention on the required *knowledge* units, definable as the information (factual or procedural) to conduct a task or job; plus a focus on the required *skills* (the level of proficiency for the execution of a task) and, on the *abilities* needed[1], being the personal traits and individual attributes, both circumstantial and psychological that determine the performance on job.

DYNAMIC CAPABILITIES AND THE PROJECT´S FUNCTIONS

Moving away from the philosophical debate between both domains (HC and RBV) and focusing more specifically on capabilities, the notion of individual capabilities refer to the set abilities owned by a person allowing the fulfillment of his/her roles, whether they are related to observation, reflection, analysis and/or action upon a given situation (e.g. to fulfill a customer need) (Hooley, Broderick and Broderick and Möller, 1998).

Individual capabilities are complemented by collective or group capabilities. These are the abilities emerged from the formal or informal interactions of individuals either in functional groups (at department-level) or other ad hoc groups (e.g. projects; teams/work cells; and other micro centers as problem-focus or research groups). The ad hoc group capabilities are formed in a project typically by the combination of gathered technical expertise and functional competences of the project team[2].

Ad hoc groups, result in a coalition of expertise (with supporting staff) into an alliance of motivations and interests in which their combinative set of capabilities is used to solve either strategic; functional; and, operational tasks. In the case of a Business Environment Analysis Project (BEAP), this type (of project) would fit into a functional task-solving with an outside-in" logic, in which the corporate capabilities aim to sense the market´s dynamics of change (e.g. emergent events; or new trends) and their underlying risks and opportunities (i.e. Market Sensing), regardless of whether the project is a pure on a hybrid BEAP (as address in Part 1, in chapters 3 and 4). In addition, it requires a set of operational capabilities, ranging from planning to processes´ design (i.e. corporate capabilities) and individual or group tasks´ completion.

Nonetheless, market sensing is a corporate-level capability of great responsibility to be build and maintained which requires the project team to have gained a ground preparatory learning about two (2) other functional domains: the spanning and inside-out view of the project and organization, which are, resource-utilization and innovation capabilities. As an example of resource utilization, as a dynamic capability, is presented in Wang et al.´s (2014) definition of knowledge utilization. It describes the past effort of the firm to learn and the subsequent use knowledge for improving future businesses. According to Wang and Ahmed (2007) an innovation capability refers to the set of abilities of a firm regarding the development of new products and/or markets. Capon et al. (1992) divide them into organizational and market innovativeness and such capability entail five major dimensions: (i) developing new products or services; (ii) identifying new methods of production; (iii) identifying new markets; (iv) discovering new sources of supply; and, (v) developing new organizational forms.

In this context, the functional-level task-solving in a project, such as a BEAP, individual-level capabilities are key to develop a focus on internal and external environment issues; an internal one (i.e. project and firm); and external (i.e. the markets) and simultaneously coordinate different skills. This encompasses at group or collective level, a capability-building upon operations and marketing and intertwining both with the capturing of innovative capabilities, oriented towards new product development (NPD). Here, the notion of marketing capability is the result of an integrative process that combines the project team´s resources and skills to fulfill customer needs, capturing the essence of the firm as to the formulation of marketing mix strategies and their portfolio options (Weerawardena et al., 2007).

As final note, I would emphasize the importance in the organization to be capability-oriented and develop particularly first-order sets of organizational capabilities, the so-called dynamic capabilities (DC). Distancing ourselves from the philosophical disputes as to the extent of contribution of different streams of thought, as the RBV, the HC and other scholars in tangent scientific fields as the Positioning School or the Industrial Economics, what is to be underlined is the broad consensus over the importance to develop incremental or regenerative capabilities to the firm´s success. This a take-away I would like the reader to consider for the project micro-sphere, i.e. capabilities are needed ex ante, on-going and ex post.

The generation of new ideas and business concepts require prior knowledge and competences, so as the project design, or the project´s structuring, or the project´s architecture (and processes delineation), or the execution of the operational tasks, or the monitoring of the progression, or the eventually need for patching (of emergent problems with new solution) or the controlling of the goal´s accomplishment and post-review of its life and internal reporting. Capabilities are needed before, during and after the project conclusion. It is expected that the project team (including the project manager), the programme manager and the whole strategic business unit or division of an organization have not solely benefited with the project, but also have learnt something for the future from it. Whether, it is considering a replication, such as in an "as… but" logic as the operations require the use of production or service systems.

LEARNING OUTCOMES

- BEAP capabilities: Molding a "project brief", "project charter", "project scope statement" and the "project management plan"
- Types of resources and capabilities used BEAPs
- Project Design: Entrepreneurial and Leadership skills
- Link between project capabilities, performance and value-appropriation
- Project functions: Members, groups and individual and collective capabilities

EXERCISE: PROJECT RESOURCES AND CAPABILITIES

Build a roadmap of resources and capabilities (R&C) for the project idealized in the previous "exercise" in chapter 7.

Considering the use of the 4D model in the previous exercise (chapter 7), now focus uniquely on the D1 phase (design) and on the types of R&Cs involved in this phase. Reflect upon possible bundles of R&C required to the particular project you´ve idealized.

Consider, in particular, the R&C needed to elaborate on the D1 the following types of documents to be presented to senior managers: a *project brief*; a *project charter*; and a *project management plan*. In sum, this exercise puts your ability to the test, regarding the delivery of the initial project paperwork.

Keep in mind that your objective is to answer these questions: *What are the R&Cs one needs for project´s design?; What R&Cs do I need to build such reporting tools)?*

In order to simply the recording of the information, you are suggested to map these R&Cs in a systematic way, as here exemplified: (i) separate items (R´s from C´s); (ii) attribute a numeric sequential number (e.g. "R01" for resource number 1); and (iii) associate the inventory of R&Cs per task (i.e. as R&C associated to the project brief; R&C´s needed to the project charter; and R&Cs to the project management plan). Finally, you are also recommended to keep a record of such an inventory in a detextualized format (e.g. a table) as exemplified below:

Table 2. Exemplified table for building an inventory of project R&Cs

R&Cs		Project areas of applicability (of R&Cs)			
		Brief design	**Charter design**	**Management planning**	**Further notes**
Code	Description				
Resources					
R01 R02 R03					
Capabilities					
C01					
C02					
C03					
Etc.					

Source: Own elaboration

CHAPTER HIGHLIGHTS

- The Resource-Based View (RBV): Link between resource and capabilities (R&Cs) and Firm-specific Advantages (FSAs)
- Outside-in versus inside-out logic: Acquire or develop R&Cs?
- The concepts of *resource, skill, ability, asset, capability, core-competence* and *dynamic capability*
- From R´s to C´s: The importance *of knowledge-possession, knowledge accumulation* and *knowledge-utilization*
- From *asset-endowment* to *asset-deployment*
- *Core-competences, core-incompetences* and *core-rigidities*
- Types of dynamic capabilities (DC) and DC essentials to the project realm
- R&Cs in projects among functional groups and ad-hoc groups

CONCLUSION

This chapter immerses itself into the resource-based view (RBV) to comprehend the formation of resources and capabilities (R&C). Leaving behind the project design and management aspects (and their links to project architecture and governance) one addressed in chapter seven, herein, the focus is the transferability, acquisition, deployment, and development of existing or new bundles of resources and capabilities in the project realm.

The chapter introduces seminal concepts to build-up a clear understanding about different constructs (e.g. *resource; skill; ability, asset; capability; core-competence;* and *dynamic capability*), especially because some of these concepts are often interchangeably used with a similar meaning lifting the business language and causing entropy in across different communication barriers across organization stakeholders.

Furthermore, the categories of resources are also presented along with the confronting logics of acquisition versus development of resources and capabilities (R&Cs). Key-ideas, such as, *knowledge-possession, knowledge accumulation, knowledge-utilization, asset-endowment,* or *asset-deployment* are also explored in the chapter, together with various types of dynamic capabilities applicable to the project realm and R&C per different types of sub-teams (*functional groups* and *ad-hoc groups*).

REFERENCES

Abrantes, B. F. (2018). Intrapreneurial Dynamics: A Case Research at the Insurance Industry in Portugal. *International Journal of Entrepreneurial Knowledge*, *6*(1), 61–75. doi:10.37335/ijek.v6i1.69

Abrantes, B. F., Preto, M. T., & Antonio, N. (2022). Unraveling collaborative learning stimuli and effective dynamic capability integration on MNCs: The global capabilities administration model (GCAM). *Review of International Business and Strategy.*, *33*(2), 272–300. doi:10.1108/RIBS-06-2021-0085

Amit, R., & Schoemaker, P. (1993). Strategic assets and organizational rent. *Strategic Management Journal*, *14*(1), 33–46. doi:10.1002mj.4250140105

Capon, N., Farley, J. U., Hulbert, J., & Lehmann, D. R. (1992). Profiles of product innovators among large US manufacturers. *Management Science*, *38*(2), 157–168. doi:10.1287/mnsc.38.2.157

Eisenhardt, K. M., & Martin, J. A. (2000). Dynamic capabilities: What are they? *Strategic Management Journal*, *21*(10-11), 1105–1121. doi:10.1002/1097-0266(200010/11)21:10/11<1105::AID-SMJ133>3.0.CO;2-E

Fortune. (2020). How the profits of Fortune 500 companies stack up in one chart. *Fourtune 500.* https://fortune.com/longform/fortune-500-companies-profits-compare-2020-chart-data/

Leonard-Barton, D. (1992). Core capabilities and core rigidities: A paradox in managing new product development. *Strategic Management Journal*, *13*(S1), 111–125. doi:10.1002mj.4250131009

Miner, J. B. (2000). Testing a psychological typology of entrepreneurship using business founders. *The Journal of Applied Behavioral Science*, *36*(1), 43–69. doi:10.1177/0021886300361003

Prahalad, C. K., & Hammel, G. (1990). The core competence of the corporation. *Harvard Business Review*, *68*, 79–91.

Teece, D. J. (2018). Business models and dynamic capabilities. *Long Range Planning*, *51*(1), 40–49. doi:10.1016/j.lrp.2017.06.007

Teece, D. J., Pisano, G. P., & Shuen, A. (1992). *Dynamic capabilities and strategic management.* Center for Research in Management, University of California.

Timmons, J. A., & Spinelli, S. (2004). *New venture creation: Entrepreneurship for the 21st century* (6th ed.). McGraw Hill Irwin.

Vega, G., & Kidwell, R. E. (2007). Toward a typology of new venture creators: Similarities and contrasts between business and social entrepreneurs. *New England Journal of Entrepreneurship, 10*(2), 1–14. doi:10.1108/NEJE-10-02-2007-B002

Wang, C. L., & Ahmed, P. K. (2007). Dynamic capabilities: A review and research agenda. *International Journal of Management Reviews, 9*(1), 31–51. doi:10.1111/j.1468-2370.2007.00201.x

Wang, Z., Chen, L., Zhao, X., & Zhou, W. (2014). Modularity in building mass customization capability: The mediating effects of customization knowledge utilization and business process improvement. *Technovation, 34*(11), 678–687. doi:10.1016/j.technovation.2014.09.002

Weerawardena, J., Mort, G. S., Liesch, P. W., & Knight, G. (2007). Conceptualizing accelerated internationalization in the born global firm: A dynamic capabilities perspective. *Journal of World Business, 42*(3), 294–306. doi:10.1016/j.jwb.2007.04.004

ENDNOTES

1 It is recommended the articulation of the discussion on KSAs with *W.E. Deming´s* concept of "thorough knowledge" introduced in chapter 9 with regard to quality´s capabilities.

2 The topic (functional/ad hoc) groups and capabilities is recommended to be articulated with the discussion held in chapter 9 regarding the "Project Management Book of Knowledge" (PMBOK) which opens the discuss for essential project-related qual capabilities, around three (3) essential Qual processes (qual-planning; qual-assurance; and, qual-control).

Chapter 9
Project Quality Management (PQM)

ABSTRACT

The chapter addresses the importance of project quality (PQ) in the mediation of the project governance´s endeavors and its outcomes (of project performance). It provides a multilateral vision of what quality is from different stakeholder´s point of view. It intertwines the seminal contribution of Deming´s theories (of profound knowledge and optimization) which influenced decisively the evolution of the project management body of knowledge (PMBOK) with the total quality management (TQM). The chapter addresses moreover the types of quality processes and enters the domain of quality assurance as a system of relevance to ensure the fulfillment of quality standards. Within the PMBOK revisits a few theorizations (as the MODest framework) and enters the realm of the total quality management (TQM).

INTRODUCTION

A fundamental aspect of any project´s success (including the BEAP) is quality. Often perceived as something fuzzy, subjective and with blurred thresholds, quality is dubbed as being difficult-to-measure (or in some cases, advocated as impossible). Recalling though the famous book of Douglas Hubbard ("*How to measure anything*"- *finding the value of intangibles in business*"), the lesson to be withdrawn is, everything is measurable. The limits reside on cognitive limitations (as "bounded rationality" and "satisficing" human nature) and/or on the accessibility to information.

Indeed, setting the parameters for running a multivariate wide range of performance checks; yes, that is what quality is all about (and more). A likely more complex configuration not comparable to the easy-to-measure (old school) quants risk analysis metrics; hence quality management is of a remarkable worthiness.

The notion of *quality* refers to an intangible resource, also of the project realm (as addressed in section *8.2. Organizational capabilities and project value* - on the previous chapter) and this mistakenly conceived idea that quality (standards) are highly subjective (such as its supporting performance metrics – far too complex to establish) and consequently, impossible to measure is a total fallacy. As a higher-

DOI: 10.4018/978-1-6684-5543-2.ch009

order or key-intangible (resource) of the firm, quality is a fundamental trait of what one does/is, being grounded on three (3) fundamental attributes:

(i) Commitment to quality is individual, and all organizational stakeholders are summoned to (the best of his/her knowledge and practice) consider it in the fulfillment of all duties.
(ii) Quality is a goal and a process all-in-one phenomenon: It ought to be embedded as something "organizational" as a collective objective, on constant observation and refinement through a bottom-up heuristic learning; however, dependent on the degree of ownership (resources) and expertise (capabilities) allocated to all activities of the micro transformational system.
(iii) Quality is an expression of corporative citizenship: It indicates a directional horizon of the internal ethical code, which is mirrored in corporate policies, principles, system of rules and operational procedures setting the line for a transversal and streamlined "expected standard behaviour."

Regardless of the layer of responsibility (individual, departmental or corporative) one assumes, this is a underlying mission, embedded in the overall of the activities across the transformational system of a firm, from inputs to outputs, perceived ultimately in the form of the products or services associated with the customer´s view as to what is delivered (Luthra et al., 2021).

PROJECT´S QUALITY AND QUALITY PERFORMANCE

Quality, in general terms, belongs to the sphere of the individual relative judgement, whether an *emotional* or a *rational* scrutiny. The emotional judgement mirrors a response to the felt or experienced while the rational a reflection about the maximization of the benefits.

However, being multidisciplinary, the concept of quality holds multiple layers of understanding and the perception of what it is, also changes with accordingly with the (internal and external stakeholders). So, what´s quality in *latu sensum?* A good starting point for such a broad question is definitely to screen the acronym ("Quality") gathering a view from multiple definitions:

Q = Quest for excellence
U = Understanding customers' needs
A = Action to achieve customer appreciation
L = Leadership
I = Involving all people
T = Team spirit for common goal
Y = Yardstick to measure progress

For end-users or clients, indulging in the act of judging the quality or its absence, perceiving it in high or low degree, they apply experiential and/or manifest knowledge to establish trade-offs (e.g. experience/benefit or cost/benefit). Project managers are, identically, urged to follow the end-user and client´s footsteps; however, the view of this latter and process is diametrically different.

On the customer´s side (including internal the customer), such phronetic cognitive process of evaluation corresponds to, a likely conscious analysis of the "goodness" of a given product or service. This includes invariably the judgment of the project taken as an internal service delivered to the enhancement of the company´s portfolio. It is an analytical process that implies inherently a comparison of the outputs of the observed entity, commonly labeled as its *performance (P)* versus the individual´s own *expectations (E)*. The expectations might derive from a multiple set of options, as a provider´s promise; a service level agreement (SLA) contractually set between parts; or even a comparison of present versus past performance (Luthra et al., 2021).

Here, the customer evaluation of virtuosity expressed in *quality (Q)* is dictated by an evaluation on a qualitative-like degree of brilliance of the output, varying across excellent, good, bad or worst. The degree of *excellence* (e) of an output *(x)* represents the maximum achievable point, or the judgement of a best (limit) performance possible. Here, performance is bigger than *expectations (E) (P >E)*. This means that the *performance (P)* is taken as positive and at an extreme value ($x > 1$), where $(x \ldots \infty]$ given the expression:

$$Quality(x) = \frac{Performance(P)}{Expectations(E)}$$

Thus, the excellence function *(P > E)* is represented by,

$$x(e) = \frac{\mathrm{P}}{1-E} \Leftrightarrow \mathrm{x} \geq 1$$

The labeling of *good (g)* quality is given by,

$$x(g) = \frac{\mathrm{P}}{E} \Leftrightarrow \mathrm{x} = 1$$

And, the negative perception assumes a ratio of quality performance, in which $P < E$, is attributed to a perception of a *low (l)* quality stance, as follows:

$$x(l) = \frac{1-\mathrm{P}}{E} \Leftrightarrow \mathrm{x} < 1$$

The *worst (w)* quality performance ratio is given by a P = = 0 (or)

$$x(w) = \frac{\mathrm{P}}{E} \Leftrightarrow \mathrm{x} = 0$$

Here, considering that the apostrophes *(P´ and E´)* correspond to the past experience the quality performance can be concurrently measured by,

$$Q(x)=\frac{(P-P')}{(E-E')}$$

Quality was until here summarily presented through the lens of the customer´s perspective and a rather quants view focused on the statistical outcomes. Yet, the main focus of the chapter is the provider, i.e. the view of the company under the eyes of the project manager.

On the provider´s side (or the project manager), quality is not a mere judgment of a degree of excellence whether is quantifiable rationally or a qualitatively taken as an emotionally satisfying feeling. Quality, means, for project managers, much more than simple judgments.

It is a responsibility attached to Project Management (PM) function, i.e. Project Quality Management (PQM) due to its mediating role in the accomplishment of the project´s objectives, in which, two variables are intrinsically connected: *Project Governance* (PG) and *Project Performance (PP)*. Such responsibility entails the *ex-ante* possession and further development of, what *W.E. Deming* calls, *thorough knowledge* (i.e. a sum of both experiential and explicit knowledge).

Project managers and its structure are required to hold an a priori set of *thorough knowledge* which are expected to put in practice in PG, namely ensuring stability through planning and subsequently in quality and risk-controlling. Furthermore, the use of such knowledge-type is expected to be applied in after-action reviews for renewing itself (thorough knowledge) on an *ex post* phase in which projects are already concluded.

So, *why is quality a responsibility in PM*? According to Haq et al. (2018), there is a relation between these two variables: project governance (PG) and project performance (PP), with the mediation of two (2) extraordinary variables, *Project Quality* and *Project Risk (PR)*. These scholars argue that quality and risk are, in turn, predictors of performance. Thus, one project managers can neither neglect one or the other. Otherwise, low extent of quality, or high effectuation of risks, or even both, will result on a substantial deviation in outcomes to the *target (x)* compared to the project objectives and plans for achieving them. Possibly, resulting in high extent of deviations above or below limits: *upper limit (y)* and *lower limit (y´)*.

$\Delta_{(x,y)} = (x - y)$; and, $\Delta_{(x,y)} = (x - y')$;

In which, the deviations are acceptable when their probability of *(P)* deviation of the results (x´) generate a scenario of

$x' = (1 - x)$

Or,

$x' = (x + \ldots \infty]$

Corresponding to the following variation:

$\Delta_{(x)} \leq y$

Or

$\Delta_{(x)} \leq y'$

As a probability general function *(U),* in which acceptable risk limit entails an additional rule, as both limits of risk (upper and lower) have to co-exist per each project objective. Taken *y* in probability theory as an *A* in probability theory and y´ as a B,

$(y=A)$, and $(y'= B)$

The probability (P) of real deviation (σ) of each project goal/objective is, then

$P(AUB) = (P(A) + P(B)) - P(A \cap B)$

The probability function, or better said the sum of probabilities of deviation (σ_x) does not correspond though to an intersection (∩) of A and B *(A∩B).* An intersection would require two sets of events, which is though theoretically impossible, since we have a single objective, at a given point in time. So, holding the target (x) equal, as the deviations cannot deviate sideways, the intersection is a null value with mutual exclusivity between A and B, and only a possible outcome. For instance, a project with a task completion date of 300 days ($x=300$) cannot deviate for a simultaneous completion in 250 days (completion before the deadline) and 350 days (completion after the deadline). In this case,

$P(A \cap B) = 0$

Thus,

$P(AUB) = (P(A) + P(B)) - 0$

As a final note, the sum of accepted deviation (σ) can be squared. It is incorrect to arithmetically account sums, avoiding the negatives by squaring them. Although, this is mathematically possible, yet not applicable in project goal´s measurement, as

$x= (y + y')$

Ought not be squared,

$x= (y + y')^2$

Since the sum of the likely deviation(s);

$\sum\sigma_{(x)} = P(AUB) = P(A) + P(B)$

Represented as A B
Is different from,

$P(A \cap B) = P(A) . P(B)$

Represented as A B
So, it is an error to represent

$$\sum\sigma_{(x)} = \sigma_{(x)}^{2}$$

Because, there only one set of results (of deviation) not two or more real sets. In this sense,

$$\sum\sigma_{(x)} \neq \sigma_{(x)}^{2}$$

Moreover, a project manager may decide to establish upper and lower limits with unequal variations, hence, non-symmetric real (ℝ) numbers. For example, accepting the same integers for the example above of a deadline for the completion of a task with a *x=300,* but now considering a y ratio of 2% y´ ratio of 10%. Thus, the limit of accepted results, assume different results *(X and X´),*

$$X = (x \,.\, y)$$

$$X = (300 \,.\, 1{,}02) = 306$$

Or,

$$X' = (x \,.\, y')$$

$$X' = (300 \,.\, 0{,}9) = 270$$

The project manager defined so a maximum and minimum range for a goal of *X=306* and *X´=270,* considering that *(y= X - x)* and *(y= X´ - x´),* in which, the whole variation is given by

$$y = (\Delta_{(x)} - x)$$

And,

$$y = (306 - 300) = 6$$

$$y' = (270 - 300) = -30$$

$$x = -30;\ 6$$

So, the project manager may have purposively defined an accepted variation of an objective with an odd setting, with a *y=6* and a *y´= 30.*

Now, one may conceive a quantitative project goal which quantification is anchored on a rational number, thus only positive figures are possible (e.g. number of defect units of a product in a continuous production line). As certainly you have figure it out, if their "non-defects" being measured, simply defects (x) so you cannot accept variations of "positive defects". The same it happens with many other goals, for example, employee´s accidents. Despite in theory, you can accept error to occur in *x* number of cases sideways, nonetheless, one cannot conceive a deviation to zero accidents to be positive or negative. It is only possible to attain an one-tailed variation, either you have accidents or not. Thus, a standard or target (x) being a natural number (e.g. 1; or $x=1$) can accept whole numbers (theoretically until plus infinite or ∞) as

$x \rightarrow \infty$; and $x \geq 0$

As one can expect, with regard to quality performance, information is critical, and the knowledge (as an intangible resource) obtained from information insights and knowledge-utilization (as a dynamic capability) empower project managers along the intelligence cycle with real competitive-gains.

The assertion of Haq et al. (2018) as to the mediating relation of quality (governance – quality – performance) is though based on the work of Khan (2012) and Wiener et al. (2016) determining that the different mechanisms of governance (G) which consubstantiate the set of project attributes influence to shaping of quality (Q) and risk (R) and ultimately performance (P); despite assuming the existence of a literature gap between the causal relation of governance and performance.

$P = G \,.\, (Q + R)$

Project Governance is defined as the set of principles of authority; accountability; control and direction; leadership; and stewardship, as to the relation of a project to the internal and external stakeholders (e.g. company´s senior management; other actors at the external environment; or the project team) (Haq et al. 2018). Here, two stream of thought collide as to PG directing principles. One considers "control" as the dominant function for benefit´s realization and project success, diverging from another seeing "trust" as the major function for the same results (Zwikael and Smyrk, 2015).

Consequently, PM, and herein, PG, implies inevitably taking quality as a serious matter and so taking significant endeavors on Project Quality Management (PQM). The latter (PQM) incorporates then three (3) *foci* (Baker, 2018): (i) *Quality Management Planning* (QMP), as a part of the overall Project Management Plan (PMP); (ii) *Quality Assurance*; and, (iii) *Quality Control*. Such control-centered approach, is based mostly on the seminal work of William Edwards Deming (whom introduced in the 1950s the initial idea of quality control) namely his foundational works, as the *theory of optimization* and *theory of profound knowledge* (Deming, 2018).

This scholar advocates that the objective of the organization should be the optimization of the entire system, in order to reach the organizational or project objectives. He argues that managerial work is better when cumulatively focused on the improvement of all parts instead of the optimization of individual systems. The latter he calls "poor management" (e.g., usage of a cheaper product/service at the expense of the work system, in turn, this will lead to an inferior output). Moreover, Deming advocates that conjugating theory and experience is the only way to generate better knowledge, thus, the combined use of senses and explicit knowledge is crucial for the fashioning and further monitoring of the progression and controlling of the outputs of the project.

Nowadays, the PQM is anchored both on the Project Management Body of Knowledge (PMBOK) mainly developed on optimization, but also, borrowing principles of Total Quality Management (TQM) as to statistical enhancement of quality outcomes regarding cost and time efficiency. So, project objectives, are drilled down to smaller operational activities to be accomplished, as small components (e.g.

scheduling or estimating) for achieving an optimal outcome (Baker, 2018). The role of project manager is in this regard diverse, being responsible for ensuring, at the same time, that seminal aspects of the project related to *cost*, *time* expenditure and *quality* are all met. Thus, a project manager need to be an expert communicator, capable of planning, budgeting and reporting to the upper management while discussing technology-related issues with the operative experts and surrounding structure (Gaddis, 1959).

The PMBOK includes three (3) types of quality processes: *quality planning*; *quality assurance*; and *quality control*. The first, quality planning or Project Quality Planning (PQP) as a part of the overall Project Management Planning (PMP) involves the identification of qualitative objectives and its underlying standards which are most relevant for the project and how they ought to be fulfilled or satisfied. This part was amply discussed above with regard to quantitative goal/objective´s setting, and moreover, as to the establishment of (upper and lower) limits of acceptance whenever measuring progression or outputs.

The *quality assurance* refers to the set of activities safeguarding the quality system to ensure that the project will meet the relevant quality standards. This is discussed further in the next section. The *quality control* refers to the monitoring of the progression of operational activities and project goals through the use of clear processes and units of measurement. Using typically a widget counting technique, regardless of the model of measurement or software utilized, the analyst is expected to cross-observe expectations against progression results and evaluate the extent of deviations and report them for a subsequent diagnosis. The measurement is focused on the standard (x) and the measurement emphasis the approximation of the progression results to the standard or target.

Therefore, on quality assurance, the critical success factors for the project entail these five (5) components: (i) the past experience in PM in quality control; (ii) the choice of methods/tools of measurement, evaluation and diagnosis of the results of progression and outputs; (iii) the use of proven technology, which the team is familiarized with; (iv) an effective controlling design, with a systematic application and clear processes as to its accurate measurement and communication; (v) effective communication and feedback systems in place; involving third parties and accepting different viewpoints at to the diagnosis and further corrective course of action.

PROJECT ASSURANCE

Governance is most concerned with the processes of planning and controlling for ensuring the completion of the project in which quality (assurance) is embedded on (Moldoveanu and Martin, 2001). Recalling the straightforward definition of Haq et al. (2018) in the previous section, as starting point for the opening of debate in this section, *quality assurance* entails to the set of activities (of planning, organizing, leading and controlling) with the purpose of safeguarding the quality system to ensure that the project will meet the relevant quality standards. The reference to "standard" describes an expected outcome of performance previously established and communicated to all project team and company´s senior managers, as a target to be achieved for a given goal. For instance, the achievement of a zero mark in industrial incidents or accidents.

Hence, project quality assurance (PQA) or simply quality assurance (QA) is dominated but two (2) sets of activities, *quality assurance planning*; and *quality assurance control*. The first, focused on the establishment of the *quality requirements*, as quality-related standard goals which compose the overall project quality planning. The second, relies mostly on the review of the *requirements artifacts*, such as, accuracy, effectiveness, or replicability for testing (or measurement). It is concerned with the solving misinterpretations, determining sufficient accuracy, spotting defects or discovering certain types of pitfalls in requirements artifacts, and diagnosing good/bad requirements quality (Femmer et al., 2017).

The *project quality assurance* function is considered, in some cases, an extension of the project itself acting as an internal auditing mechanism. The quality assurance specialist is largely focused on quality planning, reviewing often the planning of the specific issues of security and safety concerns to account that the potential impact on the project conditions and surrounding environment, to ensure that those where not properly evaluated and kept under barely risk-level.

However, the quality assurance function varies in scale and depth in a direct proportion to the project´s complexity. Indeed, managing large-scale projects, or with higher requirements of knowledge/technology, is the same of saying managing more embedded complexity, as they impose further challenges. With this regard, complexity is for QA specialists a barrier which starts with the definition of the *assurance scope,* as to the typology of requirements which ought to be screened as to the extent of requirements quality and reviewed as to the operability of the system. This constitutes the first challenge which is to delimit the *verification scope* and the *controlling scope*.

Here, the use of the *MODest Framework* can be of great utility for moving away from the initial chaos to structure them in terms of the mapping of complexity items. This framework encourages a thinking about the origin of such complexity. This means looking into the expected (or faced) difficulties, risks and barriers of performance (Maylor, 2010). This framework suggests the compartmentalization of those challenges into five (5) parameters: *mission; organization; delivery; stakeholders*; and *team*. On chapter 7 we have addressed some of those on the issues. For instance, as to the latter point (teams) I have addressed the psychological barriers of the norming phase, namely, importance of gaining concertive control to evolve to a performing phase (Boddy, 2017; Barker, 1983).

The first parameter (mission) of the MODest Framework suggests one to consider whether the path, such as the goals, may be clearly defined as something SMART; or to classify the urgency and importance of the goals; and their interaction with other projects; and uncertainty (i.e. novelty; impact and possible risks/rebounds). Secondly (organization), leads to the understanding of how can one coordinate work (where are the teams?); and accommodate differences: cultural (e.g. linguistic barriers); functioning (data or software access); or intelectual barriers (e.g. differences in human capital – as types of skills or abilities). Thirdly, (delivery), do we have a methodological matrix that will serve us as the backbone for a common practice? What are the resource constraints (e.g. financial, skills)? What´s the time horizon for the completion of the project? How´s communication across team members and timely decision-making like? What´s the room for maneuvering, adaptation to change and flexible seeking of alternative solutions if something fails?

Fourth (stakeholders), it is crucial to consider the number of stakeholders to be involved based on the project requirements. For instance, have we accounted staff at the D1 – definition phase when drawing the project proposal? Have we constituted a coalition of interest and engaged already the necessary human resources to the project? Are we experiencing any lack of commitment from key-stakeholders? What about tensions and problematic inter-relations across team members (especially in the team´s norming and performing phases)? Finally (team), is someone with lack of business or project experience, or with a deficit in skills, or requiring training and/or mentoring? Is there someone with low motivation?

Project assurance is an important tool also for tackling these question-marks about the project´s complexity, and reviewing quality requirements and defects. Naturally, project assurance has a solid planning dimension, envisioning the future of projects and their underlying performance. It provides also an oversight into possible deviating paths from the standard performance. Furthermore, *project assurance frameworks* integration into the PMO´s role allows the anticipation of emergent corrective courses of action to bring operations back on track (Agnoletto, 2020).

Hence, project assurance is a critical function of project structures, even though, many times is withheld in detriment of others, and incorporated in the PMO strategic management/communication, development of methodologies or learning conversions to the organizations. Surely, it can play a decisive role from the D1 (definition) to D4 (doing) of the 4-D model, from planning, passing through organizing (of activities – setting priority schemes), monitoring (risks) and controlling of performance, avoiding waste, duplication or work and effective risk).

However, project assurance may entail different activities, as *Requirement (Bad) Smell Analysis (RSA)*; *PMO Maturity Assessments* (PMO-MA), *Light Health Checks* (LHC); *Gated Reviews (GRs)*; or *Embedded Assurance (EA)*. The PMO-MAs assess the tools and methods in place and develop a scenario with an improved prioritization of activities for gains of efficiency in the operations, as a "*prioritized improvement roadmap*" (Agnoletto, 2020, p. 6; Femmer et al., 2017).

The RSA aims to solve a constantly dyad of issues faced issue by many project managers, as follows: (i) faster feedback requirements; and, (ii) the existence of imperfect knowledge in the project communication cycle (Femmer et al, 2017). Hence, the RSA is centered on the identification of needs for faster feedback and or communication gaps in content and pace. Moreover, it seeks to identify languages gaps, between natural language written in the quality requirements and the formal semantics requirements of portfolio expertise, namely with regard to quality defects not detectable automatically with more vague/natural language.

The LHCs refer to an on-going check of performance and risk-level, by monitoring the progression of the overall performance indicators (PI) and risk indicators (RI). GRs are focusing on thorough analysis at key project stages, while the EAs are the regular control focused on operational key deliverables and tasks, together with their effective timely completion which a preventive of upcoming operative risks.

These QA specialist´s reviews, quite productizible due to the clear circumscription into sub-auditing functions of QA´s scope, are executed in specific "packs of analysis" assumed that can be performed either manually (*Manual QA*) or computer-assisted (*Automatic QA*), as both approaches may allow, distinctively I suppose, the discover of vagueness or ineffective requirements, defects, violations to procedures and leapfrogging of some sequential steps in processes and specially in serial activities.

For an automatic QA approach, software apps as *Intellect, Scilife, BizzMine, TrackMedium, Integrum, Arena QMS* or *Compliance Quest* seem to be most broad in coverage of multiple QA processes, as corrective and preventive actions (CAPA); defect tracking; training, compliance, and audit management; document coding and control; or supplier quality control.

TOTAL QUALITY MANAGEMENT

The link of project management (PM) with TQM have been analyzed for over two decades. Scholars (mostly) in UK, such as, *David J. Bryde*; and, *Sarah T. Meegan; W. Andrew Taylor;* and others as*; M.T. Hildes;* Zahir *Irani; John M. Sharp;* and, *I. Polychronakis* have focused on the understanding of the firm-level benefits of introducing the principles of PM as a mean of a successful implementation of a TQM program.

Accordingly, they studied furthermore the impact of introducing TQM in *project-based organizations (PBO)*, as the ones carrying out work on a project-by-project basis. Of course, this includes first-timer projects, whether or not of a sub-typology of a Business Environment Analysis Project (BEAP) (Taylor and Meegan, 1997). Moreover, they analyzed the influence of transitioning from the traditional Quality Assurance (QA) encapsulated in the ISO9000 certification into TQM practice.

The traditional view (ISO9000) resembles though a mere instrumentalization of a "technocratic device" at an operational-level. Quality, in the ISO9000, is seen as a mechanism that ensures the "*conformance to requirements*". Unlike such vision, TQM "*is a dynamic concept that evolves as customers' requirements evolve, and therefore is more flexible*" (Hides et al., 2000, p. 412).

During this chapter, while TQM is unraveled to you, these differences will emerge indeed. On one side (ISO9000) observes a reasoning with the dominance of (formal) *compliance*, actually, more pronounced than the (voluntary) *conformance* aspect. At the end, you will certainly be asking yourself whether compliance is the solution in all splendor for continuous and effective improvement in any type of organization. You may wonder, it carries the burden of being inhibitor (of individual freedom) and so an adversary of further development, invalidating further entrepreneurial actions. On the other side (TQM), you will have these two (2) attributes explained: *dynamics* and *flexibility*, and described by opposition to other continuous improvement tools often confused with it (as, *Kanban, Kaizen, PDCA* or *Six Sigma)*.

The definition of total quality management (TQM) may be laid down as "*a philosophy of management that is driven by customer needs and expectations and focus on continually improving work processes*" (Boddy, 2017, p. 598). Hence, TQM clearly advocates, that continuous individual efforts are the engine for a common good for the whole organization, i.e. incremental changes and (visibly significant) effective improvements.

From the above, hope you do not misinterpret my words about non-TQM quality practices. Don't get me wrong when I refer to quality. I do not intend, at all, to ostracize the benefits of implementing quality systems for managing human processes of internal transformation (and in turn generating better outputs to the market, especially the customer). Not at all! Many companies are quite not there at this stage. Most especially SMEs with the aggravating factor of having an urgent need to grow in (their critical understanding of their own) *structural maturity* and develop consistency at work recovering from the marked deficit regarding the *formalization of management processes* (Hilde et al., 2000). These firms have still a mountain of things to reflect upon and execute in the near future.

Over one hundred years ago, *Frederick Winslow Taylor* created the foundations for one of the greatest legacies in Management Sciences (if not the greatest), i.e. the idea of *scientificity* of work. The bottom line of this idea is, work can be studied. One can plan, organize, analyze and evaluate. Thus, organizations can hold work processes and people accountable, become thinking entities, with a certain degree of criticality, and improve every day. Taylor´s notion of *efficiency* abstracted itself from the individual task and moved towards the goodness for the corporate organism. It had the virtue to demonstrate in multiple forms (e.g. as the time and motion studies; or the differential piece-rate system) that work can be studied scientifically and be object to a rigorous experimental approach (Ries, 2019).

Just wipe out any thoughts from your head as far as it comes to bad thoughts about quality or possible misconceptions related to the interpretation of my words. The same with quality assurance which is crucial for governance. In section 9.1., I have introduced an acronym (*Q.U.A.L.I.T.Y.*) which incorporate also action and dynamic features of improvement, exactly as in TQM (*Quest for excellence; Understanding customers' needs; Action to achieve customer appreciation; Leadership; Involving all people; Team spirit for common goal; Yardstick to measure progress*).

However, there is a fundamental difference in action. The fundamental difference is, when one abides to compliance, or the focus on fulfilling the quality standards in ISO9000, ISO10006 or ISO21500. This is the philosophical assumptions one may hold. But, for TQM, is not (and will never be) a matter of whether quality is good or bad *per se*, is a matter of *how* (not simply what) one can implement and exercise the best continuous improvement practices. It accounts what are the methodologies to adopt, but also, very important, how to best exploit the Taylor´s notion of "efficiency". This means, to shift your gear in quality management: *from best methods, to best practices* (that better accommodate those methods). You can holds the most fantastic weekly or monthly Kaizen meetings with the most sophisticated analytics in the world, and you believe them to be truly insightful. You might be lucky enough to have the most intrapreneurial Quality Control (QC) circles in world; however, if one company is not populated with a whole team with an embedded spirit of "breathing quality", "living quality" and thinking quality", thus, one is still miles away from TQM, which is believed to some notches above.

I will make now in this paragraph a parentheses in the narrative in order to make a quick remark. Both in sections 9.2 and 9.3. I have elaborated on standards, regarding the quality assurance (QA) function. The standards were the safeguarding institutions of the quality system that regulated the execution of activities (planning, organizing, leading and controlling). Standards are thus the set of requirements, specifications, guidelines, or characteristics of a task or a bundle of them (aka, process).

This same word is going to be regularly used in the next chapter as well, but with a different meaning. So, here is the clarification, the notion of *standard* varies with the scientific domain in which is applied to. This concept used in two chapter 9 is different from the concept used in chapter 10 of this book. Despite we are employing the same word, the meaning varies. This is a phenomenon called *polysemy*. A word with two different meanings. In this chapter *standard* (used in the context of Quality Management) identifies, as mentioned above, the operative procedure (i.e. the requirements, specifications, guidelines, or characteristics of task or set of tasks (aka, process). In chapter 10, a *standard* is a concept utilized in the context of Corporate Strategic Management, and within the sub-field of Strategic Performance Measurement (SPM). Here, standard means a quantitative measurement unit related to a goal of a performance indicator.

Returning to the discussion of TQM versus non-TQM, I would recall from section *9.1. Project´s quality and quality performance*, that the notion of qualitative is a perceptive phenomenon, involving a dyad of factors: performance *(P)* and expectations *(E)*: *(Q= P/E)*.

Consequently, the degree of quality output is determined by whom the judging individual is (i.e. yourself; your manager, or the colleague/s, the client/s; other firms' representative, and so forth).The extent of goodness is given by the extent of the gap between numerator (P) and denominator (E):

$$1 \leq Q_{(x)} \geq 1$$

This means the difference in the perceptional fraction between *P* and *E*,

x= P > E *(excellence)*

P = E *(goodness)*

Or,

$(x = P < E)$ *(badness)*

By goodness or badness one is not referring to an intention to favor or harm, but the ability or inability to produce better results and satisfy the degree of expectations of a given stakeholder. However we are looking to quality with the micro-lens, at individual-level, since logically, quality is a subjective evaluation, differently registered by everyone. However, when it comes to TQM this entails a fairly common understanding of quality inside of the organization.

$$Q(_x) = \{E_1, E_2 ..., E_n\}$$

And so, in TQM, the collective expectation of the organizations employees (e) and managers (m) in notation is,

$$E(_x) = \sum ((e_1 + e_2 ... + e_n) + (m_1 + m_2 + ... m_n) + (\varepsilon_e) + (\varepsilon_m)) / (N + \oplus)$$

To be model as a regression to be further represented vectorically as,

$$Y_{(E)} = \beta_0 + \beta_1 e_1 + \beta_2 e_2 + ... + \beta_n e_n + \beta_{n+1} m_1 + \beta_{n+2} m_2 + \beta_{2n} m_n + \varepsilon$$

In which, the sum or error ($\oplus$) is represented as the total uncertainty as the aggregate of deviating expectations,

$$\oplus_{(E)} = \varepsilon (e + m) . N$$

The residual values of employee or manager error, correspond to the deviating points of view regarding the expectations that hamper the mean even being accounted in the total number of organizational-stakeholders *(N)*. Thus, the sum of error (*E* or sum of ε) corresponds to, the employees and managers deviations or differences of thought/action against the company´s expectations. The real challenge in TQM is then the elevation of company´s standards together with the elevation of the individual standards and their conformity in thought and action. In sum, TQM requires a company-wide initiative with a timescale of many years, and as such undertaken with great caution.

However, the properties of the TQM is frequently mistaken with the *Kaizen* methodology and vice-versa, as they possess a similar role and intervention in the firm´s qualitative development. One could then raise this question:

Is Kaizen a redundant terminology to identify a TQM program?

The answer is a straightforward, No! In a simpler way, *Kaizen* can be described as a philosophy within another philosophy. *Kaizen* even in its fullness, accounting the whole methodological framework, represents a part of the TQM, as the latter is broader in scope. Despite, sharing similar assumptions and beliefs about the heuristics of quality and envision together a company-wide behavioral concern oriented toward quality enhancement, TQM goes beyond the first. Nonetheless, *Kaizen* is a sophisticated pure *bottom-up* approach to quality enhancement, with a vision of 180 degrees, symbolizing half the world of what the TQM is. Pro TQM theorists would assert that the Kaizen methodology only sees one flank for the solution it seeks (i.e. changing improvements) while the TQM represents a dual approach (*bottom-up* and *top-down*). Some insurgent voices started more recently defending the parity as to the breadth of their scope/s.

The closest the Kaizen comes TQM is, though the operationalizing of the quality system through *cross-functional management*. This methodologies advocates on the formation of three-levels of the system: a *management-oriented* Kaizen; a *group-oriented* Kaizen; and *individual-oriented* Kaizen. This is neither vertical, horizontal nor diagonal. It is a transversal approach, considering the effort toward a common behaviour across functional areas (i.e. *cross-functional management*) as a blueprint for an intra-organizational alignment, involving all parts of the organization. Yet, follows a heterarchical type of methodology, hence, non-hierarchized. Below, addressing the three (3) anchors and the five (5) principles of the Kaizen methodology I will elaborate furthermore on my justification to clarify why Kaizen does not hold a dual approach as the TQM.

As originally modelled by *Maazaki Imai,* the father of the Kaizen method, it requires *"involving everyone – managers and workers alike"* (Kaizen, online*)*. This is the first reason why Kaizen is not in parity as to the breadth of scope with the TQM. This exact statement (*"involving everyone – managers and workers alike")* uncovers a fundamental incompatibility. It is not a rupture in both philosophies, but a seminal difference in their reasoning. The *Kaizen* does not value the overlapping of a bottom-up with a top-down approach, even for the excellence or goodness of the initiatives leading to inherent positive externalities, such as, to the cost-benefit trade-offs. *Mr. Imai´*s book published in 1986 (entitled "*Kaizen: The Key to Japan's Competitive Success*"), followed by another blockbuster sequel in 1997 with "*Gemba Kaizen - a common sense, low-cost approach to management"* is argued to be a systematic approach for continuous business improvement, and subsequently, a formula for yielding superior results.

Kaizen, became something new in the vocabulary many of business managers around three decades ago, and this thesis of Kaizen derived from the combination of two Japanese words, *kay* (meaning "change") and *zen* (as something new modified "for better"). In short, the book advocated a methodology focused on the development of *changing improvements*. Companies were summoned to apply such methodology, considering three (3) anchors of action:

(i) Focus on process improvement (instead of results)
(ii) Involve everyone – managers and employees alike
(iii) Take everyone accountable (responsibility is an individual thing)

As the Kaizen methodological framework has some degree of complexity though with relevance for the successful lean implementation of any project, and moreover, its context overlaps the TQM, I´ll try to shortcut an explanation of these anchors (very briefly discussed above) and continue bringing the soul of this philosophy, the five (5) principles explanatory of the how´s, or the underpinnings of how this methodology ought to be implemented like. As referred above these principles consubstantiate my second argument of a non-parity in scope of these two philosophies of management. The five (5) principles of Kaizen are:

1. Know your Customer
2. Let it Flow
3. Go to *Gemba*
4. Empower People

5. Be Transparent

Those principles are supported on a myriad of tools. For instance, the *3M´s* (*Muda, Muri* and *Mura*), or the 5-S (*Seiri; Seiton, Seizo; Seiketsu; Shitsuke*); or the 5-W´s (*What, Why, Where, When,* and *Who*) - an adaptation for the western world by the *KAIZEN Institute Consulting Group (KICG); or* others like the *One-H (How);* or the *4-M* (*Man, Machine, Material, Method*). Like the 5-S, the 3M is inspired in Japanese words. In the 3Ms three (3) words provide, altogether, the operative guidelines for achieving a concept highly valued with regards to the management of efficiency at work (i.e., *Lean* production). The 3Ms explores the case of Toyota´s Production System, as to its principles and behaviour (the "Toyota Way"), developed around the elimination of the three (3) types of deviations that demonstrate an inefficient allocation of resources: *Muda* (or waste); *Muri* (overburden); and *Mura* (unevenness).

Likewise, you will find other *lean* tools describing the Kaizen process, as the 5-S, which respectively, mean: (i) *Seiri*: to set things in order (by eliminating or reducing the useless); (ii) *Seiton:* the shiness or cleanliness of the workplace; (iii) *Seizo:* the purity (or self-discipline) respecting the company´s policies and rules; (iv) *Seiketsu:* the standardization of rules and policies*;* and, (v) *Shitsuke:* the commitment to ground these behaviour in daily habits. Moreover, it covers the fundamental ideas comprised in *Walter Shewhart* and *W. Edwards Deming*´s Plan Do Check Act (PDCA) cycle. You will revisit this latter framework on the last chapter.

As one can easily deduce from these Kaizen tools above, managers and employees share a fairly equal individual responsibility and the same kind of *self-discipline*, a vital component to them all. The organization is the big-brother, holding an overall governance and managerial responsibility. It is a parsimonious vision of the organization, with a spark of equalitarianism as to the organization of lean work and strict abiding to standardized rules to the crowd. The job of strategic thinking and governance (e.g. in the form of, policy-making; managerial processes; budgetary and other type of resource´s allocation; and setting administrative procedures and, controlling measures), so crucial because it lays down the ground for the operational activities, is downgraded to a nearly operative and quasi-mechanic task resolution of "things" with undermined significance and criteria. The Kaizen methodology makes a fundamental assumption that we all effectively contribute equally to the prosperity of the company. Using *Alexander Dumas*´s words, is like a, somehow, naïve vision of "*all for one and one for all*". A faithful reliance on the virtues of a transversal type method (rather than a pure horizontal one) and its inferential virtues to the benefit of the firm. I can only designate it, a bottom-up approach.

Moreover, the three (3) major types of work advocated are oriented towards the achievement of a structure, and embedded culture, of continuous improvement. Those major categories of work are: *lean*; *innovation*; and *maintenance*. Again, I have to emphasize here, that this philosophy promotes a partial alienation of the manager's role for donating his/her working and thinking time to the reinforcement of operational interaction with the rest of the teams. Firstly this is routed in one of the Kaizen principles ("*Go to Gemba*"). This is the argument that managers should take time to visit the shop floor, conceived as the real place where value is created. Go to Gemba has the purpose of making managers understand what is happening there, and so, put them more in tune with the rest of company. Secondly, is grounded on Mr. *Imai*´s belief that *maintenance* is one the dominant activities of a company, because it sets things in order. This is the conjecture of the *seiri* contained in the 5-S. Thirdly, it advocates that managers ought to allocate a significant portion of time working on the promotion of innovation.

Nonetheless, Kaizen and TQM philosophy share still several commonalities, as the vision of a *true improvement* being dependent on proactive managerial intervention of proximity beginning with *hoshin kanri,* a Japanese expression for policy deployment. Both are grounded in other subjacent philosophies as the *Kanban* and *Six Sigma. Kanban* referring to the managing of work related to the balancing of demands with available capacity and solving the bottlenecks comes from any unbalanced condition. The *Six Sigma* referring to the removal of the causes of defects and minimizing variability in manufacturing and business processes. Furthermore, deriving from these two (Kanban and Six Sigma) they are aligned also as the importance of T*otal Productive Maintenance (TPM) and Total Quality Control (TQC)* practices and their inherent seminal tools as, Control Points; QC circles; Suggestion Systems; Just-in-Time; or Zero Defects.

The cumulative quality of the processes dictates the perception of the outputs, and so influences the results. In turn, both philosophies advocate process first, results at last. Also, the *locus* of the attention is the customer satisfaction. The accomplishment of the latter is dependent on a customer-centric view of the business realm, in which, the customer inputs (ideas) are considered a decisive *market-in* imperative to be taken in great account. A response to them requires the ability to adapt internal processes to market a *product-out* on a similarly way, fulfilling the (changing) expectations. One can tell, Kaizen is a part of the TQM. It is inspired on a company-wide notion of quality as the vision of business continuous improvement. Yet, the TQM features primarily focus on customer's satisfaction through improvement of quality, both top down and bottom up, comes at the expense of a more costly implementation, compared to Kaizen.

LEARNING OUTCOMES

- Quality: Project controls and performance
- Project qual and the customer perspective
- Measurement of quality as to the functions of "good", "excellent", "low" and "worst"
- Standards/targets, limits, range of variations and probability of deviation
- The role of project governance (PG)
- Project Management Plan (PMP): Qual Assurance (QA) and Qual control (QC)
- The QA activities
- QC and the theories of optimization and profound knowledge
- The Project Management Body of Knowledge (PMBOK)
- Distinction of TQM and Kaizen

REFLECTION QUESTIONS

What´s the difference between *TQM* and *Kaizen*?

How do these two (2) philosophies (*Kanban* and *Six Sigma*) relate to *Total Productive Maintenance (TPM)* and *Total Quality Control (TQC)*?

How does the 5S related to the Kaizen and the PDCA cycle?

What variables may you use in the functions *P* and *E* to measurement quality?

What´s a *Control Point* and *Quality Circle*?

CHAPTER HIGHLIGHTS

- Quality: a responsibility; an ethical action and a resource)
- Quality function and the balance of P´s and E´s
- Layers of qual responsibility
- The colliding customer and firm´s view of quality
- Standards and accreditation
- The scope of Quality Assurance: planning and control
- QA: Manual or computer?: the work of the specialist, software and "packs of analysis"
- The range of QA tools and activities
- The 5 principles of Kaizen
- TQM, TQC and TPM

CONCLUSION

The chapter addresses role of quality in the firm and its projects. It discusses the *qual function* as a measurement of inputs-outputs (expectations and performance) and confronting the company view with the consumer´s expectations. It establishes measures of *quality performance* (good, bad and worse) in relation to the standard.

The layers of responsibility of the firm are briefly presented: *individual; department and corporative.* The *quality assurance* as a system is described in its two major domains: Quality assurance planning (QAP) and Quality assurance controls (QAC). Moreover, is discussed in relation to the philosophy of continuous improvement and with reference to the PDCA cycle. Herein, were also discussed the five (5) principles of the Kaizen philosophy (and distinguished against the TQM).

Entering the QA (in section 9.2.), a plethora of methods were also described (e.g. RSAs; PMO-Mas; LHC; GR; and EAs) due to the complementarity to the others, and herein, discussed the logic of pack-of-analysis and computer QA.

In the last section (9.3) a distinction is made between two philosophies of "true improvement" (i.e. *TQM* and *Kaizen).* In addition, is presented the five (5) five principles of the latter and the three (3) levels of adoption of the Kaizen system: *management-oriented*; *group-oriented* and *individual-oriented*), together with the Total *Quality Control (TQC)* practices and their inherent seminal tools as, Control Points; QC circles; Suggestion Systems; Just-in-Time; or Zero Defects.

REFERENCES

AgnolettoJ. (2020). *Project Assurance Fundamentals.* PricewaterhouseCoopers. https://www.pwc.com.au/assurance/internal-audit/Project-Fundamentals-Slides.pdf

Baker, B. (2018). Project quality management practice & theory. *American Journal of Management, 18*(3), 10–17.

Boddy. (2020). *Management: Using practice and theory to develop skill, (8th ed.).* Pearson Education Limited.

Bosch-Rekveldt, M., Jongkind, Y., Mooi, H., Bakker, H., & Verbraeck, A. (2011). Grasping project complexity in large engineering projects: The TOE (Technical, Organizational and Environmental) framework. *International Journal of Project Management*, *29*(6), 728–739. doi:10.1016/j.ijproman.2010.07.008

Bryde, J. D. (1997). Underpinning modern project management with TQM principles. *The TQM Magazine*, *9*(3), 231–238. doi:10.1108/09544789710169037

Femmer, H., Fernández, D. M., Wagner, S., & Eder, S. (2017). Rapid quality assurance with requirements smells. *Journal of Systems and Software*, *123*, 190–213. doi:10.1016/j.jss.2016.02.047

Gaddis, P. O. (1959). *The project manager*. Harvard University.

Haq, S. U., Liang, C., Gu, D., Du, J. T., & Zhao, S. (2018). Project governance, project performance, and the mediating role of project quality and project management risk: An agency theory perspective. *Engineering Management Journal*, *30*(4), 274–292. doi:10.1080/10429247.2018.1503038

Hides, M. T., Irani, Z., Polychronakis, I., & Sharp, J. M. (2000). Facilitating total quality through effective project management. *International Journal of Quality & Reliability Management*, *17*(4/5), 407–422. doi:10.1108/02656710010298427

Hubbard, D. (2014). *How to measure anything: Finding the value of intangibles in business*. John Wiley & Sons, Inc.

Kaizen Institute. (n.d.). *What is Kaizen*. Kaizen Institute. https://www.kaizen.com/

Khan, M. E. (2012). *Relationship between project attributes, project performance, and project governance dimensions-building the theoretical framework*. 2012 PMI Global Congress Proceedings, Marseille-France.

Luthra, S., Garg, D., Agarwal, A., & Mangla, S. K. (2020). *Total Quality Management (TQM): Principles, Methods, and Applications*. CRC Press. doi:10.1201/9781003053156

Martin, R. L. (2014). The big lie of strategic planning. *Harvard Business Review*, *92*(1/2), 78–84.

Rhodes, R. A. W. (1996). The new governance: Governing without government. *Political Studies*, *XLIV*(4), 652–667. doi:10.1111/j.1467-9248.1996.tb01747.x

Ries, E. (2019). *The lean startup. How constant innovation creates radically successful businesses*. Penguin Random House.

Rodriguez, P., Uhlenbruck, K., & Eden, L. (2005). Government corruption and the entry strategies of multinationals. *Academy of Management Review*, *30*(2), 383–396. doi:10.5465/amr.2005.16387894

Roquebert, J. A., Phillips, R. L., & Westfall, P. A. (1996). Markets Vs. Management: What drives profitability? *Strategic Management Journal*, *17*(8), 653–664. doi:10.1002/(SICI)1097-0266(199610)17:8<653::AID-SMJ840>3.0.CO;2-O

Ruhanen, L., Scott, N., Ritchie, B., & Tkaczynski, A. (2010). Governance: A review and synthesis of the literature. *Tourism Review*, *65*(4), 4–16. doi:10.1108/16605371011093836

Rumelt, R. P. (1991). How much does industry matter? *Strategic Management Journal*, *12*(3), 167–185. doi:10.1002mj.4250120302

Schwartz, M. S., & Weber, J. (2006). A business ethics national index (BENI) measuring business ethics activity around the world. *Business & Society*, *45*(3), 382–405. doi:10.1177/0007650305285395

Semke, L. M., & Tiberius, V. (2020). Corporate foresight and dynamic capabilities: An exploratory study. *Forecasting*, *2*(2), 180–193. doi:10.3390/forecast2020010

Shadfar, S. (2013). Application of SORF Analysis in Formulating Businesses Strategies. *International SAMANM Journal of Marketing and Management*, *1*(2), 96–102.

Skubana. (2020). *Walmart Supply Chain [2021]: Why It Continues To Dominate*. Skubana. https://www.skubana.com/blog/walmart-leading-way

Taylor, A., & Meegan, S. (1997). Factors influencing a successful transition from ISO 9000 toTQM. The influence of understanding and motivation. *International Journal of Quality & Reliability Management*, *1*(2), 100–117.

Teece, D. J., Pisano, G., & Shuen, A. (1997). Dynamic capabilities and strategic management. *Strategic Management Journal*, *18*(7), 509–533. doi:10.1002/(SICI)1097-0266(199708)18:7<509::AID-SMJ882>3.0.CO;2-Z

Weihrich, H. (1982). The TOWS matrix—A tool for situational analysis. *Long Range Planning*, *15*(2), 54–66. doi:10.1016/0024-6301(82)90120-0

Wheelen, T. L., & Hunger, J. D. (1987). Using the strategic audit. *S.A.M. Advanced Management Journal*, *52*(1), 4–27.

Whittle, R., & Myrick, C. B. (2016). *Enterprise business architecture: The formal link between strategy and results*. CRC Press. doi:10.1201/9781420000207

Wiener, M., Mähring, M., Remus, U., & Saunders, C. S. (2016). Control configuration and control enactment in information systems projects: Review and Expanded Theoretical Framework. *Management Information Systems Quarterly*, *40*(3), 741–774. doi:10.25300/MISQ/2016/40.3.11

Worthington, I., & Britton, C. (2009). *The business environment*. Pearson education.

Zwikael, O., & Smyrk, J. (2015). Project governance: Balancing control and trust in dealing with risk. *International Journal of Project Management*, *33*(4), 852–862. doi:10.1016/j.ijproman.2014.10.012

Chapter 10
Strategic Project Auditing

ABSTRACT

Historically sparse, the body of literature in strategy auditing (SA) has grown in number and array of scholarly endeavors since the 1980s. Dominantly centered upon the instrumentalization of Robert Grant´s strategic management process (SMP), which linearity and forward-orientation of this framework outlines the number of "processes" and its "workflow," the SA is a disciple of a major school of thought (i.e. the planning view) postulating that corporate planning and strategic controls are the two most nuclear functions of the strategist. So, where is "the analysis" (and particularly the business environment analysis – BEA) realized in a SA? The strategy audit symbolizes the "big picture" outlining a full cycle of the business-level strategy execution, while the BEA is one process within the SA as a system. The embeddedness of the BEA (projects) in the SA is addressed in this chapter while summarily describing the aspects of contextualization, positioning and association with other SA-processes directly linked to it.

CONTEXTUALISING THE STRATEGY AUDIT (SA)

The notion of strategy audit (SA) refers to a mechanism of strategic control that covers key-aspects of the strategic management process in multiple steps of action and places them within the decision-making framework (Wheelen and Hunger, 1987). It contains several stages of intervention upon the internal environment and external environment ranging from *selection*, *implementation, evaluation* and *control.* Acquainted with this general notion of SA, one may wonder…

How are Strategy Audit and Business Environment Analyzability connected?

What type of knowledge-gains derive from the comprehension of such association (SA-BEA)?

With regard to a business environment analysis project (BEAP), the macro external environment analysis is something that constitutes likewise part of the Strategy Audit of the firm. Whether the scrutiny surrounds a whole business unit, or exclusively a program or project, the BEA is a piece of the whole puzzle. The SA provides a general outlook of fitness between environments (internal and external) and

DOI: 10.4018/978-1-6684-5543-2.ch010

performance (*environment-performance*). Furthermore, between environment and strategic alignment (*structure &strategy-performance*) in a given moment in time (as discussed in chapter 2 – section 2.2. Organization´s Strategic Fit). Therefore, one could well say, the SA is the larger picture in which the analysis function intertwines its various typologies and the BEA is embedded in it, as a business process within a system (and that´s correct!).

Hence, a strategy audit is realized for assessing strategic business units (SBUs) but also its micro-enterprises (of the project´s realm) of a corporate division, as each project assumes a micro-structure and ventures qualifying for an identical auditing scrutiny.

Commonly associated to the general public as being part of the corporate finance lexicon, as an in-depth analytical endeavor of the accountant, financial auditor and reviser, the expression "strategy audit" (SA) is though not a financial audit at all (even incorporating some principles of it). More than a catchword and larger than the prior, SA gathers a multiplicity of analytical efforts from multiple systems, involving several functional areas of a firm. Just in case SA is a concept totally new for you, let me tell you that several scholars have for decades quarried into it and explored the scope of the strategy audit and nowadays its boundaries are fairly clear to SM theorists. The 1980s was rather prolific in this field with scholars as *David Hunger, Milton Lauenstein, Thomas Wheelen, Mike Wahl* and others giving had a considerable impulse to this phenomenon.

Auditing is without any doubt, an apparatus of "control" fundamentally applied in organizations with a typical purpose of "looking at own belly" and with a medical gaze diagnose own ailments. This means to control critical sub-systems as Corporate Finance or Quality Assurance. This explains the growth in popularity of them. However, a larger audit of the strategic design of an entire SBU or a project holds also a tremendous utility, regardless size and dispersion of its operations. First, it follows the intelligence cycle as inputs (i.e. data), separately taken or cross-observed, empowering managers for more rational decisions for the economic maximization of value. Second, potential knowledge-gained from an SA has the virtue to open horizons to the anticipation, on a timely manner, of unseen problems or opportunities (e.g. a bottlenecking task or, underperforming result; or untapped activity).

The strategy audit comes though with a fundamental difference in scope from the two other forms of auditing above-mentioned, even though, they share a common denominator, auditing is a process-based approach. Thus, in essence, is heuristic, accounts the past practice and experience-gained and involves a high degree of complexity and depth. Until here, nothing is new; all forms of auditing assume such contours. Nonetheless, with a wider breadth than the scope of others forms of auditing, SA balances heuristics and holism, which makes it unique. Strategy auditing focusses, simultaneously, on multiple strategy-related domains while keeping a *composite depth* nature, as the analysis function entails an immersion into all these domains. The figure below exemplifies such singularity of the SA.

Indeed, a Strategy Audit does not solely affect a single organizational area but somehow multiple domains, as projects, programs, team/work groups, centers, subsidiaries or departments. Undoubtedly, has a larger in scope than the others covering altogether the financial and quality subsystems, and more. It is like a large umbrella of liabilities (such as consulting; planning; or assessment) holding typically a descriptive-assessment purpose accounting both quantitative and qualitative outputs as seminal (and inseparable) measurements units of organizational success.

Lauenstein (1984, p. 90) refers to *strategy audit*, as a collection of auditing endeavors of a corporate strategy to multiple tests of: (i) validity; (ii) consistency; (iii) and (probable) effectiveness.

Table 1. Strategy audit versus quality audit: Breadth and depth

	Quality Audit Process	Strategy Audit
Latitude or Breadth	General Quality (Narrow)	Investor´s Strategy Portfolio´s (or Business Unit) Strategy Program/Project-specific Strategies (Broad)
Degree of Specificity or Depth	Plan, Goals Team, tasks and Modelling Checklists Reporting Follow-up	Plans and Goal´s appraisal Market Assessment Strategy-Structure Gaps Performance Diagnosis

Source: Own elaboration

Wheelen and Hunger (1987, p. 6) identifies somewhat acceptable as a definition of SA, the set of endeavors to offer an integrated view of the strategic management in action, covering the key-aspects of the *strategic management process (SMP)*, placing them within a decision-making framework.

Moreover, its large spectrum of analyzability makes it a task of high exigency and responsibility, as the intertwining of the strategy function with a multitude of enterprise quadrants (e.g. finance; logistics; marketing; production; research; or sales) affects direct and indirectly the future of the whole organization´s stakeholders in terms of, for instance, asset-acquisition/development, human capital formation, competitive-gains and future wealth. Therefore, strategy has such a consultative and review power over governance and senior management influencing markedly the decision-making while exerting an indisputable meta-influence in the remaining domains of the organization.

In general, simply reflecting on the scope of corporate strategy we can quickly understand its reach. It sets firstly a direction: who one firm is or believes to be; its ethical thresholds and dilemmas; the path is willing to take; and, whom it wants to be. This is so commonly termed of corporate vision, mission, values, ethics and citizenship. Furthermore, it establishes the corporate portfolio: the type of business units; the programmes and the projects to adhere to and their prioritization (i.e. the so called portfolio scope). Also, it sets the number of business units and their risk approaches; the meanders of the venturing, as to the partnering, networking, synergizing and internationalization options, whether combining organic or non-organic business mechanisms (or the business growth and diversification); and, cumulatively these tree (3) strategic pillars (i.e. vision; portfolio; and, growth) influence all the other organizational dimensions as the structural configuration and international coordination models (parenting strategies), or the asset´s allocation, budgeting, capital-distribution per division and business units and/or the financial controls (resources-allocation strategies); or even lastly the procurement, choice and relations with potential investors, capital owner´s or stockholders and their typology and expectation´s matching (investor´s strategy).

Despite the breadth of its scope and complexity, with multiple ties and crossed-organizational levers, SA is a vital mechanism of goal-performance management and an extraordinary insightful tool for the diagnosis of performance and underlying success. It has the virtue to open avenues for further creation/innovation and questioning the corporate thinking of the future. Hence, it has the ability to redefine strategic plans and markets positions, reducing the external uncertainty in the markets; restoring some degree of firm control by scanning the assertiveness of the path and contributing for the sustainability of the organizational body.

In short, the strategy audit follows a particular view (the Mintzberg "P" - Plan) designated the *Planning View*, where the SA-practice goes along the "Strategic Management Process". Auditing entails the fulfillment of *Walter Shewart* and *Edward Deming´*s vision from the 1950s encouraging small-scale improvements, ideas which transposed into their *PDCA (Plan-Do-Check-Act)* framework. The PDCA is a pre-establishment of a set of intended commitment decisions, for a given business unit/project, being monitored on-going basis or even post-reviewed. The SA follows a heuristic logic, and the analysis function (namely in the BEAP) is a part of the whole auditing system. The next section begins depicting the formulation of strategic objectives, i.e. an essential premise of strategizing that triggers all subsequent endeavors of the SA, namely the *widget counting* as the core aspect of performance measurement also addressed in the section.

STRATEGIC OBJECTIVES AND PERFORMANCE DIAGNOSIS

Setting goals for one´s life is something natural to humankind; as a matter of personal governance, something grounded on the aspirations and own desired path that is realized both consciously and inadvertently. This happens as humans are thinking individuals endowed with natural capacity to take advantage without effort of the use of the front lobe of the cortex (part of the) brain, benefiting then of a set of cognitive skills as the major abilities to perform valuable exercises of planning, organizing work and initiating/executing tasks or delegate them (as addressed in chapter 1 – *Human Quest for environment control and the microfoundations of management*).

Likewise, organizations are semi-rational entities with memory, ability to learn, a vision of its societal relevance, and a sense of mission of their way. The reader might consider it a naïve vision of an organization, maybe romantic, and certainly this statement may be object of critique for several scholars following the great organizational theorists of seminal human relations and corporate responsibility models (as *Mary Parker Follett; George Elton Mayo*; *Henry Mintzberg*; Archie B. Carroll; *Christine Bader*; Adam Lindgreen and so as others). Judgments aside as to the romanticism of the "humanized organization", of relevance is simply to mention in this context that companies also set for themselves goals and objectives.

The difference between individuals and organizations resides in the degree of sophistication of the goal´s set (of course, also the radius of its impact) and the mechanisms adopted to appraise their accomplishment. In general, collective entities possess clearly more means to set the anchor for a strategy audit than individuals do. Nonetheless, the degree of those means vary substantially among practitioners. Rule of thumb is, large enterprises have resources to possess (and allocate) more resources to an audit than smaller enterprises. In practice, such advantages may fade away with time depending on the managerial decisions, as governance and management constitute either a stimuli or a barrier to such auditing mechanisms. Furthermore, investors/stockholders and employees make constitute an additional hidden obstacle to SA-implementation in SBUs and at the project realm, especially due to their lack of awareness regarding of the importance of its enforceability.

Bringing here some clarity to such SA discussion, a strategy auditing is fragile when the self-imposed goals for the company are unclear. Thus, the first thing to do, recalling Wheelen and Hunger´s (1987) idea of a strategy on action, covering the strategic management process, is to define clear sets of goals, not in head but written down to paper format, to be shared with the whole organizational-stakeholders and other product-market stakeholders (aka, suppliers) directly participating at any phase of the value chain/s.

Hence this section deals which the importance of goals in performance diagnosis of a strategy. It addresses five (5) fundamental goal-related aspects, essential for the comprehension of this theme:

(i) Hierarchy of goals
(ii) Modes of goal-setting
(iii) Types of goals
(iv) Morphology of goals
(v) Approaches for measuring goals

About these 5 themes aforementioned, you are recommended to taken them into account whenever initiating a new project in business environment analysis. Undoubtedly, the accuracy of objectives is a strategic starting point that must be taken seriously as it regulates the rest of the phases of the BEAP and conditions so the future success of the firm, whether being your employer, client or any other institution you´re collaborating with.

Goals have various levels of importance. This is called the *hierarchy*. Three (3) levels of hierarchy classify organizational goals as *high*, *medium* (or *intermediate*) and *low*-level goals (see figure below).

Table 2. Hierarchy of goals

Tier	Identification	Description
High	Strategic Goals (SGs)	Strategic planning of the whole organization, divisions or SBUs
Intermediate	Operational Goals (OGs)	Fitting the scope of strategic planning and fitting the SGs, OGs are planned expectations, defined at departmental level (for the whole department; and its programs and projects)
Low	Activity Goals (AGs)	Individual or teamwork goals related to one´s function and the execution of tasks

Source: Boddy (2017)

High level goals, commonly designated as *Strategic Goals* (SGs) correspond to the sphere of goals that identify the desired-to-reach overall accomplishments in a certain moment in time for a division, an SBU, a program, a project, or a subsidiary. The medium/intermediate goals are established within the framework of the directive planning of each the department. Being department-specific, these OGs derive, firstly, from the guidelines set in the corporate planning (and underlying SGs) and secondly from the directive planning established by the middle manager/s assigned to such functional areas to explore own resources for the accomplishment of those SGs but also their portfolio-related agendas[1]. The lower-level goals or activity goals (AGs) have a shorter time horizon since they are goals related to the execution of specific tasks that are part of an operational process, or workflow (e.g. a job/service shop; batch; or task belonging to the mass or continuous production or service) typically with a pre-established delivery lead time (whether as an engineer-to-order; make-to-order/stock; assembly-to-order).

This logic of hierarchy unravels at first multiple degrees of importance, and consequently, an inter-dependence of across tiers as the lowest-tier goals, the activity goals (AGs) are dependent on the direct upper tier (operational goals), and in turn, this latter ones are formed depending on the distribution of operational responsibilities outlined by senior managers while conducting back and forth corporate planning discussions with middle and line managers across functional areas to finalize the strategic goals at a certain moment in time. One can say, that SGs unfold in a set of GCs and the latter give rise to the organization work/ distribution of tasks by individuals and teams (AGs) as represented below.

Figure 1. Cascading of Strategic Goals (SGs)

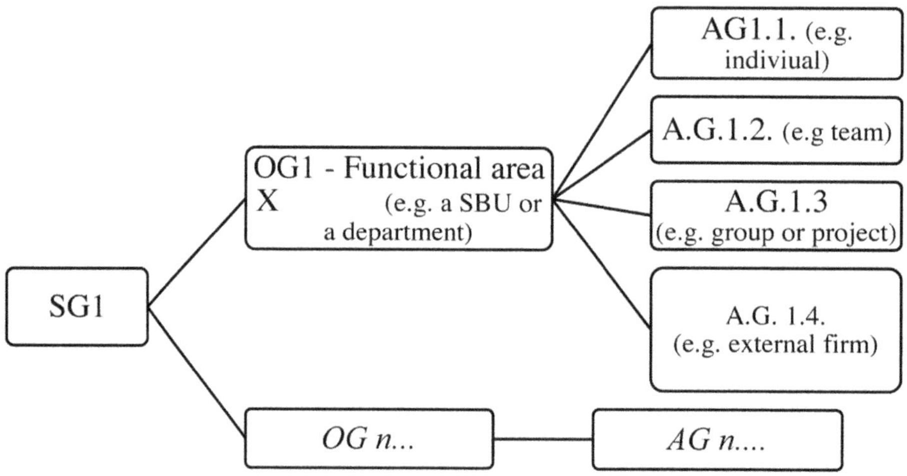

This figure expresses the association *SGs, OGs, AGs* uncovering tough two fundamental ideas. First, goals are set on a top-down manner, from higher-tiers goal´s accomplishment being dependent on lower-tier´s accomplishments altogether,

SGs →OGs → AGs

(Forward and Downward-oriented strategic design process)

However, this forward and downward-oriented strategic design process, is though dependent on the success of its reversion. I mean, individual SGs depend also on the accomplishment, altogether, of lower-tiers goals. Hence, this is also a backward process, identical to a mathematical commutative function, in which, the execution of primary activities determines the results is interdependent of cumulatively efforts across areas (and often, involving others partners)

SGs ← OGs ← AGs

(Backward and Upward-oriented Operational Execution process)

The interaction of these two processes (of Strategic Design and Operational Execution) being "cumulatively indispensable" for goal´s achievement is the reasons why the nodes across SGs/OGs/AGs in the figure above (Figure 1) are not represented with arrows indicating the direction.

There is embedded in such system a forward (and downward)-thinking logic an underlying assumption that currently set strategic goals but shared across units and fulfilled in the future, if and only if (iff):

a) With the continuity in activity of the firm
b) Goals are communicated to everyone
c) Areas ought to positively contribute to such plan

Thus, "living the company´s strategy" seems a motto, but actually represents a joint-strive for the success and wealth of the firm, expressed mathematically (see the explanation at the footnote).

$\exists$ SG(x) $\Leftrightarrow$ $\forall$ SG(x)[2]

The bottom line is, setting SGs is an essential task! Without these, one is sailing without a route, and worse, without any destiny. As the famous quote goes "*Though we cannot control the wind, we can adjust our sails so as to profit by it*". This is in short an organizational imperative in the modern world which not just managers ought to abide to, but all organizational-stakeholders. Making an analogy with a hypothetical character of a fictional movie, let us say the "worthless student" (if that exists), as the young man or lady taking a new course at their university, randomly chosen but without having any purpose for attending it; and having no thoughts about how this might upskill him/herself, and even is not interested in gaining any ECTS´s nor to conclude any educational program on that theme. *Does it sound odd…*? (it definitely does!); *Does it make sense …?* Surely not! The same can happen in an organization if professionals are unprepared (and an uninstructed) across entire divisions or business units; hence, totally left to their mercy (or luck).

Your project/BEAP would look like this also (left to drift or totally lost – relying on luck) if those goals were not set, and communicated clearly across all team-members. As one of the components of the *Planning View*, "setting goals" is therefore a task (within the realm of Strategic Planning) of an enormous responsibility. It should be something that you (not only) *plan*, but *learn* from such process, while is *negotiate*d along the way.

Indeed, organizations are expected to plan. *Plan…. What?* Organizations, Plan their destiny! As if a person were (e.g. planning your next trip, studies, marriage, or the future of your children). Those plans constitute the baseline for envisioning one bright future (for them and others in the civil community they are represented on). Setting goals constitutes so a landmark on decision-making as to the setting of milestones for approximating the present (what the company is) and the envisioned future (what it wants to be). The starting point of planning is a rational-expected corporate discussion, based in facts and incorporating new knowledge (*Learning View*) in which the formulation of these goals accounts not solely the corporate willingness "to be" (aka, vision; mission; values), but also the achievements (that one "knows about") and the collective intelligence grasped until the date. These two views are still mediated by the process of debating and bargaining (i.e. Political View) among the board of directors and the top management team members that a final concertation of ideas and opinions leads to a commitment of goals and objectives.

Setting goals obeys henceforth to this joint action of the three (3) views:

- Rational planning (Planning View)
- Updateness of (Learning View):
    - the organizational re-learning – the overall set of managerial knowledge, skills and abilities (KSAs) to be utilized in the goal´s setting process
    - the business environment´s dynamics, as inputs, and inherent built intelligence

- Equilibrium of reason and emotions:
  - ideas Vs. opinions;
  - conflict of individual/group interests Vs. company interests;
  - bargaining skills Vs. decisional powers and hubris of each manager (Political View)

Thus, planning (as herein, as the first step, setting goals) is not a fully rational exercise, neither a fully emotional. Reason and (conflictual) interests, hubris and personalities are balanced in a formula that balances them all.

From the recognition of a hierarchy of goals (that ranks them by importance), and the existence of an *ex ante* configuration (i.e. the whole goal setting process), assumed to be fuzzy and semi-rational combining three divergent (though non-incompatible) views of strategy (plan; learning and politics), let us know dig into the typology of those goals and how one can set them.

As an US Army´s military leader (*General Douglas Hastings Macarthur*) once said in the 1950s, "*rules are made to be broken…*". In the modern business world this can be interpreted on the employee-side as, "I won´t have to abide to these goals". Is this a total non-sense? Not really! *Are you surprised?.*

Rules, are disclosed instructions for a particular time and context, which serve a specific purpose (a goal x, y or z). Thus rules are wrapped up in a set of conditions guiding one stakeholder toward such end (the goal). Although goals are commonly associated to "*something to achieve*", in many cases they are established as a mechanism of:

(i) Exposure of the corporation (i.e. *what we want you to think, about what we think or do*);
(ii) Gaining positional externalities (typically the use of tactical tools for marking the territory with competitive entrenchment moves, aiming to influence and deter others firms´ maneuvers)

From the above, one can certainly discern that organizational-stakeholders work exclusively with the goals that concern them, the ones designed for own internal consumption/utilization. The others (goals) targeting external product-market and/or capital stakeholders or even regional/national authorities are, regardless of, the target group, just paving the way for the internal-administered goals to be successfully realized. Hence, one can separate two groups of goals, designated as s*tated goals* and *real goals* (Boddy, 2017). Basically, stated goals are externally-oriented while real-goals are the internal ones that one firm is actually pursuing.

Nonetheless, while setting goals for a BEAP, as any other project or business unit, one wants to consider a triad of determinants:

(i) Volume (How many goals …?)
(ii) Duration *(For how long …?)*
(iii) Nature (What is/are to be specified …?)

The *volume* entails the number of generally established aims that fulfill (altogether) the vision of the project-owner or senior manager to pursue such project or such aspiration for a business unit. *So, how many goals are enough?* The paradoxical decision about quantity is a singular versus plural one. Is the company better of focusing on one "super-goal", or on the contrary pursuing several al the same time (*multiple-goal´s* plans). *Single-goal* plans are what two renowned strategy-thinkers (*David Norton* and *Robert Kaplan*) designated of a *Strategic Destiny Statement* (SDS), as a milestone that requires both strategic themes (STs) and strategic goals (SGs). They wrapped these ideas in a famous management framework, the *Balance Scorecard (BSC)*, developed during the two decades of the 20th century.

The orientation towards single or multiple goals planning structures, is arguable dependent on the cognitive ability of the decision-makers (typically the senior managers) to make emerge the full spectre of attainable aims they are ambitioning. Moreover, it depends on the gap between internal/external contexts and these strategic ambitions. The wider the gap, the more number of goals (if feasible) one is likely to embrace.

The *duration* refers to the length of each goal (e.g. an annual business revenue set for the year 2023; or the integration of a merger deal in a time horizon of 5 years). Here the one-year of five-year rounds are the unit of maximum duration. Thus, the goal is to be met until that time (deadline). Depending on the hierarchy of the goal and the size of the strategic cycles in a focal firm, goals can vary significantly in its duration, even among firms in the same industry. Typically business goals are set on an annual/biannual basis being and corporate goals every 3 to 5 years. The latter ones involving larger matters, such as, the mission/portfolio/investment reviews are termed as *long-term goals* as they last for over a year. However, the adoption of these conceptions vary significantly. Thus, if you are a Management Consultant, or Strategy Advisor working for a partnering company, a good piece of advice is, to glue yourself to their metrics for avoiding communication entropy (e.g. noise or dissonance) which wear out and mine any provider-customer relation.

Regarding the *nature*, we saw above goals are differently established as to the nature, varying on their target, as internally-oriented and externally-oriented. The external ones, less concern is placed on their administration, as they are not the ones one works at work. They are so, more simplistic built as a rule of thumb, and do not company accompanied with metrics for an on-going monitoring of their progression. These are your *stated-goals*; thus, usually less relevant in the strategy design and consequently with incipient influence on organizational-stakeholders, as they do not directly affect their professional lives.

Conversely, the internally-oriented goals, the *real-goals* have a more sophisticated composition. For instance, are connected to business milestones or super-goals, the strategic destiny statement (SDS) as discussed above, in many cases, they are grouped into types of accomplishments, i.e. strategic themes (ST). All together these themes explain the aspired destiny:

$$SDS_{(x)} = \sum(ST_1 + ST_2 + ST_3 + ST_n\ldots)$$

Moreover, *real-goals* being the ones to work with inside the firm, they are often transformed into more clearly assessable ones (i.e. *objectives*), which come supplemented with qualitative or quantitative attributions as,

- *targets* (or standards)
- *limits* of accepted deviation
- performance *indicators*
- *scales* of observation (of progression or results)

Hence, real and stated goals hold substantive differences in their morphological composition. Real-goals are more specific while stated-goals provide a general impression of what the goal is about.

Nonetheless, stated-goals are market-oriented (mostly targeting the media, investors and other product-market stakeholders). They are those prominent in company publications and websites. Thus, the message conveyed is, either a simplified version of intended goals (i.e. further explored internally in real-goals), or unlike that, in many occasions, a statement with a subversive meaning and hidden entrenched agenda surrounding competitiveness issues, that is (purposively) illusive of the corporate´s real-goals; the strategic intentions; assets; and the preparedness-to-business.

However, as we do not wish to deceive the reader with stated-goals, on the contrary, I provide here three (3) examples of hypothetical real-goals applicable on the context of a business environment analysis project (BEAP):

(i) to map the national risk/s of pervasiveness[3] in the municipalities' administration of public tenders in country X by Dec 31st 2023;
(ii) to determine the extent (amount of losses) of observed violations (number of lawsuits) on Intelectual propriety rights (IPR) between 2012 and 2022 in country X and industry Y
(iii) to make an inventory of all natural risks and/or disasters in region X between 1920-2020 with material hazards

Of course, those are just examples of a myriad of goals that your company/client/s may be asking to work on in the future. *Have you noticed any specificities on these goals?* I would invite to look again to measurement aspects, as these goals contain incorporated variables to be instrumentalized as *observation indicators*. For example, the variable number – "…of lawsuits"; the material value – "amount of losses"; or time horizon – year "2023". I would suggest you to take some time to reflect upon these examples, break them into workable parts and compared with your own experience (if applicable).

Returning to the real/state-goals distinction, one can assert that stated-goals whenever reflect literally an intended goal, they can be seen as *directional goals*. Directional goals are a sub-set (of real-goals) aiming to tell others "the way to go". As the American musician *Jimmy Ray Dean* stated for the Reader Digest once: "*I can't change the direction of the wind, but I can adjust my sails to always reach my destination*". The opposing sub-set of the first are the illusory goals, aiming to deviate the attention from the real-goals or confuse their meaning or inner properties. Real-goals are a more detailed version of directional goals, accounting informational relevant aspects to support their accomplishment, therefore, they are consider to be *specific goals. How different are they directional and specific goals?* Look at the two pictures taken from Google and try to figure out what is directional and what is specific.

I brought these two images, as both represent an intention to move to the right, but in disclosed in a very different way. This symbolizes the differences to encounter between stated and real-goals. The first image, more generalist (such as stated-goal) is merely directional, indicates the way, or the desired output (i.e. where to go; something indicated by the shape and disposition of the arrow doing the job of a road sign). On the other hand, the picture in the Exhibit 93 shows some also sort of direction, because contains a map guiding toward the right hand-side. However this map has more information and so is more detailed. It is an example of an itinerary from one of our campus of *Niels Brock Copenhagen Business College* (i.e. located at Bispetorvet) to the Queen´s palace (Amalienborg). It contains several pieces of information, such as roads´ names, a suggested trajectory, traffic info, alternative routes and other points of interest (just to point the major things). This is how your real-goals look like to others when presented to your employees/clients. They provide information (not observed in Figure 2) which serve as guiding tool for proceeding with operational plans and activities, regardless of the amount and corporate communication about them and the ability of the messenger to explain them. The table below highlights the major differences between stated and real-goals.

Figure 2. Directional Goals

Figure 3. Specific Goals

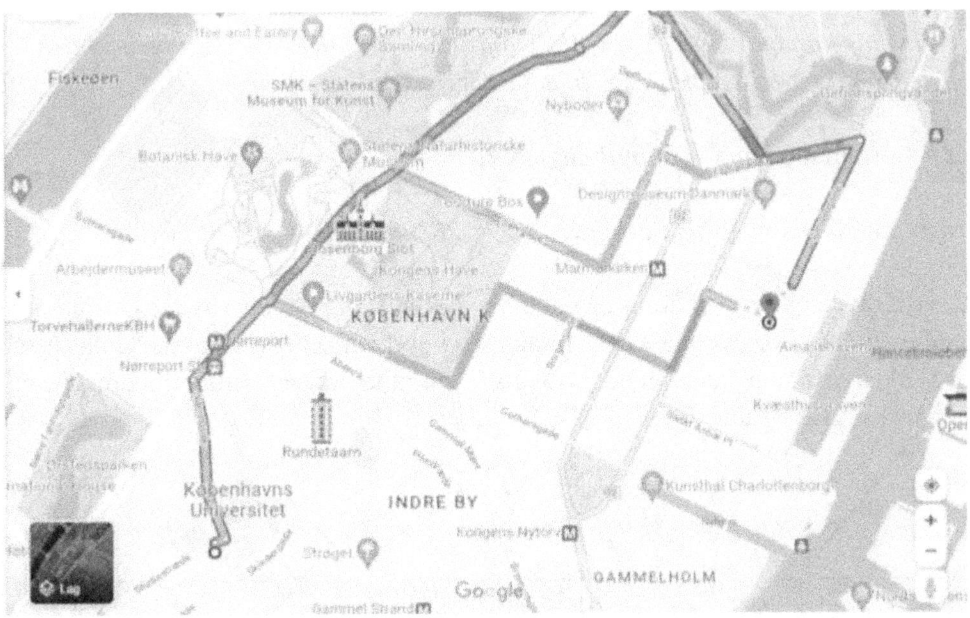

Below are presented three (3) other examples of these goals, not only circumscribed to the BEAP or the project realm, but covering all corporate planning with an application to three (3) distinctive sub-categories of real-goals (business, finance and sustainability goals):

Table 3. Differences between stated and real-goals

Dimensions	Characteristics of Stated Goals	Real Goals
Morphology	Directional (vague or incomplete in composition)	Specific (with details and data about its composition)
Communication-target/s	External	Internal
Management	Irrelevant for measurement	Reflect the manager´s priorities Enables measurement
Measurement	Hard-to-assess (as does not lead to success/ failure)	Better- to-assess (lead to success/failure[4]
Importance	Less attention given to them	More attention given to them
Typology	Not SMART[5] (Non-effective)	SMART (Effective)

Source: Own elaboration

Example 1 (formulation of a *business goal*):

"…. To reduce our customer churn (CC) ratio in SBU_1 *in 2023 to 0,01 of the total current portfolio of institutional[6] customer-base"*

Example 2 (formulation of a *financial goal*):

"To reach an average annual revenue of 12M Danish Krone (DKK) in a newly established subsidiary in the first 3 years of operation (2023-25) in a Southern Asia"

Example 3 (formulation of a *sustainability goal*):

"To implement a waste management program by Q4-2022 applicable to all facilities"

Regardless of the longevity (or duration) of the real-goals, these three (3) sub-sets are intertwined in the planning function to express one´s determination over diverse types of aims. Goals established in a sub-category hold a common denominator with goals with the same classification, regarding their *focus* and general *purpose* (*vide* Table 39).

Table 4. Sub-categories of Real-goals: Focus and Purpose

Sub-category	Focus on…	Purpose
Business goal/s	→ Corporate Portfolio	Expectations towards business operations´ achievements
Financial goal/s	→ Corporate Wealth	Aimed financial outputs (Corporate wealth)
Sustainability goal/s	→ Corporate Citizenship	Environment and social responsibilities and aspirations

Source: Own elaboration

Looking at these 3 categories of real-goals, one unavoidable issue across typologies is the quest for *effectiveness. What does constitute an effective goal?* Effective goal setting is something that entails the fashioning in such a way that the goal becomes a drive of/for action. As a motto, *Goals should drive Action!*

The effectiveness of goals, as to the assertiveness of the design, does not exclude the managerial responsibility to communicate and control its execution. However, caution and wise reflection about its nature is an initial starting point for the compliance of results with objectives. Moreover, caution it implies taking into consideration the mutual influence of one goal on another.

Below you can observe the different formulation of one of the goals exemplified in previous pages of this chapter, regarding the objectives set for the internationalization process of a firm to an Asian market. The design of the same goals varies (being a stated and real goal) according to the target audience.

Example 4 - Formulation1:

$SG_{(x)}$: *"Expand to the emergent markets of Southern Asia"*
(Stated-goal format)

Example 4 – Formulation 2:

$SG_{(x')}$:: *"Establish a Sales Representative in New Delhi (India) by the end of 2022"*
(Real-goal format)

Without any doubt the SGx´ is the one who drives the action, containing pieces of relevant information to which employees ought to pay attention to, as they are a guidance for future endeavors. For instance, the information about how (to internationalization). It indicates a preference for the use of a specific market entry-mode (MEM), i.e. nomination of local representativeness via a third party; and furthermore indicate the country region and the time horizon. Underlying to all this information is, for senior and middle managers, the understanding of "sales representative" as being goal that is anchored on risk-control and expectancy of near-future inputs of information to decide upon the future of possible investments and long-term market commitments of increased risk or on an opposing direction, eventual withholding of resources or retrieving for the market.

Again, an unavoidable question surrounding the *effectiveness of the goal setting process* is, *How do set effective goals?* A couple of pages above, in Exhibit 94 – *Differences between stated and real-goals* I present in the last row of that table to the "typology" of real-goals, whether SMART or not and between parentheses you have your answer… the S.M.A.R.T goals correspond to the effective ones.

Such nomenclature "SMART" introduced in the Management Sciences lexicon by *George Doran, Arthur Miller* and *James Cunningham* stands for an acronym, indicating the five (5) crucial aspects to consider when fashioning the individual design of a goal. It has to be:

Specific and…*Measurable* and…*Attainable* and…*Realistic*… and *Time-bound*!

So,

Effective goals = Sum (S + M + A + R + T)

This means, there is no effectiveness if one´s does not transform a directional strategic goal into an exploitable strategic objective (SO). Thus, strategic goals lead to strategic objectives,

SG => SO

And, effective strategic goals (ESG) are equivalent to …

ESGs ⇔ SMART Objectives

In this book we expand the SMART. We argue effective goals are better shield with "*SMARRRT*", goals that are cumulatively: specific; measurable; attainable; relevant; realistic; rewarded; and, time-bound!

Depicting the SMARRRT goals, a first attribute is their expectation to be *specific.* They means abandon the vagueness of narrative fallacies with unclear formulations. Instead be clear and accurate as to the content, identifying what it contains. The set of specific *variables (n)* in use their accompanying quantitative or qualitative *targets*, as units of measurement of the desired level to be reached on such variables.

Example 5 (Specified goal):

A company elected as an *SG, to act upon* "efficient waste management". The SO is "*to recycle 80% of production waste by the end of 2020*" This SO on waste management transforms an SG into a SO *[SG ~ SO]* and it becomes specific (alias, pointing to action) when it defines a working variable (*recycling* – of production waste) and defines a target of recycling of minimum 4/5 (or 80% of all waste) and even set a time horizon (i.e. the end of the year 2020).

A goal is *measurable* when it denotes specification. It specifies a combination of variable and target and the latter is also easy-to-measure quantitatively or qualitatively. It is a *S+M.* goal:

Example 6 (SM goal):

A Danish software development company is internationalizing. One of its strategic goals is "*opening of a sales office in South Asia by the end of the year". Their objective is "to be in fully operative in sales in New Delhi by the end of Q4-2022"*

They established as a strategic objective´s variable i.e. "market entry" and associated it with a deadline. Hence, the achievement of a qualitative goal, is typically as a *binary measurement* of a "yes" (observed action) or "no"(not-observed) that makes it a clearly objective. It is not a quantitative one, as you cannot claim that the company is, for instance, 60% operating in this market. Either is or is not their fully established in India. However, in case you would like to broaden the binary measurement to a more descriptive measure of the reality, the use of rating or ranking methods are strongly advised, as exemplified below.

Example 7 (qualitative scale for example 6´s SG):

1. Not achieved (0%) (i.e. Inaction)
2. Break-off (initiation) (<50%) (i.e. Action with Failure)
3. Partially achieved (≥ 50%) (i.e. Action with partial success)
4. Totally achieved (100%) (i.e. Action and total success)

This example of a four (4) points of an itemized rating scale for application with direct observation over qualitative goals, has the virtue of exploring the extent of non-achievements. One (1) indicates inaction, while 2 and 3 indicates some extent of action, despite having not fully succeeded. One (1) denotes that no initiatives were taken ("not achieved) so indicating a total inaction, while Two (2) indicates action combined with failure (e.g. difficulties in hiring local resources – such as a law firm; or still stuck in paperwork formalities for establishing the firm or celebrating initial contracts; or obtaining initial licensing approvals). Sometimes the duet (variable + target) as a performance indicator, or any other performance indicator replacing the first is not fully achieved due to some technicalities or unexpected constraints that does not stain the amount of effort and so the performance of the firm.

Another idea to introduce here, as briefly mentioned in the previous chapter is, *variable*, *target* and *indicator* are three (3) separate but complementary constructs. Imagine a company which needs to increase the extent of satisfaction of their customer-base and so established as a SG "*enhance the purchasing experience*" or "*increase the overall satisfaction with our products*". As you know, a SG to be effective needs to be SMART (thus, become a SO). However, I might have a goal with a specific focus (variable) with one or several other specifications (indicators) that are measured cumulatively to such variable.

Example 8 – Financial goal (variable and indicators):

Company X wants to "*improve financial results*" (SG_x) and set as a SO "*increase of annual growth rate in sales by 5% a year until 2025*"

Here the variable "revenue" may be measured by different *performance indicators (PIs)* as, margin-related PIs (as "gross margin"; "operative margin"; or" net margin" or other ratio variables, as "return on sales"; "return on investment", and so forth. This is a primary quantitative financial measure. However, let us now iterate the example 9 to business goals.

Example 9 – Business goal (variable and indicators):

The same company X (as in example 8), recognizes a direct relation between customer satisfaction of their product portfolio and the fluctuation of their revenue and operational inflows of cash. The company conducted an internal study involving two areas (marketing and finance) with the direct supervision of their directors. The study was conclusive on a strong correlation between those variables). Managers decided to set another goal

SG_y: "*increase overall product satisfaction*" and transformed this SG into a SO_y: "*increase overall product satisfaction by 20 percentage points". To achieve this* $SO_{y,}$ defined several PIs.

These following three (3) PIs were considered the most essential ones, and so classified as key performance indicators (KPIs). Without their accomplishment (KPIs), the goal (SGy) becomes comprised and so will be likely unmet. Their operational plans and activities accounted these SG/SO and KPIs. The established KPIs were, "complaints number" (PI_1); "customer churn ratio" (PI_2); and "degree of customer involvement"; (PI_3). These KPIs were set with the following correspondence to linear targets per KPI_n:

(i) KPI 1 (complaints): with a target of, reduction by 80%
(ii) KPI 2 (churn): with a target of, total elimination (100%)
(iii) KPI 3 (involvement): with a target of, interaction[7] increased by 400%

A third aspect of SMARRRT goals, hence is their attainability. To be *attainable*, the design of the type of goals (and the associated targets to them) need to be compelling, and trigger further action. Goals are deemed to incorporate two (2) fundamental attributes to be successful: to be "challenging" and "realistic". As to the first (challenging), is crucial to understand the borderlines. Bt "borderline" the aspects of the goal that makes become either a "challenge" or simply an "acceptance" or "acquiescence", in which, employees agree to abide to them. In the latter case, the acceptance is followed by a sentiment of neutrality (or occasionally, near-disagreement) as their trivial, uninteresting or unworthy of investment upon. Moreover, a negative perception of a goal may escalate from acquiescence to confrontation (or direct opposition), in which, "acceptance" and "contendment" is replaced by resistance and further defiance. Here, one may count with initial attempts to replace them subsequent boycotting of results.

On the positive perception side, the variance from acquiescence to challenging has a lower positive perception (i.e. "satisfaction") and upper-level ("inspiration").

Figure 4. Goal´s perception and attainment risks (using a Stapel scale)

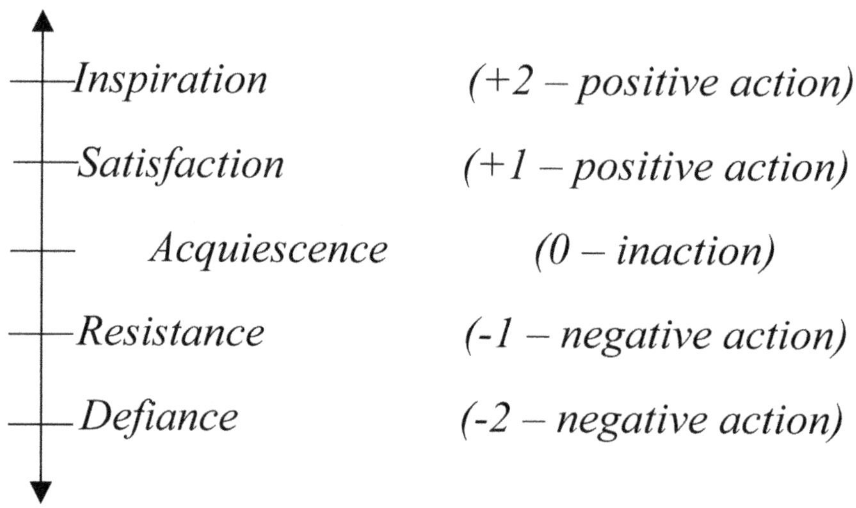

Indeed, both negative (against) and positive (in favor) sentiment towards a goal, have in their origin motivational and ethical causes preceding the individual perception (opinions or feelings), and determine the individual formal position about it. Surveying those opinions/feelings and negotiating goals across divisions, business units, departments, programs, projects and partners is an essential preliminary step one ought not to ignore. Under such logic, goals are outputs of the intertwining of the three strategic views (planning; learning; negotiation).

Another aspect to account as to the attainability issue is, the interdependence of first attribute (challenging) with the last (realistic). A wise, hence *realistic*, formulation of strategic goals is shaped by the Political View. Managers take into serious account the motivations and feelings about their initial propositions, particularly any *divergent views*, and further considerations about *alternatives* and are open to inherent *bargaining* process. Yet, before communicating any draft of goals across functional areas, or even prepare to negotiate them individually or collectively, managers are summoned to revise their own pool of initial goals and subsequently eliminate goals or targets that are over-optimistic of the reality, over-estimating the performance or unreasonably difficult to achieve. On the contrary, any easy-to-achieve ones ought also to be refined.

The conscientious establishment of fair and motivational (or inspirational) goals constitute the basis for realistic and attainable SGs; moreover they have spill-overs to the rewarding of the action. Here, the notion of *reward* is understood as, the recognition of merit as to the direct or indirect actions taken leading to the accomplishment of the goal, and the subsequent compensation of the effort and the (partial or total) contribution for its attainment. Compensations are often delivered in a proportion to the extent of attainment (partial of total achievement of the goal (*vide* example 7 above) and distributed per the involved areas and individual-achievers. Rewarding follows Jeremy Bentham´s *carrot and stick approach* of motivation. The Benthamite´ s theory explores the principles of reinforcement of the behaviour, in which, the old story of the donkey is used as an analogy to illustrate that putting a carrot in front of the animal and jab him with a stick from behind is the best way of moving him forward. Such approach is brought right in the strategy realm to introduce the notion of compensation associated with merit. Typically, in the form of an extrinsic pecuniary recompense (e.g. a bonus; a share of net-profits, or firm stocks), rewards are designed beforehand with the rest of planning units (e.g. variables, targets, indicators or limits) per each SG.

The notion of *time-bounded* goal defines the time over which it is expected to be achieved. Otherwise, the non-limitation of the time of achievement is fuzzy and leaves to the employee own interpretation. Here, some would tend to believe in one of two realities. Firstly, the absence of time-limit indicates that the goal has unlimited time *(+∞)*, which opens another doubt as to the likelihood of being of undetermined continuity (or unknown length). Secondly, is the assumption that the goal is yearly set or business cycle-bounded. In the majority of the cases goals are set for a year or business cycle. However, the clarification of whether is one or the other is essential, as companies establish many times non-yearly business cycles with accompanying goals.

In the next and final section, is explored the subsequent aspects of goal-setting, as the pure strategic controls function, from the approaches to measurement, passing through the widget counting and analysis of results to performance evaluation and subsequent steps of strategic action that follow the diagnosis of performance.

WIDGET COUNTING AND DIAGNOSIS OF PERFORMANCE

As briefly referred in the last paragraph of the previous section 10.2., the *strategic control* of a project or business goals is a process that begins at a second phase, after the collection of initial data and setting the goals. So, let us start working with controls and immerse into the widget counting of the project´s outputs of progression or results.

Hypothetically, you have a BEAP in hands that is a totally new project. As denominated in PM, this is first-timer type of project. Imagine you were requested to analyze, at your boss or client´ request, the national political risks of pervasiveness due to corruption in public tenders in a given country (e.g. Chile, in South America). Let us say, that the company detected an opportunity indirectly conveyed through a business partner in Spain, to establish themselves in another country in a partner of the partner. Thus, you are confronted to, what *Igor Ansoff* termed as a "market penetration" strategic intention (such as, is presented in the product/market matrix in section 3.2.).

Let us imagine now, your company has the aspiration to enter the market (alias, an intended strategic goal); however, the setting of such goal is dependent on *ex ante* market-research which may bring the decisional inputs to determine whether to move in or not.

Your company is an IT security-related expert in cybersecurity, namely on protection and shielding services for public institutions. In your portfolio you have services as deception technology, market surveillance, threat monitoring, security analytics, and so forth). However, a quick scan of market data raises issues of financial losses by other multinationals operating in Chile with annulment of contracts, bending of rules/requirements established in public tender specifications. This is a confusing scenario, and you are now mandated to run an analysis within the next 180 days and deliver a final report of the BEAP. Certainly, you will need to revise the most essential ideas of BEAP conception presented in section 4.5; 5.1 and 5.2 of this book. Surely, we won´t be rolling out here any data, fake or real, about the number possible lawsuits of MNCs in Chile´s courts, neither bring any ratios from the corruption-related indexes neither visit any commercial data from some of the sources and apparatus referred to in sections 5.3., 5.4 or 5.6. The most important to message to retain so far is, no decisions are taken without a fairly secure decisional ground. Hence, data is the baseline for organizational planning. Check below the five (5) elements of planning.

On the center of the diagram you have *gathering information. Why is information central (and to what)....?* A question alike has a straightforward answer. The starting point of your planning is always data! This happens in this fictional BEAP project (as exemplified above) but also in any other type of projects (as a "*first-timer*"; an "*as ...but*" or a "*painting by numbers*"), as addressed in chapter 7. This is an execution activity (gathering and analyzing data – political risk/cases of corruption in public tenders in Chile), which comes before a design activity (setting a goal – deciding about a market-entry opportunity and the specifics of the goal). These three types of activities (*design; execution*; and, *controlling*) are intertwined, also co-occurring, in many cases, and revisited as the intended and realized plans are explored, back and forth, in multiple of set activities of these three categories. Thus, gathering information is key and it kick-starts (and enhances) the remaining planning elements.

Figure 5. Five generic elements in planning (view)

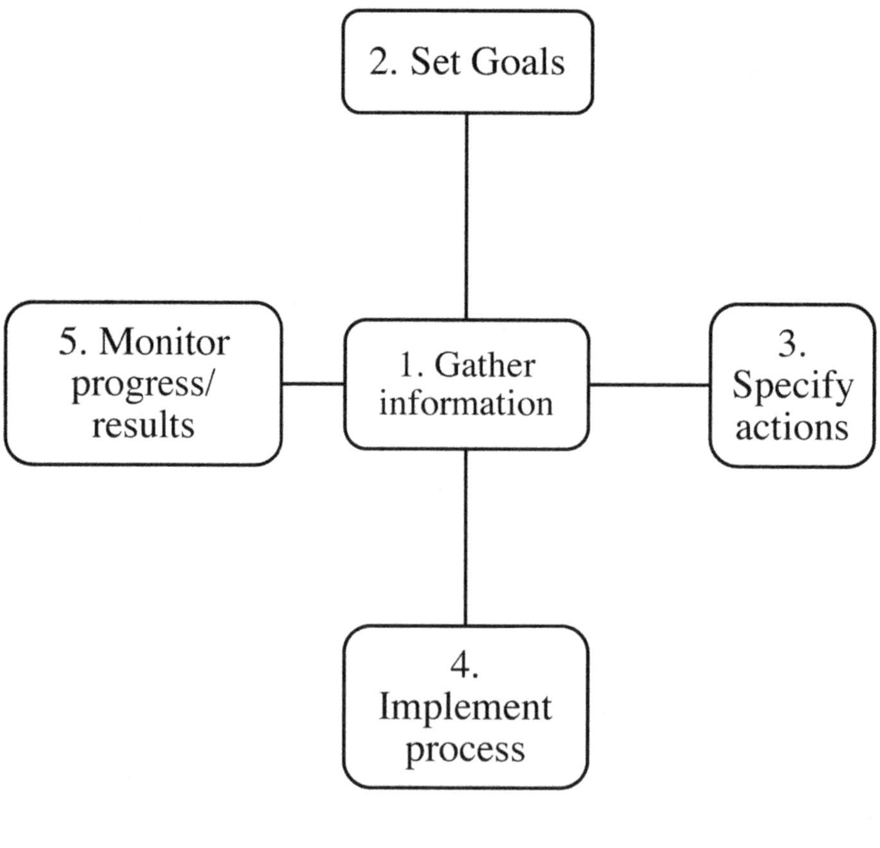

On the other hand, execution is a pivotal embedded element of planning observed across all the remaining four (4) elements. Planning is not a reality until taken to practice. In short, someone/somehow has to be executing. Hence, strategic execution is a bridge between design and control (of the design), as companies execute a design and execute controls´ activities.

The strategic control is the final part one of the planning elements. It requires the intended plans to become realized (as "official" strategies), and subsequently cascaded into operative goals (i.e. element 3, *Specific actions*) and operational activities (*4. Implementing processes*), so that strategic controlling can start its work. This section is about the final part of a plan, the controlling.

Basically, once your goals are set and approved (such as the activities needed to their accomplishment) it begins the epic work of measuring them. Controlling these goals entails a seminal choice/decision: *what do you want to measure?* Do you want to monitor the indicators that express the progression of the goal? Thus, *are you looking for applying measurement procedure focused on your on-going temporary results?* Or, *would you like to verify the final results (i.e. targets per indicator and overall goals of your last year or business cycle which already ended?*

These two ways of measurement are not different in style. They hold a different purpose and utility. *Monitoring*, is a process of following on-going activities and accompanying their performance and evolution. It is oriented towards (corrective) action upon the progression of short-termed measurement.

The latter, *verification* is a confirmatory way of looking at final results, which you cannot amend for depicting the specifics of the results, extrapolate lessons and take-aways, and prepare future plans. However final results cannot be edited. For instance, any sales in 2023 cannot be placed in the fiscal year 2020. The tax year of 2020 is closed and my invoicing has to be placed in the same year 2023. This mean looking at the past, means looking at confirmed/final results for apprenticeship in learning for the future; however, does not allow any corrective actions (as I am not in 2020) to implement additional strategic maneuvers to lift my sales up.

Consequently, one of the most elementary decisions to make with looking into data is, what do I want to measure, the performance of my present operation of the results of my past operations? Here, you have two (2) main measurement approaches. The *leading goal´s measurement* and *lagging goals´ measurement*. The table below makes a summarized distinction of both methods.

Table 5. Strategic performance: Leading versus lagging measurement methods

Measurement	Horizon	Observation	Activity	Logic	Focus
Lead measurement method	Present Future	On-Going and Forward-looking	Monitoring	Predictive analysis	Alignment and Correction of deviation/s Measuring *Progression* Forecasting; Generating Options Scenario-planning and analysis
Lagging measurement method	Past	Backward-looking	Assessment	Prescriptive analysis	Compliance Evolution/Continuity Results

Source: Own elaboration

First of all, the terminology leading and lagging can be a bit opaque. Leading measurement is applicable to an analysis horizon of present and future goals, while lagging measurement the opposite, it looks at the past. Considering this terminology used in SPM particularly used in the latter case ("lagging goals´ measurement"), I would recommend to avoid any interpretation of meaning based on the etymology of the word "lag". This method (measuring lagging goals) does not correspond to the measurement of goals with underperformed results. Instead, it refers to goals that were set in the past and with a timely horizon also in the past; hence, goals already expired. Thus, whenever you use such technique you need to be aware that the measurement, and further actions won´t alter the final result. Any eventual corrections or improvements can only be made to an equivalent goal in the present or future, identical to one in the past.

Leading goal´s measurement is controlling activity undertaken on an ongoing basis. Thus, is focused on the measurement of current goals. In this method you are monitoring the progression, as you wish to ensure compliance of the progression outputs with the desired results (i.e. the target/s) in the present and future. Hence, they are predictive of future outcomes/results and have room for strategic actions to correct gaps, improve results and modify operational approaches to the accomplishment of goal (e.g. the redistribution of the center/s of responsibility per department and person; the modification of scope of these tasks; reconsidering the material requirements - or even the timeline).

Another aspect to account in performance measurement is the typology of the real-goals, which my hold a qualitative target. In this case the *qualitative measurement* is centered on units of behaviour, as presented in example 7, in section 10.2., being on its quantification dependent on: (i) the *observation* of the behavior; (ii) the creation of a qualitative *scale* for measuring the outcomes of a potential behavioral pattern, as specifiable actions though non-quantifiable in their iterations. Such type of measurement emphasizes the development of ability/ies (e.g. adapt to change; collaboration, communication; or, learning).

The quantitative measurement is made by the use of a metric which often combines:

(i) A measurement unit, self-defined, as the *performance indicator (PI)* or key-performance indicator (KPI) for the core PIs of seminal importance which influence the whole sequence of other PIs and their non-fulfillment compromises a goal.
(ii) A *target* associated with the PIs/KPIs
(iii) Use *of widget counting* as a core methodological procedure

The combination of these three elements allows one firm to grasp the direct measurement of its success or failure at a certain moment in time. For someone not so accustomed in dealing with SPM metrics in projects or business units, I would like to emphasize the averaging targets, by breaking it down the, for example, annual SG into 12 equal parts, one per month, does not work in many cases,

$$SG =(x / 12)$$

This is due to other circumstances, as the industry´s seasonality, or other specificities of the task/s or even the goal itself. For instance, a SG averaged on sale revenue depending on large accounts of clients with fix-quantity orders placed often, let us assume it, at the end of the year. Then, the daily, or monthly, or even the quarterly results (until Q3), if the rest of the business is not altered will be in minus at to such goal. To monitor some expected deviation to the target, several companies utilize in their measurement, something called, *accepted limits* to the goal/s. The limits presuppose an active supervision, even though, not acting upon the results to correct them. The company decides these limits as the threshold of acceptance of deviations. They can be set as an *upper limit (y)*, a *lower limit (y´)*, or both. *Limits* express a unit of variation (Δ). It considers the maximum accepted gap (or accepted *range*) between the *expected performance (z)* (i.e. the target fulfillment) and the standard.

The target corresponds to your *x* variable, and its full accomplishment may be represented as

$x = 1$ (as a SG totally achieved)

In this ideal scenario, the variation *(x, y)* and *(x, y´)* is null,

$$[y, y'] = \{z \mid y' \leq z \leq y\} = 0$$

Thus,

$$\Delta(x, z) = 0$$

So, the aggregate or composite variation,

$$\sum(y' + y) = 0$$

Such ideal scenario is applied to limits in variables even of non-negative lower limits, as

$\|y'\| > 0$ *or* $\|y'\| = 0$.

This target *(x* variable) is also known as the *standard*, as it measure corresponds to a full achievement, where the status of deviation is null. The standard and limits are vectorically represented in the next figure.

Figure 6. Targets and limits to a goal
Source: Own elaboration

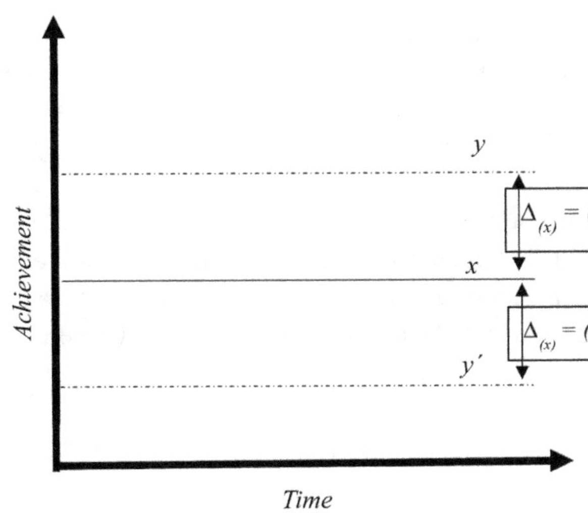

It should be emphasized here, that the sum of accepted limits is not a measure of central dispersion equivalent to a standard deviation (σ) or variance (σ^{2}. Simply, limits can vary casuistically and even encounter asymmetry and different types of metrics, as to their approximation to the x.

Hence, is incorrect to plot symmetric deviations ($z \leq 2y$) or ($z \geq 2y'$), or squared deviations y^2 or y'^2 or sum of squares, the latter as,

$$SS=(y, y')^2 \text{ or } y^2 + y'^2$$

Noticeably these limits may encounter multiple types of asymmetry as:

- null lower deviation ($y' = 0$)
- null upper deviation ($y = 0$)
- null deviation ($y + y'=0$)
- range of upper limit bigger than the range of lower limit: $\Delta\ (y, x) > (x-y')$
- range of upper limit smaller than the range of lower limit: $\Delta\ (y, x) < (x - y')$

Based on these concepts above (targets, performance indicators and limits), the challenge of practitioner is, to comprehend how to best utilize in the process of, an on-going basis, monitor the progression of a bundle of goals. This process of measurement is known as the *widget counting*. In simple terms, is the counting per strategic or operational goal´s progression figures and compare it against the target goals previously set, to understand the extent of compliance or deviation, and infer the likelihood of future accomplishment of the goal and/or the need to immediately react upon those numbers. The exercise below, is a mock business case I used once in the classroom in the academic to make my postgraduate students in strategy more familiarized, in practice, with these concepts.

Exercise 1 – Goals, targets and limits:

Mr. Simon Jørgensen, Managing Director of the firm *DK&Y, A/S* is looking at the monthly stats (Mar-2022) of the Assembling and Packaging (A&P) business unit, of three SBUs of the company. He found about "sales revenue" the following results (see table below) which he then compared with the target (or "standard") and limits set for the same strategic goal, established in the same year (2022) and the year before.

Considering the table above, students were initially asked to look at this goal, and observe how its design evolved (as a real-goal) from one year to the other: *How did the sales revenue changed in the Assembling and Packaging (A&P) business unit from 2021 to 2022?;* and among other questions to determine the upper and lower limits (y; y´): *What´s the target and upper/lower limits of the strategic goals (SOs) for 2022?*

In this exercise, the answers to the questions are straightforward, as we can find it directly from the reading of the table. The same goal increased 10% target, encountering a symmetric limit of acceptance, hence double-tailed, and with a 20% per each (upper and lower) limit. The company set, an unlikely limit, but adequate for academic observation, in which the accepted variation of forty percentage points (40%), a 2/5 variation to the target:

$$z = \underline{2x / 5}$$

$$[y, y'] = \{z \mid y' \leq z \leq y\} = 0.4;$$

Table 6. Mock case (DK&Y, A/S) - Goal, targets and limits [8]

	Temporary Results (2022)		Objective (2021)	Objective (2022)		Deviation Limits (2022)			
	Standard (DKK)	**Standard (%)**	**Standard (DKK)**	**Standard (DKK)**	**Standard Var. (%)**	**Upper DKK**	**Upper %**	**Lower DKK**	**Lower %**
Dez-22	-	-	12,5	13,75	10				
Nov-22	-	-	12,5	13,75	10				
Oct-22	-	-	12,5	13,75	10				
Sep-22	-	-	12,5	13,75	10				
Aug-22	-	-	12,5	13,75	10				
Jul-22	-	-	12,5	13,75	10				
Jun-22	-	-	12,5	13,75	10	16,5	20%	11	20%
May-22	-	-	12,5	13,75	10				
Apr-22	-	-	12,5	13,75	10				
Mar-22	20	.455	12,5	13,75	10				
Feb-22	10	(.273)	12,5	13,75	10				
Jan-22	5	(.636)	12,5	13,75	10				
Sub-Total	**35**	**(.152)**	12,5	13,75	10				
SUM2022	-	-	-	**165M**	**10%**	> 198	>20	≤132	≤20
SUM2021	**150M**	-	**150M**	-	-	-	-	-	-

Source: Own elaboration

or

$\Delta(x, y) = 0{,}4$

And, in which, the range of interval between the target and the upper limit *(y)* is set, here represented as aa an interval of rational numbers,

$[1/100, 20/100] = \{0.01, 0.02, \ldots;0{,}2\}$_

or

$[0.01, 0.2] = \{0.01, 0.02, \ldots;0{,}2\}$

Intervals between the target and the lower limit *(y´)* are set, falling into the same logic, with negative numbers (excluding non-zero positive number; hence natural numbers):

$[-0{,}01, -0{,}2] = \{1, 2\ldots;5\}$

In practice, widget counting fits into the middle of the workflow a strategy audit, being similarly applied to any projects (and replicable to a BEAP-type of project), such as, used also in SBUs.

This workflow follows these five (5) traditional sequential steps (or phases):

(i) Phase 1: Firm´s Outlook: inputs (Goals) and outputs (overview)
(ii) Phase 2: Performance measurement: Plotting of indicators and widget counting
(iii) Phase 3: Performance appraisal: Evaluation and diagnosis of performance (through the cross-observation of widget-counting and business environment intelligence)
(iv) Phase 4: Preparing to change (planning): Generation of strategic change options (SCO), course of action (CoA); and drafting of an implementation plan
(v) Phase 5: Reporting the auditing findings and conclusions; and recommendations (implementation plan) as foundations for new corporate/business planning

The workflow of the strategy audit requires, initial data from the planning function (i.e. goals) and ends with the reporting of the planning-for-change. This type of audit, thus, embraces the link between *strategy design* and *strategy execution*, as an exercise beginning with the collection of data from the plan/s (i.e. the goals) and going further along the analysis of multiple pieces of information, which conclusions, support the execution of future strategies.

The strategy audit arguably fulfills the vision of *Donald Sull* in his model (the "Strategy Loop"), as it make use of the sequence of his circular model bridging both design and execution in a fairly identically sequence (Sull, 2007): *Make Sense; Make Choices; Make Things Happen; Make Revisions.*

However, as the Strategy Loop is a holistic model with the purpose of putting "strategy in action", instead of exercises of planning or auditing, he has obviously features different from the audit. Firstly, as mentioned above, this framework is circular. On the contrary, the strategy audit, holds a project nature, typically first-timer, and do not carry continuity (circular or non-circular).

Consequently, the strategy audit does not fit into the "arch-rival" of the Strategy Loop, i.e. Robert Grant´s *Strategic Management Process,* describing strategy-making as a being a linear process. Secondly, is oriented towards action (as aforementioned briefly). You should note, I will provide below an example of a BEAP applying the Strategy Loop, clarifying its utility for practitioners. Thirdly, the model does not oppose to the revisiting of early stages (e.g. Make Sense), nor denies a back and forth journey along the cycle, which is crucial for strategic success. Specially, revisiting data is important along the auditing process (about past performance, goals and the markets). Finally, the Strategy Loop invites to a link between corporate and business planning (alias, *Make Choices*) with the operational planning and operational activities´ programing (*Make it Happen*). This latter connection is not observed so explicitly in the Strategy Audit, since the operational specifics revisited in the form of information, are not planning guidelines (as budget, materials, timelines, etc.), but the specifics of informational outputs (as indicators and target results that explain a goal). For instance, an audit may likely depict a goal related to the growth in sales revenue (as used in the example above) and unfold it into multiple explanatory information pieces of performance, as sales over capital employed *(S/CE)*, used data related to creditor turnover[9]/sales or the or the sales over PPE[10].

Abandoning now this model (Strategy Loop) and returning to the strategy audit, then workflow is now explained stepwise. The first step (or phase 1) of any auditing project is the collection of the primary (goals). One needs to gather such inputs by mapping the strategic goals of all kinds, as business, financial, social, environmental, or ethical. Once collected, you focus on a second wave of data collection (now the outputs). Outputs offer an overview of the reality and reveal the business/financial/sustainable major successes (and/or nonsuccesses) of a given civil or tax year, or the whole project/business cycle (phase

3). Outputs vary in form, structure and nature, and there is a myriad of potential information may be inclined to focus on than other. Recovering the idea above of a financial overview/analysis, you might depict sales-related data to focus on sales/CE, or instead (or even altogether), in sales margins (COGS[11]/ sales; or depreciation/sales; or SGA[12] expenses/sales).

In phase 2, is a crossing-observation of expected results as a standard/target and the outcomes. Performance-related data (either temporary outputs or final results) is counted individually per PI/KPI and related to the overall goal target (as the sum of targeted goals of the overall PIs). Typically, companies use several instruments for registered the widget counting and preparing for the conduction of further analysis, such as a *Performance Measurement Matrix (PMM)*, many times incorporated inside *Performance evaluation matrices (PEM)*. Other sophisticated tools may also be applied for the further exploring of results, as the *Optimal Strategic Performance Positioning (OSPP)* Matrix, or the *Objective and key-results (OKR)* model for monitoring operational activities and to have helicopter-type of view of strategy in a single spreadsheet you have the *Strategy Maps (SM)*. The latter being a essential tool of a management framework referred to the part one of this book (i.e. the *Balanced Scorecard*), which also the virtue of summarizing the information of the strategizing of change through future planning exercises (in phase 4 and 5). This phase culminates with the diagnosis of achievement of the strategic goals subsequent to the evaluation of results.

Phase 4, entails a cross-observation of the results of assessment with the market data. Here, one maps, the strategic priorities of the company, i.e. the Strategic Change Options (SCO). The options elected to focus on, due to odds such as non-compliance/non-achievement/underperformance, and/or because constitute substantial risk, or a serendipitous new chance, or an opportunity to be better explored, or eventually an unpredictable favorable scenario already explored to be even more efficiently exploited.

Working with SCOs implies the reflection upon the routes opened by these options, outlining possible scenarios and predictable outcomes. We are in the realm of the "unknown" doing the sensitive work (that may affect decisively a company), setting directions for future recommendations. Obviously, we are glancing at the darkness of the world in the future, as I like to call it, "doing futurology" (less hideous perhaps than "guess-logy"[13]), attempting to rationalize over options, envisioning the cost of its opportunities and risks, which come at the expense of a second prioritization task in phase 4, i.e. defining the course of action (CoA). Exploring and laying down fundamental pillars of such CoA is the first draft of your recommendation of an implementation, transferable to a more respectable reporting format in phase 5. In this last phase you are summoned to justify your CoA and pillars of the implementation plan, through a personal reflection upon chosen strategic options, actions and activities, using what is called a *Suitability, Feasibility, and Acceptability (SFA) analysis*.

The SFA is a useful way to self-evaluation your criteria and outputs (recommendations) delivered in the implementation plan. Such ultimate or posterior self-reflection has the purpose to enlighten the manager/decision-maker/client with an understanding of the reasons for your proposals in the context of a surrounding environment that is operating. *Suitability* expresses the why´s this direction is the "better for the company" in a certain moment and context. It is advisable, for delivering of a convincing S-suitability argumentation line, to make use of a summary of OT´s of the market and SWs. Decision-makers don´t need in most cases to dig into the depth of your analytical work, data or simulations (not even their visual representation in the form of graphs). But, they will certainly need to understand, in short, though your conclusions, recommendations (and their rationale: the why´s for those recommendations). Both, the SWOT and TOWS, demonstrated in chapter 5, are adequate tools for presenting you recommendations in a sound manner.

However, if you are narrative in the report is now explaining the *feasibility* of your suggested implementation plan, note first, that feasibility is all about the success of the implementation: *Can these recommendation be implemented?* And, moreover, *Do they account a reasonable/bearable cost?* A self-assessment of the feasibility of your implementation plan is an appraisal of the resources they consume, and they likelihood to be acquired or allocated at reasonable and manageable cost. Thus, here the scale of changes need to be justified in terms of resource terms, as to their needs. A narrative about feasibility ought to indicate what resource and capabilities are required at both managerial and operative levels, answering to potential questions/doubts like: *How will the organization find these resources/technology/skills?; Is the organization capable (and why) to performance at that level?;* Or, *Can these managerial/operational recommendations be internally/externally funded?*

Regarding the *acceptability,* the twist is, a customization of the reporting considering whom are your reporting to? (e.g. a client; a manager; a head of division; of board of directors). All stakeholders are in different positions different expectations and needs. Moreover, expectations are not job-specific, but also personality-specific, very unique of each individual. Two managers in the side division with hypothetical identical SBUs size, results, payment-checks and bonus and identical ambitions (and not even competing against each other) may hold diametrically different ideas about the value of your recommendations. They may receive them very differently as they are two unique persons with own values, personalities and perceptions of the reality. For instance, one may be risk-taker, while the other a stability-seeker with no desire to see any changes to the status quo.

Considering those difference beforehand is key for tailoring the reporting of your implementation plan to these particular recipients´ interests. Together with S and F criteria, acceptability is also key for concord, successful acceptance, and approval. This can be a difficult task!. Addressing some of the areas/personal concerns is essential, for instance narrating on potential questions like: *How may possibly may the function (or hierarchy and staff relations) be affected in a certain division/department?; What´s the likelihood of acceptance by the local community?; What are this risks and the benefits?; How those recommendations link to the general expectations within the company?*

Naturally, a preliminary *stakeholders´ mapping* and *stakeholders´ profiling* is of great utility for preventing upcoming obstacles. Actually, the evaluation of stakeholder expectations may be crucial. The application of this method not only increases the chances of acceptability of your recommendations, but if instrumentalized as a pre-testing tool (enquiring stakeholders before deliberating on ant recommendation - if acknowledge whom they will be), your work on SCO analysis can be articulated with an enquiry which will facilitating the effective formulation of their content toward a more acceptable one. Complementary to stakeholders' analysis, other tools, as portfolio or value network analysis are also of enormous utility.

LEARNING OUTCOMES

- Project Quality-Auditing and Strategy-Auditing (breadth and depth)
- Project goals´ setting and their typology and hierarchy
- The planning and the learning views
- Project processes (strategic and operational): Forward/downward-oriented and backward / upward-oriented
- Widget counting and diagnosis of performance

- Project performance: leading vs. lagging measurement methods
- Strategic and Project change options (SCO/PCO), further courses of action (CoA)
- Implementation plans (IP)
- Suitability, Feasibility and Acceptability (SFA) analysis and matrix

REFLECTION QUESTIONS

How are Strategy Audit (SA) and Business Environment Analyzability (BEA) connected?
What´ the difference between Project Quality-Auditing and Project Strategy-Auditing (PSA)?
What type of knowledge-gains derive from the comprehension of such association (SA-BEA)?
What´s "widget counting" in PSA?
What are the five (5) major phases of PSAs?
What the difference between a strategic or project change option (SCO; PCO) and a course of action (CoA)?
What the FSA analysis for in project strategy-auditing?

CHAPTER HIGHLIGHTS

- Definition of Strategy Auditing (SA) and uniqueness in comparison to other auditing systems (breadth and depth)
- Key concepts (as *standard, indicator, limit; change option; or course of action*) were addressed
- The Planning View/Strategic Management Process: influence in strategy auditing
- The measurement techniques (*lagging* and *leading* measurement)
- Types of strategic/project goals and essentials on their delineation
- The upstream side of the diagnosis of project performance: *change options*; choice of *course of action/*s and *implementation plan/*s
- SA´s assessment: the *Suitability, Feasibility, and Acceptability (SFA) analysis.*

CONCLUSION

The chapter addresses the definition of *strategy audit (SA)* and criticizes the theoretical diversity of their positioning. It discusses furthermore the proximity of the SA to *Mintzberg´* Planning View of strategy and to *Grant´*s Strategic Management Process. In addition, is distinguished the proximity of the SA components to *R. Grant´*s framework to build a system that combines strategy-design and strategy realization fulfilling *D. Sull´*s vision of strategy in action.

The different types of goals (as *programmed*; *structured; real* or *stated*) were addressed along with key-aspects of measurement, as the notion of *qual/quants goals, standards, limits, range* of *variation* and *indicators*. Time is instrumentalized as an essential component of strategy auditing from the delimitation of the object (goals) to be appraised, accounting multiple instances of measurement (*inputs, process* or *output measures), time-horizon* (cross-sectional/longitudinal) and considering typology of the *outputs* (as progression data-monitoring or final results).

Over a dozen of examples of strategic/project goals were used to demonstrate both their formulation and controls. On the latter function (strategic controls) the monitoring of the accomplishment of these goals takes through a *widget counting* procedure, in order to assess progression units or final result/s.

From this point the reader is taken into of journey into the downstream of the widget counting, blending strategic controls with re-formulation. Firstly, addressing the assessment and diagnosis of performance; secondly, extracting data from these two functions (assessment + diagnosis) to generate *SCOs*; and thirdly, initiating the strategy-design (for a new business cycle) using the diagnosis and SCOs as inputs for strategy reformulation, and using tools as the choice of *CoAs*, the *IPs* or the *SFA analysis* for drafting new business-level strategies.

REFERENCES

Bereskie, T., Rodriguez, M. J., & Sadiq, R. (2017). Drinking water management and governance in Canada: An innovative Plan-Do-Check-Act (PDCA) framework for a safe drinking water supply. *Environmental Management, 60*(2), 243–262. doi:10.100700267-017-0873-9 PMID:28424879

Boddy, D. (2020). *Management: Using practice and theory to develop skill* (8th ed.). Pearson Education Limited.

David, F. (2009). *Strategic management concepts and cases* (12th ed.). Pearson.

Doran, G. T. (1981). There's a SMART way to write management's goals and objectives. *Management Review, 70*(11), 35–36.

Grant, R. M. (2021). *Contemporary strategy analysis*. John Wiley & Sons. https://johnsohn.dk/2019/08/03/strategy-evaluation-sfa-analysis/

Johnson, G., & Scholes, K. (1997). *Exploring Corporate Strategy* (4th ed.). Prentice Hall.

Lauenstein, M. (1984). The strategy audit. *Journal of Business Strategy (Pre-1986), 4*(000003), 87. https://www.proquest.com/scholarly-journals/strategy-audit/docview/209883161/se-2

Sull, D. N. (2007). Closing the gap between strategy and execution. *MIT Sloan Management Review, 48*(4), 30–38.

Wheelen, T. L., & Hunger, J. D. (1987). Using the strategic audit: Quarterly journal. *S.A.M. Advanced Management Journal, 52*(1), 4. https://www.proquest.com/scholarly-journals/using-strategic-audit/docview/231216911/se-2

Zuboff, S. (2019). The age of surveillance capitalism: The fight for a human future at the new frontier of power: Barack Obama's books of 2019. Profile books.

ENDNOTES

1 With this explanation does not intend to reduce OGs to a single role of compliance to strategic planning. However, this type of debate has a better fit (and so more space) in research-based books theorizing on the specific operative themes.

2 If and only if (iff), there is a given strategic goal *(SG)* called *x*, when the SG is for all stakeholders (thus, not just for managers to work with).

3 *Pervasiveness –likelihood to find ambiguity and corruption in transactions*

4 Real goals have a set of attributes designated as "SMART" and so clearly specified the "target"

5 SMART is an acronym that stand for "Specific"; "Measurable"; "Attainable"; "Realistic" and "Time-bound"

6 An "Institutional customer" is a term used in several companies to distinguish some customer from "Commercial customers". The institutional is one rebuying and/or with an account manager; and the commercial one has only performed one single transaction or multiple of a small sum.

7 The interaction towards an higher "customer involvement," typically, accounts all means of communication as newsletters; e-mails; website visits; or orders.

8 Standard/s and deviation/s in Danish Krone (DKK) are rounded to the Millions (M) of DKK.

9 Given by the expression of the sales over receivables

10 Property, plant and Equipment (PPE), used in calculation of fixed asset turnover

11 Cost of goods sold (COGS)

12 Service, General and Administrative (SGA) expenses, commonly identified as the overhead cost/s

13 Without being apologetic, as I don't believe I need to, I explain though the provocation of calling "futurology" to SCO analysis. Multiple are likely to be the mistakes you may incur at this stage, as *Nassim Nicholas Taleb* correctly pinpoints in one of his books (e.g. the "scandal of prediction," or the "confirmation error," or "retrospective distortion")

Conclusion

Since we are now coming to an end, I would like to congratulate you first for having joined me until this point and express my gratitude to have dedicated me a part of your precious time to the reading of my thesis. Hopefully, you enjoyed it as much as I did. It was trully a pleasure to join all these ideas the last couple of years. In Danish one would say to you, *godt gået* (well done!); exactly as I pronounce it many times to my students on their academic accomplishments when I have the pleasure of witnessing them or even be part of.

From its inception, this book intended to be like a "stone thrown into a pond" and shake the somehow calm waters of the current mainstream strategy theory, something very agreeable with, but with a rather slow evolution. Nowadays, it seems the world spins faster than what scholars are able to grasp, at least strategy scholars. Naturally, I am excluding the so-called (by *Nassim Nicholas Taleb)* "black swans", not because of their pace but due to their element of total surprise. Beforehand, I should say, that I acknowledge humans are terrible predictors (worse, discoverers) of anything. It seems something totally against our essence and way above and beyond our capacity.

The aim of this book, may echo like an "anti-Blue Ocean" (here paraphrasing here a famous book also addressed in Part One). However, this is not an opposition at any sort, to *Chan Kim* or *Renée Maugborne´s* brilliant research track, is just to demonstrate that I intended to contribute to the agitation of the water in strategy towards, kind of, a "Red Ocean" (i.e. a concept *Chan Kim* or *Renée Maugborne* have developed years ago), and so being co-responsible for the widening of the ideas in the strategy realm. The bottom line is, the theoretical framework of Corporate Strategic Management has lived through times of some stagnation in last decades and is craving for substantial contributions injecting some optimism and new thoughts as to the scholarly horizon in the future. This is, for instance, the case of *Martin Reeves* with his recent book ("*The Imagination Machine*") introducing a line of investigation that pushes clearly the understanding of the strategy function towards a totally different perspective. Likewise, in one of my recent articles published in the *Review of International Business and Strategy* (entitled "*Unraveling collaborative learning stimuli and effective dynamic capability integration on MNCs: the global capabilities administration model (GCAM)*") my reflection flows on the same direction.

Consequently, this book on external business environment analyzability (EBEA) is a modest and unpretentious contribution for the understanding of the surrounding world, not solely in a rational way, but in a more likely updated and eclectic vision of it. Strategy has a huge responsibility at microeconomic level to the understanding of universe at firm-level. Perhaps, egoistically thinking, it responsibility derives from the hidden commitment to the business that pay for such knowledge-development, consulting services and individual knowledge of own employees. Hence, strategy-making has a mission of sustaining business and subsequently shape the corporate (and the community´s) wealth and well-being. By corporate wealth, I ask you not to consider it only in economic-financial terms, but to extend this idea to all forms of wealth, as the wealth deriving from experiential richness, effective learning and subsequent up/reskilling; or in terms of healthier internal environments embedded in integrative cultures of positivity that stimulate happy-living, creativity, intrapreneurial action, action-oriented research and all forms of innovation. That is a more *lato sensum* conception of wealth.

In sum, the book has accomplished what it was set out to do. Explored and developed an undermined area of strategy (i.e., external business environments) with less publications than other more nobles subfields. The book managed to refrain from entering into some other juicy areas (but overpopulated) within the micro external environment analyzability domain, as the marketing to, evolution or competitiveness of business ecosystems or industry environments and so managed to keep the narrative in line with the plan. It unraveled multiple external business environment phenomena related to the analysis function, as a triad of criteria of analyzability unseen in other strategy books, unfolding the analysis function with regard to EBEA and conceptualized the business environment analysis project (BEAP) using an elasticity of content, from old to modern times, mixing concepts, theories and critical reflections with anecdotes, cases, questions, examples and exercises Moreover, transformed text-based reflections into numbers, by making use of mathematics, econometrics, statistics and even physics. Part one contains also the learning outcomes per chapter and a chapter highlights, for the benefit of tertiary education students taking a strategy course.

Now, making a quick recap of the panorama of content here poured along the ten chapters, one may well say you were invited to dwell around several levels of reflection, swinging from higher to lower depth and vice-versa in a quasi-random manner, as I inflicted sudden turns, back and forth, at my own style (free-reading) and pleasure of writing. From epistemological and ontological issues surrounding the philosophy of management (and analyzability) you were also taken towards management theories (mostly related to corporate strategy), and revisiting societal information blended with a personal discussion of their context, meaning and potential space in present and future. Often, the narrative became unstructured and nearly chaotic.

A discussion of the analysis function, started with primary concepts of *analyzability* as the full scope of analytical options, opposing to *analysis*, the actual options taken and realized work of the analyst or strategist. We have described the primitive environment and its evolution until the modern environment and the underlying aspect of the evolution of the human judgment and behaviour. Then, explored, in the contemporary world, the perceived environmental features of our times (aka, the *VUCA*). Furthermore, the types of events occupying the external business environment, such as, *fads, trends, wild cards, noise*, and *grey* and *black swans*.

Key-issues related with the prediction or anticipation of the dynamics (and subsequent adaptation) of the external business environment (EBE) contexts were also debated. Inherently, also were accounted the impacting issues of the EBE. The threating/risky or advantageous phenomena, were considered regardless of the extent of their impact at firm-level. Seminal conceptions were also considered in relation to dynamic capabilities (DC) of the firm to comply with the EBE, as *patching*; *strategic awareness* or *strategic innovation*. Moreover discussed the pros (i.e. strategic flexibility and fit) and cons (strategic drift), as a result of corporate (in)adaptability.

Unavoidable, one explored also the human need for control (particular, the control of the surrounding world/environment), and moved into the related aspects of personal governance, and corporate governance. Here, distinguished the (cumulative) importance of governance, management and leadership functions in an organization´s context to resolve uncertainty issues. The microfoundations of management were explored and subsequently the management function in modern times. We looked into several aspects of strategic management (SM), with emphasis on two seminal sub-functions of SM (strategic planning and strategic control).

With focus on EBEs, distinguished the notion of *external business environment* against markets, marketplaces, marketspaces, business ecosystems and industry environments. Furthermore, explored the layer of external business environment (EBE), particularly the external business environment (EBEA) function. We depicted in EBEA, other aspects as the analyzability workflow (or process), the segments, factors, selection criteria, types of EBEA, models of analyzability and the importance of benchmarking and computer-assisted data analytics and big data.

Entered in the second part of the book the realm of the business environment analysis projects (BEAP), which were distinguished in terms of typology to other projects supported on project management theory. Moreover, elaborated on the project architecture (of systems), information and technology´s (ICT) infrastructures, the project´s quality, quality assurance (QA), the latter from non-Total Quality Management philosophy to a pure TQM, and its variations explained by Kaizen and other continuous improvement, lean production/services tools and Kanban, Six Sigma and the PDCA cycle. Finally, entered the project auditing cross-observing the planning (specifically project goals) and controlling (their evaluation and diagnosis), with emphasis placed on the aspect of measurement (e.g. indicators, targets/standards, limits, or widget counting) and from here inferred how a post-project review can be integrated into further reporting from the future business cycles, using change option´s analysis, definition of course of action, implementation plans and self-evaluation.

Bruno F. Abrantes
Niels Brock Copenhagen Business College, Denmark

List of Acronyms

AAR – Above Average Returns
ABV – Attention-Based View
AHP – Analytical Hierarchical Process
AIM – Affect Infusion Model
ANP – Analytical Network Process
BoT – Balance of Trade
BD – Big Data
BDA – Big Data Analytics
BA – Business Architecture
BENI – Business Ethics National Index
BIS – Business Intelligence System
BE – Business Environment
BEA – Business Environment Analyzability
BEAP – Business Environment Analyzability Project
BERI – Business Environment Risk Index
BESS – Business Environment Scanning System
BI – Business Intelligence
BLS – Business-level Strategy
BNV – Business Network View
BTE – Barriers-to-Entry
CAGE – Cultural, Administrative, Geographical and Economic
CBBIS – Computer-Based Business Intelligence System
CG – Corporate Governance
CLEAR (goals) – Challenging; Legal; Environmentally Sound; Agreed; Recorded
CR – Concentration Ratio
CoA – Course of Action
CoPI – Consumer Price Index
CPI – Corruption Perception Index
CIM – Cross-Impact Matrix
CUA – Complexity and Uncertainty Analysis
DC – Dynamic Capability

DCF – Dynamic Capability Framework
DCV – Dynamic Capabilities View
DAM – Digital Assets Management
DEEPLIST – Demographic, Economic, Ecological, Political, Legal, Informational, Social and Technological
DEMATEL – Decision Making Trial and Evaluation Laboratory
DI – Democracy Index
DWL – Deadweight Loss
EBE – External Business Environment
EBEA – External Business Environment Analysis
ECI – Economic Complexity Index
EPE – External Project Environment
ERP – Enterprise Resource Planning
EPISTELS – Environment, Political, Informative, Social, Technological, Economic, Legal, and Spiritual
ETPS – Economic, Technical, Political, and Social
EsV – Ecosystem View
EI – Education Index
EPI – Environmental Performance Index
EIS – Ethics Index Score
EI – External Interface
FS – Factor Score
GCB – Global Corruption Barometer
GCI – Global Competitiveness Index
GDI – Gender Development Index
GDP – Gross Domestic Product
GEI – Global Entrepreneurship Index
GFSI – Global Food Security Index
GHSI – Global Health Security Index
GDPR – General Data Protection Regulation
GFRQ – General Focus Research Questions
GNI – Gross National Income
GROW – Goal, Reality, Options, Will
GSI – Global Cybersecurity Index
GTI – Global Tourism Index
HDI – Human Development Index
HRM – Human Resources Management
HSAF – Hybrid Situational Analysis Framework
Ia – Impact (criterion)
Io – Importance (criterion)
IEF – Index of Economic Freedom
IET – Index of Economic Transformation
IC – Intelligence Cycle
IPT – Index of Political Transformation

ICTDI – Information and Communication Diffusion Index
IPE – Internal Project Environment
ISOC – Information Security Operations Center
IE – Internal Environment
II – Internal Interface
IPM – Individual Performance Management
IRS – Itemized Rating Scale
IS – Information System
ISM – Information Systems Management
ISIC – International Standard of Industrial Classification
KBV – Knowledge-Based View
KM – Knowledge Management
KPI – Key Performance Indicator
KSF – Key Success Factor
LT – Lead Time
LEI – Life Expectancy Index
MBV – Market-Based View
MCDA – Multi-Criteria Decisional Analysis
MEEA – Macro External Environment Analysis
MiEEA – Micro External Environmental Analysis
MIS – Management Information System
OAS – Office Automation System
ORI – Operations Risk Index
PCS – Process Control System
POLC – Plan, Organize, Lead, and Control
PD – Power Distance
PDI – Power Distance Index
PEST – Political, Economic, Socio-Cultural and Technological
PESTLE (or PESTEL) – Political, Economic, Sociological, Technological, Legal and Environmental
PESTLIED – Political, Economic, Socio-Cultural, Technological, Legal, International, Environmental, Demographic
PESTILE – Political, Economic, Sociological, Technological, International, Legal and Environmental
PRI – Political Risk Index
PSI – Political Stability Index
PPI – Producer Price Index (PPI)
PCI – Product Complexity Index (PCI)
PMO – Project Management Office
PSO – Project Support Office
PURE – Positively Stated, Understood, Relevant and Ethical (goals)
PSAF – Pure Situational Analysis Framework
R&C – Resources and Capabilities
RBV – Resource-Based View
REDI – Regional Entrepreneurship and Development Index

RLI – Rule of Law Index
SA – Strategy Audit
SBU – Strategic Business Unit
SCO – Strategic Change Option/s
SCORE – Strengths, Challenges, Options, Responses, and Effectiveness
SD – Strategic Drift
SLEPT – Socio-Cultural, Legal, Economic, Political, Technological
SM – Strategic Management
SMART (goals) – Specific, Measurable, Attainable, Rewarded, Time-bound
SO – Strategic Objectives
SOs – Strength and Opportunities
SOAR – Strengths, Opportunities, Aspirations, and Results
SOFT – Strengths, Opportunities, Faults, and Threats
SPM – Strategic Performance Management
STs – Strengths and Threats
STEPE or STEEPLE – Social, Technological, Economic, Environmental, Political, Legal and Ethical
STEER – Socio-cultural, Technological, Economic, Ecological, and Regulatory
STP – Segmenting, Targeting and Positioning
SWOT – Strengths, Weaknesses, Opportunities, and Threats
TAIDA – Tracking, Analyzing, Imaging, Deciding, Acting
TAG – Technical Advisory Group
TBV – Technology-Based View
TPS – Transactional Processing System
TPM – Total Productive Maintenance
TQC – Total Quality Control
TQM – Total Quality Management
VUCA – Volatility, Uncertainty, Complexity and Ambiguity

Glossary

Ability: Personal traits and individual attributes (circumstantial and psychological) that determine the performance on job

Action: Initial deeds and follow up endeavors related to predetermined goals

Actor: Individual, group, organization or authority with a likely interest in the issue or system under analysis

Agency Theory: Examines the relationships between a *shareholder* and a *principal* (a company) with the purpose of aligning interests between these two groups

Ambiguity: Multiple external influences (complexity) in a certain moment in time, with some events being difficult to perceive (or uncertain)

Analyzability: Full scope of theoretical options for the conduction of (future) analytical activities at a full range within a delimited problem

Analysis: Interpretation of inputs of data, sense-making/giving (namely as to the consequences perceived from a bundle of information), and generation of scenarios

Assets: effective endowed resources allocated to a certain business unit or project

Behaviour: A directly observable action taken by a person

Black Swan: An unpredictable event, which is unlikely to occur

Bottleneck: Limitation in a system constituting a constraint to growth or development

Brief: Document describing the nature of Business Environmental Analysis Project. The brief determines the likelihood of the proposal´s approval and the extent of the resources to be released.

Business Architecture: The central plexus of any organization connecting and integrating all of the architectures (sub-systems) of the enterprise in a formal and disciplined manner

Business Environment (BE): An external business context, accounting physical and digital attributions, interplaying with a specific internal environment of a focal firm

Business environment (BE) analyzability: Entire set of (likely) activities to be chosen from, for the complete examination of a BE

Business environment analysis: Set of activities effectively taken to exam the BE

Business environment factor: Elements of information within each segment of the external or internal business environment

Business environment scanning system: a set of systematic processes for the identification of early signals, patterning dynamics trends prior the recognition of effective change

Business Intelligence: is a bundle of critical information united, as a by-product of the collection of organizational and market data, and its combination and transformation into subsets of information with strategic interest

Business model: Design of a system of interdependent activities of a focal firm with its partners and the surrounding mechanisms of interrelation for the creation of value to stakeholders and subsequent capture of a portion of value

Business relationship: process established and maintained, to create or improve the position in a network and ensure the long-term survival of the firm

Capabilities: set of abilities allowing the firm, to plan, organize, lead, coordinate and manage the execution of its activities

Challenge: Event in process of change, or morphological mutation and/or with some degree of risk

Commensurability: Distinct phenomena with complementary traits

Complexity: Multiple and multifaceted events occurring on the external business environment

Conceptualization: Refining an idea/thought and removing the obscurity of its identity and/or nature

Core-competences: The capabilities with higher contribution to value creation

Corporate Foresight: Forecasting activities to predict future states of the business environments to pre-empt them and shape its attributes

Corporate Governance: The system (of rules) by which companies are directed and controlled

Corporate Nexus: The fundamental and essential links that unite the enterprise to form a harmonious whole (i.e. the system)

Counter-intelligence: set of activities to prevent the opponent/competitor use of intelligence

Critical scenario: Future condition, which occurrence, may yield likely high effects on the firm

Decision: Specific commitment to action. On a "BEAP" (project) entails the judgment of multiple sets of data and specific choices regarding its utilization

Dystopian scenario: Future scenario with most negative effective imaginable to a firm ("worse scenario" or "real nightmare" scenario).

E-marketplace: a technical infrastructure with a virtual or digital nature (known as platform) where multi-lateral trade occurs, often administered by a single platform provider

External Business Environment (EBE): Part of the Business environment exterior to a focal firm

Event: Phenomenon observed in the present, or expected to occur in the future

Fact: Measurable event on the internal or external business environment with value (positive or negative) or value-free potential or a firm

Fad: Short-term shift observed in the Business Environment

Factor: A unit of a segment (see definition of "segment") with the ability to influence the competitive action/response of a firm.

Factor Score: Importance given to a factor (ratio), based on prior quantitative parameters set for its assessment of its relative strength

Forecast: Prediction of a probable future under present conditions

Foresight: Identification of possible futures, potential issues, tendencies, and uncertainties, often using scenario methods.

Goal: a desired future result for an activity or organisational unit.

Governance: The design of a system of rules, comprised of policies, processes and ensuring their compliance

Guanxi: business networking practice based on the establishment of social connections to secure favors in personal relationships

Image/ing: Cognitive exercise of visual representing an image of what a future scenario might looks like It identifies possibilities and generate visions of what is desired.

Intelligence: the ability to acquire and apply knowledge and skills

Influence: An attempt to mobilize power resources in order to modify the behaviour of other people.

Interface: a direct interaction of, the strategy function with a part of the business environment

Knowledge: as the information (factual or procedural) to conduct a task or job

Leadership: Ability to move an organization from a current to future states – new strategy/ies and culture/s -, creating a new vision (for new opportunities) and influence other organization-stakeholders to commit to change by instilling new concepts, processes and/or technology.

Market: Set of companies engaged in the production of identical bundles of products and/or services

Marketplace: Physical infrastructure shared by multiple agents interested in establishing commercial agreements, owned by one or multiple entities.

Management: A human and/or automated function seeking alignment, predictability and certainty over the universe´s phenomena, to gain, maintain or renew a sense of physic comfort about potential hazards in society.

Netography: Method focused on specific explorative qualitative data about consumer trend

Normative Scenario: The one that describes a future scenario as desired (or undesirable) future reality

Objective: a specific desired result that an organization seeks to achieve the pursuing of its basic mission

Option: The strategic scenario encompassing a risk trade-off register between the utility of a decision, against other possible choices.

Organization: Collective arrangement with a specific purpose guiding its ventures and social exchange with third parties

Organizational management: a firm-level function, breakdown into multiple processes, utilizing a set of own resources, in other to attain alignment, predictability and uncertainty- reduction, and generate added-value.

Organizational strategy: Framework for making choices and trade-offs; and identifying resources, methods, actions, and value-creating objectives that sustain the organization over time within an ever-changing context.

Planning: An iterative activity comprising, the setting of organizational, implementation of a course of action for their achievement and evaluating of the outcomes.

Power: Ability to constrain the process of decision-making and behaviour of others, to produce the intended effects

Power Distance: The extent to which a society accepts that power in institutions is unequally distributed

Program: A group or related project (including business-as-usual activities) with joint coordination for ensuring that a high-level of benefits are realized

Project: a temporary effort to create value through a unique product, service or result

Project Brief: Check in the glossary the definition of "brief"

Resources: Stocks of available factors owned or controlled by a firm

Risk:A state of uncertainty where some of the possibilities involve a loss, catastrophe or other undesirable outcome

Satisficing: Choice of a course of analytical action most satisfactory under certain circumstances, believed to deliver results good enough to achieve the project goals

Scenario: A broad picture of what we can be found in the future, as a description of a future state, and a path to that future

Scenario planning: an analytical procedure of weighting self-generated cognitive options (or future hypothesis)

Segment (of an External Business Environment): One category of the whole dimensions in the broader society which influence the industries and firms

Skill: the level of proficiency for the execution of a task

Social events: subjective occurrence deriving from interaction

Strategy: an integrated and coordinated set of commitments and actions designed to explore core competences and gain competitive advantage

Strategic intelligence: Corporate skills and insights about the present or future of business environment contexts for fostering a flexible strategic positioning and rationality to decision-making.

Strategic planning: Task of setting out the overall direction for an organization covering all its major activities.

Strength: Capability possessed on a (positively) distinctive level from other competitors

Target: (degree of) accomplishment of a goal or objective

Tracking: finding traces of change and signs of threats and opportunities

Trait: Aspect of personality influencing individual behaviour

Trend: Event that represents a deeper change than a fad.

Uncertainty: The lack of complete certainty, that is, the existence of more than one possibility. The true outcome/state/result/value is not known.

Uncertainty Avoidance: The extent to which a society feels threatened by uncertain or ambiguous situations.

Utopian scenario: Best-case scenario that lacks in plausibility, lying beyond the space of possible, credible futures, hence disregard as to the evaluation of firm´s (future) strategic options

Volatility: Business environment in constant change

Wild Card: Event generator of business environmental discontinuities in the development curve

Compilation of References

Abrantes, B. F. & Ostergaard, K. (2021) Digital footprint wrangling: are analytics used for better or worse? A concurrent mixed methods research on the commercial (ab)use of dataveillance. *Journal of Marketing Analytics*, *10*(2022), 187-202. https://doi.org/ doi:10.1057/s41270-021-00144-5

Abrantes, B. F. (2018) The internationalization paradigm and dynamic capabilities of Portuguese firms: contributions from case studies in the metallurgical and metal-mechanic sectors. *Repositório do ISCTE.* http://hdl.handle.net/10071/16556

Abrantes, B. F. (2018). Intrapreneurial Dynamics: A Case Research at the Insurance Industry in Portugal. *International Journal of Entrepreneurial Knowledge*, *6*(1), 61–75. doi:10.37335/ijek.v6i1.69

Abrantes, B. F. (2020). Are Neoclassic Internationalization Models Enduring? A Case-Review of the Uppsala Paradigm. *SAGE Open*, *10*(2). doi:10.1177/2158244020932535

Abrantes, B. F. (2020). Governance of academic laboratories and the capabilisation of higher education students. *International Journal of Management Education*, *14*(2), 135–158.

Abrantes, B. F. (2020b). Tech-innovation and spillovers on corporate-defensiveness: Evidence from the Lisbon startup ecosystem. *International Journal of Business Competition and Growth*, *7*(1), 68–100. doi:10.1504/IJBCG.2020.108439

Abrantes, B. F., & Fernández, R. L. (2023). Digital competition and capabilities' augmentation on international cohorts: Evidence from the 'case competition 2019'. *International Journal of Education Economics and Development*, *14*(1), 100–122. doi:10.1504/IJEED.2023.127628

Abrantes, B. F., Preto, M. T., & Antonio, N. (2022). Unraveling collaborative learning stimuli and effective dynamic capability integration on MNCs: The global capabilities administration model (GCAM). *Review of International Business and Strategy.*, *33*(2), 272–300. doi:10.1108/RIBS-06-2021-0085

Abrantes, B. F., & Venkataraman, A. (2022). Environment kinesis and organizational adaptability: Effects of EU's General Data Protection Regulation on the Danish software industry. *International Journal of Learning and Change*, *14*(1), 22–45. doi:10.1504/IJLC.2022.119516

AgnolettoJ. (2020) *Project Assurance Fundamentals.* PricewaterhouseCoopers. https://www.pwc.com.au/assurance/internal-audit/Project-Fundamentals-Slides.pdf

AgnolettoJ. (2020). *Project Assurance Fundamentals.* PricewaterhouseCoopers. https://www.pwc.com.au/assurance/internal-audit/Project-Fundamentals-Slides.pdf

Aguilar, F. J. (1967). *Scanning the business environment*. McMillan.

Amit, R., & Schoemaker, P. (1993). Strategic assets and organizational rent. *Strategic Management Journal*, *14*(1), 33–46. doi:10.1002mj.4250140105

Amit, R., & Zott, C. (2015). Crafting business architecture: The antecedents of business model design. *Strategic Entrepreneurship Journal*, *9*(4), 331–350. doi:10.1002ej.1200

Andersen, P. (2013). *Performance management: A handbook for small business banks and microfinance institutions.* Practical Action Publishing. doi:10.3362/9781780447926

Ansoff, H. I. (1965). *Corporate strategy: An analytic approach to business policy for growth and expansion.* McGraw-Hill Companies.

Arrow, K. J. (1956). The Role of Securities in the Optimal Allocation of Risk Bearing. *The Review of Economic Studies*, *31*(2), 91–96. doi:10.2307/2296188

Baker, B. (2018). Project quality management practice & theory. *American Journal of Management*, *18*(3), 10–17.

Bakos, J. Y. (1991). A strategic analysis of electronic marketplaces. *Management Information Systems Quarterly*, *15*(3), 295–310. doi:10.2307/249641

Barker, J. R. (1993). Tightening the iron cage: Concertive control in self-managing teams. *Administrative Science Quarterly*, *38*(3), 408–437. doi:10.2307/2393374

Barney, J. B. (1996). The resource-based theory of the firm. *Organization Science*, *7*(5), 469–469. doi:10.1287/orsc.7.5.469

Beer, M., Voelpel, S. C., Leibold, M., & Tekie, E. D. (2005). Strategic management as organizational learning: Developing fit and alignment through a disciplined process. *Long Range Planning*, *38*(5), 445–465. doi:10.1016/j.lrp.2005.04.008

Bennis, W., & Nanus, B. (1985). *Leaders: The strategies for taking charge.* Harp & Row.

Bereskie, T., Rodriguez, M. J., & Sadiq, R. (2017). Drinking water management and governance in Canada: An innovative Plan-Do-Check-Act (PDCA) framework for a safe drinking water supply. *Environmental Management*, *60*(2), 243–262. doi:10.100700267-017-0873-9 PMID:28424879

Bhaskar, R. (2008). *Dialectic: The pulse of freedom.* Routledge. doi:10.4324/9780203892633

Biron, B., & McDowell, E. (2021) Inside the wild and tumultuous history of Toys R Us, a once beloved children's brand that just closed its last 2 stores in the US. *Business Insider*. https://www.businessinsider.com/the-tumultuous-history-of-toys-r-us-photos-2020-8?r=US&IR=T

Blacker, F. (1995). Knowledge, knowledge work and organization: An overview and interpretations. *Organization Studies*, *15*(6), 1021–1046. doi:10.1177/017084069501600605

Blok, V. (2019). Xenophon's philosophy of management. *Handbook of Philosophy of Management*, 1-19. Bloomberg Coupang Corp. https://www.bloomberg.com/profile/company/COUPAZ:KS

Bloomberg. (2022) *Data and Operations.* Bloomberg Professional Services. https://www.bloomberg.com/professional/expertise/data-and-operations/

Boddy. (2020). *Management: Using practice and theory to develop skill, (8th ed.).* Harlow – UK: Pearson Education Limited.

Boddy. (2020). *Management: Using practice and theory to develop skill, (8th ed.).* Pearson Education Limited.

Boddy, D. (2017). *Management: Using practice and theory to develop skill* (8th ed.). Pearson Education Limited.

Bosch-Rekveldt, M., Jongkind, Y., Mooi, H., Bakker, H., & Verbraeck, A. (2011). Grasping project complexity in large engineering projects: The TOE (Technical, Organizational and Environmental) framework. *International Journal of Project Management*, *29*(6), 728–739. doi:10.1016/j.ijproman.2010.07.008

Boxall, P., & Purcell, J. (2000). Strategic human resource management: Where have we come from and where should we be going? *International Journal of Management Reviews*, *2*(2), 183–203. doi:10.1111/1468-2370.00037

Bradfield, R., Wright, G., Burt, G., Cairns, G., & Heijden, K. (2005). The origins and evolution of scenario techniques in long range business planning. *Futures*, *37*(8), 795–812. doi:10.1016/j.futures.2005.01.003

Brouthers, L. E., Gao, Y., & Napshin, S. (2014). *Keiretsu centrality: Profits and profit stability: A power dependence perspective.* CORE.

Bryde, J. D. (1997). Underpinning modern project management with TQM principles. *The TQM Magazine*, *9*(3), 231–238. doi:10.1108/09544789710169037

Cadbury, A. (1992). *The Financial Aspects of Corporate Governance (Cadbury Report).* The Committee on the Financial Aspect of Corporate Governance (The Cadbury Committee). http://www.ecgi.org/codes/documents/cadbury.pdf

Capon, N., Farley, J. U., Hulbert, J., & Lehmann, D. R. (1992). Profiles of product innovators among large US manufacturers. *Management Science*, *38*(2), 157–168. doi:10.1287/mnsc.38.2.157

CaseCoach. (2021). The The Top-10 Strategy Consulting Firms Compared. *Case Coach.* https://casecoach.com/b/the-top-10-strategy-consulting-firms-compared/

Central Intelligence Agency. (n.d.). *The World Factbook.* CIA. https://www.cia.gov/the-world-factbook/

Chaffey, D. (2021). SWOT analysis template examples. *Smart Insights.* https://www.smartinsights.com/marketplace-analysis/swot-analysis/swot-analysis/

Chandler, A. D. (2020). *Structure and strategy.* Harvard University Press.

Chao, G. T., & Moon, H. (2005). The cultural mosaic: A meta-theory to understand the complexity of culture. *The Journal of Applied Psychology*, *90*(6), 1128–1140. doi:10.1037/0021-9010.90.6.1128 PMID:16316269

Chesbrough, H. (2010). Business model innovation: Opportunities and barriers. *Long Range Planning*, *43*(2/3), 354–363. doi:10.1016/j.lrp.2009.07.010

Cisco (online) *Acquisitions by year.* CISCO. https://www.cisco.com/c/en/us/about/corporate-strategy-office/acquisitions/acquisitions-list-years.html

Cisco. (n.d.). *Acquisitions by year.* Cisco. https://www.cisco.com/c/en/us/about/corporate-strategy-office/acquisitions/acquisitions-list-years.html

Cohen, M. D., March, J. G., & Olsen, J. P. (1972). A garbage can model of organizational choice. *Administrative Science Quarterly*, *17*(1), 1–25. doi:10.2307/2392088

Conforto, E. C., Amaral, D. C., da Silva, S. L., Di Felippo, A., & Kamikawachi, D. S. L. (2016). The agility construct on project management theory. *International Journal of Project Management*, *34*(4), 660–674. doi:10.1016/j.ijproman.2016.01.007

Cooper, R. G. (2008). Perspective: The stage-gate® idea-to-launch process—update, what's new, and NexGen systems. *Journal of Product Innovation Management*, *25*(3), 213–232. doi:10.1111/j.1540-5885.2008.00296.x

Cooper, R. G. (2010). The stage-gate product innovation system: from idea to launch. In *Encyclopedia of Technology and Innovation Management* (pp. 157–167). John Wiley & Sons Ltd.

Cooper, R. G., & Edgett, S. J. (2008). Maximizing productivity in product innovation. *Research Technology Management*, *51*(2), 47–58. doi:10.1080/08956308.2008.11657495

Cooper, R. G., & Sommer, A. F. (2016). Agile-Stage-Gate: New idea-to-launch method for manufactured new products is faster, more responsive. *Industrial Marketing Management*, *59*, 167–180. doi:10.1016/j.indmarman.2016.10.006

Cotton, D. (2010). *The Business Strategy Toolkit*. Gloucestershire: UK: Management Books 2000.

Critical Mass. (2021). To be the best, be like Lego. *Critical Mass*. https://www.criticalmass.com/think/detail/to-be-the-best-be-like-lego

David, F. (2009). *Strategic management concepts and cases* (12th ed.). Pearson.

Debreu, G. (1959). *Theory of value*. Wiley.

Dinçer, Ö. (2004). *Stratejik yönetim ve işletme politikası*. Beta Yayınları.

Doran, G. T. (1981). There's a SMART way to write management's goals and objectives. *Management Review*, *70*(11), 35–36.

Duke, L., & Birkinshaw, L. (2011) *The rise and fall of Nokia*. Think at London Business School Magazine. https://publishing.london.edu/cases/the-rise-and-fall-of-nokia/

Duke, L., & Birkinshaw, L. (2011). *The rise and fall of Nokia*. Think at London Business School Magazine. https://publishing.london.edu/cases/the-rise-and-fall-of-nokia/

Dun and Bradstreet. (2021) *Our analytics*. DNB. https://www.dnb.com/

Dunning, J., & Kim, C. (2007). The Cultural Roots of Guanxi: An Exploratory Study. *World Economy*, *30*(2), 329–341. doi:10.1111/j.1467-9701.2007.00885.x

Economist Intelligence Unit. (2005). *Business 2010: embracing the challenge of change*. Economist Intelligence Unit: London, U.K.

Economist Intelligence Unit. (2005). *Business 2010: embracing the challenge of change*. Economist Intelligence Unit: London, U.K. EEA (online) About EEA indicators. Available at: https://www.eea.europa.eu/data-and-maps/indicators/#c0=30&c12-operator=or&b_start=0

Eisenhardt, K. M., & Martin, J. A. (2000). Dynamic capabilities: What are they? *Strategic Management Journal*, *21*(10-11), 1105–1121. doi:10.1002/1097-0266(200010/11)21:10/11<1105::AID-SMJ133>3.0.CO;2-E

Erikson, R. S., & Tedin, K. L. (2003). *American Public Opinion* (6th ed.). Longman.

EU. (2020). *EU data protection rules*. EU. https://ec.europa.eu/info/priorities/justice-and-fundamental-rights/data-protection/2018-reform-eudata-protection-rules/eu-data-protection-rules_en#documents

EU. (2020). EU data protection rules. *Europea*. https://ec.europa.eu/info/priorities/justice-and-fundamental-rights/data-protection/2018-reform-eudata-protection-rules/eu-data-protection-rules_en#documents

Eur-Lex. (2016). Regulation (EU) 2016/679 of the European Parliament and the Council of 27 April 2016, *Official Journal of the European Union, L119/1*. https://eurlex.europa.eu/legal-content/EN/TXT/PDF/?uri=CELEX:02016R0679-20160504&from=EN

Eur-Lex. (2016). Regulation (EU) 2016/679 of the European Parliament and the Council of 27 April 2016. *Official Journal of the European Union, L119/1*. https://eurlex.europa.eu/legal-content/EN/TXT/PDF/?uri=CELEX:02016R0679-20160504&from=EN

Euro Monitor. (n.d.). *How passport helps*. EM. https://www.euromonitor.com/our-expertise/passport

Euromonitor International. (2021). Explore insights. EI. https://www.euromonitor.com/

European Central Bank. (2022). Statistics. ECB. https://www.ecb.europa.eu/stats/html/index.en.html

European Data Protection Supervisor (EDPS). (n.d.). *The History of the General Data Protection Regulation*. Europea. https://edps.europa.eu/data-protection/data-protection/legislation/history-general-data

Femmer, H., Fernández, D. M., Wagner, S., & Eder, S. (2017). Rapid quality assurance with requirements smells. *Journal of Systems and Software*, *123*, 190–213. doi:10.1016/j.jss.2016.02.047

Fenwick (2020) *Coronavirus Impact on M&A and Other Strategic Corporate Transactions*. Fenwick. https://www.fenwick.com/insights/publications/coronavirus-impact-on-m-a-and-other-strategic-corporate-transactions

Fenwick. (2020) Coronavirus Impact on M&A and Other Strategic Corporate Transactions. *Fenwick*. https://www.fenwick.com/insights/publications/coronavirus-impact-on-m-a-and-other-strategic-corporate-transactions

Fischer, B., Lago, U., & Li, F. (2015) *The Haier Road to Growth*. Strategy + Business. https://www.strategy-business.com/article/00323.

Fischer, B., Lago, U., & Li, F. (2015) *The Haier Road to Growth*. Strategy + Business. https://www.strategy-business.com/article/00323.

Forgas, J. P., & George, J. M. (2001). Affective influences on judgments and behavior in organizations: An information processing perspective. *Organizational Behavior and Human Decision Processes*, *86*(1), 3–34. doi:10.1006/obhd.2001.2971

Fortune. (2020). How the profits of Fortune 500 companies stack up in one chart. *Fourtune 500*. https://fortune.com/longform/fortune-500-companies-profits-compare-2020-chart-data/

Friedman, V. J., & Antal, A. B. (2005). Negotiating reality: A theory of action approach to intercultural competence. *Management Learning*, *36*(1), 69–86. doi:10.1177/1350507605049904

Friesner, T. (2011). History of SWOT analysis. *Marketing Teacher, 2000-2010*. https://www.researchgate.net/publication/288958760_History_of_swot_analysis/citations

Gaddis, P. O. (1959). *The project manager*. Harvard University.

Gartner Inc. (2021). *Gartner Forecasts Worldwide IT Spending to Reach $4 Trillion in 2021*. Garter Inc. https://www.gartner.com/en/newsroom/press-releases/2021-04-07-gartner-forecasts-worldwide-it-spending-to-reach-4-trillion-in-2021

Geiss, C., Geiss, S. (2009) *An introduction to probability theory*. Jyväskylän yliopisto.

Ghemawat, P. (2001). Distance still matters. *Harvard Business Review*, *79*(8), 137–147. PMID:11550630

Goldratt, E. M. (1990). *Theory of constraints*. Croton-on-Hudson: North River.

Grant, R. M. (2021). *Contemporary strategy analysis*. John Wiley & Sons. https://johnsohn.dk/2019/08/03/strategy-evaluation-sfa-analysis/

Grant, R. M. (2021). *Contemporary strategy analysis*. John Wiley & Sons.

Graves, T. (2006). *An introduction to SCORE: Beyond SWOT analysis: strategy, capability, and effectiveness*. https://documen.site/download/introduction-to-score-tetradian-consulting_pdf

Grundy, T. (2006). Rethinking and reinventing Michael Porter's five forces model. *Strategic Change*, *15*(5), 213–229. doi:10.1002/jsc.764

Gürkan, E. (2012). The efficacy of Ottoman counter-intelligence in the 16th century. *Acta Orientalia (København), 65*(1), 1–38. doi:10.1556/AOrient.65.2012.1.1

Hansen, C. (2020). Daoism. *The Stanford Encyclopedia of Philosophy (Spring 2020 Edition),* Edward N. Zalta (ed.). https://plato.stanford.edu/archives/spr2020/entries/daoism/

Haq, S. U., Liang, C., Gu, D., Du, J. T., & Zhao, S. (2018). Project governance, project performance, and the mediating role of project quality and project management risk: An agency theory perspective. *Engineering Management Journal, 30*(4), 274–292. doi:10.1080/10429247.2018.1503038

Hawawini, G., Subramanian, V., & Verdin, P. (2003). Is performance driven by industry-or firm-specific factors? A new look at the evidence. *Strategic Management Journal, 24*(1), 1–16. doi:10.1002mj.278

Hides, M. T., Irani, Z., Polychronakis, I., & Sharp, J. M. (2000). Facilitating total quality through effective project management. *International Journal of Quality & Reliability Management, 17*(4/5), 407–422. doi:10.1108/02656710010298427

Hitt, M. A., Ireland, R. D., & Hoskisson, R. E. (2016). *Strategic management: Concepts and cases: Competitiveness and globalization*. Cengage Learning. Hofstede Insights (online) National Culture. https://hi.hofstede-insights.com/national-culture

Hitt, M. A., Ireland, R. D., & Hoskisson, R. E. (2016). *Strategic management: Concepts and cases: Competitiveness and globalization*. Cengage Learning.

Hubbard, D. (2014). *How to measure anything: Finding the value of intangibles in business*. John Wiley & Sons, Inc.

IMD. (2021). *China and US pursuing markedly different digital transformations*. IMD. https://www.imd.org/news/updates/China-US-pursuing-markedly-different-but-equally-competitive-digital-transformations-WCC/

International Trade Centre. (n.d.). International trade statistics 2001-2020. ITC. https://www.intracen.org/itc/market-info-tools/trade-statistics/

Jofre, S. (2011). *Strategic Management: The theory and practice of strategy in (business) organizations*. DTU. https://backend.orbit.dtu.dk/ws/portalfiles/portal/5705108/rapport1.11.pdf

Johanson, J., Mattsson, L. G., Hood, N., and Vahlne, J. E. (1988). Strategies in global competition. *Strategies in global competition, 14*, 75-81.

Johanson, J., & Vahlne, J. E. (1977). The internationalization process of the firm—A model of knowledge development and increasing foreign market commitments. *Journal of International Business Studies, 8*(1), 23–32. doi:10.1057/palgrave.jibs.8490676

Johnson, G., & Scholes, K. (1997). *Exploring Corporate Strategy* (4th ed.). Prentice Hall.

Johnson, G., Scholes, K., & Whittington, R. (2008). *Exploring corporate strategy: Text and cases*. Pearson education.

Kaizen Institute. (n.d.). *What is Kaizen*. Kaizen Institute. https://www.kaizen.com/

Karampatsis, R. M., Babii, H., Robbes, R., Sutton, C., & Janes, A. (2020, October). Big code!= big vocabulary: Open-vocabulary models for source code. In *2020 IEEE/ACM 42nd International Conference on Software Engineering (ICSE)* (pp. 1073-1085). IEEE.

Karlström, D., & Runeson, P. (2006). Integrating agile software development into stage-gate managed product development. *Empirical Software Engineering, 11*(2), 203–225. doi:10.100710664-006-6402-8

Khan, M. E. (2012). *Relationship between project attributes, project performance, and project governance dimensions-building the theoretical framework.* 2012 PMI Global Congress Proceedings, Marseille-France.

Krogerus, M., & Tschäppeler, R. (2017). *The Decision Book: Fifty models for strategic thinking (New Edition).* Profile Books.

Lauenstein, M. (1984). The strategy audit. *Journal of Business Strategy (Pre-1986), 4*(000003), 87. https://www.proquest.com/scholarly-journals/strategy-audit/docview/209883161/se-2

Leonard-Barton, D. (1992). Core capabilities and core rigidities: A paradox in managing new product development. *Strategic Management Journal, 13*(S1), 111–125. doi:10.1002mj.4250131009

Lindgren, M., & Bandhold, H. (2009). *Scenario Planning*. Palgrave MacMillan.

Luthra, S., Garg, D., Agarwal, A., & Mangla, S. K. (2020). *Total Quality Management (TQM): Principles, Methods, and Applications*. CRC Press. doi:10.1201/9781003053156

Lynch, R. (2009). *Strategic management*. Pearson Education Limited.

Lynch, R., & Cross, K. (1991). *Measure Up! Yardstick for Continuous Improvement*. Blackwell.

Mackay, B., Arevuo, M., Mackay, D., & Meadows, M. (2020). *Strategy: Theory, practice, implementation.* Oxford University Press.

Markit, I. H. S. (2021) *Economics and country risks.* IHS Market. https://ihsmarkit.com/products/global-industry-forecasts-analysis.html

Martin, R. (2022). Why Planning Over Strategy? *Medium.* https://rogermartin.medium.com/why-planning-over-strategy-88555015af3c

Martin, R. L. (2014). The big lie of strategic planning. *Harvard Business Review, 92*(1/2), 78–84.

Maylor, H. (2010). *Project Management* (4th ed.). Pearson Education Limited.

Maylor, H., Vidgen, R., & Carver, S. (2008). Managerial complexity in project-based operations: A grounded model and its implications for practice. *Project Management Journal, 39*(1, suppl), S15–S26. doi:10.1002/pmj.20057

McCrae, R. R., & John, O. P. (1992). An introduction to the five-factor model and its applications. *Journal of Personality, 60*(2), 175–215. doi:10.1111/j.1467-6494.1992.tb00970.x PMID:1635039

McGahan, A. M., & Porter, M. E. (1997). How much does industry matter, really? *Strategic Management Journal, 18*(S1), 15–30. doi:10.1002/(SICI)1097-0266(199707)18:1+<15::AID-SMJ916>3.0.CO;2-1

Miller, G. A. (1953). What is information measurement? *The American Psychologist, 8*(1), 3–11. doi:10.1037/h0057808

Miller, T., Kim, A. B., & Roberts, J. M. (2021). *Index of Economic Freedom.* Heritage Foundation. MA. https://www.heritage.org/index/pdf/2021/book/index_2021.pdf

Miner, J. B. (2000). Testing a psychological typology of entrepreneurship using business founders. *The Journal of Applied Behavioral Science, 36*(1), 43–69. doi:10.1177/0021886300361003

Mintzberg, H. (1987). The strategy concept I: Five Ps for strategy. *California Management Review, 30*(1), 11–24. doi:10.2307/41165263

MIT Technology Review. (2021). *Tech policy: This company delivers packages faster than Amazon, but workers pay the price.* MIT. https://www.technologyreview.com/2021/06/09/1025884/coupang-amazon-labor-costs-worker-death/

Moon, H. C., Rugman, A. M., & Verbeke, A. (1998). A generalized double diamond approach to the global competitiveness of Korea and Singapore. *International Business Review*, *7*(2), 135–150. doi:10.1016/S0969-5931(98)00002-X

Morris, P. W., Jamieson, A., & Shepherd, M. M. (2006). Research updating the APM body of knowledge. International Journal of Project Management, 24(6), 461-473.

Mui, C. (2012) How Kodak Failed. *Forbes*. https://www.forbes.com/sites/chunkamui/2012/01/18/how-kodak-failed/?sh=778c51d76f27

Negash, S. (2004). Business Intelligence. *Communications of the Association for Information Systems*, *13*(15). doi:10.17705/1CAIS.01315

Negash, S., & Gray, P. (2008). Business intelligence. In *Handbook on decision support systems 2* (pp. 175–193). Springer. doi:10.1007/978-3-540-48716-6_9

Nickols, F. (2016). *Four Strategies for Managing Change*. Nickols. https://nickols.us/four_strategies.pdf

Nielsen. (2021). Insights. Nielsen. https://www.nielsen.com/us/en/

Nokia. (2021) *Our history*. Nokia. https://www.nokia.com/about-us/company/our-history/. Accessed on the 22/10/2020.

Nordman, E. R., & Tolstoy, D. (2014). Does relationship psychic distance matter for the learning processes of internationalizing SMEs? *International Business Review*, *23*(1), 30–37. doi:10.1016/j.ibusrev.2013.08.010

Ohmae, K. (1982). *The Mind of the strategist: The Art of Japanese Business*. McGraw-Hill Observatory of Economic Complexity (OEC) Data. https://atlas.media.mit.edu/en/resources/data/

Organisation for Economic Co-operation and Development (n.d.). *Data*. OECD. https://data.oecd.org/

Panagiotou, G., & van Wijnen, R. (2005). The "telescopic observations" framework: An attainable strategic tool. *Marketing Intelligence & Planning*, *23*(2), 155–171. doi:10.1108/02634500510589912

Pellegrinelli, S. (1997). Programme management: Organising project-based change. *International Journal of Project Management*, *15*(3), 141–149. doi:10.1016/S0263-7863(96)00063-4

Performance Consultants. (2021). *What is the GROW Model?* PC. https://www.performanceconsultants.com/grow-model

Performance Consultants. (2021). *What is the GROW Model?* Performance Consultants. https://www.performanceconsultants.com/grow-model

Phillips, M. E., & Sackmann, S. A. (2002). Managing in an era of multiple cultures: Finding synergies instead of conflict. *Graziadio Business Review, 5*(4).1-11. https://gbr.pepperdine.edu/2010/08/managing-in-an-era-of-multiple-cultures/

Pickton, D. W., & Wright, S. (1998). What's SWOT in strategic analysis? *Strategic Change*, *7*(1), 101–109. doi:10.1002/(SICI)1099-1697(199803/04)7:2<101::AID-JSC332>3.0.CO;2-6

Porter, M. E. (1979). How Competitive Forces Shape Strategy. *Harvard Business Review*, *57*(2), 137–145. PMID:18271320

Porter, M. E. (1980). *Competitive Strategy*. Free Press.

Prahalad, C. K., & Hammel, G. (1990). The core competence of the corporation. *Harvard Business Review*, *68*, 79–91.

Project Management Institute. (n.d.). *What is Project Management?* PMI. https://www.pmi.org/about/learn-about-pmi/what-is-project-management

Proquest. (2022). Culture Grams. Proquest. https://www.proquest.com/products-services/culturegrams.html

Rarick, C. A. (2009). The historical roots of Chinese cultural values and managerial practices. *Journal of International Business Research*, *8*(2), 59–66.

Rhodes, R. A. W. (1996). The new governance: Governing without government. *Political Studies*, *XLIV*(4), 652–667. doi:10.1111/j.1467-9248.1996.tb01747.x

Ries, E. (2019). *The lean startup. How constant innovation creates radically successful businesses*. Penguin Random House.

Rodriguez, P., Uhlenbruck, K., & Eden, L. (2005). Government corruption and the entry strategies of multinationals. *Academy of Management Review*, *30*(2), 383–396. doi:10.5465/amr.2005.16387894

Roquebert, J. A., Phillips, R. L., & Westfall, P. A. (1996). Markets Vs. Management: What drives profitability? *Strategic Management Journal*, *17*(8), 653–664. doi:10.1002/(SICI)1097-0266(199610)17:8<653::AID-SMJ840>3.0.CO;2-O

Rosling, H. (2019). *Factfulness*. Flammarion.

Rugman, A., & Cruz, J. (1993). The "double diamond" model of international competitiveness: The Canadian experience. *MIR. Management International Review*, 17–39.

Ruhanen, L., Scott, N., Ritchie, B., & Tkaczynski, A. (2010). Governance: A review and synthesis of the literature. *Tourism Review*, *65*(4), 4–16. doi:10.1108/16605371011093836

Rumelt, R. P. (1991). How much does industry matter? *Strategic Management Journal*, *12*(3), 167–185. doi:10.1002mj.4250120302

Saaty, T. L., & Takizawa, M. (1986). Dependence and independence: From linear hierarchies to nonlinear networks. *European Journal of Operational Research*, *26*(2), 229–237. doi:10.1016/0377-2217(86)90184-0

Schneider, R. S., & Barsoux, J. (2002). *Managing Across Cultures, 2nd*. Upper Saddle Rivier.

Schoemaker, P. (1993). Multiple scenario development: Its conceptual and behavioral foundation. *Strategic Management Journal*, *14*(3), 193–213. doi:10.1002mj.4250140304

Schumpeter, J. A. (1942). *Capitalism, socialism and democracy*. Harper and Brothers.

Schwartz, M. S., & Weber, J. (2006). A business ethics national index (BENI) measuring business ethics activity around the world. *Business & Society*, *45*(3), 382–405. doi:10.1177/0007650305285395

Semke, L. M., & Tiberius, V. (2020). Corporate foresight and dynamic capabilities: An exploratory study. *Forecasting*, *2*(2), 180–193. doi:10.3390/forecast2020010

Sethi, R., & Iqbal, Z. (2008). Stage-gate controls, learning failure, and adverse effect on novel new products. *Journal of Marketing*, *72*(1), 118–134. doi:10.1509/jmkg.72.1.118

Shadfar, S. (2013). Application of SORF Analysis in Formulating Businesses Strategies. *International SAMANM Journal of Marketing and Management*, *1*(2), 96–102.

Skubana (2020). *Walmart Supply Chain [2021]: Why It Continues To Dominate*. Skubana. https://www.skubana.com/blog/walmart-leading-way

Skubana. (2020). *Walmart Supply Chain [2021]: Why It Continues To Dominate*. Skubana. https://www.skubana.com/blog/walmart-leading-way

Smith, C., & Brooks, D. J. (2012). *Security science: The theory and practice of security*. Butterworth-Heinemann.

Snihur, Y., & Zott, C. (2015). Towards an institutional perspective on business model innovation: how entrepreneurs achieve robust business model design. *Working paper*, IESE Business School, Barcelona, Spain.

Sommer, A. F., Hedegaard, C., Dukovska-Popovska, I., & Steger-Jensen, K. (2015). Improved product development performance through Agile/Stage-Gate hybrids – The next-generation Stage-Gate process? *Research Technology Management*, *58*(1), 34–45. doi:10.5437/08956308X5801236

Sprague, L. (2007). Evolution of the field of operations management. *Journal of Operations Management*, *25*(2), 219–238. doi:10.1016/j.jom.2007.01.001

STA Group. (2021). *What is Business Architecture*. STA Group. https://www.stagrp.com/architecture/business-architecture/what-is-business-architecture/

Startup Talky. (2021) Why Did Kodak Fail?: Kodak Bankruptcy Case Study. *Startup Talkey*. https://startuptalky.com/kodak-bankruptcy-case-study/

Sternberg, R. J. (2009). The nature of creativity. *The Essential Sternberg: Essays on intelligence, psychology and education*, 103-118.

Sull, D. N. (2007). Closing the gap between strategy and execution. *MIT Sloan Management Review*, *48*(4), 30–38.

Svejvig, P., & Andersen, P. (2015). Rethinking project management: A structured literature review with a critical look at the brave new world. *International Journal of Project Management*, *33*(2), 278–290. doi:10.1016/j.ijproman.2014.06.004

Taylor, A., & Meegan, S. (1997). Factors influencing a successful transition from ISO 9000 toTQM. The influence of understanding and motivation. *International Journal of Quality & Reliability Management*, *1*(2), 100–117.

Teece, D. J. (2018). Business models and dynamic capabilities. *Long Range Planning*, *51*(1), 40–49. doi:10.1016/j.lrp.2017.06.007

Teece, D. J., Pisano, G. P., & Shuen, A. (1992). *Dynamic capabilities and strategic management*. Center for Research in Management, University of California.

Teece, D. J., Pisano, G., & Shuen, A. (1997). Dynamic capabilities and strategic management. *Strategic Management Journal*, *18*(7), 509–533. doi:10.1002/(SICI)1097-0266(199708)18:7<509::AID-SMJ882>3.0.CO;2-Z

Thatcher, J. (2014). Big data, big questions| Living on fumes: Digital footprints, data fumes, and the limitations of spatial big data. *International Journal of Communication*, *8*(19), 1765–1783.

Timmons, J. A., & Spinelli, S. (2004). *New venture creation: Entrepreneurship for the 21st century* (6th ed.). McGraw Hill Irwin.

Trice, H. M., & Beyer, J. M. (1984). Studying organizational cultures through rites and ceremonials. *Academy of Management Review*, *9*(4), 653–669. doi:10.2307/258488

Tricker, R. I. (1984). *Corporate governance: Practices, procedures, and powers in British companies and their boards of directors*. Gower Publishing Company, Limited.

Tsai, D. F. (2005). The bioethical principles and Confucius' moral philosophy. *Journal of Medical Ethics*, *31*(3), 159–163. doi:10.1136/jme.2002.002113 PMID:15738437

Tuckman, B. W., & Jensen, M. A. C. (1977). Stages of small-group development revisited. *Group & Organization Studies*, *2*(4), 419–427. doi:10.1177/105960117700200404

United Nations Educational, Scientific and Cultural Organization. (n.d.). *Reports*. UNESCO. https://en.unesco.org/gem-report/statistics

Varum, C., Valente, H., Resende, J., Pinho, M., Sarmento, P., & Jorge, S. (2018). *Economia industrial* (2nd ed.). Edicoes Silabo.

Vega, G., & Kidwell, R. E. (2007). Toward a typology of new venture creators: Similarities and contrasts between business and social entrepreneurs. *New England Journal of Entrepreneurship, 10*(2), 1–14. doi:10.1108/NEJE-10-02-2007-B002

Volberda, H. W., Morgan, R. E., Reinmoeller, P., Hitt, M. A., Ireland, R. D., & Hoskisson, R. E. (2011). *Strategic Management: Competitiveness and Globalization (Concepts & Cases)*. Cengage Learning.

Wang, C. L., & Ahmed, P. K. (2007). Dynamic capabilities: A review and research agenda. *International Journal of Management Reviews, 9*(1), 31–51. doi:10.1111/j.1468-2370.2007.00201.x

Wang, Z., Chen, L., Zhao, X., & Zhou, W. (2014). Modularity in building mass customization capability: The mediating effects of customization knowledge utilization and business process improvement. *Technovation, 34*(11), 678–687. doi:10.1016/j.technovation.2014.09.002

Waterman, R. H. Jr, Peters, T. J., & Phillips, J. R. (1980). Structure is not organization. *Business Horizons, 23*(3), 14–26. doi:10.1016/0007-6813(80)90027-0

Weerawardena, J., Mort, G. S., Liesch, P. W., & Knight, G. (2007). Conceptualizing accelerated internationalization in the born global firm: A dynamic capabilities perspective. *Journal of World Business, 42*(3), 294–306. doi:10.1016/j.jwb.2007.04.004

Weihrich, H. (1982). The TOWS matrix—A tool for situational analysis. *Long Range Planning, 15*(2), 54–66. doi:10.1016/0024-6301(82)90120-0

Wheelen, T. L., & Hunger, J. D. (1987). Using the strategic audit. *S.A.M. Advanced Management Journal, 52*(1), 4–27.

Wheelen, T. L., & Hunger, J. D. (1987). Using the strategic audit: Quarterly journal. *S.A.M. Advanced Management Journal, 52*(1), 4. https://www.proquest.com/scholarly-journals/using-strategic-audit/docview/231216911/se-2

Whittle, R., & Myrick, C. B. (2016). *Enterprise business architecture: The formal link between strategy and results*. CRC Press. doi:10.1201/9781420000207

Wiener, M., Mähring, M., Remus, U., & Saunders, C. S. (2016). Control configuration and control enactment in information systems projects: Review and Expanded Theoretical Framework. *Management Information Systems Quarterly, 40*(3), 741–774. doi:10.25300/MISQ/2016/40.3.11

Willen, C. (2002). Airborne Opportunities. *Intelligent Enterprise, 5*(2), 11–12.

World Bank. (2022). *Databank*. World Bank. https://databank.worldbank.org/data/home.aspx

World Trade Organization. (n.d.). *Documents and resources*. WTO. https://www.wto.org/english/res_e/res_e.htm

World Values Survey. (n.d.). *Findings and insights*. WVS. https://www.worldvaluessurvey.org/WVSContents.jsp

Worthington, I., & Britton, C. (2009). *The business environment*. Pearson education.

Xin, K. K., & Pearce, J. L. (1996). Guanxi: Connections as substitutes for formal institutional support. *Academy of Management Journal, 39*(6), 1641–1658. doi:10.2307/257072

Yüksel, I. (2012). Developing a multi-criteria decision making model for PESTEL analysis. *International Journal of Business and Management, 7*(24), 52–66. doi:10.5539/ijbm.v7n24p52

Zanakis, S. H., Theofanides, S., Kontaratos, A. N., & Tassios, T. P. (2003). Ancient Greeks' practices and contributions in public and entrepreneurship decision making. *Interfaces, 33*(6), 72–88. doi:10.1287/inte.33.6.72.25177

Zott, C., & Amit, R. (2008). The fit between product market strategy and business model: Implications for firm performance. *Strategic Management Journal, 29*(1), 1–26. doi:10.1002mj.642

Zuboff, S. (2019). The age of surveillance capitalism: The fight for a human future at the new frontier of power: Barack Obama's books of 2019. Profile books.

Zuboff, S. (2019). *The age of surveillance capitalism: The fight for a human future at the new frontier of power: Barack Obama's books of 2019*. Profile books.

Zwikael, O., & Smyrk, J. (2015). Project governance: Balancing control and trust in dealing with risk. *International Journal of Project Management, 33*(4), 852–862. doi:10.1016/j.ijproman.2014.10.012

About the Author

Bruno Abrantes (Ph.D.) is an Associate Professor at De Monfort University (DMU) (UK) and Niels Brock Copenhagen Business College (NBCBC) (Denmark) in the field of Corporate Strategic Management. Currently, is the interim Program Manager for the Master of Science (MSc) program in International Business and Management (IBM) at NBCBC (Denmark). He is also an Integrated Researcher at ISCTE University Institute of Lisbon (Portugal). With a past record of Strategic Advisory of Executive Boards in the Banking and Consultancy industries, he holds as an educational background with a doctoral degree (Ph.D.) in Management Sciences with a specialization in Strategy and Entrepreneurship from ISCTE University Institute of Lisbon, which complemented his postgraduate studies in Economics and Business Administration at ISG - Business and Economics School (Portugal). Awarded with a Senior Fellowship of Higher Education Academy (SFHEA), is moreover an affiliated member of the Strategic Management Society (SMS), the European University Network on Entrepreneurship (ESU), and the Institute for Mergers, Acquisitions and Alliances (IMAA). He has collaborated with several other universities, as a Visiting Professor, Guest Speaker, Supervisor, and External Reviewer; also with academic publishers, as an Editor and Peer-Reviewer. His research interests encompass the fields of internationalization processes; global dynamic capabilities and contemporary crisis, topics he holds several publications on, including on top-ranked internationally peer-reviewed journals.

Index

A

Assembling Packaging (AnP) 292

B

BEAP 25, 58-59, 63, 67, 69, 71, 88, 90-95, 97, 103, 105, 107-108, 110-118, 122-123, 127-128, 131-132, 136, 138, 140, 143, 145, 148, 151-153, 156-157, 162, 166, 169, 171, 173, 176-177, 180, 182-183, 191, 198, 201-202, 207-211, 213-214, 216, 225, 227-229, 231-232, 234, 236-237, 240-242, 244, 247-248, 252, 262, 271, 274-275, 277-278, 280-281, 287-288, 294
Business Architecture 184, 192, 209, 218, 225-229, 237-239, 270
business environment (BE) 3-6, 10, 12, 23, 25, 32-33, 38, 40-41, 44-47, 50-53, 55-63, 65, 67-76, 78-81, 83, 85-89, 94, 96-97, 100, 107-112, 115, 120-122, 125-126, 128-129, 139, 145, 161, 170-171, 178, 181, 183-184, 191, 195, 197, 201, 207-208, 210, 218-219, 225, 228-231, 234, 236, 240-242, 247, 262, 270-271, 275, 277, 280, 294, 297
business environment analyzability (BEA) 23, 38, 69, 297
business-to-consumer (B2C) 50, 90, 135, 175

C

Chesbrough´s innovation 196, 202
Chief Strategy Officer 197, 202
Cisco System 28
Clear thinking 221-222, 227, 236
comparative design 135, 149, 152, 173, 175
competition models 93
competitive advantage 34, 40, 83, 108, 111, 145, 197-198, 209, 229
computer-based information 191-192, 198, 203
computer-based information systems 191-192, 203
contemporary business 8, 22-23, 106
corporate governance 10-11, 17-20, 22, 24-25, 70, 106, 192, 222
corporate thinking 14, 74, 84-85, 115, 123, 273
Coupang Corp 129, 181, 185

D

design themes 226-227
digital competitiveness 199-200, 203-204
digital footprints 138, 189, 201-202
digital transformation 199-200, 202

E

Environment analysis 10, 12, 23, 25, 33, 38, 41, 55-57, 61, 63, 65, 67, 76, 89-90, 93, 97, 107-108, 110-111, 120-121, 128, 167-171, 173, 184, 191, 197, 201, 207-210, 228-229, 231, 234, 236, 241-242, 247, 262, 271, 275, 280
epistemological assumption 71, 86, 88, 115
External Business 6, 12, 33, 50-52, 57, 66-70, 74, 80, 89, 94, 100, 107-108, 110, 112, 115, 120-122, 145, 161, 170-171, 191, 197, 210, 218, 228
external business environment 6, 12, 33, 50-52, 57, 68-70, 74, 80, 89, 94, 100, 107-108, 110, 112, 115, 120-122, 145, 161, 170-171, 191, 197, 210, 218, 228
external communication 196, 203-204
external environment 38, 52, 62, 79, 89-90, 93, 107, 111, 139, 157, 161, 165, 173, 182, 212, 219-220, 237, 247, 258, 271

F

firm-specific advantages 74, 241, 246, 249
first-order sets 246, 248

G

general environment 88-91, 103, 108, 111, 120-122, 125, 132, 134, 147, 168-170, 173, 219
greenhouse gas (GHG) 36-37

H

Heritage Foundation 135, 176, 188
hybrid approach 70, 82
hybrid model 170, 224, 236-237, 240

I

Industrial Economics 48, 66, 248
industrial organization 48, 72-73, 78, 85, 107, 109
Information Systems (IS) 191-192, 198, 203
intelligence cycle 191, 193-194, 202-203, 258, 272
intelligence tools 133, 136-137, 181-182
internal fitness 85, 223

J

Just-in-Time 217, 267-268

L

Life Expectancy 180
low-end competitors 57, 66

M

macro analysis 111, 118, 120, 122
market intelligence 33, 44, 133, 136, 181

N

non-organic growth 27-28, 45

O

organizational capabilities 26, 32, 50, 53, 59, 73, 77, 80, 85, 219, 241-243, 246, 248, 252
organizational ecology 47, 59, 63, 67, 88, 101, 125, 179
organizational levers 26, 32, 46, 73, 77, 85, 107, 219
organizational management 1, 6, 11-12, 19, 22-24, 26, 33, 94, 106, 192, 219

P

philosophical stance 88, 113, 122, 143, 171
POLC cycle 26, 32, 35-36, 40, 44-46, 208
product development 174, 190, 196-197, 238-239, 247, 250
project architecture 209, 217-218, 223, 228-229, 231-232, 236, 240, 244, 249
Project assurance 184, 234, 259-261, 268
Project Management (PM) 70, 128, 140, 183, 185, 188, 207-209, 213, 217, 224, 228, 231, 234-240, 242, 248-249, 251-252, 255, 258-259, 261, 267, 269-270
project manager 210, 232, 234-235, 248, 255, 257, 259, 269
Property Rights 135, 176

Q

quality assurance 217, 252, 258-260, 262-263, 268-269, 272
quality performance 59, 253-254, 258, 263, 268

R

rational decisions 140, 219-220, 272
relative importance (RI) 113
resource-based theorists 120, 168, 244
resource-based view 70, 72-73, 85, 241, 249
resources allocation 207, 228, 235

S

self-managed teams 195-196
senior managers 23, 162, 194, 210-212, 223, 248, 259, 275, 279
strategic decisions 9, 79, 94, 110, 118-120, 137
Strategic Goals 20, 37, 81, 130-131, 158, 218, 221, 275-276, 279, 283-284, 286, 292, 294-295
strategic management (SM) 1, 7-8, 12, 22-24, 26, 33-35, 38, 42-43, 46-47, 49, 52, 69-70, 74, 83, 91, 97, 106, 108, 120, 129, 183, 185-189, 215, 237, 239, 243, 250, 261, 263, 269-271, 273-274, 294, 297-298
Strategic Planning 24, 35-36, 40, 45-46, 60, 66-67, 71, 93, 128-129, 131, 141, 169, 183, 213, 225, 230, 269, 277, 299
Suitability, Feasibility, Acceptability (SFA) 59
survival-responsive function 1
sustainable policies 122, 131-132

T

technological advancements 62, 64, 169, 192, 196, 210
theoretical domains 10, 17

Total Productive Maintenance (TPM) 267

V

visual representation 84, 86, 295

W

widget counting 45, 58, 259, 274, 287, 290, 292-298

X

Xenophon´s philosophy 7-9

www.ingramcontent.com/pod-product-compliance
Lightning Source LLC
LaVergne TN
LVHW060420300926
849162LV00006B/1475